JUTTA AND HILDEGARD:
THE BIOGRAPHICAL SOURCES

Brepols Medieval Women Series

Jutta and Hildegard:
The Biographical Sources

ANNA SILVAS

THE PENNSYLVANIA STATE UNIVERSITY PRESS
UNIVERSITY PARK, PENNSYLVANIA

Published in 1999 in paperback by The Pennsylvania State University Press.
University Park, PA 16802

First published in 1998 in a clothbound edition by Brepols Publishers in the
'Medieval Women: Texts and Contexts' series

ISBN 0-271-01954-9 (paper)

Library of Congress Cataloging in Publication Data
A CIP catalog record for this book is available from the Library of Congress.

Printed in the European Union

Printed on acid-free paper

Dedicated with deepest gratitude to
a very dear elder, sister, and friend,

Sr Marguerite Burke OSB
1904 – 1997

and to the Prioress she looked up to in her youth
Dame Mary Joseph Brady OSB
1878 – 1949

and to all the foremothers of
the Benedictine monastery
of 'Subiaco', Rydalmere, NSW
2 Feb 1849 – 19 Dec 1957

CONTENTS

PREFACE AND ACKNOWLEDGMENTS

THE YEAR 1998 MARKS the nine-hundredth anniversary of the birth of St Hildegard of Bingen (1098–1179), the outstanding female religious figure of twelfth-century Germany. As a contribution to this celebration, this book is offered as a comprehensive dossier of her biographical sources, many of them appearing in English translation for the first time.

My involvement began in 1984, when Brother Terence Kavenagh OSB, the editor of *Tjurunga, an Australasian Benedictine Review* invited me to translate the *Vita S. Hildegardis* (the *VH*). The only Latin version readily available at the time was Migne's edition in PL 197. My translation appeared in *Tjurunga* 29 (1985), 30 (1986), 31 (1986) and 32 (1987).

In 1993 a major critical edition of the *Vita S. Hildegardis* was published in the Brepols CCCM series by Monika Klaes. Sr Kym Harris OSB, the then editor of *Tjurunga*, put it to me that I revise my translation in the light of this edition and publish it as a book.

Several factors worked to change the complexion of the project and considerably expand its scope. As I grappled with Klaes's stringent scholarship, it became clear to me that there was no question of simply revising my translation. It had to be a completely new work. Klaes's edition of the *VH* also contains editions of a number of other documents supplementary to the *VH*, which also merited translation for the book. Sr Kym introduced me to Dr Constant Mews of Monash University in Melbourne, who has been an enthusiastic supporter all through the undertaking. From him I learned of the *Life of Jutta* (the *VJ*), a newly rediscovered and published *vita* of Hildegard's *magistra*, Jutta of Disibodenberg. This would definitely have to be included in the book. Whereupon, Guibert's Letter 38, the *Letter to Bovo*, could scarcely be omitted either. Through the generosity of Julie Hotchin in Canberra, then working on a thesis under the direction of Dr Mews, I became aware of a range of other documents supportive of the life and times of Jutta and Hildegard. Finally, the *Acta Inquisitionis*, which proved every bit as interesting as I suspected it might be, completed the ensemble of documents.

For such a project, debts to many friends and colleagues have naturally been incurred. Among other Benedictines I have to thank are Abbess Benedicta Philips of Jamberoo Abbey, Srs Joan Malony and Genevieve Harrington OSB of Lammermoor, Qld, and Sr Ancilla Ferlings of St Hildegard's abbey, Eibingen. I mark my link with the Benedictine tradition by dedicating the book to a dearly loved spiritual mother and friend, Sr Marguerite Burke OSB, and to one I came to esteem through her, the prioress of her youth, Mother M. Joseph Brady OSB.

When I moved to the Department of Classics and Ancient History at the University of New England in 1996, Professor Greg Horsley went out of his way to make me welcome. He has consistently backed me in this project and also in another research topic on the Cappadocian Fathers (and with St Macrina, Mothers) and monastic life. I found the Classics department, which this year celebrates, along with the University, the sixtieth anniversary of teaching and research, a congenial setting in which to settle down to work. The outstanding philologist, Dr Alan Treloar, gave invaluable help in cross-checking my translations for accuracy. Others in the University and in Armidale have provided help in various ways: Dr Lynda Garland, Gina Butler, Tom Pollak, and Nathan Westaway. Most encouraging was the Bishop of Armidale, Kevin M. Manning, now transferred to the Diocese of Parramatta (western Sydney), very near the 'Vineyards', or 'Subiaco' as it became known, where Archbishop Polding OSB first brought the Benedictine nuns to Australia exactly 150 years ago in 1848.

Thanks are owed to other friends, Esther Nott of Sydney, Barbara Shea of Melbourne, Margaret Watts of the Catholic Institute, Sydney, and Sabina Flanagan of the University of Adelaide, who gave timely help with certain difficulties in the *VJ*, also to Bärbel Würth, whose family occupies the site of Rupertsberg, for most helpful answers to my enquiries. Bärbel sent the eighteenth-century sketch of the Rupertsberg ruins, included in the appendix.

I have a special debt of gratitude to Dr Barbara Newman, the academic reader, who approved, praised and so strongly recommended the work to Brepols. Thanks to her, I was able to put the book through another sieve of fine detailing. Thanks are owed to the Brepols editorial team who promoted this book as the first of a new series, Medieval Women: Texts and Contexts. A very special thanks is due to the typesetters, Elizabeth Wall and Peter Binkley.

I express my gratitude also to my treasured parents, Theodor and Margaret Silvas, in whose home an early stage of the work was done, and who followed its fortunes with loving attention and support. My mother, however, did not live to see it to the end, but died early this same year, 1998.

Almost any page of this book should show that I work very much from 'within the tradition', not only from within the same religious and ecclesial faith as Jutta and Hildegard, but even as a sometime heir like them of Benedictine monastic culture. It goes deeper than that. When all the strenuous academic work is done, I am not one to hang back as an impartial 'genre critic' of Jutta and Hildegard's 'hagiographies'. I take heart at the courage and tenacity with which they played out their lives in their own times, and run to catch up with them in the same immense venture of holiness, a client of the same Spirit of Grace, a member of the same believing, struggling, and praying Church they belonged to, if facing the peculiar challenges of another age. So finally, to Jutta and Hildegard themselves, these inspiring sisters and foremothers in the Faith, I say 'thank you'.

Anna Silvas
School of Classics and History
University of New England, Australia
Feast of St Hildegard, 17 September 1998,
900th anniversary year of Hildegard's birth.

GENERAL INTRODUCTION

HILDEGARD EDITIONS AND TRANSLATIONS

ON THE PRIMARY LEVEL of the critical Latin texts available for Hildegard studies, recent years have been very generous to us. Fittingly, the pioneers of renewed Hildegard studies in this century were three learned Benedictine nuns of St Hildegard's Abbey in Eibingen, Germany, i.e. Sisters Marianna Schrader, Adelgundis Führkötter, and Angela Carlevaris. In 1978 the critical edition of *Scivias*, by Führkötter and Carlevaris appeared. In 1988 Barbara Newman provided for both scholars and general readers alike a Latin edition and English translation of Hildegard's hymns and sequences. In 1993 Monika Klaes published the critical edition of the *Vita Hildegardis*. In 1995 the edition of the *Liber Vite Meritorum* (*The Book of Life's Merits*) appeared, and in 1996 the last of Hildegard's major theological works, the *Liber Divinorum Operum* (*The Book of Divine Works*), appeared. Since 1991, two volumes of the critical edition of Hildegard's correspondence have appeared, although, due to the death of Lieven van Acker, the third and final volume is pending. The letters of Guibert of Gembloux, indispensable for Hildegard studies, were published in 1988 and 1989.

On a secondary level, a growing body of worthy and responsible English translations of Hildegard's works might fairly be looked for. It is to be hoped that *Jutta and Hildegard: The Biographical Sources* will make a valuable contribution to that end.

THE AIM OF THIS BOOK

THIS VOLUME AIMS TO present in English translation a comprehensive collection of the biographical sources available for St Hildegard of Bingen (1098–1179) and for her spiritual mother, Bl. Jutta of Disibodenberg (1092–1136). I have endeavoured to provide English translations of these sources that will be accurate and sensitive enough to stand on their own merits, even without notes, for those whose primary purpose is to engage in spiritual reading. But in addition to that, for the benefit of Hildegard studies in English, an apparatus of detailed and up-to-date introductions, notes, and appendices is included.

The present volume has evolved its own integral character and structure. Indeed the entire compilation may be looked upon as a comprehensive presentation of Hildegard and Jutta for the twenty-first century, using a wide range of primary sources, and addressing in the introductory sections questions of a textual and historical nature. In a very real sense, this work is simply carrying out afresh Theodoric of Echternach's original commission: to collate and arrange the available sources in a comprehensible sequence, interspersed with commentary.

THE CORE OF THE COLLECTION: THREE *VITAE*

THE FOUNDATION OF THIS collection is a translation of Theodoric's already well-known *Vita S. Hildegardis, The Life of Saint Hildegard* (hereafter referred to as *VH*). Admittedly, this *vita* has already appeared in a variety of English translations, either whole or in part,[1] but, with the appearance of Monika Klaes's ground-breaking Latin edition in 1993, it was time for a new and searching translation to be made from the Latin, together with an attempt to communicate to English readers a good measure of the German scholarship connected with it.

To this *Life of Hildegard* there are added, above all, two other documents: the *Life of Lady Jutta the Anchoress* (hereafter referred to as *VJ*), and Guibert's *Letter to Bovo* (hereafter referred to as Ep. 38), containing his unfinished *vita* of Hildegard. These three documents may be considered the 'core' of this volume.

The three documents are in the nature of *vitae*, i.e. 'lives' of saints or holy persons, allowing for the fact that Guibert's Ep. 38 began its existence as a letter. I would briefly propose that the idea of a *vita* is to present a memorial of its subject in the form of a 'verbal ikon', i.e. a

---

[1] See *The Life of the Holy Hildegard*, trans. by James McGrath (Collegeville, Minnesota: Liturgical Press, 1995). This is a translation of Führkötter's German translation of the *VH*, including her notes: Godfrey of Disibodenberg and Theoderich of Echternach, *Das Leben der Heiligen Hildegard*, trans. by Adelgundis Führkötter (Salzburg: 1980). See also Anna Silvas, 'Saint Hildegard of Bingen and the *Vita Sanctae Hildegardis*', *Tjurunga*, 29–32, and *The Life of the Saintly Hildegard*, trans. by Hugh Feiss OSB (Toronto: Peregrina, 1996). Large selections of Hildegard's autobiographical texts are translated by Peter Dronke in 'Hildegard of Bingen', in *Women Writers of the Middle Ages* (Cambridge: CUP, 1984), pp. 144–201.

narrative of the history of his or her life, virtues and 'wonders', calculated so as to bring out his or her exemplary holiness, with the aim of moving the readers to admiration and imitation of the holy person depicted, and of inspiring them to have recourse to his or her advocacy in heaven.[2] It assumes a considerable degree of shared Christian and ecclesial faith between the subject, the author, and the reader.

These three particular *vitae* together form a more or less continuous historical narrative, beginning in the *VJ* with the family origins of Jutta and her birth in 1092, Jutta's early attempts at a religious vocation, her choice of what we know from other sources was the newly refounded monastery of Disibodenberg, and her enclosure there in 1112.

The *VJ* is also our first introduction to Hildegard herself, as she was in the days before her public fame. She glows like a background presence in the entire work, for she was the one who roused Abbot Cuno to commission it as a memorial to Jutta, her *magistra* or spiritual mother, and also the spiritual mother of the monks. As if that were not enough, the *VJ* is also our introduction to the person of the monk, Volmar, the same who later became Hildegard's beloved secretary and provost. As I demonstrate in the Introduction to the *VJ*, he is almost certainly the author of the *VJ*. I also broach the whole problem of the historiographical discrepancies between the *VJ* and Hildegard's later autobiographical recollections concerning her 'oblation' and early religious life. I argue in favour of evidence in the *VJ*: that Hildegard may well have spent the years of her childhood 'oblation' not at Disibodenberg, but at Sponheim with Jutta, before being enclosed with her at Disibodenberg in 1112.

Since this volume is not only Jutta and Hildegard's volume, but also Volmar's, I have chosen to insert immediately after the *VJ* a translation of the one surviving letter of Volmar to Hildegard, in order that the reader may be able to make some immediate comparisons.

The remaining document of the three, Guibert's *Letter to Bovo* (Ep. 38), to a considerable extent, maintains the focus on Jutta, giving additional biographical material about her not found in the *VJ*. Guibert in particular brings out the 'transitions' of Jutta's anchorhold, describing in

---

[2] The promotion of this latter objective will be all the more important if the *vita* is part of an effort to achieve the formal canonization of the holy person, as it is in the case of the *VH*. Not all putatively holy persons had the charism of 'canonizability', so to speak. That lay in the competence of Church authorities to judge. By early in the century after Hildegard, the process became definitively centralized in Rome.

detail the solemn enclosure in 1112, the eventual expansion into a small 'school', and after Jutta's death in 1136, the election of Hildegard as *magistra* in her stead, and subsequently her formal constitution as prioress of a small cenobitic monastery of nuns. He then describes her call to prophetic leadership some years later, where the surviving text suddenly breaks off.

Thus Ep. 38 leads us almost seamlessly into the *Life of Hildegard* itself. This *Life* begins by briefly revisiting the person of Jutta in the first two chapters, and then surges forward with its subject, Hildegard, continuing on its magnificent trajectory, incorporating large tracts of her own autobiographical writing on the way, and leading eventually to her death in 1179.

Thus, these three major works are like a trilogy, covering the interwoven lives of two holy women over a period of nearly ninety years, from 1092 to 1179.

A PENUMBRA OF SUPPORTING DOCUMENTS

ARRANGED AROUND THESE *VITAE* is an outer cluster of documents which have a valuable contribution to make to what we can recover of the lives of Jutta and Hildegard.

A fitting prelude to the entire collection consists of selections from the *Annales Sancti Disibodi* or the Chronicles of Disibodenberg (hereafter referred to as *AD*). These Chronicles record significant events at the monastery during the first half-century of its existence, and, most importantly, mention both Jutta and Hildegard in the entry for the year 1136. They communicate a good deal of the spiritual and intellectual thought-world of the monastery during the period when Jutta lived out her entire monastic vocation there, and Hildegard lived out the first half of hers.

A perfect epilogue to the collection is provided by the *Acta Inquisitionis* (hereafter referred to as *Acta Inq.*), a document which is the fruit of early efforts made towards Hildegard's canonization, i.e. the formal authentication and proclamation of her sanctity. Amid a host of miracle reports, this document preserves some precious anecdotes about Hildegard we would not want to be without, as well as introducing us to Hildegard's *Nachleben* (afterlife), in the memory of later generations.

Filling in the space between the prelude and the epilogue and the three central *vitae*, are collections of shorter ancillary sources, which help us to anchor the lives of Jutta and Hildegard in the historical and social context of their time and place. A good few of these documents are legal charters issued by the Archbishops of Mainz, in favour of Disibodenberg for example, or for Rupertsberg. There are also a couple of texts deriving from or relating to Theodoric's *Life of Hildegard* itself, which nevertheless contain items of valuable information in their own right. Two most interesting texts connected with the abbey of Sponheim are included. One is the only contemporary attestation of Hildegard's father, the other a kind of summary statement by Trithemius as he looks back over the whole phenomenon of the holy nuns attached to the monks' monasteries that had once been part of the local Benedictine tradition to which he belonged.

Such then is the overall structure of this volume of biographical documents.

THE GENEALOGICAL TABLES

AMONG THE APPENDICES ARE included genealogical tables I have compiled from several sources, of which the most important are researches into the Sponheim and Formbach genealogies by Johannes Mötsch, Wilhelm Wegener, and Anneliese Naumann-Humbeck. By far the most interesting find here was the close connection of the Sponheim family, through Sophia, with Lothar von Supplinburg, i.e. Emperor Lothar III. Still, genealogical research goes on among the German archivists, and who can tell what other surprising connections or emendations to historical family trees may yet have to be made.

BIOGRAPHICAL MATERIAL NOT INCLUDED IN THIS VOLUME

THERE ARE OTHER SOURCES of biographical information about Jutta and Hildegard not included in this volume.

The most important source is, of course, the large corpus of Hildegard's own writings.

The next most valuable source is the correspondence of Guibert. In this volume, only the single most valuable item among them, Letter 38, *The Letter to Bovo*, has been translated. Nevertheless, passages from Guibert's other letters are liberally noted and translated here and there where appropriate. Hildegard studies in English will be well served if ever a translation of Guibert's letters becomes available, although it would be no easy task, for his Latin is very highly wrought.

Another source is an abbreviation of Guibert's revision of the Life of Hildegard found in an Utrecht manuscript of the late fourteenth to early fifteenth century, examined by Klaes on pp. 178–180*.

Apart from the one representative sample I have translated, Abbot Johannes Trithemius also has a fair deal to say in his historical works about Hildegard, and a certain amount about Jutta too. Admittedly, he is not himself a contemporary source, he makes demonstrable errors, and his reportage has to be treated with caution when not corroborated by contemporary sources. Still, he had access to documents and to local oral tradition not available to us, and was a late representative from within of that particular local Benedictine tradition to which Jutta and Hildegard had belonged.

Trithemius alleges a visit of St Bernard to Rupertsberg (*Chron. Hirsaug.*, p. 132), Hildegard's visit to Hirsau (ibid., pp. 145–147), the existence of Hiltrude, supposedly a daughter of Meinhard and a favourite nun of Hildegard's at Rupertsberg (ibid., p. 156); there is much too about Kraffto, a son of Meinhard and Abbot of Sponheim, the unique information that Hildegard transmitted her visions *partly in Latin, partly in German* (*Chron. Sponh.*, p. 257), Hildegard's authorship of a work against the Cathars on the Eucharist: *On the Sacrament of the Altar* (*De Luminaribus*, p. 138; *Chron. Hirsaug.*, p. 148), and a notice about the struggle over leadership among the nuns at Rupertsberg in the year 1210 (*Chron. Sponh.*, p. 261). There are many reports about people and events at other nearby monasteries. Trithemius is invaluable in giving us the whole texture and colour of that local Benedictine tradition in the *Rhineland-Pfalz* region to which Disibodenberg, Rupertsberg, and Sponheim all belonged.

THE GENESIS OF THE HILDEGARD *BIOGRAPHICA*: AN OVERVIEW

IT BUT REMAINS TO introduce the reader to the genesis and the historical relationship of the biographical material concerning Hildegard and Jutta. Much more detail on this topic will be found in the introductions to the major documents.

The Life of Lady Jutta the Anchoress, a *vita* of Hildegard's spiritual mother, Jutta of Sponheim, was composed in the first half of the 1140s. Its author is almost certainly Volmar. In his prologue he reveals that the instigator of the *Vita* was no less than Hildegard herself, so the *VJ* is, in effect, the first fruit of Hildegard and Volmar's collaboration. Coming as it does from a period before the developed cult of Hildegard, even in her lifetime, the *VJ* has much light to shed, and questions to raise, in comparison with the subsequent documentary record.

The first attempts to compile material for a *vita* of Hildegard herself took place while both she and Volmar were still alive. To this end, he edited the first systematic collection of her correspondence. It seems likely that it was for Volmar's use in a projected *vita* that Hildegard wrote out, or dictated, her autobiographical notes. Volmar, however, died in 1173, six years before Hildegard herself. Subsequently a monk was sent from Disibodenberg, Godfrey, who implemented the project, and composed a *libellus* or 'little book' of her life, which survives now as the first seven chapters of *VH* I. But Godfrey died in 1176, too soon to finish his projected work.

His successor was Guibert, a learned monk from the monastery of Gembloux in Brabant, who stayed at Hildegard's monastery during the last two or three years of her life, enjoying her trust and friendship. Monika Klaes stresses the pivotal role of Guibert in the transmission of the corpus of Hildegard's *biographica*. He was urged to take up the matter of her *vita* by Hildegard's friend, Archbishop Philip of Cologne, while she was still alive. Consequently, he canvassed the written sources already available at Rupertsberg and assembled them in preparation for the project. There is also what he was able to obtain from oral tradition: his conversations with Hildegard herself, and with members of the community, as well as interviews he carried out, such as with the monks at Disibodenberg. A breakdown of his stock of sources may be found in the Introductions to Guibert's Ep. 38 and to the *VH*.

After Hildegard died (1179), and while he was still resident at Rupertsberg, Guibert commenced writing the *vita*. But some time late in 1180, he was suddenly called away, and had to break off his work. He was never able to return to it. But he left the collection of biographical sources behind him, while taking his own unfinished *vita* with him. Years later, in 1209, near the end of his life, he was editing the collection of his letters when he took the opportunity to graft his own unfinished *vita* onto a letter he had sent to a confrère at Gembloux soon his first arrival at Rupertsberg in 1177. So it survived among his works in the form of Ep. 38, *The Letter to Bovo*.

At this same time Guibert was also sent a copy of the *vita* as finally edited by Theodoric, i.e. the *VH*. Guibert made his own version of the *VH* (*not* to be confused with his own Hildegard *vita*), adding to it and altering it here and there. This revision he left among the corpus of his works. Important sections of it are included in this volume under the title *Guibert's revision of VH*, while other interesting variations are entered in the notes to the *VH*, simply under 'Guibert'. In working on this document, I came to the tentative conclusion that while he was still at Rupertsberg Guibert may have made a copy of Hildegard's biographical texts for himself, and taken this copy with him when he left in 1180, and thus had it available when revising the *VH*. If so, Guibert's revision of the *VH* may well contain some original phrases from Hildegard not included in the *VH*, though it is a very careful matter to try and discern these from Guibert's many stylistic 'improvements'.

Within two years or so of Guibert's departure from Rupertsberg in 1180, two abbot friends of Hildegard, Ludwig of Echternach and Godfrey of St Eucharius commissioned Theodoric, the learned *Magister Scholarum* at Echternach, to restart the lapsed *vita* project. Unlike Guibert, it seems Theodoric never knew Hildegard personally, but was dependent for his knowledge of her solely on the stock of written materials left behind by Guibert. This surely worked to our benefit, as he approached the task by deciding to include intact and acknowledge his sources to a far greater degree than did Guibert, who was more inclined to paraphrase them in his own style. It was Theodoric who at last brought the project to a conclusion. The end product, *The Life of Holy Hildegard*, is without doubt one of the outstanding *vitae* of the century, and something of a literary watershed for its generous inclusion of verbatim autobiographical passages of its subject.

Also translated for the first time in this volume is *Eight readings to be read on the Feast of St Hildegard*. This is largely a summarized account of the *VH*, made by Theodoric himself after he had finished the *VH*, but before 1188. It was intended to provide a worthy text for liturgical use on Hildegard's projected feast-day. Despite its largely derivative character, this document nevertheless preserves a few unique biographical items, in particular the note about Hildegard's Profession before Bishop Otto of Bamberg. Clearly, Theodoric was possessed of more information from his sources than he included in his final draft of the *VH*.[3]

In *VH* III, 21, Theodoric commenced the text of an exorcism ritual composed by Hildegard for the famous Sigewize incident of 1169, but he did not write it out in full. He had a copy of it among his stock of sources, probably among Hildegard's letters, and evidently assumed that the reader too would be able to consult a copy. And indeed this exorcism text has survived in an independent transmission to this day. It is translated here, but I have inserted it in the appropriate place in the *VH*, in the narrative sequence where Theodoric had in mind that it should be read.

Other documents included in this book are not strictly a part of the corpus of Hildegard's *biographica* as above described, but are ancillary to it, being primarily legal or annalistic in character.

Except for the *VJ* and Guibert's Ep. 38, the Latin texts of all the above sources are to be found in Klaes's critical edition.

THE APPROACH TO TRANSLATION

BEFORE CONCLUDING THIS INTRODUCTION, some indication of my general approach to translation and the use of language is in order.

Detailed surveys of Latin style and problems of translation may be found in the introductions to individual documents. Of most interest in this regard will be the section in the introduction to the *VH*: 'Observations on translating terms in the *VH*'.

Let the reader be assured that here, a loose, overly 'interpretive' approach to translation has been purposefully avoided. The work began with an attempt at a strict literal translation, and was refined after many revisions and consultations, and much re-evaluation over a long period of time, to something like a mature form. I have made it my business to prefer standard English. It is to be hoped that something of the different character of each author comes through even in English, as, for example, Hildegard's spiritually charged immediacy, or Guibert's cultured periodic style.

---

[3] Another likely example of material he had available which he excluded from the definitive version is the episode of the five-year-old Hildegard and the unborn calf, reported in *Acta Inq.* VIII.

Hopefully, there are those wishing to read with a spiritual and theological perspective even today, who will ask from a translation more than so many kilobytes of bald, instant 'information' on the one hand, or a 'hermeneutic' ricochet of their own evanescent moods and prejudices on the other. Such readers will be prepared to lay aside the chronological snobbery of secular progressivism, which seems to have invaded so much of contemporary religious discourse. They will accept that they might be profitably confronted, even 'critiqued' by religious texts from an earlier age, an age which might even have evinced resources of spiritual strength seriously wanting in our own. They will be prepared, in a way, to let the text, the 'word', read *them*. To take this approach is to speak from and to a tradition of *Lectio Divina*. Readers disposed in this way will appreciate a language of accuracy and substance, with something additional of beauty, resonance, and depth; it is to be hoped that in the translations presented here such qualities have not gone completely missing.

ABBREVIATIONS

Acta Inq.	*Acta Inquisitionis de virtutibus et miraculis S. Hildegardis*, ed. by Petrus Bruder, *Analecta Bollandiana*, 2 (1883), 116–29.
AD	*Annales Sancti Disibodi*, ed. by G.W. Waitz, in MGH SS 17, pp. 4–30.
'Aus Kindheit'	'Aus Kindheit und Lehrzeit Hildegards: Mit einer Übersetzung der Vita ihrer Lehrerin Jutta von Sponheim', introduction to and German translation of the *VJ* by Franz Staab, in *Hildegard von Bingen: Prophetin durch die Zeiten, zum 900 Geburtstag*, ed. by Abbess Edeltrude Forster and the Community of St Hildegard's Abbey, Eibingen (Freiburg: Herder, 1997).
Chron. Hirsaug.	Trithemius, Johannes (1462–1517), *Chronica Insignis Monasterii Hirsaugiensis*, in *Johannis Trithemii Opera Historica*, ed. by Marquand Freher (Frankfurt: 1601; repr. Frankfurt/Main: Minerva, 1966), vol. 2, pp. 1–235.
Chron. Sponh.	*Chronicon Monasterii Sponheimensis*, ibid., pp. 236–435.
CCCM	Corpus Christianorum Continuatio Mediaevalis, the series of critical Latin texts published by Brepols at Turnhout, Belgium.
Derolez	*Guiberti Gemblacensis Epistolae*, ed. by Albert Derolez, CCCM, 66A (Turnhout: Brepols, 1989).
Guibert	'The Revision of *VH* by Guibert of Gembloux', in *Vita Sanctae Hildegardis Virginis*, ed. by Monika Klaes, CCCM, 126 (Turnhout: Brepols, 1993), pp. 91–106.

Klaes

The introduction (pp. 17–194*) and critical apparatus of *Vita Sanctae Hildegardis Virginis*, ed. by Monika Klaes, CCCM, 126 (Turnhout: Brepols, 1993).

Ep. 38

Guibert's Letter to Bovo, Epistola XXXVIII (Letter 38), in Derolez, pp. 366–79.

LDO

Hildegardis Liber Divinorum Operum (*The Book of Divine Works*), ed. by A. Derolez and P. Dronke, CCCM, 92 (Turnhout: Brepols, 1996).

MGH

Monumenta Germaniae Historica.

MUB 1

Mainzer Urkundenbuch, vol. 1, *Die Urkunden bis zum Tode Erzbischof Adalberts I (1137)*, ed. by M. Stimming (Darmstadt: Arbeiten der Historischen Kommission für den Volkstaat Hessen, 1932; repr. 1972).

MUB 2

Mainzer Urkundenbuch, vol. 2, 1–2, *Die Urkunden seit dem Tode Erzbischof Adalberts (1137) bis zum Tode Erzbischof Konrads (1200)*, ed. by Peter Acht (Darmstadt: Selbstverlag der Hessischen Historischen Kommission, 1968–71).

PG

Patrologia Graeca (Migne).

PL

Patrologia Latina (Migne).

Pitra

Hildegard, *Analecta Sanctae Hildegardis*, ed. by J-B Pitra, in *Analecta Sacra*, vol. 8. (Monte Cassino: 1882; repr. Farnborough: Gregg, 1966).

RB

The Rule of Benedict, as published in *RB 1980: The Rule of St Benedict in Latin and English with Notes*, ed. by Timothy Fry et al. (Collegeville, Minnesota: Liturgical Press, 1981).

Van Acker

Hildegardis Bingensis Epistolarium I–XC, ed. by Lieven van Acker, CCCM, 91 (Turnhout: Brepols, 1991).

Van Acker 2

Hildegardis Bingensis Epistolarium, pars secunda XCI–CCLr, ed. by Lieven van Acker,

CCCM, 91A (Turnhout: Brepols, 1993).

VH *The Life of Hildegard*, the Latin text as edited in *Vita Sanctae Hildegardis Virginis*, ed. by Monika Klaes, CCCM, 126 (Turnhout: Brepols, 1993), pp. 1–71.

VJ *The Life of Jutta*, the Latin text edited as Appendix 2 in Franz Staab, 'Reform and Reformgruppen im Erzbistum Mainz. Vom "Libellus de Willigisi consuetudinibus" zur "Vita domnae Juttae inclusae"', in *Reformidee und Reformpolitik im Spätsalisch-Frühstaufischen Reich. Vorträge der Tagung der Gesellschaft für Mittelrheinische Kirchengeschichte vom 11. bis 13. September 1991 in Trier*, ed. by Stefan Weinfurter, Quellen und Abhandlungen zur Mittelrheinische Geschichte, 68 (Mainz: Selbstverlag der Gesellschaft für Mittelrheinische Kirchengeschichte, 1992), pp. 119–87. Appendix 2: *Vita domnae Juttae inclusae* (edited text), pp. 172–87.

THE CHRONICLES OF DISIBODENBERG

INTRODUCTION

The selection of texts presented here is translated from the *Annales Sancti Disibodi*, edited by G.W. Waitz, in *Monumenta Germaniae Historica*, Scriptorum, 17 (Hannover: 1861; repr. Stuttgart: Anton Hierseman, 1963), pp. 4–30. The Chronicles survive in only one early fourteenth-century manuscript, comprising 116 smaller folio-size leaves. A note on the inside cover refers to a 'lord Wernher' whom Waitz takes to be Abbot Werner of Disibodenberg, 1294–1305. Another note on the last leaf informs us that the manuscript has been given to the monastery of St Bartholomew in Frankfurt. From there it made its way to the public library in Frankfurt as Codex Nr. 104.

Waitz determined from the internal evidence that a single Disibodenberg monk composed the bulk of the Chronicles in the years 1146–1147. For the history of earlier centuries the author made use of a number of other chronicles and documents, e.g. the Chronicles of Marianus Scottus, of Charlemagne's Chancellor Eynhard, of Fulda, and especially of St Alban in Mainz. For more recent times he also used a number of popular rumours about Henry IV, and gives some first hand reports, e.g. from his own visit to St Anselm's monastery at Bec. After the year 1147, he ceased working on it. Various authors continued the Chronicles in a much more cursory fashion up to the year 1200, under which date is the last entry.

The Chronicles are of general historical value for the period of late eleventh to early twelfth century history,[1] due to the number of letters included, some of them surviving nowhere else, and due also to the dates and locations which the author consistently supplies, such as what year

---

[1] The *Cambridge Medieval History*, vol. 5, *Contest of Empire and Papacy*, ed. by J.R. Tanner (Cambridge: CUP, 1957) has a detailed political history of the Chronicler's period. See Chapter II, 'Gregory VII and the First Contest between Empire and Papacy' and Chapter III, 'Germany under Henry IV and Henry V', by Z.N. Brooke, and Chapter X, 'Germany 1125–1152', by Austin Lane Poole.

and where the Emperor spent the annual liturgical feasts of Christmas and Easter. More specifically, they are a primary source for the early history of Disibodenberg, and thus provide invaluable background for the lives of Jutta and Hildegard.

For a brief sketch of the ecclesiastical and political background of the *Chronicles*, we may go back to the 1080s, when Cardinal Otto of Ostia, sometime prior of Cluny and later Pope Saint Urban II, was papal legate in Germany. He worked tirelessly to strengthen the alliance between three forces: (1) the determination of the Popes to extricate the Church in Germany from its submergence in civil (imperial) polity and to raise the spiritual level of the clergy, (2) the contemporary movement of monastic renewal led by Abbot William of Hirsau, and (3) the political opposition to Henry IV and the Salian dynasty on the part of the free nobility which was focussed particularly in Saxony.

The Disibodenberg Chronicler writes entirely within the perspective of this axis of interests: pro-papal, pro-monastic, and anti-Salian. Such dispositions were very much shared by the Counts of Sponheim, the Formbach family of Jutta's mother, and the entire social and religious milieu in which the lives of Jutta and Hildegard took their shape. According to *VJ* III, Jutta's brother Meinhard was instrumental in her choice of an anchoress's life at the newly refounded Disibodenberg. As Count, Meinhard was also a promoter of the Hirsau type of monastic life. In 1124 he founded a monastery at the church of Sponheim itself. Hildegard's father, Hildebert , was one of the lower free nobility closely connected with the Counts of Sponheim. Sophia, mother of Meinhard and Jutta, was first cousin of Hedwig, mother of Lothar, Duke of Saxony, who became the 'Church's choice' for Emperor, when largely through the efforts of Archbishop Adalbert I of Mainz, the Salian dynasty was defeated at the imperial election of 1125. Count Meinhard was there, participating in the election of his second cousin.

Quite apart from the historical information they contain, the Chronicles convey much of the intellectual, spiritual and monastic culture, i.e. the 'climate' or 'tonality' of Disibodenberg from its foundation up to the year 1147. Thus, they are a fitting prelude to what immediately follows that watershed year in the life of Hildegard.

The most obvious comment to make about the intellectual culture of the Chronicles is that it is marked by a very *theocentric* approach to history, much like that of the historical books of the Old Testament. Certainly, the Chronicler is concerned to ground his account soberly in the annalistic world of names and dates and cited documents, yet at the same time his 'theological' history tends through its eschatological perspective and its interest in signs, wonders and most pertinently *visions*, to an incipient apocalypticism. Allowing for the differing foci of the *AD* and the *VJ*, it is notable how much consistency of outlook and method there is between this writer of 'historiography', and the writer of Jutta's 'hagiography'.[2]

It is argued later in this volume that the anonymous author of the *VJ* is Volmar, Hildegard's secretary in the second half of her life. Could it possibly be that this same Volmar is the anonymous Chronicler as well? Admittedly, this would seem to be too much of a good thing—it would be too bad for a twelfth-century Benedictine monastery if it had only one really literate monk! The disagreement between *VJ* III and *AD* 1136 on the number of those enclosed with Jutta in the year 1112 does appear to rule out the same author for both documents, though there is the fact that even Staab, the editor of the *VJ*, acquits himself of the same confusion.[3] To some extent the consistency of outlook remarked above may be attributed to shared commonplaces of the time and setting.

Still, there are some circumstances worth pondering. It is at least a strange coincidence that the Chronicler stops work precisely in 1147, that pivotal year of Hildegard's, and *ipso facto* Volmar's, life. Of course the Chronicler may have died or been assigned to other duties.

Both the author of *AD* and the author of the *VJ* are concerned to anchor their narrative with concrete dates and names, in particular of abbots, archbishops and emperors. Aspects of the Chronicler's presentation of St Anselm seem at times like an uncanny forecast of Hildegard's life, gifts, and interests. Both documents embrace reports of miracles and visions. The passage about a 'temptation of the flesh' in *VJ* VI and the one in *AD* 1194, share some common vocabulary and perspectives, and, at the very least, indicate a similar degree of trust reposed in the author/confidant.

---

[2] These genre categories were only coined in the setting of mid- to late-nineteenth-century German secularism and nationalism. Felice Lifschitze closely examines them with regard to pre-scholastic literature, and shows the distinction between 'historiography' and so-called 'hagiography' to be completely anachronistic: 'Beyond Positivism and Genre: "Hagiographical" Texts as Historical Narrative', *Viator*, 25 (1994), 95-113. In medieval Latin, the term *hagiographa* referred not to saints' 'lives', but to the Scriptures.

[3] See the note on this text at *AD* 1136.

Similar formulas can be detected such as, 'in order to avoid tediousness, we will dispense with inserting it here, and hasten on' (*AD* 1094), and 'which we will avoid inserting here because it would take too long' (*VJ* III). Then there is a similar, bare mention of 'Hildegard' by name only, without any honorific, in both *AD* 1136 and *VJ* VIII.

But surely there were other Disibodenberg monks competent for such work apart from Volmar? The sources suggest that Disibodenberg did not have an oversupply of adequately qualified monks or priest-monks. Why did the monks' chapter have to fetch the 'priests' of the neighbourhood in Ep. 38, VIIII, in a report which Guibert emphasizes he had from the brothers? Why did Cuno have to be 'ordained' when assuming the office of Abbot (*AD* 1136)?[4] Why, in the early 1150s, did a prior of Disibodenberg speak of the needed 'salvation' of his monastery at the time of Hildegard's departure?[5]

Intrinsic to Hildegard's submission of her prophetic call for approval was a request for Volmar's help.[6] If Volmar was the best that Disibodenberg had to offer, perhaps fulfilling a role of *magister scholarum* and *armarius* (keeper of documents, archivist) like Theodoric at Echternach, it would partly explain the extent of Hildegard's struggle with her Abbot and the monks to have Volmar also sent with her to Rupertsberg. If Volmar and the Chronicler were one and the same, it would explain why the Chronicler stops work in 1147, and no-one with

---

[4] 'The twelfth century was a period of transition: before then, few Benedictine monks were ordained, whereas by the thirteenth century, a nonordained monk would be the exception', from a note to me by Barbara Newman, whom I thank for sounding a caution about the idea of Volmar as the Chronicler. To Newman, the Chronicler savours of a very different style and viewpoint from that of Volmar in the *VJ*.

[5] J.L. Baird and R.K. Ehrmann, *Letters of Hildegard of Bingen*, vol. 1 (Oxford: OUP, 1994), Letter 78, pp. 172–73. See the last footnote to the Introduction to the *VJ*.

[6] See Ep. 38, XIII and XIIII, and Hildegard's *Scivias*, ed. by Adelgundis Führkötter and Angela Carlevaris, CCCM 43 (Turnhout: Brepols, 1978), Protestificatio, p. 5, in the translation by Columba Hart and Jane Bishop (New York: Paulist Press, 1989), p. 60: 'In My love she searched in her mind as to where she could find someone who would run in the path of salvation. And she found such a one and loved him, knowing that he was a faithful man, WORKING LIKE HERSELF ON ANOTHER PART OF THE WORK THAT LEADS TO ME. And holding fast to him, she worked with him in great zeal so that my hidden miracles would be revealed. And she did not seek to exalt herself above herself but with many sighs bowed to him whom she found in the ascent of humility and the intention of good will.' Is there a hint here of Volmar's other literary activities?

the same commitment or competence is found to replace him at the task, and also why in the years that followed Abbot Cuno tried to retrieve Volmar, incurring Hildegard's fulminations thereby: 'if you try to take away the shepherd of spiritual medicine [Volmar] then again I say, you are sons of Belial, and in this do not look to the justice of God'.[7] In the end she had to resort to canonical sanctions to prevent his recall.[8]

The shortage of learned monks and priest-monks, or some kind of internal trouble at Disibodenberg, seems to have worsened as time went on, for after Volmar died in 1173, Hildegard had such difficulties in trying to obtain a replacement from Disibodenberg that only her obtaining an intervention from the Pope himself had the needed effect. In the following decade, the 1180s, the nuns were relying on the monastery of Siegberg for a priest, since Disibodenberg did not have the priests to spare.[9] By 1224, Trithemius says, 'religious life had dwindled so much in the monastery of Disibodenberg', that the nuns of Rupertsberg 'became more daring' and obtained the agreement of Archbishop Sifrid of Mainz for their transfer from the charge of the Abbot of Disibodenberg to the Abbot of Sponheim. Eventually, Trithemius says, the character of religious life degenerated at Sponheim too, and the nuns became free of any abbot.[10]

None of the above amounts to conclusive evidence of the identity of the Chronicler. Volmar may have been the one, or may not. The question remains open.

In the following translations, SMALL CAPITALS are used for all texts dealing directly with events at Disibodenberg and for items concerning Bishop Otto and the Archbishops of Mainz. Texts are included which illustrate attitudes to women and texts which show the Chronicler's sense of the precariousness of human events and his religious evaluation of them, which completely buttress Hildegard's own characterization of the times in which she was born (*VH* II, 2). Examples of the Chronicler's

---

[7] *Explanatio Symboli Sancti Athanasii* (PL 197, 1066). The translation is from Peter Dronke, *Women Writers of the Middle Ages* (Cambridge: CUP, 1984), p. 153.

[8] See Archbishop Arnold's second charter for Rupertsberg, 1158.

[9] See Guibert's Ep. 33, Derolez, p. 344.

[10] See Trithemius, *Chron. Sponh.*, p. 268. In *Chron. Hirsaug.*, p. 191, Trithemius reports that in the year 1259 Disibodenberg was transferred to the Cistercian Order.

openness to reports of miracles and visions, which play such a role in the *vitae* of both Jutta and Hildegard, are here presented; so too, instances of his 'symbolic' reading of meteorological and climatic phenomena. The entire entry on St Anselm for the year 1094 is translated, for the Chronicler presents here not less than a verbal ikon of an ideal monastic father, and of Bec as his ideal monastery, which he seems to have personally visited.

At the end, a few historically relevant items from the Chronicles after 1147 are added. The note about a famine in 1151 is of interest, since that was during the early years at Rupertsberg, when the nuns experienced much want and hardship (*VH* II, 5). We suitably conclude with a mention of Archbishop Willigis, with whom the account began.

In summing up the overall impression made by the Chronicler, one could hardly do better than repeat with Sabina Flanagan:[11]

> Even from this short selection of entries it can be seen that, as far as the Disibodenberg chronicler was concerned, contemporary events illustrated sudden reverses of fortune, shifting allegiances, and a world where the balance of good and evil was constantly fluctuating. In fact, he only seems to recognize unequivocal progress when his gaze is withdrawn from the wider world and concentrated on the establishment and growth of the monastery of Disibodenberg itself, culminating in the dedication of the chapel of St Mary by Henry of Mainz in 1146.

---

[11] *Hildegard of Bingen, 1098–1179: A Visionary Life* (London: Routledge, 1989), p. 21.

THE CHRONICLES OF DISIBODENBERG

SELECT ENTRIES

975   In this year Rupert, the most honourable Archbishop of Mainz, died. IN HIS PLACE, WILLIGIS WAS CONSTITUTED. HE BUILT THE MONASTERY OF ST STEPHAN, WHERE HE IS BURIED. HE ALSO RESTORED THE DIVINE SERVICE AT MOUNT ST DISIBOD WITH CANONS, WHICH HATTO HIS PREDECESSOR, OR RATHER THE PREDECESSOR OF ARCHBISHOP RUPERT, HAD DISMANTLED WHEN HE EXPELLED THE MONKS FROM THERE.

1075   In these times, but not all in the same year, there arose a great and savage discord in the Teutonic kingdom, that is, between Henry and the princes of Saxony.

... By means of priests given to concubinage, that is, heretics, Henry did not fear to defile and besmirch the unique and beloved bride of the Lord (cf. Rev. 21:2) *whom he redeemed* from the enemy *with his* own *precious blood* (Acts 20:28; 1 Pet. 1:19), while in the manner of Simon (cf. Acts 8:18–21) he put up spiritual offices for sale, that is, the free gifts of the Holy Spirit, through iniquitous transactions contrary to Catholic faith. Catholic men saw and heard these things, and likewise the other disgraceful and unheard-of crimes of King Henry, which were to be found in the Church at that time. Then, like the prophet Elijah *they were filled with zeal for the Lord of Israel* (1 Kg. 19:14) and sent messengers to Rome, to Alexander, high-priest of the Apostolic See, deploring in tears and lamenting before him both by letters and the living voice these and many other things which the senseless simoniac heretics said and did in the Teutonic kingdom with Henry as their instigator and protector ...

1088   Wezil the Archbishop of Mainz died. THE LORD RUTHARD SUCCEEDED HIM.

1093   The Lord Emehard was ordained on the sixth day before the Kalends of April [27 March] at Würzburg. Bratislav, Duke of Bohemia suddenly fell off his horse at the hunt and instantly died the death.

Conrad, son of the Emperor Henry[12] rebelled against his father for this reason. King Henry took to hating Queen Adelheid,[13] whom he had taken as wife, so that his hatred became greater than the love with which he had formerly loved her. He even placed her in custody and allowed many to use force against her. He is said to have reached such a pitch of madness as to have urged his son mentioned above to go into her. When he refused to pollute his father's bed, the king addressed him not as his own son but declared that he was the son of a stranger, that is to say, of a certain Swabian prince to whose appearance Conrad bore a great resemblance.

After this Queen in her innocence had had many unheard-of kinds of evil brought against her, it was as if she were set free by the mercy of God from the custody in which she was held, and making her escape she fled to the most powerful woman of that time, called Matilda,[14] who took the Queen into her protection and led her to that venerable man, Urban, high priest of the Apostolic See. She cast herself at his feet and, pouring out her tears and racking with sobs, she made known to him the whole horror of the calamity which had been brought against her.

When that Apostolic Lord learnt the Queen's calamity he was moved with human compassion for her wretched plight, and having called an assembly of Catholics[15] he freshly excommunicated King Henry for the unlawful, criminal deeds, unheard-of in all the centuries, which he had perpetrated against his lawful wife.[16] Then the Queen returned to her own

---

[12] Henry IV, 1056–1106.

[13] Praxedis, daughter of the Grand Duke of Kiev.

[14] Matilda, countess of Tuscany 1046–1115, *La Gran' Contessa*, 'hand-maid of St Peter', 'heroine of Christian Italy'. Matilda interceded for Henry IV at her castle of Canossa in 1077, but after his breach of faith became an indefatigable supporter of the Popes and their aims. She was the close friend of Popes Gregory VII and Urban II and Abbot Hugh of Cluny. She combined ascetical and mystical inclinations with the most vigorous political and indeed military activities. She was known to sometimes don armour and lead her troops herself during her intermittent wars with Henry IV. In 1634 Pope Urban VIII re-interred her remains in the new St Peter's at Rome, in a tomb with the inscription: 'This warrior woman disposed her troops as the Amazon Penthesilea used to do. Thanks to her, through so many contests of frightful war, man was never able to conquer the rights of God.' See Antonia Fraser, *Boadicea's Chariot* (London: Weidenfeld & Nicolson, 1988), pp. 131–50.

[15] The Council of Piacenza in 1095.

[16] In 1094 when Pope Urban's position was more secure, he had also excommunicated

country where she entered a monastery and, as some say, became an abbess.

There was an eclipse of the sun at the third hour of the day, and a dragon became visible. Whence, Conrad, when it appeared above, rebelled against his father and came to Pope Urban. Absolved from excommunication, he reigned in Lombardy against his father. This Conrad is said to have been outstanding for his goodness and upright conduct, humble, modest and charitable. However, he lived only a few years after his coronation and died before his time.

1094 There was a great plague. At this time there flourished in the church of Canterbury, Archbishop Anselm most blessed and worthy before God. His truly orthodox and illuminating books,[17] which may be found in many communities, are a testimony to his holiness. Before he was called to the episcopate this blessed man was the Father of monks at the monastery of Bec. All his zeal was to instruct them in the paths of righteousness by means of the word of doctrine and the carrying out of most sacred works, that they might be formed to a love of the life of their heavenly homeland. How greatly there flourished in this monastery the zeal for reading in the liberal arts along with the practice of the monastic way of life! Accordingly, among the varied studies of the students, some applied themselves to the reading of secular books, some to the reading of sacred books.

There occurred in the same region a deadly plague, and on all sides, a great number of people were succumbing to the fatality. That unrelenting disaster had already taken over the monastery itself. So, when some of the brothers were dying, fear was troubling all of them, and very many prayers were offered to the Lord. But one night, an angel wielding a spear appeared to the brothers as they rested in the dormitory; he indicated with a touch each one who was going to die in turn. He came to a certain young man who had applied his mind to the epistles of the blessed Paul. When the one striking was stood by and hesitated, the angel of the Lord said: 'Why do you stand still?' He replied: 'I am sparing'. The angel said, 'Strike! Why do you leave off?' He replied, 'I am sparing the one who is faithful'. To this the angel replied: 'Whom? - the boy Paul.' The angel

---

King Philip I of France for putting away his wife Queen Bertha and marrying Bertrada, wife of Count Fulk of Réchin.

[17] *cuius sanctitatem praestant libri eius rectissimi et luculenti.*

said, 'thank so great a master, through whom you have escaped death.'[18]
And thus the plague was calmed.

In the same monastery a certain youth underwent a severe temptation
of the flesh. He confessed it to the blessed Father, from whom he received
unfailing support, so that he controlled himself most carefully in every
way. Now the youth was following the counsel of the blessed Father with
all his might, when suddenly that organ became so distended with a
tumour that he could scarcely walk. But the distress could not remain
hidden from the blessed Father of the brothers. On being asked by him
what the nature of his distress was, he confessed his suffering, though
with a blush. That blessed Father raised his hand and made the sign of the
cross saying: 'I believe in my God that from this hour you shall be freed.'
And immediately the entire tumour was healed and the suffering of the
flesh was soothed.[19]

In that same monastery I heard of a certain event which was truly
marvellous[20] and worth commending to the memory of many.

One day the brothers were sitting at table. Among them was a very
devout senior much given to contemplation. He deserved to have the eyes
of his mind opened by the Lord, with the result that he saw what was
going on in a way that the others could not, and this was in order that
many might be corrected.

So it happened one day that he was caught up in contemplation and
perceived a little Ethiopian, very short, clad in rags, standing in the midst
of the refectory. He was letting down a sizeable basket from above on a
rope. He placed it in the middle and then scurried around in every
direction under the tables of the brothers while they ate, collecting the
crumbs which fell into their laps through their carelessness. When these
were collected he most carefully conveyed them to the basket above
mentioned. Then he pulled on the rope and drew up the basket into the
air. When he had seen these things the senior almost fainted for fear. But
he saw the same thing again after a few days. So he rose from table, and
summoned the Ethiopian in the name of the Lord. He asked who he was,

---

[18] This is a literal translation. The text seems quite confused as if there are sentences or
phrases which have dropped out.

[19] This story is unknown elsewhere. Possibly the author heard it from the youth when
visiting Bec as he goes on to describe.

[20] *In eodem monasterio audivi rem contigisse valde mirabilem.*

what he was doing and how long he had been doing it. He answered in front of all: 'If you desire to know who I am, look at my form. But my task, you should know, is to carefully note your [*plur.*] negligences, in order that I may have something to accuse you of in the presence of the most just Judge on the day of Judgment. I began to carry out this task on the day this place was founded, and I have kept it up without a break to this very hour.'

Alas, how very cleverly and resourcefully the enemy of the human race stalks us wretches with his snares! Accordingly, we wish that all equally, brothers and lords, rich and poor of both sexes be warned so that they may lay these things to heart, and not misuse the gifts of the Lord, but rather fill the laps of the needy from those things which seem to you less abundant, from the crumbs I say, yes even from fragments.

The blessed Father Anselm was still serving in the above-mentioned monastery in the office of Abbot, when a certain cleric[21] in France presumed to make this extravagant assertion: 'If', he said, 'there are three persons in God, and only one substance[22] (and not three substances, each one separately, just like three angels or three souls, although so as to be entirely the same in will and power), therefore, the Father and the Holy Spirit became incarnate with the Son.' Though the originator of this perverse teaching was outwitted and convicted by the Fathers and the Doctors of the Church's faith, and was almost handed over to death by the people, it was said that in order to escape death he abjured his error. Against this error Father Anselm began a letter while abbot, which he completed when bishop, in which he wrote to Urban, high priest of the Apostolic See.

He also wrote a letter to Walram, bishop of Nuremberg, on the procession of the Holy Spirit. He begins by vigorously taking Bishop

---

[21] Roscelin of Compiègne, called to task for tritheism at the Council of Soissons in 1092. He figures in the early development of medieval nominalism, and is mainly known through the writings of his adversaries, Anselm and Abelard. His basically anti-realist position found it hard to concede any but a verbal existence to universals, so that, for him, each *res* was an individual reality or subsistence. The passage within the brackets represents his own line of thinking. It is not that Roscelin asserted that all three persons of the Trinity *were* incarnate, but that this would be the consequence if they were only one *res*, i.e. one 'reality.' Instead he thought they were three *res*, or *substantia*, in effect, three gods.

[22] *Si, inquit, in Deo tres personae sunt, una tantum res ...*

Walram to task for favouring Henry, and declares himself compliant and obedient in all things to the pronouncements and sanctions of the Apostolic Lord Urban:

> Anselm, servant of the church of Canterbury to Walram, Bishop of Nurem-berg. I curtly address one who knows—if I were sure that your prudence does not favour the successor of Julius Caesar and Nero and Julian the Apostate, against the successor and vicar of the Apostle Peter, I would most gladly greet you as 'very dear and reverend Bishop'.
> Since you ask for the defence of the truth against the Greeks, we ought not fail in this as far as we can. So I have sent you a small work which I wrote against them concerning the procession of the Holy Spirit. But concerning the Sacrifice, in which the same Greeks do not think in agreement with us, it would seem to many reasonable Catholics, that just because this is what the Greeks do, it is not against the Christian faith ...[23]

Because this letter is so very long, like the one above, in order to avoid tediousness, we will dispense with inserting it here, and hasten on to other things.

He also wrote a short letter to William the Abbot of Hirsau [d. 1091], in which, using the most searching discernment he gave a response that was humble indeed, but confirmed by the authority of the scriptures, to questions addressed to him about a certain count who had been excommunicated by the Apostolic See, about the wives of priests, about those fallen away who had holy orders, about those polluted by secret offences who have confessed, about those who are too ashamed or stupid or stiff-necked to willingly confess, and yet who proudly seek office. With divine authority he also composed books of great power, one on the Incarnation of the Lord which is called *Cur Deus Homo*, the second which is named *Monologion*, a third entitled *Proslogion*. He laboured greatly in the composing of his meditations and prayers, sometimes sweating over verses of his which survive, well-constructed in hexameters and pentameters.

---

[23] This refers to the dispute over the use of leavened or unleavened bread in the Eucharist, mooted particularly by Photius Patriarch of Constantinople (820–891). Whereas Anselm defended on doctrinal grounds the Western addition of *Filioque* to the Niceno-Constan-tinopolitan Creed, and refuses Photius's censure of the West over the use of unleavened Eucharistic bread, he does not support the imposition of the Western Eucharistic practice on them, but allows the opinion that the Greek custom of using leavened bread for the Eucharist is valid.

1095   Adelman, abbot of Saint Alban's died. Margrave Lupold and Henry, Count Palatine died.

In the year of the Lord 1095 and the following, that is 1096, certain heavenly portents threatened the world, things never seen or heard before were predicted through frequent signs. Let us mention two of them, so that our credibility about the rest may be strengthened. An apparition of fire in the form of a lightning bolt, shaped like a spear, but broader, moving about on the very brightest day in the blaze of the sun itself, struck the eyes of beholders with an unexpected terror, though it injured no-one. In addition to this, one day, when the sun was setting in the west, something like fire-balls erupted in the air in various places; they then withdrew themselves into other parts of the sky. Some people thought that this was not fire, but the angels called 'Powers', prefiguring the tumult of the nations, which is what followed.

While such things were still before people's eyes, behold, there arose a certain anchorite in the regions of Spain, called Peter, who left his enclosure and set in motion the whole world.[24] He carried around a certain document, which, he asserted, had fallen from heaven, containing the message that the whole of Christianity from all parts of the world was to put on armour and go to Jerusalem, cast out the pagans from it, and so possess it and all its borders forever. Moreover the Gospel witness confirmed it, *And Jerusalem*, said the Lord Jesus, *shall be trod down by the nations until the time of the nations is fulfilled* (Lk. 21:24). Whereupon not only country people, but even kings, dukes and other powerful ones of the world were stirred, and I shall go on to greater things: bishops, monks and the other orders of the Church were moved to make this journey.

At length when all these mentioned were agreed in purpose, kingdoms were left empty by their rulers, cities by their pastors, villages by their inhabitants. Not only men and boys, but many women also took part in this journey, for a marvellous spirit in those times impelled people to take up this journey. Indeed females went forth on this venture dressed as men and marched in armour.

When all who had crossed themselves to make this journey had assembled, they entered into a scheme that wherever they found Jews,

---

[24] *inclusus ... claustris egressus totum commovit orbem*—*inclusus/inclusa* is the same term used of Jutta and Hildegard at Disibodenberg, i.e. not just a 'hermit', but one dedicated to enclosure in an anchorhold.

they would draw them into Christianity, either willingly or forcibly, so that the memory of the Jewish name should not remain anywhere, and all those would be killed who did not embrace the name of Christian by signing themselves with the cross of the faith. And so it came about that some of the Jews, although unwilling, took refuge in Baptism, in order that they might not lose their lives as well as their fortunes. Many, however, were killed and their wealth seized by the Christians. The distress was so dreadful that the Jews were driven to stab and kill each other with knives. The men did not spare their wives nor their relatives; they put to death their mothers, sons and daughters.

And so, pressing on with the journey to Jerusalem, they reached a city of Pannonia which is called Mersberg, where a great part of them was killed. And deservedly! Since men were marching together with women as mentioned above, unclean deeds of fornication and abomination transpired among them. For this reason they well deserved the wrath of God.

1097   Henry returned from Italy and allowed to those Jews baptized under duress the preceding year their Jewish law and custom.[25] Praxedis the Queen departed from the Emperor.

1098   RUTHARD THE ARCHBISHOP OF MAINZ WOULD NOT CONDONE THE EXCOMMUNICATED KING, AND SO LOST HIS FAVOUR;[26] HE WITHDREW

---

[25] Jews were instrumental in the mercantile development of the Rhineland towns—e.g. in 1086 the Bishop of Speyer was careful to establish Jews in his town for its commercial advantage, and granted them special privileges. An important part of Henry IV's power base was the support of Rhineland townspeople and the Jews. Mainz itself held the leading Jewish community and the largest rabbinical school in Europe. The first crusade was diverted into persecution of the Jews, especially in the Rhineland by some of the nobles who were in debt. They did this on a pretext of including Jews with Moslems as 'infidels'—no matter that this was not Palestine on a war footing. On 27 May 1096 there was a great massacre in Mainz led by Count Emich of Leisingen who invaded the bishop's palace, where many had taken refuge. Some Jews fled to Rüdesheim, but were pursued and attacked there by Emich. In the second crusade (1146–47) St Bernard of Clairvaux visited the Rhineland and had to intervene very strongly to stymie a recurrence of anti-Jewish violence. Cf. Bernard Dov Weinryb, 'Mainz', *Encyclopaedia Judaica* (Jerusalem: Keter, 1972), vol. 11, cols 788–92.

[26] There may be something more to his disappearance from Mainz. Henry, at the time of his son's election at Mainz, wanted to open an enquiry into Ruthard's performance during the Mainz pogrom of 1097. The Archbishop was legally the protector of the Jews. See Peter Rassow, 'Über Erzbischof Ruthard von Mainz 1089-1109', in *Universitas: Dienst*

INTO THURINGIA AND STAYED THERE FOR SOME YEARS.

1099 The Emperor celebrated Easter at Regensburg, where there was a deadly epidemic, in which Rabod, the Count Palatine, died and many others. Conrad, Bishop of Utrecht was cruelly killed on the fourth day of Easter by the merchant Fresico. Burchard was constituted in his place. Herman the bishop of Cologne died, to whom Frederick succeeded. Conrad, bishop of Eichstadt died. Conrad was constituted in his place.

Pope Urban, also called Otto, died. Abbot Reynher, that is Paschal, succeeded him, the 151st since Peter, for eighteen years. After Urban died, his death was revealed to a certain religious in a vision. To the one who asked who was going to be Pontiff after him, the one who appeared to him replied: 'Abbot Reynher'. When asked again how long he might live, he said, 'Look at the kneeler in your choir-stall.' When he looked at it, he saw a small parchment sheet lying there, one part of it with bristles, the other part smooth. It was inscribed with a few letters like this: 'Three, three fours, and three,' which added up together make eighteen. So he enquired of him again why the parchment sheet was partly bristly, partly smooth. He replied, 'The time of his pontificate shall be partly placid and serene, partly turbulent and chaotic.' Subsequent events proved this was destined to be very true.

In these times there arose a band of monks, who are clothed not in black but in grey attire. Their founder, some say, was Adam[27] ...

On the Ides of July [15 July] Jerusalem was taken by the Christians, on the same day in which the dispersal of the Apostles took place, while Godfrey, the leader of the army was in command there; and immediately the Christians set him up as king over themselves.

1100 The event of this year is as follows:

To the Lord Paschal, Pope of the Roman church, and to all bishops and every follower of the Christian faith, from the Archbishop of Pisa and Duke Godfrey, by favour of the Church of God, now protector of the Holy Sepulchre, Regemund Count of St Egidius, and the entire army of God

---

an Wahrheit und Leben: Festschrift für Dr. Albert Stohr, ed. by Ludwig Lenhart (Mainz: Matthias-Grünewald-Verlag, 1960), pp. 55–56.

[27] I.e. the Cistercians. Cf. Hildegard's very long Letter 84r, in reply to Meffrid prior of Eberbach, subtitled 'to the Grey monks' and containing a theology of monastic life. She also had contacts with Ebrach near Bamberg, founded in 1127 from Morimund. Its first abbot was an Adam (d. 1161) venerated in the order as Blessed.

which is in the land of Israel, greetings and many prayers and supplications
of prayers in all joy and exultation in the sight of God, for God has
magnified his mercy, bringing to completion in us what was promised in
ancient times.

For when Nicea had been captured, the whole army set out from there.
There were more than thirty thousand in arms. Yet though it was so great a
multitude, which could have occupied all of the Byzantine world and could
have drunk up all the rivers, and eaten all the cornfields in one day,
nevertheless the Lord led them with so great a plenitude that a levy of
scarcely twelve sheep and oxen was accepted. And although the leaders
and kings of the Saracens rose up against us, by God's will, they were
easily conquered and trampled down.

Because some became puffed up at these successful deeds, God put
Antioch in our way, unassailable by human strength. He kept us there for
nine months, and in the siege outside, he so humbled us that in the whole
of our army scarcely a hundred good horses could be found. God opened to
us the bounty of his blessing and mercy, and led us into Antioch where the
Turks and all of them paid tribute to our ascendancy. But since we held on
to these things as if we had acquired them by our own strength, and did not
worthily magnify God who had offered them to us, we were besieged by a
great multitude of Saracens. No one dared leave the great city. At length
the famine became so strong that there were some who scarcely restrained
themselves from human flesh. It would take a long time to tell all the
miseries in that city. But God looked on the people whom he had scourged
so long, and in his kindness consoled them. To begin with, as if in
recognition of our tribulation, he conferred on us his lance, that rueful
blessing from the time of the Apostles, as a pledge of our victory ...

1102   The nineteenth cycle began, and the tenth indiction. The emperor
celebrated the Nativity of the Lord at Mainz. The Emperor entered
Flanders with an army and restored peace. RUPERT THE BISHOP OF
BAMBERG DIED; OTTO[28] WAS CONSTITUTED IN HIS PLACE. Hartwig,

---

[28] St Otto of Bamberg (1060/62–1139) was appointed as Chancellor by Henry IV early in
1102 and then on 25 December of that year, Bishop of Bamberg. Otto went to Italy in
1106 and in May established concord on the matter of investiture between Pope Paschal II
and Archbishop Ruthard, who was technically his Metropolitan. Thereupon Otto was
ordained Bishop at Anagni by the Pope. He accompanied Henry V on his 1110–1111 trip
to Rome, receiving the pallium on 15 April 1111. He had a great reputation as a
peacemaker and an arbitrator between parties. While he supplied episcopal duties for
Adalbert and eventually ordained him bishop in 1115, their relationship had its strains. At
one time he was even placed under anathema by Adalbert (Brooke, *Cambridge Medieval*

Archbishop of Magdeburg died; Henry was constituted in his place.

1105 Henry, son of Emperor Henry, invaded the realm and began to reign while his father was still living. Moreover, the elder Henry wanted to invade Saxony with a hostile force on account of certain Catholics there, but he was able to accomplish very little, for his son detested him, as did also many of the faithful, because he had been denounced as excommunicate by three prelates of the Apostolic See, that is, Gregory, Urban and Paschal. During that very expedition, while he was trying to enter Saxony, his son, with a few others, escaped from the army. Henry was grieved over the secession of his son;[29] his schemes having fallen through, he gave up his expedition and returned. But his son was making for Swabia, where he was absolved of his excommunication[30] by the legate of the Roman pontiff, Gebhard Bishop of Constance, and so was restored to the bosom of mother Church. When matters had been sorted out with the Church there, he sought Bavaria and Saxony, deposed the usurpers through synod, but suspended from office others who favoured the heresiarch, forcing them to submit to examination by the Apostolic Lord.

RUTHARD THE ARCHBISHOP OF MAINZ WAS RESTORED TO HIS OWN DIOCESE EIGHT YEARS AFTER HE HAD DEPARTED. The Emperor celebrated the Nativity of the Lord at Mainz, and Easter likewise. Emehard, the bishop of Würzburg died.

1106 The Emperor was captured by his son before the Nativity of the

---

History vol. V, p. 104). This 'Father of Monks', called by Trithemius 'one of our order'(*Chron. Hirsaug.*, p. 128, and *Chron. Sponh.*, p. 249) founded up to thirty monasteries in his lifetime, speaking of them as 'inns which we erect on the road to eternity'. He sponsored especially the Hirsau Benedictines, Cistercians and Premonstratensians. Another well deserved epithet was 'Apostle of Pomerania'. He lead two missionary ventures there, one in 1124–1125, the second, with more lasting results, in 1128. He was canonized in 1189 by Pope Clement III. See the monk Ebbo's *Vita Ottonis Episcopi Babenbergensis*, in MGH SS 12, ed. by Rudolf Köpke, and R. Bartlett, 'The Conversion of a Pagan Society in the Middle Ages', *History* 70 (1985), 185–201, especially the long bibliographical note on p. 185.

[29] Henry V 1106–1125, was anointed king in 1099 with oaths of fealty to his father. He rebelled in 1104, successfully fought against his father and began to reign as king in his stead, though his position was not secure till his father's death.

[30] The younger Henry had incurred a penalty for flagrantly breaking a solemn public oath of fealty to his father which he had sworn preparatory to his crowning as 'king'.

Lord. King Henry celebrated the Nativity of the Lord at Mainz, where he held a meeting to arrange for peace. When the leaders had given their advice, he presented his father to his court. At Ingelheim, on the day before the Kalends of January [31 December], he had handed over his kingdom to his son above-mentioned, in the presence of certain leaders. Even though he had done this, in no way did he obtain from his son what was necessary for peace.

A comet star appeared. Magnus, the Duke of Saxony died. Since he had no heir, Count Lothar, son of Gebhard, obtained his dukedom.[31] The younger Henry besieged Cologne to the injury of his father. But meanwhile his father died; he was made ready at Liège and transferred to Speyer where he was deposited unburied in a certain small church, because he had remained excommunicated for so long a time by so many and such great fathers.[32]

I will complete the onerous history of this man with a brief epilogue.

It is manifestly clear in every way that Henry was a perverse man and cast out from the Church by a just judgment. For he sold all spiritual offices, was insubordinate to the Apostolic See, and advanced a usurper to this very see through supplanting Gregory with Guibert, exceeded all Christian bounds against his lawful wife, and made light of the judgment of the Pope. Out of this there arose a very great strife in the Church of God, for one exacted vengeance on another, brother maligned brother, one favoured the king while another the Pope, whence it happened that many perished. This evil increased to such an extent that the Apostolic censure was held for nothing, and even excommunication itself was all but ignored.

That I might not omit anything about him he was, to be sure, very merciful. There were some, who, wanting to run him through while he was seated for the necessities of nature, were caught and convicted and confessed. Yet he ordered them to depart unpunished. There were many

---

[31] He was assigned it by Henry V, who thus helped the advancement of the one who was to succeed him as king, in 1125.

[32] Henry had been excommunicated under Popes Gregory VII, Urban II and Paschal II. When in Rome in 1111, Henry V wrung from Paschal II not only the imperial crown and the concession of lay investiture, but also the posthumous absolution of his father who had died excommunicate. On his return to Germany he held a memorial service for his father on 7 August, 1111, whose body was then interred in the Salian family vault in Speyer Cathedral.

leaders, who had committed many offences against him, and had attacked him with great contempt. But as soon as they had prostrated themselves before him, he pardoned them everything. Yet though he was indeed compassionate and merciful in alms to the poor, because of his obstinacy of mind he remained excommunicate. These things hung like a cloud over all the works of his generosity. When his father was sick at Botfeld—for he had eaten death in the liver of a deer—he summoned to him the princes, and requested them insistently, and indeed commanded them, that they should swear to reserve the Empire for his son, which indeed they did when he was eight, and as yet unbaptized.

Henry V began his reign of twenty years; he was the 96th Roman Emperor, son of Emperor Henry III.

1108 The King celebrated the Nativity of the Lord at Aachen. King Henry entered Pannonia where, on account of the faithlessness of certain princes, he accomplished nothing worthy of memory. In the same year, almost three thousand Bohemian men were put to death by their own Duke.

THIS YEAR, THAT IS 1108, CONSTRUCTION BEGAN OF THE NEW MONASTERY AT DISIBODENBERG. BURCHARD OF LOVING MEMORY, THE ABBOT OF SAINT JAMES IN MAINZ WHOM THE LORD ARCHBISHOP RUTHARD HAD APPOINTED AS FIRST ABBOT OF THE COMMUNITY OF ST DISIBOD, PLACED THE FIRST FOUNDATION STONE ON THE SECOND DAY BEFORE THE KALENDS OF JULY [30 JUNE] BY COMMAND OF THE ABOVE MENTIONED PRELATE.

1109 The King celebrated the Nativity of the Lord at Mainz. In the same year, he betrothed to himself the daughter of the King of England.[33] RUTHARD THE ARCHBISHOP OF MAINZ DIED. TO HIM SUCCEEDED ADALBERT THE KING'S CHANCELLOR.[34]

---

[33] Matilda (1102–1167), only daughter of Henry I of England, and his designated heir. She and Emperor Henry V were formally married in 1114. 'Empress Maud', as she was known in England, had a turbulent career in later life, from 1139 to 1148 prosecuting an ultimately unsuccessful civil war against King Stephen for the English throne, then retiring to the Norman estates of her second husband, Geoffrey Plantagenet of Anjou, and exercising considerable influence on Stephan's successor, her son, Henry II of England. See *AD* 1125 and footnote.

[34] Adalbert, son of Count Sigehard of Saarbrücken was initially the protégé of Henry V, who made him chancellor in 1106, before the death of Henry IV, and nominated him Archbishop of Mainz, highest episcopal office in Germany, over the largest ecclesiastical

1112 The Emperor celebrated the Nativity of the Lord at Goslar. ADALBERT THE BISHOP WAS IMPRISONED.

1113 The Emperor celebrated the Nativity of the Lord at Erfurt. BURCHARD THE ABBOT OF SAINT JAMES DIED, WHO WAS ALSO THE FIRST ABBOT AT DISIBODENBERG. TO HIM SUCCEEDED FOR FIFTEEN YEARS THE LORD ADILHUN, A MAN VIGOROUS IN EVERY UNDERTAKING AND CON-SPICUOUS IN ALL THINGS FOR THE PROBITY OF HIS CONDUCT.

1115 The Emperor celebrated the Nativity of the Lord at Bamberg, and after the octave of Epiphany fought with the Saxons, losing many of his own. When he returned he celebrated Easter at Mainz. ADALBERT THE BISHOP WAS FREED FROM HIS CAPTIVITY.

1116 The Emperor celebrated the Nativity of the Lord at Speyer. After the octave of the Epiphany ADALBERT THE ARCHBISHOP WAS CONSECRATED AT COLOGNE BY OTTO THE BISHOP OF BAMBERG ON THE FEAST OF ST STEPHEN THE PROTO-MARTYR.[35]

1117 At dusk on the octave of St John the Evangelist [3 January] an earthquake occurred twice through the whole world. There was such a jolting that many buildings collapsed and people scarcely escaped. It was especially severe in Italy, where it was so perilous and frightening that people were in expectation of the revelation of God's judgment upon

---

province in Europe after Rome. Before investing him however, Henry took him on his expedition to Italy, 1110–1111, where Adalbert's political skills assisted him in his successful attempt to dominate Pope Paschal II. On returning to Germany, Henry invested Adalbert, who, though not yet ordained a bishop, entered into possession of the temporalities of the diocese, till then accruing to Henry, as they had accrued to Henry IV during the exiles of Archbishops Siegfried and Ruthard. This question and other canonical matters became a very sore point with Adalbert. Within the year his comportment towards the Emperor changed dramatically and he came out as a strong supporter of Pope, Church, and nobles, particularly in Saxony. The rupture between the two came in November 1112 (note!) with a violent manifesto from Henry who thereupon imprisoned Adalbert, and subjected him to severe mistreatment from November 1112 to December 1115, when a revolt by the citizens of Mainz forced Henry to release him. Adalbert was quickly ordained Bishop on 26 December, 1115, by Otto of Bamberg. Adalbert and Henry remained implacable lifelong foes. On Adalbert see Brooke, *Cambridge Medieval History*, vol. 5, pp. 156–60.

[35] There is an inconsistency here. St Stephen's feast is 26 December, and the octave of the Epiphany, 13 January.

themselves. In various places of Italy, cities, castles and towns where people were staying suddenly perished in clefts of the earth. For mountains were torn and rivers were swallowed up by the earth and dried up so that those who wanted to, could cross on their feet. Why, the river Po even lifted itself from its bed and extended itself on high in the form of an arch, so that a way opened up between the earth and the water. By the raising of the waters we can clearly understand that an exodus from the world was impending. For when the water was hanging like this for a time, it let itself down in a thunderous clamour, so that the roar of it was heard by thousands.

At such marvellous and awesome signs, spread about in all sides, everyone throughout Italy engaged in prayer and fasting for three days. At Cremona a certain baby, lying in his cradle covered in wraps, opened his mouth contrary to nature and gave utterance in speech for the first time. His mother was giving food to his elder brother who had been crying and demanding bread. The baby checked her for this care of the body, asserting that he could see Mary the Mother of God standing before the judgment seat of Christ, imploring him with the most urgent prayers on account of the judgment which he was intending to give the world because of its sins. After this the baby laid aside his speech until the time that was proper for the human condition.

Despite such great and frightening wonders, those who saw them and who barely escaped the dangers of death, were not pierced with mindfulness. They did not give thanks to God for their escape. Those who heard of such stupendous signs did not give glory to God, but remained impervious in their vicious ways, and added still greater sins to those they had already done. For in this same year many were the evils perpetrated: conspiracies of injustice, acts of arson, murders, the burning of churches and filchings of the things used for the service of God there. It was especially so in the regions of Gaul where citizens rose up against citizens, imprisoned those who did not concur with them, snatched goods, destroyed and set fire to cities, castles, houses and farms. Human beings—in a way no longer human but more like herd animals—tore each other to pieces and killed.

Twice in this year there was an eclipse of the moon, that is the sixteenth day before the Kalends of July [16 June] and the third day before the Ides of December [11 December]. A marvellous sign appeared in the sky in an array of colours, on the seventeenth day before the Kalends of January [16 December].

1125 The Emperor Henry IV, the fifth of this name as king, died. LOTHAR, DUKE OF SAXONY WAS CONSTITUTED IN HIS PLACE[36] AT MAINZ ON THE THIRD DAY BEFORE THE KALENDS OF SEPTEMBER, [30 AUGUST] AND WAS CROWNED ON THE IDES OF SEPTEMBER [13 SEPTEMBER] AT AACHEN BY FREDERICK ARCHBISHOP OF COLOGNE. Honorius, 154th Pope after Peter, sat for five years, two months and eight days. Queen Mathilda journeyed to England, to her father, taking with her a hand of St James. Through this, irreparable damage was done to the kingdom of the French ... Cardinal Gerhard and the Bishops of Cambrai and Verdun were sent as legates to Rome for his confirmation as king.

1128 The King celebrated the Nativity of the Lord at Würzburg, where he appointed Embrich as Bishop. Speyer was besieged from the Ides of August [13 August], till the Kalends of November [1 November]. Alexander the bishop-elect of Liege received investiture at Mainz from the King. Bernard was constituted Bishop of Paderborn. Andrew, the provost of Liège, was ordained Bishop of Utrecht. The King celebrated Easter at Mersberg in royal style. Here, on Holy Saturday, he received from the baptismal font[37] the son of the Duke of Bohemia, who had been sent for this purpose.

ADILHUN, THE SECOND ABBOT OF DISIBODENBERG PASSED AWAY ON THE FIFTEENTH DAY BEFORE THE KALENDS OF JULY [17 JUNE]; FULCARD SUCCEEDED HIM AS ABBOT.

1130 Speyer was induced to capitulate. Honorius, 154th Pope, died. In his place two were constituted, Gregory, who is called Innocent, and Peter, whose other name is Anacletus, son of a certain powerful man among the Romans called Pierleoni. At the monastery of Cluny, the monk Berthold, Bishop of Hildesheim died, in whose place Bernard, the

---

[36] Henry V died childless on 23 May 1125, the last of the Salian line. Before he died he entrusted the royal insignia to his wife, Empress Matilda, and designated his Hohenstaufen nephew Frederick, Duke of Swabia, as his heir and successor. However Archbishop Adalbert 'by means not too reputable, if we are to believe Bishop Otto, succeeded in persuading the Empress to surrender the insignia' (Poole, *Cambridge Medieval History*, vol. 5, p. 335), and, having the prescriptive right of 'first voice' in the election of a king, was able to skilfully manage the electors so as to reject Frederick and choose a candidate more suitable to Church interests, Duke Lothar of Saxony. Thus it was due to Adalbert that the elective principle was rendered effective again and established from then on. Lothar's reign was marked by his conciliatory friendship toward Pope and Church.

[37] I.e. the King Lothar was his god-father.

Magister of students, was constituted. Volpert, the Abbot of St Alban's died, in whose place Werner was constituted. Burchard, Bishop of Cambrai died. Udo of Frankenleuf was killed by the henchmen of Count Adalbert. Herman of Winzburg invited Burchard of Lochenheim, a man most loyal to the King, to a meeting, and killed him. Ludwig received the Countship, removed from Herman at his judgment, from the King in Zürich. The Castle at Nuremberg was handed over to the King.

THE ALTAR TO SAINT STEPHEN, SITUATED IN THE SOUTHERN PART OF THE NEW MONASTERY, WAS DEDICATED BY THE LORD ADALBERT ARCH-BISHOP OF MAINZ IN HONOUR OF OUR LORD JESUS CHRIST, AND OF THE BLESSED VIRGIN MARY, AND SPECIALLY OF ALL THE MARTYRS, IN PARTICULAR SAINTS STEPHEN THE PROTO-MARTYR, LAURENCE, VINCENT AND ALBAN.

1136   The Emperor returned to Italy with a second army against Roger, king of Sicily. ON THE FIFTH DAY BEFORE THE IDES OF NOVEMBER [9 NOVEMBER] FULCARD OF LOVING MEMORY DIED; HE WAS THE THIRD ABBOT OF DISIBODENBERG. THE LORD CUNO SUCCEEDED HIM, BEING ORDAINED[38] ON THE SIXTH DAY BEFORE THE KALENDS OF JANUARY [27 DECEMBER] BY THE LORD ADALBERT SENIOR, ARCHBISHOP OF MAINZ.

IN THE SAME YEAR, ON THE ELEVENTH DAY BEFORE THE KALENDS OF JANUARY [22 DECEMBER] THE LADY JUTTA OF DIVINE MEMORY DIED, HAVING BEEN ENCLOSED FOR TWENTY-FOUR YEARS AT DISIBODENBERG; SHE WAS THE SISTER OF MEINHARD COUNT OF SPONHEIM. THIS HOLY WOMAN WAS ENCLOSED ON THE KALENDS OF NOVEMBER [1 NOVEMBER] AND THREE OTHERS[39] WITH HER, THAT IS HILDEGARD AND TWO OTHERS

---

[38] *Cui successit dominus Cuono, ordinatus 6. Kalend. Ianuarii a domino Adelberto seniore Moguntino archiepiscopo.* It is just conceivable that being 'ordained' here might mean being appointed, installed or constituted. The Chronicler however does use the verb *constituere* for this sense elsewhere. The sense of the verb *ordinare* as referring to the sacrament of Holy Orders, was quite strong in twelfth-century church Latin: see Du Cange, vol. 4, p. 58. A likely explanation is that the new trend for choir monks to be ordained as priests was not yet established at Disibodenberg, and Cuno was ordained as a priest for his new pastoral role as abbot, whether before or after he became abbot is not sure.

[39] Through awkwardly revisiting Jutta's enclosure in the same mention as her death, the Chronicler has confused the number of those preparing her body as reported in *VJ* VIII with the number of those enclosed 'in homage of the Trinity' on 1 Nov 1112 as reported in *VJ* III. He seems to have tripped over permutations of the number three, as have most commentators since. Most remarkably Staab himself trips over it, who despite the manifest

SHARING HER NAME, WHOM WHILE SHE LIVED SHE STROVE TO IMBUE
WITH HOLY VIRTUES.

1137 The Emperor returned from Italy, having accomplished many great deeds, and passed away on the third day before the Kalends of December [29 November] at a certain castle of the Duke of Bavaria. But his body was taken into Saxony and buried in his own monastery at Lutter.[40] Adalbert the Archbishop of Mainz died on the ninth day before the Kalends of July [23 June]. Our founding monastery in Mainz was burnt along with some part of the city.

1138 An assembly of princes was held at Koblenz in the cathedral of Saint Peter, where they constituted Conrad, nephew of Emperor Henry through his sister, as King. Then on the Sunday of mid-Lent he was consecrated by Cardinal Ditwin of Aachen.

THE ALTAR OF THE CONFESSORS WAS DEDICATED IN THE SANCTUARY OF THE NEW MONASTERY AT A PLACE IN THE NORTHERN AISLE BY THE LORD SIWARD, BISHOP OF DESSAU, IN HONOUR OF OUR LORD JESUS CHRIST AND ALL CONFESSORS, BUT PARTICULARLY OF SAINT CLEMENT, POPE AND MARTYR, POPE GREGORY, SAINT MARTIN AND SAINT NICHOLAS, BISHOPS. THIS VENERABLE PRELATE HAD BEEN UNJUSTLY CAST OUT OF HIS OWN CHURCH AND CAME TO THE DIOCESE OF MAINZ. SINCE AT THAT TIME IT WAS WITHOUT A PRELATE, HE CONSECRATED MANY CHURCHES AND ALTARS THERE WITH THE AGREEMENT OF THE CHURCH OF MAINZ.

IN THE SAME YEAR ON THE SAME DAY THE ALTAR OF SAINT BENEDICT, LOCATED BEHIND THE TOMB OF SAINT DISIBOD, WAS DEDICATED BY THE SAME PRELATE IN HONOUR OF SAINT BENEDICT AND ALL CONFESSORS.

IN THE SAME YEAR, ON THE FOURTH DAY BEFORE THE KALENDS OF MARCH [26 FEBRUARY], AN ALTAR WAS DEDICATED BY THE SAME BISHOP IN THE SANCTUARY AT A PLACE IN THE SOUTHERN AISLE IN HONOUR OF SAINT JOHN THE EVANGELIST, MARGARET, AGATHA, LUCY AND ALL HOLY VIRGINS. THESE THINGS TOOK PLACE UNDER THE LORD CUNO, FOURTH ABBOT OF DISIBODENBERG.

---

text of the *VJ* edited by himself, asserts in his introduction (p. 164) that Jutta was enclosed 'mit drei Schülerinnen'! This 1136 entry proves the Chronicler had the *VJ* available to him, but the error either counts against his identity with the author of the *VJ*, or if Volmar is the Chronicler, he anticipated Staab in making the same mistake.

[40] Today, Königslutter near Braunschweig.

Conrad, 98th Roman Emperor and the third of this name began his reign. The king celebrated Easter at Cologne. Then he came up to Mainz three weeks after Easter and was received with great favour by the clergy and the people. There Adalbert, nephew of the dead Archbishop through his brother, with the common consent of all, having been given the king's preference, was designated Archbishop. At Pentecost the King held court in Bamberg, where the princes of the whole realm gathered except for Henry Duke of Bavaria, son-in-law of the dead Emperor Lothar. Adalbert of Mainz was chosen on the Saturday of twelve readings, and, being ordained priest, was, on the following day, that is, the octave day of Pentecost, consecrated Bishop by Otto, the prelate of that church. Legates were sent from the King to Henry, Duke of Bavaria. Having received the regalia at Regensburg, they went to meet the King.

IN THIS SAME YEAR, ON THE GOOD FRIDAY OF THE PASCHAL FESTIVAL, WHICH WAS THE KALENDS OF APRIL [1 APRIL], SHORTLY AFTER MATINS HAD BEEN CELEBRATED, THE SEPULCHRE OF OUR MOST HOLY FATHER DISIBOD WAS OPENED BY THE BROTHERS IN THE PRESENCE OF VENERABLE PERSONS, THAT IS, THE LORD CUNO, FOURTH ABBOT OF THIS VERY PLACE, THE LORD GERHARD ABBOT OF SAINT MAXIMIN AT TRIER AND THE LORD BERNHELM FIRST ABBOT AT SPONHEIM, WITH THE ENTIRE ASSEMBLY OF THE SAME COMMUNITY, WHILE A BROTHER BROUGHT OUT THE RELICS OF THE SAME FATHER UNDER SEAL. THEY WERE DISCOVERED IN THE OLD MONASTERY, WHERE THEY HAD BEEN INTERRED BY THE LORD ARCHBISHOP WILLIGIS.

1139   The King celebrated the Nativity of the Lord at Goslar. Henry the Duke of Saxony died. Count Adalbert took the dukedom in his stead, but nearly all the leaders of Saxony fought against him. The Empress Richenza died. ON THE KALENDS OF NOVEMBER [1 NOVEMBER] THE RELICS OF SAINT DISIBOD WERE TRANSLATED FROM THE OLD CHURCH TO THE NEW MONASTERY; THE ENTIRE COMMUNITY MADE THE MOVE AS ONE UNDER THE ABOVE MENTIONED LORD ABBOT CUNO.

1140   The cycle of the fifth decade began, the third Indiction. The King spent the Purification of Holy Mary[41] at Worms. OTTO OF BAMBERG DIED. Adalbert Bishop of Mainz was called by Pope Innocent and went to Rome where he was received with kindness. The Castle at Winzburg was

---

[41] I.e. Candlemas, or the Presentation of the Lord in the Temple, followed by an 'octave' of eight days.

besieged by the King. In this siege, Welf, the brother of Duke Henry, took his place against the King in the same war, on the Saturday of twelve readings. The King however emerged the victor. Many of those of Welf, above-mentioned, were killed, some were captured, and shortly afterwards, the castle was taken. The King gave the abbey of St Maximin to St Peter in Trier.

1141   The King held his court in Regensburg at Pentecost. Some of the Saxon leaders stayed away. Adalbert archbishop of Mainz fought with the Saxons against the King, and not long after, died on the sixteenth day before the Kalends of August [17 July]; Markolf was constituted in his place.

1142   The King celebrated Easter at Würzburg, and passing on from there came to Frankfurt on Mercy Sunday. There he held his court, where almost all the Teutonic princes of the Teutonic realm assembled; there, the Saxons came into the King's favour, and the son of Duke Henry received the dukedom of Saxony, whose mother the King joined in marriage to his own brother the Margrave Henry, and gave him the dukedom of Bavaria.

MARKOLF, ARCHBISHOP OF MAINZ DIED, IN WHOSE PLACE HENRY, THE HEAD OF THE CATHEDRAL CLERGY WAS CONSTITUTED. He accepted his investiture from the King at Frankfort in the presence of the Cardinals Gregory and Ditwin.

THE CHAPEL OF THE HOSTEL WAS DEDICATED IN HONOUR OF OUR LORD JESUS CHRIST AND SAINT NICHOLAS ON THE FIFTH DAY BEFORE THE KALENDS OF JUNE [28 MAY] BY THE LORD GUIGO BISHOP OF BRANDENBURG; ON THE NEXT DAY OF THE SAME YEAR THE CHAPEL OF THE INFIRMARY WAS DEDICATED BY THE SAME PRELATE IN HONOUR OF BLESSED MARY MAGDALENE; THIS WAS ON THE FOURTH DAY BEFORE THE KALENDS OF JUNE [29 MAY].

1143   It was a hard winter. Adalbero, Archbishop of Trier, having put out the senior monks of Saint Maximin, constituted one called Suger as Abbot there; Celestine was 155th Pope.

IN THIS YEAR, THE SIXTH INDICTION, OUR NEW MONASTERY AT DISIBODENBERG WITH ITS HIGH ALTAR WAS DEDICATED BY HENRY, ARCHBISHOP OF MAINZ, IN HONOUR OF OUR LORD JESUS CHRIST AND HIS GLORIOUS MOTHER MARY, AND THE BLESSED EVANGELIST JOHN, AND OUR MOST BLESSED FATHER DISIBOD, CONFESSOR AND HIGH PRIEST.

IN THE SAME YEAR, ON THE SAME DAY AN ALTAR WAS DEDICATED IN

THE VESTRY OF THE MONASTERY BY THE ABOVE MENTIONED ARCHBISHOP IN HONOUR OF THE ALL-CONQUERING CROSS AND SAINT JOHN THE BAPTIST. MOREOVER, ON THE SAME YEAR AND DAY THE RELICS OF SAINT DISIBOD OUR FATHER, HAVING BEEN PLACED IN TWO LEAD RELIQUARIES WERE FRESHLY SEALED AND BLESSED IN A STONE TOMB-SHRINE BEHIND THE HIGH ALTAR BY THE ABOVE MENTIONED PRELATE ON THE THIRD DAY BEFORE THE KALENDS OF OCTOBER [29 SEPTEMBER]. ONE OF THE RELIQUARIES, THE SMALLER, CONTAINS THE BONES, THE OTHER, THE LARGER, THE ASHES. THERE WERE ALSO PLACED IN THE SAME TOMB-SHRINE THREE BODIES OF THE COMPANY OF THE ELEVEN THOUSAND VIRGINS,[42] AND CERTAIN BODIES OF THE THEBAN LEGION. THESE THINGS WERE DONE IN AGREEMENT WITH THE LORD CUNO, FOURTH ABBOT OF THIS PLACE.

1145 The King celebrated Easter at Würzburg. Eugene was constituted 158th Pope. A comet appeared in May. This year Rohas was captured by the Saracens on the sacred night of the Nativity of the Lord. Their King is a certain Sanguin by name.

1146 THIS YEAR THE CHAPEL OF THE HOLY VIRGIN MARY WAS DEDICATED ON THE KALENDS OF NOVEMBER [1 NOVEMBER] BY THE LORD HENRY, ARCHBISHOP OF MAINZ, IN HONOUR OF OUR LORD JESUS CHRIST AND HIS HOLY CROSS, AND SPECIALLY TO THE PRAISE AND GLORY OF MARY, THE EVER-VIRGIN MOTHER OF GOD AND OF OUR MOST HOLY FATHER DISIBOD, AND OF POPE FELIX THE MARTYR AND OF ALL THE SAINTS.

The King celebrated the Nativity of the Lord at Magdeburg. This year there was a great earthquake in fifteen places.

1151 There was a great famine from which people died.

1152 Herman, the Count of Winzburg and his wife were killed. During January there was an immense flood in the Rhineland regions. King Conrad died on the fifteenth day before the Kalends of March [15 February]. Frederick, 99th emperor of the Romans, cousin of king Conrad, began to reign.

1153 A sign appeared in the sun on the seventh day before the Kalends

---

[42] Trithemius records that Abbot Bernhelm of Sponheim also acquired relics of the 11,000 virgins at about the same period: *Chron. Sponh.*, p. 250, for the year 1143.

of February [26 January]. HENRY ARCHBISHOP OF MAINZ WAS DEPOSED AT PENTECOST BY ORDER OF POPE EUGENE, AND ARNOLD THE CHANCELLOR WAS ELECTED. Henry archbishop of Mainz died on the Kalends of September [1 September].

1155 Frederick was made Emperor at Rome by Pope Adrian. There was a war between Archbishop Arnold and Herman, Count Palatine. THE LORD CUNO, FOURTH ABBOT OF DISIBODENBERG DIED ON THE SIXTH DAY BEFORE THE NONES OF JULY [2 JULY]. TO HIM SUCCEEDED THE LORD HELENGER, FIFTH ABBOT, ON THE SIXTEENTH DAY BEFORE THE KALENDS OF AUGUST [17 JULY].

1156 Archbishop Arnold was called by certain persons to the Apostolic presence, and went to Pope Adrian, who received him with honour. He merited appointment as apostolic legate and returned to an honourable reception at Mainz. This year the Emperor Frederick took as wife Agnes, daughter of the Duke of Burgundy, having previously repudiated his lawful wife at Constance. Out of this there arose a very serious schism in the Church.

1160 The Emperor ordered a council to be held after the Octave of Easter at Pavia, at which Pope Victor was present, but Alexander was absent. Hence Victor was confirmed while Alexander was rejected. After these events, Bishop Arnold returned to Mainz, and on the Nativity of St John the Baptist [24 June] was killed in the monastery of St James. That monastery was set fire and all its fields laid waste.

After the crime had been carried out, the authors of the crime together with the clergy though under duress, substituted Rudolf, son of the Duke of Zahringen as bishop, once they obtained his trust, for they had earlier given him into the hand of the Emperor.

In the time of Emperor Otto, the third of this name, Archbishop Willigis of worthy memory presided over the church of Mainz. He educated Otto himself while he was still a young boy and Emperor, and for a span of sixteen years ruled the Roman empire. He made a golden cross and placed it in the monastery of Saint Martin. The crosspiece itself was made of cypress, covered over with gold layers and precious stones; the image was gold,[43] as declared by the verse worked into it:

---

[43] I.e. the cross included a corpus or figure, in solid gold, which was taken advantage of by later archbishops who progressively melted down parts of it for the financing, it seems, even of simoniac practices.

This cross contains six hundred pounds of gold.

Bishop Markolf removed one of the feet of this image and sent it to Rome for the pallium. Bishop Arnold received the other foot and the legs, and with it, rebelled against Herman Count Palatine.

CHARTERS OF DISIBODENBERG

CHARTER OF RUTHARD, ARCHBISHOP OF MAINZ

The following is a translation of the beginning and ending of Document 413 in *Urkundenbuch zur Geschichte der mittelrheinischen Territorien*, vol. 1, *Von den ältesten Zeiten bis zum Jahre 1169*, ed. by Heinrich Beyer, Leopold Eltester, and Adam Goerz (Koblenz: 1860; repr. Hildesheim: Georg Olms, 1974), pp. 473–74. Beyer edited his text, he says, 'from the archives of the monastery held in Darmstadt'. This is the foundation charter of Archbishop Ruthard's re-establishment of Disibodenberg as a monastery, in which he describes his replacement of canons with monks, and records the properties made over to them up to the present.

Date: 11 May 1107.

IN THE NAME OF the holy and undivided Trinity.

I desire it to be known among all the faithful in Christ both those in time to come and those present that I, Ruthard, by the grace of God Archbishop of the See of Mainz, have, with consultation, displaced the canons at Disibodenberg and substituted monks, thereby remedying an easy-going and careless life with a stricter and better way of life. I have enlarged the goods of the same community, and desire to enlarge them still more, for the salvation of my soul and all my predecessors, both bishops and my own parents.

So that this may be understood and be able to remain irreversible and without just cause for complaint, I have allayed the protest of the canons with appropriate compensation of ecclesiastical and other benefices to their satisfaction. Moreover, the right hand of the Most High and the patronage of the servant of God lying at rest there, and the beauty of the place fires my will to this change, and above all because I found, through popular report, that the same way of life and religious community had once existed in that very place. I do not know by what wrath of God, but the monastery was burnt down, its goods were dispersed, and this hill of the service of God was reduced to an utter wilderness until the time of the venerable Archbishop Willigis[1] my predecessor, who indeed placed canons there but did not restore again the earlier way of life.

Therefore, I was greatly moved on account of this, and applied myself to raising up again the way of life of monks in religious community, according to the Rule, which was there formerly. To this end, I have increased the estates of the same community with the properties written out below[2] ...

Accordingly I have lawfully transferred all these things to St Disibod, issued my bann, and as is just, have finally confirmed and established my transfer of property by the affixing of my seal. Henceforth, this transfer is in effect. On the fifth day before the Ides of May [11 May], in the year of the Lord's Incarnation MCVII, in the first indiction, during the reign of Henry V, king and Roman Emperor, under the reign of the lord Jesus Christ over his Church,[3] by whom all good will is initiated and on whom depends the piety of our deeds and the recompense of our rewards.

Of this, these are the witnesses: Dideric Abbot of St Alban, Burchard Abbot of St James, Embrich provost of the greater monastery, Anselm provost of St Stephen, Odo provost of St Victor, Regezo provost of St Mary in the fields, Frederick and Richmund canons, Arnold count of the city, Emich count of Schmudeberg and his son Emich, Bertolf count of Nuring, Gerhard count of Berbach, Ludwig count of Arnestein, Cuno of Mandendale, Henry of Conradsdorf, Ortwin of Budinsheim, Helich of Haginhausen and his brother Sigewin, Arnold of Quecbrunnen, Bubo of Aldevila, Ezzo of Windeness, Werner of Roude, Vulveric, Ludwig, Embrich the deputy, Richard, Richelo.

CHARTER OF ADALBERT, ARCHBISHOP OF MAINZ: SELECT ENTRIES

The following is a translation of sections of Document 462, *Urkunden-buch zur Geschichte der mittelrheinischen Territorien*, vol. 1, pp. 518–22.

---

[1] 975–1011.

[2] At this point the catalogue of properties begins.

[3] Note the 'relativizing' of Henry's role as king in relation to the Church.

Beyer also edited this document 'from the archives of the monastery at Darmstadt'. Here, Archbishop Adalbert rehearses the beginnings of the re-establishment of Disibodenberg under Archbishop Willigis, and then records in historical sequence the properties donated to the monastery. There is mention of an Uda who, if we interpret *iam ibidem defuncte* rightly, died at Disibodenberg. That a woman died there, presumably having lived there, is in itself intriguing. It seems doubtful, however, that this could be the Uda who was Jutta's *magistra*, for the donation is recounted as though taking place during the time of Archbishop Willigis, a century too early. A translation of the entire text from Willigis to Ruthard is supplied so that the reader may be able to judge. Adalbert recounts how Ruthard converted Disibodenberg into a monastery under the Rule of St Benedict; he also gives information about Jutta and her mother Sophia in connection with a report of a property given by Count Meinhard of Sponheim for his sister. The sections on Uda, Meinhard, Jutta and Sophia are presented in SMALL CAPITALS. Since no abbot of Disibodenberg appears among the witnesses, the document may be assigned to a period sometime after Abbot Adilhun's death on 17 June 1128 (*AD* 1128), when Archbishop Adalbert had returned to Mainz (*VJ* VI), but before the installation of Fulcard as Abbot.

   Date: second half of 1128.

IN THE NAME OF the holy and undivided Trinity.

   I, Adalbert, Archbishop of Mainz and legate of the Apostolic See, desire it to be known among all the faithful of Christ, both those in time to come and those present, how our predecessors of blessed memory, the venerable Archbishops Willigis, Lupold,[4] Siegfried,[5] Ruthard[6] and other faithful, being aflame with zeal for God, did, among other signs of their piety by which they showed themselves generous to God and holy Church, increase, augment and raise to a better state the community of St Disibod through their own contributions and benefactions. We have caused to be written out and noted down below their gifts and devout offerings and this with the purpose that a worthy, abiding and fixed

---

[4] 1051–1059.

[5] 1060–1084.

[6] 1089–1109.

memory of such great fathers should exist and be maintained in every age by all those holding the Christian faith.

Among these fathers, the most reverend Willigis, Archbishop by the will of almighty God, whose mercy inspired him not a little, wished that the first fruits of his devotion, such as they were, be offered to God. Since the time of St Disibod's commemoration was at hand, he ascended the hill of the aforesaid confessor. Though he could see that the place was utterly desolate and that the divine worship there had come into utter neglect, he was moved by heartfelt piety and commanded that a church be founded and built there. Since he was not entirely able to restore a foundation of monks under the Rule, he only set up twelve clerics there in a canonical state, while wishing it understood that, of course, if the circumstances or means should become available, he wished to restore in its integrity the earlier way of life which the above mentioned patron [St Disibod] had set up in the beginning.

These then are the estates which the same illustrious man handed over to Saint Disibod in his generosity of mind: he donated in Sobernheim two houses with a court to which he attached the church which he dedicated, in such a way that the tithe of the same land would be wholly assigned with the same endowment; he offered the church itself in Sobernheim with all its tithe. For the repair of the church and for the ongoing maintenance of the roof, he so arranged and ordained it concerning the individual villas adjoining the hill, that the right side of the holy place be maintained by Odernheim and the left by Studernheim, that Odernheim should support the right choir and Studernheim the left. Concerning the demesne at Boos, the tithe of Studernheim should support the right half of the sanctuary of the chapel of St Mary, Odernheim the left. Concerning the demesne at Studernheim, Ilusen and Royde should support the right half, and Robura the left half. He added also to the same church twenty houses in Osterna paying a yearly rent, with sallow[7] land, woods and fields, pastures, roads and tracks, watercourses, with every right, and beyond that gave two churches, the one in Osterna the other in Ovenbach, and all its legal right and use, and since the entire tithe of all new land cleared from the woods belonged to the same, he ordered three churches to be built in the same forest. Their names are: Bollenbach, Hunzbach and

---

[7] I.e. land with willows or wattles for 'pollarding', or the farming of the trees for rods used in the thatching of roofs.

Meckenbach, which he made tributary to Disibodenberg with the whole tithe of the land then cultivated and which would be cultivated later.

Next, because he had nothing in the forest called Sane, when he acquired a *huba*[8] from a certain cleric called Wezelin, he built a church at the end of an estate called Monzech, giving it the name of Gehinkirche, offering the entire tithe of the land cultivated then and in the future, to the same church with all its tithes; he then gave it all to Disibodenberg. But afterwards, because of the length and breadth of the forest, all those who dwelt in the villages could not congregate at this same church, so he acquired a clearing in the same wood in a *huba* belonging to St Alban's, built a branch church in it and dedicated it, giving it the name of Semendisbach, making it and all that belonged to it a dependency of the church at Gehinkirche, and laid it down that it should always be managed by the same cleric who managed that church.

Also at that time Duke Cuno of Beckilneim and his wife Jutta, from the resources of their wealth and the authority of their high state, at the instigation and request of the venerable Archbishop handed over as property to St Disibod for the well-being of their souls AND IN MEMORY OF THEIR DAUGHTER UDA, WHO HAD LATELY DIED THERE, two fields containing twenty acres of sallow land according to true and sure reckoning by men, two manses occupied by serfs in the estate of Boos.

The same abovementioned Archbishop also wanted to make arrangements for the benefit in perpetuity of the brothers serving under the above named confessor, and, wishing to indicate how much of the mountain they were allowed by right, assigned to their property whatever was included within the old embankment. He set an advocate over the same place, and decreed what should be owed each year to that justice, 12 pence, that is, 12 pence for meat, 12 for bread, a jar of wine and 20 sheaves of wheat for the feeding of horses, and this on the Nativity of our Lady.

The reverend Archbishop Lupold succeeded him. He, learning of the generosity of his predecessor, himself also extended to St Disibod the hand of his own piety and added to the goods above-mentioned four *hubas*, two at Sobernheim, and two at Crebezhul, with such legal right

---

[8] An approximate measure of land containing 30 *Morgen*, or acres; see Heinrich Beyer, Leopold Eltester, and Adam Goerz (eds.), *Urkundenbuch zur Geschichte der mittel-rheinischen Territorien*, Vol. 1, *Von den ältesten Zeiten bis zum Jahre 1169* (Hildesheim, Georg Olms, 1974), p. 366.

and use as applied to himself and his predecessor. Moreover in the case of the same estate Sobernheim he added that a half offering should be presented on Holy Thursday at Mainz.

When he had entered on the way of all flesh, Siegfried succeeded him in the governance of the same See, and was of no less a generosity. Having learnt of the benefactions of the bishops whom we mentioned above, he too was moved with compassion, and by gifts and donations himself also lightened the poverty of the brothers in the following way: there was a certain payment which was owed to him from all the churches belonging to the same mountain. All three parts, two from the brothers, and one from the parish priests themselves, he assigned to the same place. Moreover the benefaction of a certain retainer of his, Ringebert by name, of Sobernheim, who had lately died, he contributed to St Disibod.

When he also had joined his predecessors, the Lord Ruthard of holy memory succeeded as Archbishop to the episcopal chair not long after. Although each of these fathers had, according to his capacity, venerated St Disibod with gifts and votive offerings, none of them had applied himself to restoring the earlier life of monks in a religious community, except this same prelate Ruthard worthy of all honour, who now restored the same monastic way of life, by which the hill had originally been distinguished. He removed from there the canons, compensating them adequately with ecclesial and other benefices.[9] Then, having entered into counsel, he appointed the lord Burchard of loving memory to the same title,[10] increasing his responsibility to this extent, that, since through the merits of St Disibod that place might become more renowned and held in greater veneration, he was to be his co-operator and in all respects his

---

[9] The dispute was not settled even by this charter, but continued into the late 1140s. In 1147 Archbishop Henry makes final property arrangements between the canons of St Mary at the Steps in Mainz and the monks of Disibodenberg. '... by this decision we have finally, at long last, established peace between the communities of Saint Disibod and Saint Mary at the Steps [Mariengreden] which have been contesting each other for so long, that is, the canons dwelling on Disibodenberg by appointment of the lord Archbishop Willigis and the monks afterward substituted there by the prelate lord Ruthard which was subsequently reiterated and confirmed by the archbishop lord Adalbert the younger, for the canons of Saint Mary had complained that certain things had been taken from them, which the brothers of that same place represented as being their own.' *MUB* 2, Document 96, pp. 185–87.

[10] Burchard was already Abbot of St James in Mainz and held the two abbatial posts concurrently.

deputy by preaching, baptizing, by burying and by receiving and gathering penitents. Besides all this he allowed, confirmed and wanted it understood that whenever there was a father of the monastery to be ordained for the same brothers, he alone would be appointed among them whom they had elected unanimously by common counsel and consent at the designation of the Holy Spirit, and should be presented to the Bishop to be invested ...

ITEM: MEINHARD, THE COUNT OF SPONHEIM, IN FULFILMENT OF THE PRAISEWORTHY VOW OF HIS SISTER,[11] THE LADY JUTTA, OFFERED WITH HER TO GOD AND TO SAINT DISIBOD THE TOWNSHIP CALLED NUNKIRCHEN[12] WITH ALL THAT BELONGED TO IT, THAT IS, THE CHURCH WITH ITS TITHES, FREEHOLD PROPERTIES, FIELDS, WOODS, MEADOWS, PASTURELANDS WHICH ARE CULTIVATED, UNCULTIVATED OR TO BE CULT-IVATED, ITS ROADS AND TRACKS, WATERS AND WATERWAYS, AND ITS MILLS.

THIS WAS DONE WITH THE SAME LIBERTY WITH WHICH HIS MOTHER, THE LADY SOPHIA, AND AFTER HER DEATH HE HIMSELF HAD POSSESSED IT. AS JUTTA HERSELF DESIRED AND MOST ARDENTLY SOUGHT, HE SECURED THE ARRANGEMENT THAT SHE SHOULD BE DIVESTED OF ALL WORLDLY POMPS AND BE ENCLOSED THERE.

THEIR MOTHER THE LADY SOPHIA, A RELIGIOUS WOMAN, HAD WANTED THE LIBERTY OF THE AFORESAID CHURCH, AND HAD OBTAINED IT FROM THE VENERABLE ARCHBISHOP RUTHARD MOST WILLINGLY, IN RECOG-NITION OF HER DEVOTION ...

These are the witnesses of this document: Henry provost of the greater church, Volpert Abbot of St Alban, Werenbald Abbot of St James, Bernhelm Abbot of Sponheim, Hartman the chamberlain, Cuno the dean, Durimbert the *Magister*, Anselm the provost of St Mary,[13] Emich the

---

[11] *sororis sue domne Iutte laudabili voto satisfaciens*; a less formal translation might be, 'fulfilling a praiseworthy wish/request of his sister the lady Jutta'. The 'vow' then, does not necessarily refer to her solemn enclosure and profession in 1112.

[12] There is also mention of this property in a document of 18 February 1948, only partially surviving, in which Pope Eugene III confirms the gifts of properties made to Disibodenberg. See *MUB* 2, Document 108, p. 209. A translation of it follows.

[13] I.e. the foundation in the city of Mainz, where the canons continued who had once occupied Disibodenberg.

provost of St Severus of Erfurt; the canons: Gosbert, Godeschal, Arnold; laymen and counts: Wilhelm of Luccilinburch, MEINHARD OF SPONHEIM, Emich of Kirberch and his brother Gerlach, Sigebracht; freemen: Roric of Merxheim and his brother Gerlach,[14] Adalbero of Hachenfels, Folmar and his son Folmar of St Albino; Servants and townsmen: Ruthard the deputy, Dudo the mayor and his brother Wignand, Embrich of Geisinheim, Conrad of Hebenhefde, Werner of Rüdesheim, Ernest and his brother Obrecht, and many others.

These things are given effect in the year of the Lord's Incarnation MCXXVIII, in the sixth indiction, during the rule of the lord Lothar, third of this name, in the fourth year of his reign; under the reign of the Lord Jesus Christ over his Church, by whom all good will is initiated and on whom depends the piety of our deeds and the recompense of our rewards; Arnold being prefect of the city, Dudo the mayor.

CHARTER OF POPE EUGENE III

The following is a translation of Document 108, *MUB* 2, pp. 207–10. The original document is lost. The sources for the document are two: a copy made by the Mainz magistrates dated 6 June 1268 in the Staatsarchiv, Darmstadt, Urk. Rheinhessen Hechtsheim Nr. 8. The second is from the correspondence book of Disibodenberg from the end of fifteenth century as preserved in the Staatsarchiv, Darmstadt, Hechtsheim Nr. 167. Here Pope Eugene takes Disibodenberg under Abbot Cuno into Apostolic protection, and confirms the gifts made to it by the Archbishops of Mainz and by the faithful. Notable among the latter is Nunkirchen, the donation made by Count Meinhard of Sponheim for Jutta his sister, as recorded at some length in Adalbert's 1128 charter. At the very time of this document, Hildegard has set in train the move to Rupertsberg. There is also mention of the Weiler estate, which reappears in *VH* I, 5. At the end of *VH* I, 4 Godfrey speaks of a letter sent by Pope Eugene to the abbot and monks of Disibodenberg congratulating them on account of Hildegard, and giving them his blessing, but of such sentiments there is no sign in the present document.

Date: Metz, 18 February 1148.

---

[14] *sic*; it seems to be a case of diplography.

... ESTABLISHING THAT WHATEVER POSSESSIONS, whatever goods the same monastery justly and rightly possesses in the present or in the future is able to acquire through the concession of Pontiffs, the endowment of kings or princes, the offering of the faithful or other just means, as the Lord provides, should remain confirmed and unimpaired to you and to your successors. In these matters we have judged that we may properly set forth these terms: that very place in which the abbey is located, as our venerable father Willigis the Archbishop of Mainz assigned to you and other successors to him confirmed;

two houses in Sobernheim and the church of the same village with its tithe, in Osterna, twenty houses, paying rent with sallow land and the church of the same village, another church in Ovenbach and other churches in Bollenbach, Hunzbach, Meckenbach, and in Gehinkirche with all that belongs to it, a chapel in Semendisbach, all of which the above mentioned Archbishop granted you through his own donation; two houses in Sobernheim, two in Crebezol, half the offering on Holy Thursday,[15] through gift of our venerable brother Lupold, Archbishop of Mainz;

a tithe for the episcopal court which is within the walled town of St Albans and attached to the village of Hechtsheim, the newly planted part of the vineyards below Rüdesheim, a vineyard in Bodenthal, and the hamlet Glefartsburg, the village of Bischofsrod in Thuringia, an estate in Merxheim and in Weinsheim, an estate of two houses in Staudernheim, as were formally given to you by our venerable brother Ruthard, Archbishop of Mainz;

a forest called Steinhart, by gift of Markolf the archbishop of worthy memory; whatever belongs to the right of the archbishop in the same village, excepting dominical and taxable land, by grant of our venerable brother Henry the archbishop of Mainz; two royal houses in Boos, an allodial property in Monzingen and in Niederwörresbach, a church and estate in Nunkirchen with all that belongs to them, a church and allodial property in Obernsdorf with all that belongs to them, possessions you have in Bingen and in Weiler, in Dürkheim, in Höchstingin, in Gensingen, in Appenheim, in Kreuznach, in Bosenheim, in Werschweiler;

---

[15] *dimidiam oblationem in cena domini*, i.e. the day when the institution of the 'Lord's Supper' is commemorated.

whatever measure of right concerning the churches belonging to the same place our venerable brother Siegfried the Archbishop of Mainz of worthy memory granted to you, and Adalbert his successor confirmed to you in his own writing ...

DOCUMENTS OF SPONHEIM

CHARTER OF ADALBERT, ARCHBISHOP OF MAINZ

The following document is a translation of Document 545, *MUB* 1, pp. 452–53. For his edition, Stimming used primarily the 'cartulary' or document-book of Sponheim from the fifteenth century, held in the Generallandesarchiv zu Karlsruhe, Kopialbuch Nr. 1346.

In this charter, Archbishop Adalbert confirms a donation made by the free nobles Udo and his wife Jutta to the monastery of Sponheim founded and endowed by the Counts of Sponheim. Here we have the only contemporary witness of the name of Hildegard's father, Hildebert, and the location of the family seat at Bermersheim. The relevant text is presented in SMALL CAPITALS. The document is examined at length in Schrader, *Herkunft*, pp. 28–31.

The protocol of witnesses should be noted. First of all there are the monastic and clerical witnesses, including Abbots Bernhelm of Sponheim, Adilhun of Disibodenberg and Folbert of St Albans. Then there follow the list of laity, in order of rank, headed by Count Meinhard of Sponheim; three names later, still among the free nobles, appears *Hiltebertus de Vermerssheym et filius Drutwin*, 'Hildebert of Bermersheim and his son Drutwin' (Hildegard's brother).

This document tends to confirm Pitra's surmise (Proemium p. V) that Hildebert was *nobilem vassallum Comitis Meginharti de Spanheim*, i.e. belonging to the lower free nobility, a property owning but untitled knight in service to the Count of Sponheim. Trithemius describes him in the *Chron. Hirsaug.*, p. 133, as *Hildebertus vir nobilis, in curia comitis Meginhardi de Spanheim nobilissimi et illo tempore potentissimi militabat, vir dives et honoratus in seculo*, i.e. 'Hildebert was a noble man, wealthy and of high station in the world, who served as knight in the court of Meinhard of Sponheim, most noble and at that time very powerful.' He is also described in the *Chron. Sponh.*, p. 133, as *Stephani Comitis nobilissimo milite*, 'a most noble knight of Count Stephan'.

Date: Mainz (?), 25 December 1127.

IN THE NAME OF the Holy and undivided Trinity. I, Adalbert, by the grace of God, Archbishop of Mainz and Legate of the Apostolic See.

We notify the faithful of Christ and the Church, both now and in the future, that a certain Udo,[1] a free noble of high station, and his wife Jutta, while still enjoying all strength of body and mind, have, for the well-being of their soul and of their parents, committed with full authority their entire estate in Bockenau and Gensingen, the church with its tithes and all that belongs to it: the servants, fields, vineyards, woods, cultivated and fallow land, meadows, pastures, mills, fishponds, watercourses and their approaches, to the altar of blessed Martin in the monastery of Sponheim, to the abbot and brothers dwelling there under the monastic rule, without objection from anyone, though the hands of the advocate Count Meinhard of the castle of Sponheim.

It has also pleased the two above-mentioned, that is, Udo and his wife, that because they have some of their servants that are more outstanding and some less so, those whose character, hard work and probity has commended them, should serve the abbot and brothers as administrative officials, that they should permit no advocate to have any say in them, but that rather, they should obtain parity and equality with full legal rights, among the priors and the higher officials of the other abbots of our diocese. But let the rest of the household remain under the royal tax system, so that they must pay a levy of eight coins each year at the altar of the above mentioned monastery.

So that this transfer may remain firm and irrevocable, we have caused this charter to be written out, and have sealed it with the impression of our seal and strengthened it with the key of this anathema, that if anyone should presume, by whatever perverse scheme, to undo and invalidate this transfer, let him be subject to our bann, and be punished by the testimony of the truth itself, and realize that he has made himself an offence to God and Saint Martin.

These are the witnesses: Abbot Folbert of blessed Alban, Wernbald,

---

[1] Anneliese Naumann-Humbeck, *Studien zur Geschichte der Grafen von Sponheim vom 11. bis 13. Jahrhundert*, Heimatkundliche Schriftenreihe des Landkreises Bad Kreuznach, 14 (Bad Kreuznach: Kreisverwaltung, 1983), p. 68, suggests this is Udo von Stade, son of the Marchioness von Stade and elder brother of Richardis von Stade, nun of Rupertsberg and of Hartwig, Archbishop of Bremen; in this case, his wife would be Jutta von Winzenberg.

Abbot of Saint James, Adilhun, Abbot of St Disibod, Bernhelm, Abbot of the above-mentioned monastery and all its community, Richard of blessed Martin from the archdeacon's house, Henry the chamberlain, Cuno the dean, Hartmann the cantor and provost, Anselm the provost of St Mary at the Steps, Bertholf a cleric of Sponheim, Ringerus a cleric, Henry a cleric, Herman provost of Schwabenheim;

Count Meinhard, advocate of the same community, Bertholf of Eppelsheim, Adalbert of Basenheim, HILDEBERT OF BERMERSHEIM AND HIS SON DRUTWIN, Roric of Merxheim and his brother Gerlac, Udalric of Stein and his son Hugo, Gerhard of Emezweiler, Gerlac of Husen, Henry of Paptenheim, Ernest the steward, Warin the magistrate, Ruthard whom they call Walbot, Erlewyn, Folpert, Lufrid, Salemann;

from the *ministeriales*: Erlolf, Herwig of Kreutznach, Marcward of Huffelsheim, Henry of Montzegin, Wolfram of Studernheim, Henry of Sobernheim, Hertwin of Henneweiler, Conrad, Adalbert, Hertwig, Otto, Berwin, Retherus, Cuno, Frederick, Vigant, Gernung of Sponheim and many others.

These things were given effect on the eighth day before the Kalends of January [25 December], in the year of the Lord's Incarnation MCXXVII, in the fourth indiction, during the rule of Lothar, Holy Roman King, in the second year of his reign.

CHRONICLES OF SPONHEIM, SELECT ENTRY

It would not be difficult to edit a series of extracts from the works of Trithemius as a kind of *Chronicle of Holy Women.* Trithemius (1462–1517), the learned Abbot of Sponheim 1483–1506, is quite within the tradition of his monastic milieu in his desire to give full recognition to the Benedictine nuns who figure in its history, and to record other holy women he has come to know about. If one had to choose a single representative text in the extensive corpus of his writings, then it is surely his entry in the Chronicles of Sponheim for the year of Jutta's death, 1136. This is presented here, translated from *Chron. Sponh.*, pp. 247–48. Trithemius composed this work in 1509, after he had ceased being abbot of Sponheim.

Considerable variety of information is concentrated in this one text. It is as if his reporting the event of Jutta's death sparked Trithemius' reflection and perhaps regret over the disappearance of the houses of nuns attached to monasteries of monks. He show himself rather house-proud of the roll-call of holy nuns in the local Benedictine tradition to which he belonged, but is a little anxious about the potential sexual ambiguity of this type of monastic set-up, which he discreetly addresses. First of all he gives an overview and a kind of *apologia* for this practice that used to be the way of life at his monastery, at Disibodenberg and elsewhere. He then goes on to tell of the cooling of the nuns' and monks' spirituality, so to speak, and the incidence of scandal that eventually led to the dismantling of the system by authority of the bishops—a move, it might be noted, that Hildegard only seems to have anticipated, if perhaps for different reasons.

This text also contains a unique report of Jutta as a wonder worker, not found in either the *VJ* or Ep. 38. It came perhaps from some local oral tradition and is partly supported by the account of Jutta's powers of healing and of reading minds in *VJ* IIII. Trithemius also states that Jutta's history and way of life were 'diligently written down', which seems to indicate that he knew or had heard of the existence of *The Life of Lady Jutta the Anchoress*, though the fact that he says Count Stephan was still alive, and that there were three, rather than two enclosed with Jutta suggests he had not read it. He agrees with the date given in the *VJ* for the enclosure of Jutta and Hildegard. One gains the impression here and elsewhere[2] that he may have noticed the historical discrepancy between this date and Hildegard's oblation 'in her eighth year', but has not quite accounted for it and quietly glosses over it.

This text excellently contextualizes the *vitae* of Jutta and Hildegard, and suitably leads us into the first of the three major documents: the Life of Jutta.

MCXXXVI

The year 1136. The most chaste virgin Jutta, daughter of Count Stephan of Sponheim and sister of Meinhard our founder,[3] rested in the Lord on the eleventh day before the Kalends of January [22 December 1136]. She was buried in the monastery of St Disibod next to the main altar towards the south.[4] Having been enclosed there with certain other

---

[2] Cf. *Chron. Hirsaug.*, p. 126 and p. 135.

[3] The document attesting the foundation by Meinhard of a monastery of monks around the church at Sponheim is dated 7 June 1124. It is edited as document 522 in *MUB* 1, pp. 457ff. Trithemius recounts the earlier history of the site under the Counts of Sponheim at the beginning of *Chron. Sponh.*, pp. 237–41.

[4] *iuxta maius altare versus meridiem sepulta*. According to the description here, this

virgins for love of the heavenly kingdom, she served the Lord in a strict rule of life for twenty-four years. She was enclosed in the year 1112, in the fifth Indiction, while Count Stephan her father was still alive, also with three other virgins, Hildegard of Böckelheim,[5] who, after her death, moved to Bingen and founded a monastery at Rupertsberg as her place is called, and Jutta another noble virgin, and another nun of the same name, most devoted to Christ.

The holy Jutta, daughter of Count Stephan, was also the *Magistra* in Christ of the virgins at Disibodenberg, above-mentioned, and under her, their numbers greatly increased. Many nobles of the region offered their daughters for the service of our Lord Jesus Christ under her guidance.

They all fought under the Rule of our Holy Father Benedict in obedience to the abbot, enclosed separately in a strict and well-walled custody. No men had access to them except the abbot. Indeed, this practice was fostered in almost all of our monasteries back then, so that the more there were men in the vicinity, the more easily the nuns would be protected by their[6] vigilance from the snares of the enemy.

This is the way it was in the above-mentioned monastery of St Disibod, also in the monastery of St John at Reingau, also at Schönau, also at St Alban's, also at St James, also at Hirsau under the holy Abbot William; likewise in Franckendal. Why, around the monastery of Limburg there were as many as three monastic houses of our Order set up for nuns, namely Sebach, Haufen and Schönfeld, of which the first is still flourishing, suitable for holy virgins, while the other two are deserted. Also at the monastery of St Martin in Trier, adjoining the walls, above the bank of the Moselle toward the north, there was the monastic house of St Symphorian, in which many very holy nuns of our Order became

---

would have been at the end of the left aisle of the main church, beyond the transept, adjacent to the chancel. Ep. 38, VIIII says she was first buried in the Chapter house, and then buried before the altar in the chapel of our Lady Queen of heaven, which was a separate small church.

[5] In the immediate vicinity of Sponheim (see Waldböckelheim and Schloßböckelheim). Despite Trithemius's statements, Marianna Schrader concluded that Hildegard was born at Bermersheim near Alzey: *Die Herkunft der heiligen Hildegard*, rev. ed. by A. Führkötter, Quellen und Abhandlungen zur Mittelrheinischen Kirchengeschichte, 43 (Mainz, 1981) p. 31). See Staab's discussion, 'Aus Kindheit', pp. 63–64. He is more inclined to credit what Trithemius may have obtained from local tradition.

[6] *eorum vigilantia*; i.e. the vigilance of the men.

renowned, of which there remains not a trace today except a single solitary column, once part of the structure of the church.

Bernhelm, the first abbot of our place as mentioned above, constructed a small monastic house at the foot of the hill on the slope in the western part of this monastery as we said above. Here, his sister Mechtild, previously enclosed at St Alban's, was secluded for love of the heavenly life with another called Sophia. In this same anchorhold many virgins succeeded each other for many years. Holy they were, and most devout, and their names I do not doubt are written in heaven.

But afterwards, due to the proximity of the sites, the nuns began to be a snare and a stumbling block for the men,[7] for they, on both sides, no longer *walked by the spirit* as before, but *according to the flesh* (Rom. 8:4 etc.). Consequently, nearly all the monastic houses of nuns adjacent to men were, by the discretion of the bishops, incorporated into the men's monasteries either when there were no more nuns, or even after driving them out. And so we have seen these places totally destroyed, either by neglect or some other cause. Thus today, only the name of the place remains with us, called Clausa, taken from the enclosure of the virgins who once dwelt there. Not a trace of the monastic house or buildings is to be seen.

But let me return to our history.

And so Jutta, the holy virgin of Christ of whom we speak, became renowned in this life for many miracles. Among other things, she changed water into wine, and often crossed over the flowing streams of the river Glan on dry foot. Her history and most holy way of life were most diligently written down.[8]

After her death, the holy virgin Hildegard was constituted *Magistra* of the sisters, under Cuno, Abbot of the above-mentioned monastery. After some years had passed she was forewarned by a divine revelation and, by permission of the Abbot, moved with the entire community of sisters to Bingen. Making use of the alms of the faithful, she built a monastery for herself and her sisters there on the hill of the confessor Rupert, which continues to this day.

---

[7] *viris in laqueum et in scandalum esse ceperunt.*

[8] Trithemius, *Chron. Hirsaug.*, p. 126, gives the same two examples of Jutta's miracles, and also says, with apparent reference to the Life of Jutta: 'her history, conduct, deeds and miracles were diligently written down'.

THE LIFE OF JUTTA

INTRODUCTION

Manuscripts and first edition

The Life of Jutta is translated from the first edition of the *Vita domnae Juttae inclusae* by Franz Staab who added it as the second appendix to his article 'Reform und Reformgruppen im Erzbistum Mainz. Vom "Libellus de Willigisi consuetudinibus" zur "Vita domnae Juttae inclusae"', in *Reformidee und Reformpolitik im Spätsalisch-Frühstaufischen Reich. Vorträge der Tagung der Gesellschaft für Mittelrheinische Kirchengeschichte vom 11. bis 13. September 1991 in Trier*, ed. by Stefan Weinfurter, Quellen und Abhandlungen zur Mittelrheinische Geschichte, 68 (Mainz: Selbstverlag der Gesellschaft für Mittelrheinische Kirchengeschichte, 1992).

Staab based his edition on two late medieval copies of the document, both of which he believes derive from a common source, but which, due to shared passages of disturbed text, was not the autograph. The first copy (C 1) is a quarto manuscript of the fourteenth–fifteenth century, the first section of which comes from Corvey, the second from Abdinghof, where both parts were bound together in the fifteenth century; it is preserved today at the Berlin Staatsbibliothek Preußischer Kulturbesitz, MS theol. lat. qu. 141, fols 119–24ᵛ (old reckoning: pp. 237–48). The second copy (C 2) is preserved in a surviving fragment of the great Lectionary of 1459–1464 from the Augustinian monastery of Böddeken in Westphalia. It is the Paderborn Gymnasium Theodorianum MS Ba 2 held in the Erzbischöfliche Akademische Bibliothek. The *Vita Juttae* may be found at fols 212–15. Only two months survive of this beautifully produced lectionary, one of them fortunately being the month of December, since it is in this month the death-day or 'heavenly birthday' of Blessed Jutta occurs.

I have supplemented this translation with many more references to Scripture and to the Rule of St Benedict than Staab provides.

Staab's *editio princeps* and notes are not without fault in some details. Some of the scripture references are not quite correct. There may also be printing errors, e.g. *examinis* instead of *exanimis* in section VI. It seems he has missed an important point in reading *supercilicium* instead of *super cilicium*, overlooking the *collocata* in *VJ* VIII, though he picked up on this in his later German translation. Some points of a factual nature indicate caution, such as note 157 where a text is attributed to the Life of Radegund by Fortunatus, rather than that by Baudonivia. On p. 164 of his article Staab contradicts the data of the text in *VJ* III on the number of those enclosed with Jutta. That he could do so, however, proved to be very useful when considering the authorship of *AD*. Disagreement with other points, such as the dating and authorship of the *VJ*, can be set down to the progress of scholarly discussion.

Genesis and authorship

The author describes in *VJ* I how his Abbot, Cuno of Disibodenberg (27 December 1136–2 July 1155) charged him with the writing of this *vita*, but not before the Abbot had been goaded by someone else to do something about it: Jutta's first disciple and successor, Hildegard (*VJ* I). So there is in effect a trio of persons behind the *VJ*: Hildegard, Abbot Cuno, and the anonymous monk of Disibodenberg who actually wrote the work. But who might he have been?

The author reveals himself as wholly and deeply formed by his monastic milieu, devout, disciplined, and self-effacing, yet ingenuous in a way, and very engaged in his topic. He is well versed in Christian classics and authors such as the Rule of St Benedict, Gregory the Great, Gregory of Tours, Sulpicius Severus and the *vitae* of female saints, but above all in the Scriptures. He has a happy propensity for recording annalistic details of dates and persons. Outbursts of personal enthusiasm or extravagant self-disclosures do not escape him the way they do, for example, with Guibert.

He had no superficial knowledge of Jutta, for he had learned many things about her, he says, *experimento* 'by experience' (VI), was privy to the difficulties she had in preserving her chastity in her youth (III), seems to have watched her at prayer (VI), was an eyewitness of some of the events connected with her, above all, her death (VII), and like his Abbot preserved a devout memory of the holy woman (X). He interviewed Jutta's disciples after her death and used their testimony extensively (X).

What he says of Hildegard in the prologue and in several passages throughout the work, and, in particular, what he relates of her vision of Jutta's soul after death in IX, shows that there is no slight degree of confidence between him and Jutta's successor, i.e. Hildegard, whom he already appreciates as her singularly gifted heir.

According to Staab (p. 172), a well founded guess as to which Disibodenberg monk composed the *VJ* does not at this stage seem possible. On the contrary, I believe there is a strong contender for authorship: Volmar, Hildegard's secretary in the second part of her life.

In Ep. 38, XIII Guibert gives us a brief character sketch of Hildegard's monk collaborator as sober, chaste and learned, an altogether very monastic kind of person, and Hildegard herself also testifies to the same in *VH* II, 2. This quite accords with the character of the author we can discern here. Earlier in *VH* II, 2, Hildegard declares that Jutta laid her (Hildegard's) case before 'a certain monk known to her'. In Guibert's revision of the *VH*, the monk is described not simply as 'known' but as *familiari*, i.e. *well* known to Jutta. Yet in her introduction to *Scivias*,[1] Hildegard says that it was only five years after Jutta's death she spoke of her visions to a 'certain monk', whose name we learn from Guibert's letters was Volmar. However, we know Hildegard was conversing with Volmar before this, because according to *VH* I, 3 and Guibert's revision of the *VH*, she had already chosen him earlier as her *magister*. Is the 'certain monk' well known to Jutta whom she consulted about Hildegard's visions the same as the 'certain monk', Volmar, whom Hildegard already knew *before* 1141?

Thus far, the circumstantial evidence is already very suggestive. Is it likely that Jutta consulted this monk about Hildegard's case and Hildegard did not learn of it at the time? Surely that would have been the occasion for Hildegard also to have broached the topic with him. In fact there is evidence that even at this early stage, i.e. sometime in the 1130s, she was discussing her visions with a monk, for in her Preface to the *Scivias* she acknowledges that even before 1141, she was speaking of her 'visions' to 'a few religious persons living in the same manner as I'.[2]

---

[1] See *Scivias* (ed. Führkötter), CCCM 43, p. 4, translated by Hart and Bishop, p. 59; *VH* II, 2; and Ep. 38, XII.

[2] *nulli hominum exceptis quibusdam paucis et religiosis qui in eadem conversatione vivebant qua et ego eram, manifestavi* (ed. Führkötter, CCCM 43, p. 4). The translation is by Hart and Bishop, p. 60; *eadem conversatione* here refers to the monastic way of life, for

What we infer is, that in 1141, Volmar did not necessarily learn of Hildegard's visionary gift for the first time. Rather, that was the occasion he heard of a *particular* vision, different in kind to any that went before, of enormous import for the future.

Conclusive evidence that Jutta's 'certain monk' and Hildegard's Volmar are one and the same is supplied by the *VJ*. The author is a single Disibodenberg monk on close terms with *both* Jutta *and* Hildegard, and, most pertinently, one to whom Hildegard was already confiding the content of her visions (*VJ* X). With such qualifications, it is clear that Jutta's 'certain monk' can be none other than Volmar. That brings us to the interesting conclusion that the *VJ* is the earliest fruit of Hildegard and Volmar's collaboration, though their *modus operandi* was set to change as Hildegard's role as prophetess developed. Here, at the beginning, Volmar speaks in the *VJ* in his own voice, and reports Hildegard's vision in the third person.

Striking confirmation that the author is Volmar comes with a phrase in *VJ* VIII: *Quaedam pulcherrima species hominis*—'a certain most beautiful form of a human being'. This is a classic 'Hildegardian' turn of phrase, by which in her later writings Hildegard referred to figures in her own visions. Barbara Newman, in a note to me, considers this is among the clearest indications of Volmar's authorship, that either Hildegard took it up from the *Life of Jutta*, or that it was Volmar who initially proposed it when working as her secretary.

The other member of the trio is Abbot Cuno. A few all-too-brief notices in the *VJ* would suggest that Domna Jutta and Dom Cuno had had a close spiritual relationship—'he was after all her beloved father, and in Christ her very dear son' (X). By about the time of Jutta's death (22 December 1136), he had succeeded as Abbot of Disibodenberg, which she had clearly foretold (VI) and over which she had prayed much. He was 'ordained' (*sic*) only five days after her death (*AD* 1136). He even seems in some sense to have been a protégé of the holy woman. These were sufficient reasons why Abbot Cuno might have set about commissioning a *vita* of one who was not only his, but also the entire community's spiritual mother. The *VJ* prologue also emphasizes Cuno's determination to uphold Jutta's arrangements for the women's

---

which there was a special vow of *conversatio morum* (*RB* 58, 17).

community, which provides an interesting backlight to his disputes with Hildegard in subsequent years.

The dating of *The Life of Jutta*

The author is noticeably meticulous in furnishing the dates and the names of persons, in particular of abbots of his community and leaders in Church and society. Thus we are able to situate Jutta's life precisely in the era of Emperors Henry V and Lothar III.

Staab assumed (p. 172) that the closing phrases of the *VJ*, 'under the aforementioned glorious Emperor Lothar, and Abbot Cuno our most loving father', indicate that the Emperor Lothar III was still alive at the time of the author's writing, so that there was only a short timespan, eleven months in all, for the work to be composed, i.e. between 27 December 1136, the commencement of Cuno's term as Abbot, to 4 December 1137, the death of Lothar.

Constant Mews, however, drew my attention to a little phrase appended to the mention of Otto of Bamberg in *VJ* III: 'of holy memory', which indicates of course that he has died. Otto died in 1139, though *AD* reports it for 1140. Therefore Staab's dating of the *VJ* is invalidated. A closer look at the author's mention of Lothar made clear that it only has reference to the time of Jutta's death, not to the time of the author's writing.

At the time of the *VJ*, Hildegard's prophetic calling has not yet found the Church approval gained in 1147 at the Council of Trier. There are signs that her standing in the Disibodenberg scene is rising, that there she is *known*, but the author still seems somewhat circumspect in presenting her. Though he frequently refers to Hildegard throughout the *VJ*, he does not expressly mention her name, except for once in *VJ* VIII, when he uses it simply without adding any honorific such as *Domna*. This is exactly how it appears also in *AD* for 1136.

Thus, the *VJ* was composed sometime from late 1139, but before Hildegard had become a public figure in the Church beyond the monastery. By 1146–1147, it was available to the Chronicler of Disibodenberg, who used it in his report under the year 1136. In general we can say that the *VJ* dates from the early 1140s, at Disibodenberg.

The early religious life and enclosure of Jutta and Hildegard

There are primary discrepancies between the 1112 date of Jutta and Hildegard's enclosure given in *VJ* III and *AD* 1136, and on the other hand, Hildegard's recollection in *VH* II, 2 that she was 'offered for a spiritual way of life' in her eighth year, i.e. in 1105/6, and the conflation of these two events by Hildegard's biographers both in *VH* I and Ep. 38, VII. The following is an attempt to piece together from the sources a probable sequence of events.[3]

From the outset we accept one firm date and event: the solemn enclosure of Jutta and Hildegard on the Feast of All Saints, 1 November, 1112. It is well corroborated by the dating in the last sentence of *VJ*, in *AD* 1136 and in Ep. 38, VII, by the mention of Bishop Otto implying Adalbert's unavailability for episcopal functions, by the mention of Abbot Burchard's last year of office in agreement with *AD*, and by the mention of Otto at Hildegard's profession in *Eight Readings* II. Trithemius also dates the enclosure to the year 1112.[4]

According to *VJ* II, Count Stephan died in 1095, in which case Jutta may well have grown up in a Sponheim family presided over by a woman, her mother Sophia. In the year 1104, when Jutta had just turned twelve, she fell very ill (*VJ* II), during which she promised herself to God in virginity if she recovered. But after her recuperation she found that she had become a very desirable marriageable prospect, coming as she did from a wealthy family of the upper nobility. She seems to have had a drawn-out crisis of vocation which she eventually solved by side-stepping her family's expectations, slipping out of home, and 'seeking out' Archbishop Ruthard from whom she obtained the religious habit and episcopal protection for her commitment to celibacy (*VJ* III). It was only in late 1105 that Ruthard was recalled from exile by Henry V, so her venture must have taken place after that, probably early in the year 1106. Jutta would have been about fourteen years of age when she undertook this provisional form of a dedicated life.

---

[3] On this dating problem cf. Constant J. Mews, 'Seeing is Believing: Hildegard of Bingen and the *Life of Jutta*', *Tjurunga*, 51 (1996), pp. 12–16, esp. nn. 12 and 16, and Julie Hotchin, 'Enclosure and Containment: Jutta and Hildegard at the Abbey of Disibodenberg', *Magistra: A Journal of Women's Spirituality in History*, 2 (1996), esp. pp. 104–08.

[4] *Chron. Hirsaug.*, p. 126, and *Chron. Sponh.*, pp. 247–48.

Jutta chose a *magistra* for herself, a devout noble widow, Uda (*VJ* III).
Where were they residing? Could they have been living at Disibodenberg
as early as 1106?[5] If so, either the first monks arrived there earlier than
the documentation indicates, and the women's arrival perhaps coincided
with theirs, or they were initially living alongside the canons who may
have been at the site till as late as May 1107.[6] By that date Archbishop
Ruthard had definitely sent in a party of monks.[7] The first abbot,
however, was not appointed and construction of the new monastery did
not commence till the following year, 1108 (*AD*). One thing is certain: in
1106, there was no properly constituted monastery to furnish the
circumstances for a solemn anchoretic enclosure. So, if the women were
there, they were living in a somewhat informal, not quite canonical
situation, something like the devout widow Trutwib, reported in *VJ* VII.

That is one scenario, fraught with difficulties. Another is that Uda and
Jutta actually remained at the family seat at Sponheim.[8] *VJ* III contains a
passage with closely interwoven references to the noble widow Uda and
Jutta's 'devout mother'. At a first reading I thought that the latter might
have been referring to Uda as her 'spiritual' mother. But if we situate
ourselves at Sponheim, all becomes clear: we are dealing with two
persons, and Jutta's 'devout mother' is Sophia, her real mother. Both
Sophia and Uda are noble and devout widows, the latter it seems hosted,

---

[5] Hildegard recalls Disibodenberg as the place she was offered (a point considered
shortly); there is also in Archbishop Adalbert's charter of 1128 an intriguing mention of an
Uda who died at Disibodenberg, though from the account it seems to have taken place
about a hundred years earlier. See Beyer et al., *Urkundenbuch*, p. 521, and *MUB* 1, p. 463.

[6] Apropos of the canons, Constant J. Mews perspicuously suggests ('Seeing is Believing',
p. 15), 'it is just possible that Uda was living alongside the canons of St Disibod (perhaps
not mentioned by Jutta's biographer, because of the long-standing animosity between the
monks and the canons they ousted).' On the other hand, it does not seem socially very
likely that women of the upper free nobility, as at least Jutta was, would have associated
themselves with canons, and canons on so precarious a footing at that.

[7] See Archbishop Ruthard's charter of 11 May 1107, which demonstrates that though an
abbot was not officially appointed till 1108, the site was already occupied by monks.
Adalbert's charter of 1128 also has details of Ruthard's reorganization of Disibodenberg
as a foundation of monks. The disgruntled canons continued their protest intermittently till
as late as 1147 when Archbishop Henry made final property arrangements between the
canons of St Mary at the Steps in Mainz and the monks of Disibodenberg. See *MUB* 2,
Document 96, pp. 185–87.

[8] On the following scenario, see also Staab, 'Aus Kindheit', pp. 64–65.

perhaps as a companion, by the former, who had still to attend to supervising the Sponheim estates. The distinction between the two is made where it says: 'But she [Jutta] stayed with her mother since she really was serving the widow.' Both older women are concerned to prevent Jutta's pious 'wanderlust'. Jutta served her 'novitiate' under Uda for a pre-arranged 'three years', perhaps until 1109/10, then sometime after that her mother was 'taken from their midst', i.e. died. Naumann-Humbeck (p. 182) suggests the year 1110 for Sophia's death; because of Bishop Otto's chronology, discussed below, I would propose the following year, 1111.

After her mother's death, Jutta made plans to set out on pilgrimage. *VJ* III describes her as wanting 'to leave her native land and her father's home for the Lord'—surely proof positive of residence at Sponheim. Her brother Meinhard was now the effective senior of the family, but, it seems, still young and not yet officially Count. Probably with the disastrous end of great aunt Richardis's pilgrimage in mind,[9] he headed off his sister's departure by appealing to their acting bishop, Otto of Bamberg. This points to a period after Archbishop Ruthard's death in 1109, although we have to take into account Otto's absence on Henry V's Italian expedition from August 1110 to August 1111. Thus, Meinhard's intervention could have been in early 1110 or late 1111. Bishop Otto, also to gain a great reputation for holiness and be called a 'father of monks', persuaded Jutta to do seemingly the very opposite of going on pilgrimage: to attach herself to a monastery of monks as an *inclusa* or anchoress, which, after all, was but a more radical and lasting form of ascetic 'exile' from ordinary life than pilgrimage. Something significant happened to Jutta at this stage, because she seems to have channelled her energies into the austere ideal of *anachoresis* with enthusiastic, if not excessive, determination.

Guibert says of this interval (Ep. 38, VI), perfectly realistically, that Jutta 'looked around' various monasteries, and was particularly attracted to Disibodenberg for its situation and the fervour of its monastic life. Through its mother house, St James in Mainz, Disibodenberg fostered the Hirsau form of Benedictine monastic life,[10] which provided for the

---

[9] See the note at *VJ* III for earlier examples of pilgrimage in the family.

[10] In *Chron. Hirsaug.*, pp. 86–87, Trithemius speaks of the 'most famous' monastery of Cluny, whose reform was taken up at Hirsau, and a 'confederation' of monasteries set up by Abbot William to which belonged St Alban's in Mainz, Hassungen, St Eucharius at

attachment of small anchorholds of women to the monasteries of monks. So Jutta had an anchorhold built in stone for herself, to be finished in time for 1 November 1112. She welcomed the 'proposal' of Hildegard's company in her anchorhold as a 'consolation' from heaven (Ep 38 VII).

Finally, Jutta in her twentieth year, Hildegard in her fifteenth and another young woman also called Jutta, were solemnly enclosed by Abbot Burchard at Disibodenberg on the Solemnity of All Saints, 1 November 1112, and later on the same day made their monastic profession before Bishop Otto of Bamberg (*VJ* III and *Eight Readings* II).

Where does that leave the child-oblate, Hildegard? It would appear, at Sponheim.[11]

According to Hildegard's recollections (*VH* II, 2) she was 'offered for a spiritual way of life' in her eighth year, i.e. in 1105/6, before her eighth birthday. We note at the outset, the approximate coincidence of Jutta's return from Archbishop Ruthard, and the date of Hildegard's 'oblation'. Hildegard in fact never explicitly mentions her solemn enclosure as such, or her monastic profession, only her 'oblation' by her parents. This is what seems to have stayed in her mind—perhaps because it was the occasion that marked her separation from her parents' household. But if so, she was certainly not enclosed in a monastic anchorhold.

Even Hildegard hints at an interval between her oblation and her solemn enclosure. For one thing, she had a 'nurse', at the same time as she had Jutta as her *magistra*. When speaking of this period of her life, Guibert's revision of the *VH* makes a clearer distinction than the *VH* itself

---

Trier, Brauweiler, St Peter's in Erfurt, and 'many others'. In *Chron. Sponh.*, p. 245, Trithemius tells how in the year 1128 Abbot Bernhelm of Sponheim organized a 'confraternity' between his monastery and others in the area, beginning with 'the brothers of St Disibod', for which he cites a document. Through Disibodenberg, St James and St Alban's in Mainz learned of this 'spiritual society' and joined it, as did other monasteries including most of those mentioned above, and the nuns of Rupertsberg.

[11] John van Engen argues in a recently published article 'Abbess, Mother and Teacher', in *Voice of the Living Light: Hildegard of Bingen and Her World*, ed. by Barbara Newman (Berkeley: University of California Press, 1998), that Hildegard remained with her own family until she joined Jutta at Disibodenberg in 1112, and was not with Jutta at all before that date. This treats her parents' 'oblation' of her at age eight as a rather tenuous statement of intention at best, to be worked out later on. Such a scenario would all the more underscore Hildegard's deliberate 're-working' of her early life, a topic I go on to broach.

between the 'certain good woman who used to nurse me' on the one hand, and the 'certain woman of very noble birth to whom I had been entrusted' on the other. This suggests a period with Jutta before their solemn enclosure, as she scarcely had a 'nurse' with her in her older years at the anchorhold. Another point is that Hildegard felt relatively at ease from the age of seven till she was fourteen, after which she felt more constrained. During that early period, she says (*VH* II, 2), she often used to speak of her visions in an artless way, so that her hearers used to wonder, but at about the age of fourteen became embarrassed about it and began to conceal it from others. So it seems that as a child 'oblate' there were people around her to a degree improbable later on in the anchorhold.

There is another historiographical discrepancy to deal with. For Hildegard, speaking in an autobiographical account, dating perhaps from the early 1160s, consistently nominates Disibodenberg as 'that place where I had been offered to God' (*VH* II, 7; 10, III, 25). Either she is fore-shortening related events in a kind of ready autobiographical shorthand, conveniently using Jutta as a strong common element (childhood 'oblation' at Sponheim *with Jutta*, and later enclosure at Disibodenberg *with Jutta*), or, in her later years had a particular interest in presenting her early history that way, i.e. eliding over her sojourn at Sponheim and the extent of her indebtedness, not to Jutta as such, but to the comital family, perhaps for quasi-political reasons. In addition, she may well be partially veiling the domestic and informal character of her earliest religious years, in the light of subsequent canonical legislation and her developed Benedictine perspectives.[12]

What further suggests that Hildegard deliberately 're-worked' her early life, are a few hints made by Staab in 'Aus Kindheit' (p. 62) that Godfrey of Disibodenberg used the *VJ* when writing what is now the *VH* I (and, I would add, *VH* II) sometime in the mid 1170s. If so, then despite the evidence of the *VJ*, Godfrey still presents the conflation of events according to Hildegard's 'canon' so to speak. True, he may have been

---

[12] Canon 26 of II Lateran Council of 1139 (*Decrees of the Ecumenical Councils*, ed. by Norman P. Tanner, vol. 1 (Nicaea I–Lateran V) (London: Sheed & Ward, 1990), p. 203) endeavours to steer the enthusiasms of religiously minded women into canonically recognized life-styles. I thank Julie Hotchin for making this connection. This canon also forbids monks and nuns to sing together in choir, and we know what a premium Hildegard set on the chant. The bearing that awareness of such legislation may have had on Hildegard's religious development in the 1140s and '50s is a question worth opening up.

relying on Hildegard's autobiographical passages, already extant, but then, he was writing at Rupertsberg itself while she was still alive to supervise. The case that in this later period Hildegard' had established a standard 'canon' of her early life may receive further support if we ask the same questions about Guibert's Ep. 38 and whether he also both used and suitably ignored aspects of the *VJ*.

The *VJ*, which had more than Hildegard's approval in her pre-*Scivias* days, casts further doubt on the face value of the later version of her early life. Nothing in the *VJ* allows us to assume that a hypothetical stay of Jutta with Uda at Disibodenberg from 1106 was going to end up inevitably in Jutta's commitment to anchoretic life there in the year 1112. All this supposes too much. The *VJ* account, stemming from the early 1140s, has a living quality about it: it conveys the tentative character of Jutta's early religious gropings. Excepting the celibacy issue, what the outcome at each stage was going to be for Jutta was not so clear-cut as hindsight would tend to read into it. So the earlier, more ingenuous document seems preferable, from which we infer that the place of Hildegard's childhood 'oblation' was not Disibodenberg but, it seems, the Sponheim family seat.

It is another of the merits of Guibert's account that, according to Ep. 38, VI and VII a suitable plan for their daughter only gradually revealed itself to Hildegard's parents. They too, it seems, were groping. Hildegard's family was close to the Sponheim family, not only socially but geographically. Though her family's seat was at Bermersheim, it may be that Trithemius is tapping some valuable local tradition by giving Böckelheim as a surname to Hildegard.[13] Böckelheim was in the immediate vicinity of the Sponheim burg, and, as Staab suggests, possibly a small possession of her family where Hildebert might stay when attending the Count of Sponheim or transacting business.[14] Jutta's return from the archbishop and her essaying of an interim, domestically based religious life under Uda's guidance and her mother's watchful eye,[15]

---

[13] See 'Chronicles of Sponheim: select entry', earlier in this volume.

[14] See Staab, 'Aus Kindheit', pp. 63–64 on this point.

[15] Though there can be no literary connections, I cannot but remark on a number of striking parallels between Jutta's career and that of St Macrina, 'Mother of Greek monasticism', elder sister of St Basil of Caesarea and St Gregory of Nyssa,. The latter describes in his *Life of Macrina* (in *Saint Gregory of Nyssa: Ascetical Works*, trans. by V.W. Callahan, Washington: Catholic University of America, 1967) how his sister, the

became an opportunity for Hildebert and Mechtild to make a tentative placement of their own unusual and precocious daughter, with a view to working out something more formal later on. Such then, was Hildegard's 'oblation', involving a concrete and religiously oriented change of setting, but which was, as yet, still only provisional in character. Meanwhile, her parents would have been able to check in on her regularly. On this analysis, all that *VH* I has to say about Jutta's education of Hildegard would have taken place at Sponheim, where Jutta had but to implement much the same program she received as reported in *VJ* II.

By the time it came to Hildegard's solemn enclosure with Jutta, it was no longer entirely up to her parents. For by then she was fourteen, and must have at least freely consented, or, as likely, personally wanted and chose to take such a dramatic step. It could well be that Hildegard herself 'proposed' it to Jutta, a mentor she had learned to admire. Monastic profession would not have been considered valid before about fourteen, when a marriage at that time could also have been contracted.[16]

---

eldest child of a wealthy and eminent family, began her youthful religious experiment by resolutely rejecting arrangements for her marriage. She then apprenticed herself as an ascetic to serve at home under her mother, a devout widow who supervised the family estates. This domestically based ascetic life evolved by degrees into a more formal monastic life, so that by the time of her death, Macrina was the much revered foundress and presiding charismatic head of its female section, if not of both sections, male and female, of a double monastery. Hers too was a vigorous moral and intellectual character, and she became renowned as a wonderworker. The stages of her religious evolution are studied by Susanna Elm in *Virgins of God* (Oxford: Clarendon Press, 1994), pp. 78–105.

[16] See Ep. 38, VI where Jutta struggles to ensure no marriage contract is written for her. This corresponds to the period after her serious illness at the age of twelve (*VJ* II). For Hildegard's warnings on the practice of child oblation, and the necessity that parents respect their free will when it comes to a choice of religious profession, see *Scivias* II, 5, 45–46.

Among the monastic rules, only the Rule of St Basil addressed the question of the reception of child oblates and at what age their commitment should be judged valid: 'We deem that any time, from the earliest age on, is favourable for receiving newcomers to instruction and to the fear of the Lord. However, the profession of virginity will only be firm from the time adult age has already begun, or at least that age which is usually considered appropriate and ripe for marriage.' Rule of St Basil, VII, 2–4, translated from *Basili Regula*, ed. by Klaus Zelzer (Vienna: Hoelder-Pichler-Tempsky, 1986). The Rule of Basil was standard spiritual reading in Benedictine monasteries, being expressly recommended in *RB* 73, 5. Contemporary with the *VJ*, we find the Rule of Basil mentioned along with those of Benedict and Augustine as one of the approved monastic rules that religious women ought to be living by in Canon 26 of II Lateran Council of

At the time of their enclosure Hildegard's *magistra* was no mature widow, but a young vital woman only twenty years of age. As Staab says ('Aus Kindheit', p. 65) one can only marvel at the courage of all parties concerned in allowing such youthful and eager spirits to take so daring a step. In childhood and adolescence, Jutta and Hildegard's difference in age (about five or six years) would have made a real difference, but by the time the younger had reached about twenty, the significance of this gap would have diminished and, without necessarily compromising the lines of religious obedience, their relationship tend to develop from mentor/disciple to that of a youthful camaraderie based on a growing sense of parity. Hildegard had in Jutta a friend sympathetic to her visionary gift, for, as the *VJ* makes clear, Jutta herself was a visionary, and for that matter, a wonder-worker.

While Jutta, if anyone, was capable of force of character, she does not seem to have been characterized by a domineering or jealous use of authority in the anchorhold, least of all towards Hildegard. She seems to have reserved the full rigour of her ascetic regimen for herself alone. A memorable line in *VH* I, 2, backed up by (borrowing from, and developing?) a line in *VJ* V, suggests her eagerness to foster the best in her charges, and even to rejoice in it when she perceived in Hildegard a disciple who was developing into a *magistra* herself and a 'pathfinder in the ways of excellence'.

The Latin style of *The Life of Jutta*

The author's Latin style is considerably different from Guibert's. He gives evidence of what one might call a well-schooled, cultivated and distinctly monastic *Latinitas*. Guibert was undoubtedly familiar with the classics of ancient Rome and affects a highly skilled classicism; there is much less of that ambience in the *VJ*.

He tends to place the main verb earlier in the sentence than does Guibert. He sometimes attempts the extended periodic style and *variatio*

1139 (see *Decrees of the Ecumenical Councils*, ed. by Tanner, p. 203). One of the major transmissions of the Rule of Basil is found in the copy of Benedict of Aniane's *Codex Regularum* which belonged to the great library of a monastery closely associated with both Disibodenberg and Rupertsberg: St Maximin in Trier (cf. *AD* 1138). It is the 9th century Codex Monacensis (see Zelzer, p. xxiii).

in his syntax, but perhaps not always skilfully. One example of this tangle of constructions is a single long sentence early in his prologue, *VJ* I, 'Since according ... observed', which is broken down in the translation. Here he is attempting a high and formal style. Translation was not made easier by ungrammatical use of the reflexive *suus -a -um*.[17] Another example of difficulty is the mixture of statement and unfulfilled condition in the passage about Uda in *VJ* III.

Sometimes he seems to forget, or the copyist has missed, auxiliary verbs like 'est' or elements of infinitives like 'esse'. One can be left wondering where the main verb is. An example is 'praeventa <est>' in the same passage, *VJ* III. This is also sometimes a feature of the autobiographical passages in the *VH*, and perhaps a small stylistic corroboration of Volmar's authorship of the *VJ*.[18]

In the way of medieval Latin, ablative gerundives seem to be used as a kind of present active participle, and indeed gerundives are used a great deal. Sometimes a narrative is constructed with a series of ablative absolutes using gerundives in present tense.

The author is given to prose-rhymes and alliterations—though nothing like to the extent of Theodoric! Examples are *inspicientes inspicere* (VI) 'looked at those who came to look at it' (VI) and *certamen foret certatura* 'was to fight the good fight' (VII) and, in as good an example as he offers, *compassionis plena, eius passione comperta* (VI)—'when she learned of his suffering (passion), she who *was filled with compassion ...*'

The importance of *The Life of Jutta*

Along with the Chronicles, the *VJ* documents the religious culture of Disibodenberg from the time of its foundation as a Benedictine monastery through its formative years up to the 1140s.

The *VJ* echoes traditional and contemporary Catholic sensibilities such as thirst for tangible contact with the holy, the felt need for the advocacy of the saints, whether male or female, still below or already beyond,

---

[17] See Guibert's revision of the *VH* II, 12 for the survival of passages which confuse reflexive and non-reflexive forms.

[18] When Guibert supplies missing auxiliary verbs in his version of the *VH*, it may well be a case of his 'correcting' mistakes which slipped Volmar's attention in editing Hildegard's text.

solicitude for the fate of the souls of the dead, a climate of acceptance of miraculous and visionary phenomena. It uses a fully weighted language of 'virtue' and 'merit', temptation, sin, punishment etc.—no ghost of linguistic nominalism here! It presents the devil very much in his biblical role as Satan, the Accuser/the Prosecutor.

With regard to monastic life, the *VJ* shares the esteem for the eschatologically oriented, ascetical and 'desert' trends of the contemporary renewal movement, exhibits a zeal for the Scriptures as encountered in the liturgy and *lectio divina*, and looks to the Rule of St Benedict as the yardstick of monastic virtue. All in all, it evinces a conscientiously Benedictine monastic culture, to be contrasted with that of the rising 'schools' on the one hand, or that of Augustinian foundations on the other. In comparison with the more personalist and devotional upswell at Citeaux, we could describe its monastic piety as somewhat archaic, in the Cluniac/Hirsau mold, though not the less deeply felt for all that. It does share with the Cistercians a concern for manual labour.

Within these traditionally Catholic and specifically monastic perspectives, the *VJ* focusses on the piety of a particular holy woman, Jutta of Sponheim. It first of all shows the domestic setting of her earliest religious experiments, and then documents that feature of the Hirsau tradition[19] whereby anchoresses were attached to male monasteries. It illustrates the context within which monks reverenced and fostered the presence of consecrated women. Indeed, within these limits, and in concert with a high spiritual ideal, the *VJ* is testimony to a considerable degree of esteem, affection, and collaboration between the sexes. It would be difficult to argue that the monk-author shows himself incapable of a deep empathy with his disciples-friends-mothers, Jutta and Hildegard, or that that he much misses their purpose in what he communicates about

---

[19] There are records of other anchoresses attached to monks' monasteries in the Mainz vicinity, e.g. Wertrude, daughter of a founder of Johannisberg across the river from Bingen, who became an anchoress there in 1108, and Mechtild who became an anchoress at St Albans in Mainz in 1118 and transferred to the monastery of Sponheim when her brother Bernhelm became Abbot there in 1125. Mechtild was also credited as a visionary. She died in 1154, leaving a little school of five disciples, and was buried in the monks' choir. Over in England there is a contemporary parallel in Christina of Markyate whose anchorhold developed into a cenobitic community, and later the women for whom the *Ancrene Wisse* was written. On anchoresses in the Mainz vicinity, see Hotchin, 'Enclosure and Containment', pp. 115–17, and on Christina, see Sabina Flanagan, *Hildegard of Bingen, 1098–1179: A Visionary Life*, pp. 29, 32, 34, 36.

them.

The *VJ* shows an anchoress who, notwithstanding an outward dependence on the monks and a lack of educational parity with the more learned among them, attained no mean ascendancy as a counsellor, healer, teacher, spiritual mother, and even divine oracle in the life of monastery, Church, and local society. And this she accomplished, not by any political scheme to bring it about, but by first of all focussing wholly on God, with the starkest tenacity of purpose, and by the inherent spiritual force of character that came of it—in short, by her manifest holiness, though other factors such as high social rank and native intelligence were also part of it. It shows how this anchoress could also attract other female disciples to join her company and the anchorhold develop into a 'school' under her direction, and then into a small monastery of nuns adjunct to the monks.

Staab suggests that as an example of hagiography the *VJ* points to 'individualistic' and 'mystical' tendencies far into the future (p. 172). Perhaps he means to refer to the Beguine and Third Order movements of subsequent centuries. As far as the presentation of Jutta goes, this may be true to some extent for the early experimental phase of her religious life, but I would prefer to characterize her mature religious life, her severely anchoretic, ascetic and 'virile' virtues, not excluding her public ministry of compassion and counsel, as harking back to an older religious tradition, to be found, for example, in the *vitae* of Saints Radegund, Monegund and other female saints of the patristic era.[20] On the other

---

[20] The Life of St Monegond (d. 530), as reported by St Gregory of Tours, shows the characteristic themes. *Virility of the woman saint*: 'He gives us as models not only robust men, but even the weaker sex, fighting not feebly but with virile vigour. He gives a place in his heavenly kingdom not only to men who fight, but also to women who take a hand in these combats by their wholesome toils: which He causes to be seen by us in our day in blessed Monegunde.' *Enclosure in a cell*: 'she had a cell made for herself where there was only a little window through which she could see the day, and there ... occupied herself only with God to whom she entrusted herself, praying for her sins and the sins of the people, having only one little girl in her service in order to get her necessary things.' *Prayer and rigorous asceticism*: 'she spent all her days in prayer, fasting and vigils ... eating only barley bread and drinking only a very little wine on feast days, diluted with much water. She did not have a soft bed of hay or fresh straw but only one of woven rushes, commonly called matting, which she put on a bench or laid on the ground.' *Expansion of the cell into a community of disciples*: 'she gathered together a few nuns there.' *A public ministry*: 'she gave to the sick a multitude of healing remedies.' Monegond moved from a cell at Chartres to one at the tomb of St Martin, which Radegund

hand, the amount of space given to visions in general, and especially Hildegard's vision in *VJ* IX, does indeed point to future developments in this field, beginning with the *VH* itself.

The *VJ* suggests that at least one of the tributaries of what became the canonical 'contemplative' life of nuns was not strictly the cenobitic life at all. The small monastery of nuns with strict enclosure, in this line of evolution, presents as an expanded anchoress's cell, i.e. a collective anchorhold, and as a practice with historically excellent Benedictine credentials, though at Disibodenberg the women's enclosure was offset by its contingency with the monastery of monks.[21]

Perhaps the *VJ* has its most surprising value as the earliest documentation of Hildegard of Bingen herself. Present in the background throughout the *VJ*, and sometimes in the foreground, is a 'pre-*Scivias*' Hildegard, a Hildegard prior to her public fame as prophetess. Here is the earliest evidence of her visionary gift. Here too, in the person of its author, we meet her collaborator, Volmar, for the first time.

The re-emergence of the *VJ* must significantly affect any future study of Hildegard's life, particularly her early life. In it we have something of a 'control' document, dating from the early 1140s, with which to weigh statements made in the later *VH* and Guibert's Ep. 38.

The *VJ* is a worthy memorial of Hildegard of Bingen's real *pietas* towards her *magistra* and friend, Jutta of Sponheim, for it was Hildegard who instigated Abbot Cuno to commission the writing of the *Vita*, and contributed much material for it. Yet it documents a type of holiness which Hildegard was to take up, modulate, and develop in directions that Jutta could scarcely have imagined.[22] In showing us a Jutta so

---

was to visit some decades later before settling in Poitiers. St Monegond shares the same feast day in the Roman Martyrology as St Otto of Bamberg, July 2. See the translation by Seraphim Rose and Paul Bartlett, *Vita Patrum: The Life of the Fathers by St Gregory of Tours* (Platina, California: St Herman of Alaska Brotherhood, 1988), pp. 278–85.

[21] In a peculiar inversion of this process, the most strictly contemplative, semi-eremitical form of canonical life for women in the Western Church, the Carthusian nuns, evolved during the twelfth century among nuns in southern France who had been heirs of a centuries-old tradition of cenobitic life for women under the Rule of St Caesarius of Arles, and who applied for affiliation with the monks. It is worth noting that monasteries of Carthusian nuns had—and have—attached to them what is in effect a small monastery of Carthusian monks, including priest-monks for the service of the sacraments.

[22] As an example of continuity yet independence, we could say that while Hildegard assumed Jutta's role as 'oracle', visionary, and wonder-worker at Disibodenberg, she

intrinsically woven into the spiritual, social, and economic fabric of Disibodenberg, the *VJ* throws into relief the enormous uprooting involved in Hildegard's drive to establish a separate community of her nuns at Rupertsberg.[23]

---

transposed it, with the help of her unique gift of 'vision', to the vastly wider field of the universal Church. *Scivias* is the instrument and first fruits of this transposition. Similarly, by earning in her own right something of the spiritual ascendancy that had been Jutta's, she carried it perhaps to a logical conclusion by her extrication of the nuns from Disibodenberg and the establishment of a separate community for the nuns. For Hildegard's shift from anchoretic to cenobitic virtues see Ep. 38, X, and notes; Constant J. Mews, 'Seeing is Believing', pp. 29–30.

[23] How greatly this uprooting affected the monks of Disibodenberg appears with much pathos in a letter written to Hildegard in the early 1150s by Adalbert, prior of Disibodenberg. As to claims that Hildegard was with them almost from her infancy, we have to bear in mind its later editing: '... We who have known you almost from the cradle and with whom you lived for many years wonder why you have withdrawn the words of your celestial visions from us who thirst for them. We remember how you were educated among us, how you were taught, how you were established in the religious life. For your instruction was appropriate only to a woman, and a simple psalter was your only schoolbook. Yet without complaint you embraced the good and holy religious life. But the will of God filled you with celestial dew and opened up to you the magnitude of its secrets. And just as we were set to rejoice in these things with you, God took you away from us against our will, and gave you to another people. We cannot fathom why God did this, but, willy-nilly, we are suffering great distress from the deed. For we had hoped that the salvation of our monastery rested with you.' (Letter 78, trans. by Baird and Ehrmann, pp. 172–73).

The structure of *The Life of Jutta*

The chapters are those of the original manuscripts. The headings are Staab's:

I	Prologue
II	Jutta's childhood, illness, and the vow she made
III	Her dedication to virginity and entrance into the monastery
IIII	Her ascetic endeavours
V	Her ministry to others and her piety
VI	Her miracles and prophecies
VII	The foretelling of her death
VIII	Her death and burial
VIIII	The testing of her soul after her death
X	Epilogue

THE LIFE OF LADY JUTTA THE ANCHORESS

BY A MONK OF DISIBODENBERG

I

HERE BEGINS THE PROLOGUE to the life of lady Jutta the anchoress, whose memorial day is the eleventh day before the Kalends of January [22 December].

Since, according to the Apostle's saying, we are those *upon whom the last times have come* (1 Cor. 10:11), we have that Gospel prophecy to fear, which says that the more *wickedness shall abound*, the more *shall the charity of many grow cold* (Mat. 24:12). Just as when the sun declines to its setting the warmth of its rays cools down, so as the world grows old and iniquity more and more abounds, zeal for the virtues grows cold. Therefore the faithful, whoever they are, ought to collect examples of holy deeds as though they were collecting sticks of firewood, with which to daily enkindle in themselves inducements to the virtues.

According to that precept of the Law, *The fire on my altar shall always be kept alight*, says the Lord, *which the priest shall feed, supplying it with wood every morning, day by day. It is a fire in perpetuity, which shall never be wanting to my altar* (Lev. 6:11–12), the lord Cuno, priest of Christ, chosen shepherd of the community of Saint Disibod, considered that it was his responsibility to feed the fire on the altar of the Lord. Therefore he decided that for the coming generation a record should be made of the life of the lady Jutta, a nun and the first anchoress of modern times in this place, to whose arrangements he scrupulously adhered, entrusting them to the care of her daughters.

The same father commanded our humble self to set forth what she had accomplished through the grace of God, for he had been warned by a divine inspiration, and spurred on by the request of a loyal disciple[24] of her mother Jutta, Christ's handmaid above-mentioned. This disciple was the one who undertook the direction of her school[25] after her death. In order that the structure of her work might not fall to ruin, the above-mentioned father resolved that a narrative of the way of life of this beloved lady be published to the praise of Christ, the edification of the generations to come, and as a memorial of her.

Now we, bereft of talent for the carrying out of so great a work, implore his mercy whose *Wisdom has opened the mouth of the dumb, and made the tongues of infants to speak* (Wis. 10:21), that we might carry out this work as his grace may inspire. For this grace we humbly beg in his name. Trusting in his help to whom the Prophet says: *In you our fathers hoped; in you they hoped and were not put to shame* (Ps. 21:5–6), we now approach to take up the task which has been set before us.

II

HERE BEGINS THE LIFE of the lady Jutta.

The blessed Jutta arose from the noblest of Gallic stock, the heir of a lineage eminent according to the esteem of this world. Her father, Stephen of Sponheim, being himself of distinguished birth,[26] obtained as his consort in marriage Sophia, truly enriched with all wisdom,[27] born of

---

[24] *rogatuque provocatus piae matris Juttae discipulae...* This is Hildegard, who succeeded as *magistra* of Jutta's school. See Ep. 38, X. In an intriguing reversal of roles Hildegard was herself asked years later, in 1170, by the abbot of Disibodenberg, Helenger, to write the life of their patron saint, St Disibod.

[25] *Eius scolam ipsius suscepit.* For the monastery as 'school of the Lord's service', see *RB* Prologue 45.

[26] On Count Stephan's genealogy see Mötsch, 'Genealogie', pp. 72–77.

[27] *Sophiam omni prudentia decoratam;* the play is on the meaning of her name. In the light of what Wisdom was to become to Hildegard, it is worth noting how often the term appears in the *VJ*. The mention of Sophia's Bavarian stock reinforces Mötsch's conclusion that her father was Count Meinhard V of Formbach and her mother Mathilde von Reinhausen. Thus, Sophia was a near relative of Emperor Lothar III, whose maternal grandfather, Frederick of Formbach, was a brother of Meinhard V. It is all the more understandable that Meinhard of Sponheim was present as an interested party at the election of Duke Lothar of Saxony as king at Mainz on 30 August 1125, Mötsch,

the most illustrious Bavarian stock. From her he acquired, among other pledges, this daughter of outstanding character.[28]

When she was scarcely three years old, death deprived her of her father,[29] but she was nurtured with great care by her widowed mother. Once she had passed the tender years of her infancy, her mother handed her over to be instructed in the learning of the sacred scriptures. In these she made good progress; whatever her capacious intelligence could absorb from them she committed to her retentive memory, and thereafter strove to implement with good deeds. Being filled with the *fear* of the Lord which *casts out sin* (Eccli 1:26), she made progress through daily growth in the virtues.

She had just completed her twelfth year of age, when she was laid low by a severe illness. At the point of despair she vowed to God that if she survived she would undertake a holy way of life. But when she recovered from this illness, she was the delight of everyone, for she was a young woman of comely appearance. Many nobles and wealthy landowners were coming to her, even from far-off places, panting to be joined to her in the marriage union.

III

BUT SINCE SHE HAD already sworn *to know nothing of the marriage bed,*[30]

'Genealogie', p. 75, esp. n. 104, and Naumann-Humbeck, *Studien*, Document 51, pp. 66–67.

[28] Of their other 'pledges', 'tokens', 'proofs', *pignora*, we definitely know of Meinhard, who subsequently carried on the Rhineland family line, and Hugo, sometime dean of the Cathedral of Cologne, who founded the Premonstratensian monastery of Knechsteden in 1131 and became Archbishop of Cologne briefly before he died in 1137. Cf. Naumann-Humbeck, *Studien*, p. 215, where the existence of another brother (or cousin) is suggested, to account for the way the Sponheim name is attested in some later documents. According to the present text, Jutta was born in 1092, before December 22. Since, in her preface to *Scivias*, Hildegard dates her birth clearly to early 1098, it emerges that she was only six years younger than her *magistra*.

[29] According to the above reckoning, the year of her father's death would be 1095, not 1118 as reported by Trithemius, *Chron. Sponh.*, p. 237. For an excursus on this dating problem see the note to Ep. 38, VI.

[30] *Nescire thorum*, timens *in delicto habitura fructum, in respectione animarum sanctarum*. The text is accommodated to Jutta's situation, whose 'sin' would be the

she feared *the fruit she would have from sin at the examination of holy souls* (Wis. 3:13). So she resisted them all vigorously,[31] such that in guarding her chastity she withstood grave dangers. But these we will avoid inserting here because it would take too long.[32]

Whereupon, despite the wishes of all her relatives, she sought out the lord Ruthard, Archbishop of the See of Mainz, and obtained from him the habit of holy religion. Warned by a divine inspiration, she also submitted herself as a disciple for three years to the lady Uda, a widow of Göllheim, who was living in the habit of holy religion. Instructed by her teaching, she advanced day by day from the good to the better, from virtue to virtue.

At that stage, she burned to go on pilgrimage while she was still young,[33] if only her devout mother had not stood in her way.[34] But she stayed with her mother since she really was serving the widow, together with her devoting herself *to the Lord day and night with fasting*, vigils and prayers (cf. Lk. 2:37), yet always waiting for an appropriate moment to slip away from her in flight. She was continually prevented, however, by her careful supervision.[35] After her mother was taken from their midst,

---

forswearing of her private vow. The Vulgate has: *felix est sterilis; et inconquinata, quae nescivit thorum in delicto, habebit fructum in respectione animarum sanctarum*: 'Blessed is the barren woman, and the undefiled woman who has not known the marriage bed in sin, for she will have her reward in the examination of holy souls'.

[31] *viriliter;* 'manfully' might be even more accurate, since Jutta's spiritual and moral 'virility' is a motif of the work.

[32] *quae his inserere devitamus causa prolixitatis;* In Ep. 38, VI Guibert enlarges on Jutta's difficulties at this stage.

[33] There was precedent for the idea in the Carinthian branch of her father's family. In 1065 Siegfried I pilgrimaged to Jerusalem, and died on his return. His wife Richardis, Jutta's great aunt, set out on pilgrimage to Santiago de Compostela but died on the way. Her body was brought back to Sponheim for burial; see Mötsch, 'Genealogie', p. 67. Such family memories may have had something to do with Meinhard's alarm; cf. Staab, *VJ*, n. 153. Jerusalem's recent recapture (1099) had reopened pilgrimage there.

[34] *Aestuabat enim tunc in teneris annis peregrinationem adire, si ei pia mater non obstitisset.* The meaning is, Jutta did really burn to go on pilgrimage, *and would have done so,* had her mother not stood in her way.

[35] *Cui* (referring back to her *pia mater*) *adhaerens, utpote vere viduae faulabatur, cum ea … vacando, semper operiens aptum tempus quo fuga laberetur ab ea, industria tamen eius iugiter praeventa custodia.* The absence of a main verb presents some difficulties for translation. I supply *est* with *praeventa* as a main verb.

Jutta made arrangements so she would not have to delay in carrying out her plan, that is, to *leave her native land and her father's house* (cf. Gen. 12:1) for the Lord.

The Lord however arranged things for her in another way. For when her brother Meinhard became aware of it, he considered that, as far as he was concerned, her departure was not to be tolerated. He worked to head off his sister's pilgrimage using the lord Otto of holy memory, prelate of Bamberg[36] as a go-between. On his counsel, and at the plea of her brother, she chose for her dwelling this place called Disibodenberg, which she entered when she was twenty years of age.

So on the Kalends of November [1 November] the venerable lord Abbot Burchard, then in the last year of his life,[37] enclosed her, with two sisters and herself the third, in homage of the divine Trinity. On that very same day, in the presence of the Father mentioned above[38] she made profession of monastic life, and, *being strengthened by the Holy Spirit* (Acts 9:31), she followed it with all her heart.[39]

---

[36] Saint Otto, Bishop of Bamberg 1103–1139. From 1112–1115 Otto was supplying episcopal duties for Adalbert of Mainz who was still only a bishop-elect, being ordained bishop by Otto himself on 26 December 1115. Adalbert was imprisoned by Henry V in the month following Jutta and Hildegard's enclosure, December 1112. On Adalbert and Otto see *AD* 1109 (and note), 1112 and 1116, and Staab, *VJ*, p. 160, esp. n. 125.

[37] Abbot Burchard of St James in Mainz and of Disibodenberg died on 3 March 1113.

[38] *praedicto patre presente*; Who is this 'father', Abbot Burchard or Bishop Otto? That it refers to Otto receives corroboration in *Eight Readings* II which reports that Hildegard received the holy veil from Bishop Otto. See Schrader, *Die Herkunft der heiligen Hildegard*. As a bishop, Otto was properly 'Father' in relation to Abbot Burchard, even if the latter was not of his diocese. On the title 'Father' as proper to bishops see A. de Vogüé, 'Twenty-Five Years of Benedictine Hermeneutics—An Examination of Conscience', *American Benedictine Review*, 36 (1985), pp. 402–52, esp. n. 53. On the other hand, at the end of *VJ* VIII, there is a case where the phrase 'above mentioned father' must refer to the abbot.

[39] *Secuta est ex toto corde*. This phrase recalls a line in the dialogue between candidate and bishop in the ancient rite of the Consecration of Virgins, which was often conflated with the monastic profession of nuns. The arch-priest (here, Abbot Burchard?) summons the candidates: 'Wise Virgins, prepare your lamps, behold the bridegroom comes, go out to meet him'. He then presents them to the Bishop, addressing him as 'most reverend Father'. A dramatic exchange, an expanding tricolon in form, ensues between bishop and candidates. Three times he invites them *venite* 'come' and three times they reply, *et nunc sequimur in toto corde* 'and now we follow with all our heart'.

IIII

SHE SHUNNED FORGETFULNESS,[40] AND, being filled with *the fear of the Lord*, which in all ways *is the beginning of wisdom* (Eccli 1:16), brooked no negligence[41] whatever, but *day and night meditated on the Law of the Lord* (Ps. 1:2). Before God and before human beings[42] she strove to advance without giving cause for complaint, anxious that not a trace of virtue should escape her. For, according to the warning of Solomon who said: *diligently work your field, so that afterward you may be able to build your house* (Prov. 24:27) she *chastised her body and subjected it* to servitude (1 Cor. 9:27), *crucifying* it along *with its vices and passions* (Gal. 5:24). She immolated herself as a *living sacrifice, a holy sacrifice* (Rom. 12:1) in *vigils*, prayers and continual *fasting, in cold and nakedness* (2 Cor. 11:27).

Among the various ways in which she inflicted relentless torments and wounds on her body she wore a hairshirt and an iron chain, by means of which she had already been accustomed to subduing her youthful limbs.[43] But from the time of her enclosure till the end of her life, she made a practice of wearing these next to her flesh except when a special feast-day or serious illness intervened, when she was obliged by order of her elders

---

[40] *Oblivionem namque fugiens* ...; *RB* 7, 10. This whole chapter is replete with references to Benedictine, monastic virtues, drawing particularly on *RB* chapters 4–7.

[41] *nil duxit neglentiae*, *RB* 31, 11.

[42] *coram deo et hominius nitens sine querela incidere*, *RB* 7, 14.

[43] Cf. the life of St Radegund (520–587), King Clothaire's estranged wife who become an extremely penitential, and also publicly influential, anchoress. See Baudonivia, *Vita S. Radegundis*, in *Handmaids of the Lord*, trans. by Joan M. Petersen (Kalamazoo, Michigan: Cistercian Publications, 1996), p. 407: 'Having clothed herself in strong armour, she gave herself unceasingly to prayers, vigils and regular sacred reading [*lectione propensa*]. She herself served meals to visiting strangers at table ... After she had assumed the habit of a religious, she made a penitential bed for herself ... so greatly did she impoverish herself for the sake of God.' St Radegund was specially revered at Hirsau where her relics were solemnly interred on the day the monastery church was consecrated in 1091. She was also venerated at Disibodenberg, for she is noted in the Martyrology of Disibodenberg, Bern Burgerbibliothek MS 226, fol. 36ᵛ, with the words: 'deposition at Poitiers of Saint Radegund, Queen, whose life and virtues are famous far and wide'. There is extant a twelfth-century copy of *Vita Radegundis* made at St Maximin at Trier, with which monastery Disibodenberg had close links. Cf. MGH SS rer. Mer. 2, p. 361, and J. Hotchin, 'Enclosure and Containment', pp. 110–13.

to abstain from these things.[44]

Her tender heart was always moved over those sick in body or soul, so that, according to the Lord's promise, *she placed her hands on the sick, and they recovered* (Mk 16:18). Through her consoling words, many were restored from all kinds of wretched conditions.

She applied herself wholeheartedly to manual work, *not eating her bread in idleness*[45] (Prov. 31:27). No less fervent in the virtue of obedience, she applied herself to reading with her mouth silent, very much on guard against whispering words under her breath and the idle talk which provokes laughter.[46]

In all things and above all things she kept her *garments shining white* with the virtue of charity, not allowing the *oil* of fraternal charity to be *lacking from her head* (Eccle 9:8). Clad in the cheapest and meanest of clothing,[47] humble in her conduct, she abhorred all pride from the depth of her heart,[48] contenting herself with the left-overs from the common table, though it be but a pauper's table. She embraced humility with all her might—as was right since it is the guardian and queen of all the virtues—*through patience gaining her soul* (Lk. 21:19).

V

IT IS BEYOND OUR powers to express how great was her wisdom both in spiritual matters and in dealing with various other needs. Not only did all those living in this place devoutly obey her sound warnings and

---

[44] Cf. Fortunatus, *Vita S. Radegundis*: 'On one occasion, she had bound three broad circlets round her neck and arms the days of Lent, and after she had implanted chains around her body, by binding herself so tightly that her tender flesh became swollen from being enclosed in the hard iron. After the fast was over, when she wished to extract the chains enclosed beneath her skin, she could not do so ...', in *Handmaids of the Lord*, trans. by Joan M. Petersen, pp. 391–92.

[45] Cf. *RB* 48, 1.

[46] *summopere cavens susurii verba et otiosa risumque moventia; RB* 6, 8, *scurrilitates vero ve verba otiosa et risum moventia*. The author quotes verbatim from *RB* here, but for *scurrilitates vero* has *susurrii verba*, possibly indicating some confusion in the text. Cf. also *RB* 4, 52,53.

[47] *RB* 7, 49.

[48] *RB* 7, 51.

counsels,[49] but all those from round about of whatever rank, nobles or common people, rich or poor, pilgrims or tenants, were asking only after the anchoress, the lady Jutta; they waited on her alone as on a heavenly oracle. She was a cause of admiration and esteem to everyone for the wisdom divinely bestowed on her, and indeed, there flourished in her the greatest discernment for all situations.

Though she was indeed *busy about many things* as Martha was, she did not forget *the better part chosen by Mary* (Lk. 21:19). Through the contemplation of *a pure heart* (Mat. 5:8) she kept herself intent on our Head, that is, Christ, and *moved forward without turning her head* (cf. Ezech. 1:9), like the *animal with eyes in front and back* (Apoc. 4:6). *Forgetting*, therefore, *the things that lay behind and stretching out to what lay ahead* (Phil. 3:13), she cared only to be as intent as humanly possible on assiduous prayer, mindful of the apostolic saying: *pray unceasingly* (1 Thess. 5:17).

In the course of her rule of life, she used to complete the entire psalter every day,[50] as well as daily reciting other additions for the living and the dead, which could not be expected of anyone else. She sometimes added a second and a third psalter, but never less than one, except when she was prevented by serious weaknesses.[51] On occasion, she went through the entire psalter standing in one place, adding a prostration between each verse, but she did this rarely because she had not enough strength for it. More often she went right through the psalter while standing erect or crouching on her knees. Sometimes she used to give herself to this work in bare feet even through the hardest and most pressing winters, so that from this labour she became afflicted by a serious debility.

Since she was truly a sheep of the good shepherd who said: *I have not come to call the righteous but sinners*, and *what I want is mercy and not sacrifice* (Mat. 9:10), she gave generously to all who came seeking her;

---

[49] *Omnes isto in loco degentes eius salutaribus monitis atque consiliis devote obtemperabant*; i.e. Jutta was spiritual mother to all the monks as well as the young women in her anchorhold.

[50] See *RB* 18, 24–25.

[51] Cf. Fortunatus, *Vita S. Radegundis*: 'throughout the fast she did not even drink two sestaria of water. Consequently she suffered so much from thirst that her throat dried up and she could scarcely say a psalm ... she spent the night-vigils continuously repeating the cycle of the psalms ... Rest itself wearied her, for whom too small a bed seemed to support her little body', in *Handmaids of the Lord*, trans. by Joan M. Petersen, p. 390.

whether to those who came suffering some affliction or to those who came as public penitents, she stretched out the hand of consolation and the help of her devout prayer.

Because of the many works of piety that so abundantly overflowed in her, the fame of her name became widely celebrated, for her house *built on a mountain could not be hidden* (Mat. 9:13). Some, absent in far-off places, sent messengers, and many others used letters to humbly seek the advocacy of her prayer. She had a care for her good name, aware that it was of more benefit to her than many treasures. For this reason it was *as oil poured out* far and wide (cf. Cant. 1:1).

All the same, she was *ardent* in her zeal *for the Lord* (Rom. 12:11)—she was not one to prop up anyone's elbow with the cushions of flattery. For those who came to see her, she mixed the *wine* of stringent correction with the *oil* of sweet and humble counsel (cf. Lk. 10:34). She accommodated herself humbly and wisely to the character and station of each person,[52] not retaining *anger* against another at *the setting of the sun*[53] (Eph. 4:26).

She taught ungrudgingly whomever she could, all that she herself had learnt from the inspiration of the Holy Spirit, the tradition of the elders and the report of the faithful. She held back none of her daughters—on the contrary, she exhorted them to do well, being herself keen to match her own words with her deeds. She did not prefer one before another unless she was found humbler, more eager for obedience and more zealous in good works.[54]

Though she strove with all her effort to conceal the treasure of her virtues, in case it should be despoiled through its being displayed in public, he who knows all secrets, whom it was all her longing to please, did not permit it that her *light remain hidden under a bushel* (Lk. 11:33).

---

[52] *conformans se humiliter et prudenter qualitati cuiusque persone ac dignitatis*; cf. *RB* 2, 32. In citing this text of the *RB*, the author uses *dignitatis* instead of the RB's *intelligentia*. *Dignitas* had strong connotations of social standing both in the classical world and in the time of the author. The *RB* reacts very strongly against the *dignitas* of the secular world; membership of the community entails that a person's secular rank cease utterly and a new order of 'rank' obtain (cf. *RB* 2, 18).

[53] Cf. *RB* 4, 23,73.

[54] Cf. *RB* 2, 21.

VI

BECAUSE SHE HAD LABOURED with such unrelenting effort for so long, and, notwithstanding the frailty of her body, had abstained from eating meat for eight years, she was eventually laid low by a serious weakness. Thereupon, by command of the lord Abbot Adilhun[55] she was ordered to use meat. She was still humbly begging to be excused from this when unexpectedly, a kind of water bird, rather large in bulk, occasionally heard in this area before, but never seen, came and settled in her window at twilight one evening. When it was found in that spot early next morning it caused a great stir. Marvellous to relate, the bird did not seek safety by flying away, but as if it were tame, just looked back at those who came to look at it.

When the said father found out about this, he drew deep sighs, dissolved into tears and said: 'Heaven has refuted my hardness of heart since for so long I have put off compassion for her infirmity.' He then commanded that she must take refreshment with the gift that heaven had sent her. She then humbly yielded to him, but she requested that she should not be put under obligation by such an order from him or his successors except for unavoidable necessity, when it would be otherwise impossible for her to recover her strength. This she obtained—though she knew that by decree of our holy Father Benedict food of this kind was permitted for the sick that they might recover their strength.[56]

The Lord of virtues and the King of glory was delighted in the beauty of his beloved (cf. Cant. 1:14), adorned as she was with such great virtues, *though these were hidden within* (Cant. 4:3). But of these *he was the judge* (Prov. 24:12) and eye-witness. He did not disdain to indicate by clear signs whatever had been concealed from our awareness till now, or if known to us had been overlooked, so that *her sweet voice* came into *the ears* of piety itself (Cant. 2:14). While there are many examples from our knowledge, and indeed from our experience, that might be to the point, a few will be enough to help us build up the faith of our readers.

So then, after our loving father Adilhun had passed on heavenwards, the

---

[55] Adilhun assumed office in 1113 according to III, 3, and died 17 Jun 1128; see *AD* 1113, 1128.

[56] *RB* 36, 9.

brothers agreed to defer the election of another in his place till lord
Adalbert the Archbishop should be present, who had then been absent for
some time.[57] She was consumed with great anxiety over this, and gave no
rest to her spirit as she offered supplication day and night concerning the
government of this place. Because her unremitting prayers were
resounding in the ears of the King of all, by a divine revelation she came
to know the venerable fathers who were to have charge of this place:
Fulcard and Cuno. We saw this fulfilled while she was still alive,[58] a third
also having been shown to her, not actually by name, but through certain
distinguishing features.[59]

Again, one of the faithful was very hard pressed as he struggled with a
temptation *of the flesh* against the spirit (cf. 2 Cor. 12:7). He thought that
it would be a help to lay his distress before this handmaid of Christ,
trusting that he would gain relief, if only he uncovered to her his wound.
And his hope did not prove false. For when she learned of his suffering,
she who *in her inmost being was filled with compassion* (Phil. 2:1) *put on
the breastplate of faith* (1 Thess. 5:8) and obtained reinforcement from
the King of Kings to help the sufferer. Thereupon he felt within himself
the access of heavenly support and his *goadings* (cf. 2 Cor. 12:7) abated,
and this was through the advocacy of Christ's handmaid.

There was the occasion she found out that a certain brother had voiced
certain things very inimical to his salvation. She is said to have been

---

[57] Adilhun died on 17 June 1128 (see *AD*). It seems that Adalbert was absent in Thuringia.
See Ludwig Speer, *Kaiser Lothar III und Erzbischof Adalbert I von Mainz. Eine
Untersuchung zur Geschichte des Deutsches Reiches im Frühen zwölften Jahrhundert*,
Dissertationen zur Mittelalterlichen Geschichte, 3 (Cologne, Vienna: Böhlau, 1983), p. 91:
'Adalbert hatte während des Jahres die Besitzungen des Erzstifts in Hessen, Thüringen
und auf den Eichsfeld bereit. Dabei hat er am 28 Mai in Fritzlar das Reichskloster
Hilwartshause in seinem Schutz genommen.'

[58] Did the author see Cuno become Abbot while Jutta was still alive? According to *AD*
1136, Abbot Fulcard died on 9 November, Cuno succeeded him and was 'ordained' (*sic*)
on 27 December, five days after Jutta's death.

[59] *quod et ipsa vivente scimus completum, designato ei, et tertio non quidem nominetenus,
sed quibusdam rebus accidentibus*; *tertio* is translated as ablative with *designato*, and the
editor's comma after *ei* is set aside. This obscure passage seems to suggest that though
Cuno was Abbot for many years after Jutta's death (till 1155), Jutta had foreknowledge as
to who would be the abbot after him. Cuno's successor was Abbot Helenger (1155–1178).

stirred by a zeal for God and to have pronounced this imprecation: 'Let the tongue which was not afraid to utter such things, fall dumb now, that in the future he may be freed from eternal punishment.' These words had not been long uttered when the signs followed in their wake. For the same brother, as everyone knows, was struck by the divine rod and suddenly rendered lifeless,[60] so that he was thought by many to be dead. After a little while he came back to himself and recovered, but for three days he was without the use of his tongue. She, however, was quite alarmed that her prayer had been heard, and poured herself out again in prayer, till the suspended use of his tongue was restored to him.

Consequently, she readily obtained whatever she wanted in the sight of Almighty God, for when she was engaged in the prayers her face was unaltered in any way; in the dignity of her conduct, she was constant towards all, ever joyful, never frivolous.

We believe that these few things should suffice to build up the faith of our elders, because one who is not satisfied with a few things, will not profit by many. For our part, we know that the apostolic saying was fulfilled in her which says: *whoever cleaves to the Lord is* made *one spirit with him* (1 Cor. 6:17), since we also know, and have learned by experience that she came to know many things from divine revelation, for it is agreed that she learned them neither through nor from any human source.

VII

WHEN TWENTY-FOUR YEARS HAD passed, during which she showed herself irreproachable in the entire integrity of her conduct, and worthy of praise for her dignity and modesty, being one who daily immolated herself as *a sacrifice to God with a humbled and contrite heart* (cf. Ps. 50:19), she began to look out for the day when she would be called, *keeping* her *loins girded* through the curbing of vices, and *carrying her lamp* alight (Lk. 35:35) through the steadfast performance of good works. Although she knew beforehand the number of years fixed for her, nevertheless she kept in mind at all times the warning of the Lord: *Keep watch, for you know neither the day nor the hour* (Mat. 25:13).

---

[60] *examinis;* presumably an editorial or typographical error for *exanimis.*

We have decided to spend some time here telling how the number of years the said handmaid of Christ was to fight the good fight in this holy purpose, and how she was to happily finish her course, was all divinely revealed long beforehand.

There was a certain old woman called Trutwib who was spending the many years of her widowhood like the *prophetess Anna* in the Gospel, haunting the threshold of the church, and serving the Lord *day and night* with vigils, *fasts* and prayers (Lk. 2:36–37). This woman had devoutly attended nocturns and lauds on the Kalends of November when the holy festival of All Saints is celebrated. At about sunrise she was going to take a little rest and was returning to the guests' quarters, where the lady Jutta was also staying with her young women on the very day she was to be enclosed.[61] Suddenly, as she approached the door of the courtyard a most beautiful form of a human being[62] divinely appeared to her, at which she took great fright. She turned round and was making a hasty retreat when she heard the apparition proclaim: 'You must know that the lady Jutta, who today is to be enclosed in this place, shall happily spend twenty-four years here, and in the twenty-fifth year pass happily from this world. That you may give all credence to my words, you must know that in a short while from today you yourself are to die.' When this was finished, this most beautiful form of a human being vanished.

The venerable old woman was, of course, utterly terrified by this vision. But she was as anxious about the passing of the lady Jutta as for her own death, and though for a while she was very hesitant, after some days she made known to the lady Jutta what she had seen and heard. Then she herself, as had been foretold to her, was overtaken by death and so paid the debt of the flesh.

When the lady Jutta learnt of her passing, her death authenticated for her the above revelation, and she gave it all credence. From then on, the more she knew the time for her to die was growing shorter, the more resolutely she forced her weakening limbs to the spiritual service of God. So, in case he should find her asleep, she stood ready at every hour keeping watch for the coming of her Spouse. She *carried oil in her vessel*

---

[61] 1 November 1112. Jutta, Hildegard and the second Jutta (Ep. 38, VII) are staying in the guest house prior to their solemn enclosure in the anchorhold later that day. I thank Barbara Newman for sorting out for me the time frames of this episode.

[62] *Quaedam pulcherrima species hominis.* This typical 'Hildegardian' phrase is strongly supportive of Volmar's authorship.

for her lamp (Mat. 25:1–4), *while her left hand did not know what her right hand was doing* (Mat. 6:3).

VIII

IN THE LAST YEAR of the number already foretold, she was aware that the Lord had decreed to set an end to her great labours, and that she was going to receive for them her everlasting reward. She began to be completely deprived of bodily strength, and cried out like the Prophet, from the depths of her heart: *My soul is longing and fainting for the courts of the Lord* (Ps. 83:3), and *when shall I come and appear before his face?* (Ps. 43:3) Well prepared by vigils and fasts and innumerable labours, she longed *to be dissolved and to be with Christ* (Phil. 1:23), *through whom the world had* already long *been crucified to her and she to the world* (cf. Gal. 6:13).

A month had passed of her twenty-fifth year and she was laid low by illness; the strength of her body was quite exhausted. Then suddenly, in the dawn light of the second of December, while she was lying neither fully asleep nor quite awake, she saw a man standing by her, tall of stature and beautiful in appearance. On seeing him, she fortified herself with the sign of the holy Cross, and then heard him say these things to her: 'Do not be afraid, for I am Oswald,[63] once king of the English people, and I have now come to you, that I might let you know the day of your departure, which you have obtained today from the Lord by your daily prayers. For this infirmity which now lays you low, shall furnish you with the end of your mortal life.' Encouraging her with these and other words, he revealed to her the day fixed for her departure, and then disappeared; and of his words there was a confirmation and proof.

After she had been burning in an acute attack of fever for twenty days, she comforted her disciples, ten of them in number, with her soothing

---

[63] St Oswald was specially venerated at Cluny, Hirsau and also at Disibodenberg. The first entry of the Disibodenberg Martyrology for 5 September records: 'among the English, Saint Oswald, king, whose acts the venerable Bede the priest commemorates in his history of that people', Bern Burgerbibliothek MS 226, fol. 25ᵛ. The cult of St Oswald among German-speaking peoples is testified to this day by churches dedicated to him as, for example, in the towns of Alpbach and Seefeld in the Tyrol, an area evangelized by Northumbrian monks in the eighth and ninth centuries.

counsels. Since she knew that *the time of her call* (cf. 2 Tim. 4:6) was drawing near, she asked for Viaticum[64] and received it, which she had been accustomed to do almost every day she was lying ill. When she sensed that the hour was almost at hand for her to be led forth from the body, she asked them to read to her the Passion of the Lord. When this was finished she counselled all who were present to give themselves to the prayers and the psalmody, *praying*, like her, *unceasingly* (1 Thess. 8:17).

In the silent hours of that very night, she surprised everyone there by asking that the holy veil be brought to her quickly. Having placed it on her head, she asked that she be placed on a hair-mat strewn with ashes,[65] earnestly appealing to the bystanders then, as she had before, that they not hinder her by their weeping from moving towards her Creator. Thus placed on the hair-mat in a place convenient for the arrival of the brothers[66] she entreated by a sign that the brothers be called. When they had prayed the litanies over her, she then fortified herself with the sign of the holy Cross, and gave up her holy soul.

In the year of the Lord one thousand one hundred and thirty-six, on the eleventh day before the Kalends of January [22 December],[67] in the first

---

[64] Holy Communion administered to the dying as provisions 'for the journey': *via*.

[65] *Supercilicium stratum cinere se imponi postulavit*. Following a suggestion of Sabina Flanagnan, I depart from Staab's text and read *supercilicium* as two words: *super cilicium*, given that in medieval manuscripts it can be sometimes difficult to separate words, and Staab's own testimony (p. 173) that the second half of the C 1 manuscript was made in a hurry and is particularly difficult to read. Indeed Staab adopts this reading in his later German translation ('Aus Kindheit', p. 77). For corroborating evidence see *VH* II, 9, where Hildegard is placed *super cilicium* as if for impending death. There is a description of this traditional way of monastic death in *The Monastic Constitutions of Lanfranc*, ed. and trans. by David Knowles, Mediaeval Classics (London: Thomas Nelson and Sons, 1951), pp. 122–24. Guibert of Nogent also says: *Quo facto hominem, ut monastici moris est, cilicio suppositum, ut videbatur in extremis … reliquimus*—'Once this was done, we left the man lying on a hair-mat, as is the monastic way, since he seemed to be very near death.' See Guibert of Nogent, *Autobiographie*, ed. and trans. by Edmond-René Labarde (Paris: Les Belles Lettres, 1981), Book 1, Ch. 21.

[66] *Supercilicium ergo loco competenti ad fratrum occursum collocatum (est), fratres convocari facto signo praecabatur*. Again, I read two words *super cilicium*, and prefer the *collocata*, as referring to Jutta, of the second manuscript C 2.

[67] 22 December 1136. The same date is given in *AD*. Jutta's name does not appear in the surviving fragments of the Rupertsberg Martyrology. See Staab, *VJ*, p. 184, n. 165 for a number of other late medieval documents in which Jutta is mentioned, but with her details

of the night vigils, she passed out of this world in her forty-fifth year, to be *crowned* (2 Tim. 2:24) with the *reward* (1 Cor. 9:24) of an everlasting kingdom for having *fought the fight well, and run the race* happily *to the end* (2 Tim. 4:7).

After her passing, three of her disciples, that is, Hildegard and two others sharing her name,[68] who were more advanced in a holy way of life and more privy to her secrets than the others, inasmuch as she herself could not keep them hidden from them, were mindful of her instruction with which she had appealed to them for many days beforehand, that after her death her body was not to be openly uncovered for washing.

So, putting out the others, they gave themselves in privacy to the task of arranging the limbs of her holy body. They declared that they were struck back by the light of the brightness of her dead body. They marvelled at the lustre of snowy whiteness which shone from her, to which we too can testify, for through the Lord's compassion we were deemed worthy to take part in her passing and funeral. These disciples of hers, watering the body of their mother and *magistra* with heartfelt tears, carefully examined it. Among innumerable other marks of her passion they discovered that a chain which she had worn on her flesh had made three furrows right around her body. Thus it became clear in her dead flesh what her soul had wrought while living in the flesh, now that her heavenly spouse was inviting it to *come from Lebanon to be crowned* (Cant. 4:8) in his heavenly kingdom.

While the brothers were keeping the due watches for her funeral rites, some of them of praiseworthy life sensed themselves pervaded by a most sweet perfume of fragrances. We need have no doubt that the King of sweetness and glory came to meet her yonder, for it was he who promised that he would come *to the mountain of myrrh and to the hill of incense*[69] (Cant. 4:6). With unmistakable signs such as these he condescended to

---

sometimes confused. The most accurate record, both as to her death day, and her being an anchoress, is to be found in the Necrology of Echternach, the monastery of Theodoric, *endredactor* of the *VH*. Jutta has continued to be venerated as *blessed* in the Bingen district up to this day. Her cult, Staab says, would require a separate study.

[68] I.e. Jutta; see Ep. 38, VII, for a niece of Jutta's also called Jutta who was the third of the original trio.

[69] Hildegard uses this verse in her Letter 5 to Pope Eugene, Van Acker, p. 12, Baird and Ehrman, p. 36.

show his approval of his beloved, who had pleased him through the mortification of her vices and the humility of her holy prayers.

How many of the faithful came together from different classes and professions, sexes, and ages! Her holy body was committed for burial rites to the venerable Father the lord Cuno who poured out an unstinting rain of tears over it, as did many others, racked by the overwhelming ardour of their affection.

We also think we should not fail to mention how she, mindful in all things that *whoever humbles himself shall be exalted* (Mat. 23:12), adjured the above-mentioned father in her last hours, that when she was dead she should not be buried in any holy place, but rather in a place where she might be daily trodden upon by passers-by.[70]

IX

WHEN ALL THESE THINGS had been reverently and fittingly completed, a certain faithful disciple[71] of the lady Jutta herself, one who had been on the most intimate terms with her while she still lived in the flesh, devoutly desired to know what kind of passage from this life her holy soul had made,[72] whose reputation among human beings was so glorious. And she was not disappointed of her desire. She was gladdened by the mercy of him who *does not despise* (Ps. 21:25) the prayers of his humble ones, for by means of a divine revelation she learned most surely and in a beautiful way that after the soul of lady Jutta had departed the body it was taken in charge by angels. They led her through the place of punishments,

---

[70] In Ep. 38, VIIII Guibert reports the brothers' testimony, that she was originally buried in the floor of the monks' chapter house, but, after certain preternatural incidents, was exhumed and then buried before the altar in the chapel of our Lady Queen of Heaven. Staab suggests (*VJ*, n. 167), without reference to Ep. 38, the entrance way of the monastery church.

[71] This is Hildegard, of which we are given indications throughout the passage.

[72] In after years Hildegard became renowned for being able to foresee the death and the merits of those still alive, and tell the fate of the souls of the dead. See *VH* II, 4. This concern with the retributive character of eternal destiny is central to her *Book of Life's Merits*. Dronke, *Women Writers*, pp. 191–92 looks at some contradictory statements in Hildegard's letters on this subject. See also Klaes, pp. 133–34* and Newman, 'Hildegard of Bingen and the '"Birth of Purgatory"'. Newman speaks of her as a potential 'Doctrix Purgatorii'!

where she saw huge balls of fire, and much *weeping and grinding of teeth* besides (Mat. 25:30). When she saw these things she realized what punishments one would have to be sifted by who did not pass out of this life free. But this happy soul, though much terrified by them, had obtained from God by her continual prayers and labours in this world that she should not be tried by these punishments.

Passing on from there, they approached the entrance of rest, that is, of the blessed dwelling of paradise. Suddenly, the enemy of the human race, not yet willing to give up, appeared *like a roaring lion* (1 Pet. 5:8) with a crowd of his minions, and tried to block her way. Those who were leading this holy soul opposed his many false accusations with the divine mandate, as if to satisfy the accuser, however false his case.

Since she was not to receive anything mean for her eternal dwelling, this happy soul was placed by the judgment of Almighty God between the spirits of the good and the spirits of evil, so that in this way the devil might see for himself whether he could find anything of his own in her.

Casting against her the *failures and the follies* and the *sins of her youth*[73] (Ps. 24:7), he tried to snatch her for his own through his malicious trickery and accusation, at which this fortunate soul took fright and alarm. Then suddenly John the Evangelist, the beloved of Christ Jesus was at her side. By his advocacy this blessed Evangelist commended all her acts from her earliest years, and especially her death. Then, together with his brother James[74] and in the company of many other blessed spirits, he bore her out of the midst of this strife, confounding and routing the crowds of demons who had contrived these provocations against her, and with a majestic dance[75] led her away with them into the rest of the citizens above.

---

[73] Cf. Sulpicius Severus, *Vita S. Martini*, 22, 4, ed. by Jacques Fontaine, Sources Chrétiennes, 133 (Paris: Cerf, 1967), 'Martin kept on replying to the devil who strove against him: "former failings are purged by a better way of life, and through the mercy of the Lord, those who have ceased to sin are to be absolved of sins".'

[74] St James was the patron saint of Disibodenberg's mother-house in Mainz.

[75] *Cum magno tripudio*. In ancient Rome the 'Tripudium' was a sacred dance or rhythmic stamping in honour of the god Mars, perhaps, as its name suggests, in a stately three-four time, like the hexameter of the epics. The dance was abolished in Christian Rome, though something of its energies was re-deployed into the great processions and marching hymns of the civic liturgy. By the Middle Ages the word *tripudium* accommodated a more general sense of joy and exultation.

Now the virgin to whom these things were shown was the lady Jutta's first and most intimate disciple, who, growing strong in her holy way of life even to the pinnacle of all the virtues, had certainly obtained this vision before God through her most pure and devout prayer. That she might be quite reassured about these things, and every scruple be completely removed from her, she was shown still other things of which she had previously been entirely ignorant, in order that what had been revealed to her might be confirmed. Though indeed the things spoken to her in the vision proved by careful examination to be completely consistent in every way, we dispense with including them here. She was divinely commanded to commit the aforesaid vision carefully to memory so that she and those hearing these things might take greater care in preparing for their own departure from this life.

Consequently, none of the faithful ought to be alarmed that the soul of this chosen one of Christ saw the place of punishment in her passage, or that the devil tried to block her way from the place of rest, for notwithstanding, she passed through all these things unscathed. Such in the sayings of Gregory,[76] was the case of Paschasius, a deacon of the Apostolic See. When a demoniac touched his dalmatic which had been placed over his bier, he was immediately saved. Nevertheless he himself sustained punishment, though very slight.[77] Again, the ancient enemy did not hold back from Saint Martin at his passing, but was conquered and vanished.[78] Just so, he departed confounded by the holy soul of whom we speak. She was even received at the moment of her departure by a multitude of the elect, although God reserved his beloved, John the Evangelist, with the above mentioned saints till the last, so that, though

---

[76] *Dialogi* of St Gregory the Great, Bk 4, Ch. 40. Book IV of the Dialogues is taken up with the fate of the souls of the dead, a special concern of the Cluniac-Hirsau monasteries, and of Hildegard herself, both in this vision and later on in her life.

[77] The force of this example is that though Paschasius was so holy that a demoniac was instantly cured in the manner described, yet even Paschasius's progress to glory after death underwent a momentary 'fluctuation'. The fault for which Paschasius had some penance to do was that after an ambiguous papal election, he had supported the one who proved to be the anti-Pope. While this would be a welcome cautionary tale in an era of Church reform which from time to time had to deal with imperially promoted anti-popes, it would hardly be applicable in Jutta's case.

[78] Cf. Sulpicius Severus, *Vita S. Martini*, 24, 8, ed. by J. Fontaine, 'at this cry he immediately vanished like smoke and filled the cell with so great a stench that he left an unmistakable indication that it had been the devil.'

his chosen one was shaken by the enemy in the final struggle at the entrance of rest, the ancient enemy would flee at their approach, as was indeed the case.

X

AS WE ARE ABOUT to bring this work to an end, we call God to witness that it was not from daring presumption that we, despite our limited abilities, sweated over this task, for we were ordered to it, for the purpose of encouragement, by the lord Cuno our Abbot, who was himself privy to the secrets of the blessed Jutta, since he was after all her beloved father, and in Christ her very dear son. We call to witness that we have inscribed in this work only what we ourselves have seen, or what we have heard from those who were formed under her teaching.[79]

Besides, we have reported only a few things concerning her holy way of life, though indeed there were many things we could have reliably reported about her, for she showed such great virtue and constancy while dwelling in this mortal life, that even if she been taken unexpectedly by an attacker, she would have offered her neck for Christ. But if she finished her life in peace, she did not miss out altogether on the palm of martyrdom, for indeed the *sword of the spirit* (Eph. 6:17) *pierced her own soul* (Lk. 2:35), since for Christ she subjected her body to many and great afflictions and sufferings while living here.

So let us for our part pluck up our courage and speak confidently in the spirit of humility. Let us implore her aid as her suppliants, that through the advocacy of her merits we too may succeed in reaching beyond, to that blessed abode where, we are confident, she now rejoices.

Under the glorious Emperor Lothar above-mentioned, and Abbot Cuno our most loving Father, after many struggles and distresses, this beloved one of Christ passed from the work-house of this world to everlasting joy, just as it was foretold, on the eleventh day before the Kalends of January [22 December], in the twenty-fifth year of her enclosure, and the forty-fifth year of her age. May we deserve to see her there, united in Christ, through his help, who with God the Father and the Holy Spirit lives and reigns as God, for ever and ever. Amen.

---

[79] *ab his, quae sub magisterio eius educatae sunt audivimus.*

A LETTER OF VOLMAR

The following is a translation of the one known letter of Volmar surviving among Hildegard's correspondence. It is taken from the edition in *Hildegardis Bingensis Epistolarium, pars secunda XCI–CCLr*, edited by L. van Acker, CCCM, vol. 91A (Turnhout: Brepols, 1993), pp. 443–45. The letter is found in two manuscripts, R,[1] the Riesenkodex, from Rupertsberg in the 1180s, and Wr,[2] a mid-thirteenth-century manuscript, containing, among the selection of Hildegard's works, a copy of Gebeno's *Pentachronon.*

Here then, is the author of the *VJ*, some twenty-five years or more further on, near the end of his own life. Volmar, writing from Rupertsberg, writes to Hildegard in her absence, probably sometime in the year 1170. Hildegard has been severely ill, and yet has been spurred on to her last preaching journey, in Swabia (*VH* III, 23). He is finding her absence hard to endure, which he tries to remedy by proposing to himself how much worse it will be if she dies. Nevertheless, he was to die in 1173, some six years before she did.

The letter is constructed in a formal epistolary style, with long, at times, tangled periods. Indeed at one point he seems to almost apologize to Hildegard for his indulgence in high rhetoric—about the futile labours of the rhetoricians at that. Comparison of Volmar's own style in the *VJ* and in this letter, with the very different style of Hildegard's autobiographical passages, argues for the disciplined minimalism of Volmar's editorial work and the authenticity of what has been transmitted under Hildegard's name. It also reveals the high standard of Latin Hildegard could take in her stride unaided, late in life.

Even in this one letter, we can identify features of the style we know

---

[1] Wiesbaden, Nassauische Landesbibliothek MS 2, described in Van Acker, vol. 91, pp. XXVII–XXIX.

[2] Vienna, Österreichische Nationalbibliothek MS 963, described in Van Acker, vol. 91, pp. XXV–XXVII.

from the *VJ*. Here are such typical items of vocabulary as *insudo* (to sweat/labour), *modernus* (modern), *adminiculo* (with the help/assistance), *obnixe* (resolutely), and above all, *experimento* (by experience). Here is the characteristic uncertainty about reflexives, and the use of an ablative absolute gerund as kind of present participle.

But above all it is the character and religious culture of the author that we are interested in, and it proves to be entirely consonant with that of the author of the *VJ*. Volmar, however, seems far less positive about the benefits of secular 'liberal studies' than was the Chronicler in his 1094 report about Anselm. Indeed, he satirizes the prevailing trends in contemporary scholasticism, as an outright corruption of the use of reason, knowledge and ecclesiastical study.

Date: Rupertsberg, c. 1170.

TO THE REVEREND LADY Hildegard, sweetest mother, most holy, most truthful and most praiseworthy *magistra* and co-worker of God,[3] Volmar[4] her son, however unworthy, and the entire united flock of her young women,[5] together with others cleaving to her and to God and to Saint Rupert, however lukewarmly, who serve in due subjection, in due obedience and with the affection of daughters, who rightly delight so *to be consoled by the breasts of her consolation* (cf. Is. 66:1) in this present world because they are being made into *participants of the heavenly fatherland after the sojourn of this exile* (Heb. 3:1).

Even if, O sweetest mother, we should see you daily with our eyes of flesh, hear you daily with our ears of flesh, and, as is just, daily cleave devotedly to you, understanding that the Holy Spirit speaks to us through you, we still do not doubt that your absence, which we cannot mention without tears, shall one day really weigh upon us when, as it pleases God, we *shall not see you henceforth* (cf. Mat. 23:39) *with the eyes of the flesh* (cf. Job 10:4). For *there is no man who shall live, who does not see death*

---

[3] *Hildegardi, Domine reverende, matri dulcissime, magistre sanctissime et symmiste Dei in cenobio beati Ruperti veracissime et probatissime.*

[4] Simply 'V' in the codices. The heading of the letter in R is 'Volmar, provost, to his beloved, the mother of St Rupert's'.

[5] *puellarum ipsius.* There is a variation, if not confusion of possessive forms here: *eius ... ipsius ... sibi.* I translate according to sense.

(Ps. 88:49).

For then our lamentation and wretchedness shall be greater than our present gladness. Where then shall be the answer to all the cases of those who petition you? Where then a fresh interpretation of the Scriptures? Where then the voice of a melody and a language not heard before? Where then the fresh sermons on the festivals of the saints not heard before? Where then the unveiling of what concerns the souls of the dead? Where then the revelation of things past, present, and future? Where then the explanation of the natures of diverse created things, which, by the gift of divine grace, with the sweetest and humblest ways and the motherly affection of your overflowing compassion towards all, we have known in you?

O how great a divine condescension there is in his gifts! O the foolish preoccupations of men! O *vanity of vanities!* (Eccle 1:2, 12:8) Why do so many go, despite the difficulties of the roads, to distant parts of the world vainly examining the teachings on different matters? Why do they afflict themselves with thirst, hunger, and cold as they sweat through the watches of the night over the profundity, or rather the riddles of learned opinions, and this for the litigious declamations of their disputations? Surely, surely, we know that they endure all these things not with the intention of *a simple eye* (cf. Mat. 6:22), but for the sake of corrupt simony?[6] Therefore, they make no progress, they comprehend very little or even less of what is to the purpose. Instead, they waste no time in extinguishing the spark of the Spirit of God in themselves by that arrogance through which they seem to themselves to be something.

The result is, that to the shame of modern scholastics who misuse the knowledge given them from above, the Spirit of prophecy and vision is now revived in the mouthpiece of a fragile vessel without the help of outward instrumentality, and utters things so great that they cannot grasp them by any reason, since the Spirit teaches what he wills and *blows where he wills* (Jn 3:8). Wherefore, that word seems to be most manifestly fulfilled which says that *God has chosen the foolish and weak*

---

[6] I.e. they engage in church-sponsored disciplines, perhaps even being ordained priests, not from a genuine spirit, but basically for pecuniary advantage: career advancement, worldly reputation and influence, etc.

things of the world in order to confound the wise and the strong (cf. 1 Cor. 1:27).

We set forth such considerations, not that we, most beloved mother, are moved by the torch of envy on account of so great a gift conferred on your simplicity because of the zeal of your discipline, and set it at lower value, or that we, who are specially yours, and who constantly stay with you and attentively listen to your voice, seek to be glorified with a foolish glory. No, it is rather to demonstrate that the application of their labour avails to achieve very little in searching out the sublimity of true doctrine by comparison with the purity of goodness and piety, for the teacher[7] moves his lips in vain outside, if the Spirit who instructs the hearts of his hearers, is not within. More marks of the virtues, more works of the marvels of God and the Holy Spirit appear in you than we could say or would want to say. Let it be for others to praise and proclaim you, but for us rather to wonder at you, reverence you, and love you.[8]

Since you know all these things by experience of the actual case better than we do, and since few things are sufficient in order to understand many, we omit saying anything more to one who is wise, but rather give thanks to God who can do all things, who gave you to us, and who illumined you with his own Spirit for the glory of his name and the salvation of many. We humbly and resolutely beseech him to bestow on you health of body and strength of mind, so that he may abundantly distribute his gift which he has poured out in you for the building up of the whole Church.

---

[7] *doctor.*

[8] *nostrum autem te mirari, venerari et diligere.*

GUIBERT'S LETTER TO BOVO

INTRODUCTION

Manuscripts and critical edition

The Letter to Bovo is here translated from the critical edition of the Latin text in *Guiberti Gemblacensis Epistolae*, edited by Albert Derolez, CCCM, 66A (Turnhout: Brepols, 1989), Epistola XXXVIII (Letter 38), pp. 366–79.

Guibert's Letter 38 survives in two manuscripts of the Bibliothèque Royale in Brussels, MS 5387-96 (G) from the late twelfth or early thirteenth century and MS 5527-34 (B) from the early thirteenth century.[1] Due to the loss of a quire, B stops at line 333, the end of section XI. Both manuscripts show the same lacunae at the beginning of the account of Hildegard's life.

Here, many references to Scripture and the Rule of St Benedict have been added, in addition to those indicated by Derolez, and also a possible reference to Ovid.

Guibert of Gembloux, 1124/5–1213

Guibert (or Wibert) was born in Brabant and attended the monastery school at Gembloux, where he achieved a very high standard of Latin literacy. There he became a monk and priest.

He lived at Rupertsberg from 1177 to 1180, remaining there for a year after Hildegard's death, when he finally complied with a recall to Gembloux. But, being greatly devoted to St Martin of Tours he first went to the monastery of Marmoutiers and stayed there for eight months before returning to Gembloux. After the great fire at Gembloux in 1185 he again

---

[1] In her critical edition of the *VH*, Klaes refers to these manuscripts as G^1 and G^2 respectively.

returned to Marmoutiers. In 1188 he was called to be Abbot of Florennes from which position he was elected Abbot of his own monastery at Gembloux in 1194. He remained in this office for ten years, resigning in 1204. He retired to Florennes where he died about the year 1213.

Klaes remarks in Guibert's character a disconcerting blend of a strong sense of his own importance on the one hand, and an inclination to excessive self-recrimination and public avowal of his faults on the other.[2] She says that he tends to 'over-stylize' both himself, others, and his environment. Though Klaes's task is that of the historical/literary critic, in assessing Guibert's character and method she may risk a certain stylizing tendency herself, through an excessively reductionist approach to her material. Her over-reflexive discourse abounds with terms like 'construct', 'formula', 'topos', and 'later emendation'. Guibert's text is treated as a tissue of these devices which it is the task of the critic to exhaustively decode, whether the matter at hand concerns a passing self-disclosure of Guibert,[3] or the character of 'holiness' itself.[4]

The letters of Guibert

Guibert's letters are a quarry of historical and biographical information about Hildegard and her network of supporters and friends. Letter 26 to Radulf of Villers, written from Rupertsberg, has the most to tell about her, after Letter 38. Here he tells how he came to know Hildegard and

---

[2] A marginal note to the *Notae Gemblacenses*, MGH SS 14, p. 598 says 'By way of acknowledging the mercy of him whose mercy fills the whole world, he [Guibert] did not blush to reveal his own miseries, as humbly and clearly as he could, that is, his failures in thought, word and, deed. This he did not only in the secret place of his own conscience before the loving and eternal high priest Jesus Christ, but also outwardly to persons of rank such as cardinals, bishops, abbots and priests. Moreover through the example of that strong woman who entered in among those at banquet and did not [hesitate?] to publicly confess that she was a sinner ...' Here the text becomes mutilated (Klaes, p. 26*, n. 11).

[3] E.g. p. 29*, Klaes typically dismisses his comment to Philip in Letter 15 about worsening the more important and better work of his predecessor as an 'obligatory humility formula'. Klaes's Guibert seems a remarkably insincere man, insufferable really, and one wonders what Hildegard ever saw in him.

[4] E.g. pp. 43–44*, Klaes assumes that Guibert depicts Jutta with the traits of holiness due to a pre-conceived idea that the teacher of a saint *must* have lived a saintly life. Klaes did not have the benefit of access to the *VJ*.

stay at her monastery, and also of the friendship between her and Archbishop Philip von Heinsberg of Cologne.[5] It is from his correspondence we learn the name of Hildegard's collaborator, Volmar.[6]

In Letter 38, here translated, there are details about Jutta not found in the *VJ*, such her looking about various monasteries before settling on Disibodenberg, the decision to open up the anchorhold and allow it to expand into a little school, and the events after her burial. Such details he could easily have had from his conversations with Hildegard herself, or from the oral tradition of the community where he was staying. He assures the reader that he personally interviewed the brothers at Disibodenberg for the events reported in Ep 38 VIIII, so he also drew on the oral traditions of the men's monastery.

He also furnishes us with details about Hildegard, not found in the *VH*, such as the information that she was the tenth child of her parents, that a suitable plan for their daughter only gradually revealed itself to them, Hildegard's election as *magistra* to succeed Jutta, and the formal reconstitution of Jutta's 'school' as a cenobitic monastery under Hildegard as prioress. He also gives a new visitor's rosy report of the nuns' way of life at Rupertsberg, a delightfully urbane character sketch of Hildegard in her maturity, and mentions the number of nuns at Rupertsberg near the end of her life.

Guibert also wrote letters to Rupertsberg after Hildegard's death, e.g.

---

[5] 'Likewise the Archbishop of Cologne, the lord Philip, a man of lofty dignity, holds himself bound to her with the greatest devotion and reverence, and constantly visits her. And he loves me not a little too, however unworthy of it I am.' Ep. 26, Derolez, p. 280.

[6] Cf. Ep. 19, Derolez, p. 238, line 82; Ep. 26, p. 278, line 289; and Abbot Godfrey's letter to him: Ep. 41, p. 388, line 28. In Letter 19, he writes to Hildegard of his visit to Villers: 'In the meantime, while I was staying there, Peter, a cleric from the monastery of Villers whom I knew, who had turned aside to your house while on the way back from Jerusalem, unexpectedly produced for us your letter. It consoled the above mentioned novices with its sweet address, but sadly added news of the bitterness of soul which afflicted you through sorrow over the death of lord Vulmar your provost.' In Letter 26, Guibert writes: 'Then, after a short passage of time, the lord Fulmar, a man of pious memory, attained the goal of his life with a good end. He had served her in the post of provost, and, receiving the series of her visions produced by her in a simple and unpolished style, had used his pen to improve them as he could. Deprived of her principal support after God, she took the advice of her friends and asked me through a letter if she might enjoy my consolation in his place.' Volmar's only surviving letter to Hildegard is signed with a single 'V', Ep. 195, Van Acker 2, p. 443.

Letter 36 to Hildegard's successor as prioress, Ida, and Letter 37, to Gertrud, a nun in Guibert's confidence.

During his last years at Florennes, Guibert collected and revised his own letters, which makes their historiographical value at times quite a complex matter. On pages 24–59* Klaes exhaustively analyses these letters with particular reference to the Hildegard *vita* material.

The setting and genesis of the Letter to Bovo

In 1160, after a turbulent recent history, the monastery of Gembloux gained a new abbot, John, who, despite the questionable circumstances of his election[7] continued in office for many years till eventually succeeded by Guibert himself. Guibert at the time seems to have been a monk of standing both within and outside his monastery, but under Abbot John his personal situation deteriorated rapidly. He came into serious conflict with developments—or devolutions as he saw them—in his own community, which he characterizes as 'irregularity'. In particular he came into conflict with his 'unworthy' abbot, whom he repeatedly accuses of simony.[8] At the same time he forged close links with the Cistercian monks of Villers nearby.

It was in such painful circumstances as these that in 1175 Guibert took the initiative of contacting Hildegard. The first exchange of letters between them has not survived.[9] What survives is a sub-collection of Guibert's Letters to Hildegard, numbered in Derolez's edition 16, 17, and 18, dated to 1175, and Letters 19, 20, 21 and 22, dated to 1176.[10] Hildegard's first surviving letter to him, called in the Riesenkodex *De modo visionis suae* and excerpted in *VH* I, 8, is Letter CIIIr in Van Acker 2, pp. 258–65. Letter 18 is his reply to it. He then made a first, short visit to Rupertsberg. In Letter 19 to Hildegard, he tells how he stopped at

---

[7] Cf. the biographical notes in Derolez, pp. vi–viii.

[8] On the relationship between Guibert and Abbot John of Gembloux, see Klaes's lengthy excursus on p. 36*, n. 49.

[9] Dronke edits what he calls 'the first letter to Guibert of Gembloux' in *Women Writers*, pp. 250–56. He uses two different versions of letters appearing in two manuscripts, one of them in G^2 and the other in R.

[10] See Ep. 16, Derolez, pp. 216–20; Ep. 17, pp. 221–24; Ep. 18, pp. 225–34; Ep. 19., pp. 235–42; Ep. 20, pp. 243–44; Ep. 21, pp. 245–47; Ep. 22, pp. 248–50.

Villers on the return journey. There his friends gave him a long list of theological questions which they wanted him to submit to her for them, which he appends to the letter. He also mentions the recent death of her assistant whom he calls Volmar.[11] Not long after, Guibert was invited to Rupertsberg to take the place of Godfrey of Disibodenberg as Hildegard's assistant. With the initial approval of his abbot he eagerly made his way to Rupertsberg in June of 1177.

Not long after Guibert arrived however, Abbot John changed his mind and wanted him back. But Guibert decided to stay. In Letter 32, he writes that he was supported in this decision by Bishop Radulf of Liège, in whose diocese Gembloux lay. Given Hildegard's turbulent relationship with her own abbot in the past,[12] it is not surprising he found in her a most supportive empathy. While at Rupertsberg he met Hildegard's friend, Archbishop Philip of Cologne, who also encouraged him to stay. They became lasting friends.

In Letter 26 he squarely places the blame for his estrangement on the situation at Gembloux, and in Letter 29 makes his return conditional on a thorough change in the community. In letter 28 he even brandishes a dire vision from Hildegard herself concerning the reasons for his staying away.[13] Meanwhile he received more than one pressing invitation to transfer to other monasteries, such as Amand-les-Eaux (Letter 26) and Villers, which he considered 'regular' or 'disciplined' monasteries. This

---

[11] It was actually Godfrey, Volmar's successor, who died in 1176. Volmar had died in 1173, but Guibert evidently substituted Volmar's name in the re-editing of his letters to give the impression that he was Volmar's immediate successor at Rupertsberg. In letter 41, from Godfrey abbot of St Eucharius, we obtain a more satisfactory sequence of events when the abbot speaks of the author of *VH* I: 'the provost Godfrey, who succeeded Fomar the first provost at that same place'.

[12] Cf. the surviving correspondence, Ep. 74, Van Acker, p. 160, and Ep. 74r, pp. 161–62, Baird and Ehrman, pp. 160–62; cf. specially the mordant Ep. 75, pp. 162–63, Baird and Ehrman, pp. 162–63. In *VH* II, 7 Hildegard mentions abbot Cuno's death, almost as if it were an incidental nuisance.

[13] 'If it were not so long, and did I not fear that they would be irritated and think it a fabrication, I would write to them a vision which my lady Hildegard has seen concerning their miseries and tribulations, a vision which is very dire and severe even to narrate, though it is not yet to be endured. Because of it I would be greatly terrified to have to return there.' (Ep. 29, Derolez, p. 325). Guibert did eventually return, and shortly afterwards, Gembloux was gutted by a great fire, in 1185. Guibert was quite traumatized by it and fills his letters 36 and 37 to *Magistra* Ida and to Gertrud with reports of it.

is what he seems to be alluding to at the end of Ep. 38, II.

Such was the setting in which Guibert wrote to Bovo, one of his fellow-monks and friends at Gembloux, soon after his arrival at Rupertsberg and two years before his Letter 28. Consequently, he composed the original letter to Bovo in the second half of the year 1177.

Guibert's unfinished Life of Hildegard

In Ep. 38 as it stands, section V to the end obviously consists of an unfinished *vita* of Hildegard. It was Herwegen who showed[14] that Guibert had grafted it onto his original Letter to Bovo. He carried out this 're-formatting' during his last years at Florennes, while arranging his writings. In his letter 40 to Godfrey, Abbot of St Eucharius, written about this time, he asks for the names of Hildegard's parents, since he says, he has written something on her. He was clearly referring to his unfinished *vita*, where these same lacunae remain.

Klaes argues that Guibert shows no hint of any intention to write a *vita* in his original letter to Bovo, and that Guibert's introductory remarks in section IIII are hardly more than an adventitious literary device to link originally disparate documents.

In Letter 15 to Archbishop Philip, Guibert devotes himself to the topic of drafting a Hildegard-*vita*, for the Archbishop had requested this of him while Hildegard was still alive. When he broached the task he found some biographical material already to hand, in particular a *Libellus*, or 'little book' whose style he describes as *humilis* and *simplex sermo*, which can be largely identified with the first book of Theodoric's *vita*, i.e. the work composed by Godfrey of Disibodenberg, Volmar's successor and Guibert's predecessor as Hildegard's assistant. To add to this *Libellus*, the nuns gave Guibert some miracle reports and an account of Hildegard's death. Most important of all, he obtained the autobiographical documents which had been entrusted to Volmar; he added to the collection her own letter to him: *On the mode of her vision*. He assembled all this source material for the *vita* project. He may also have had the Life of Jutta as a source document, which will be discussed below. Last but not least, he had living contact with the oral tradition of

---

[14] Ildephonse Herwegen, 'Les collaborateurs de Sainte Hildegarde', *Revue Bénédictine*, 21 (1904), pp. 396–401; cf. Klaes, pp. 36*-39*.

the sisters, and the benefit of his conversations with Hildegard herself.

During the months following Hildegard's death in September 1179, while Guibert was still at Rupertsberg, he commenced his writing of the *vita*, but suspended it when he had suddenly to depart sometime in 1180. The description of these circumstances in Letter 42 to Abbot Godfrey, line 131, supports the dating. Passing comments in the Ep. 38, e.g., the end of section XI, indicate his presence at Rupertsberg while writing.

The generous space allocated to the person of Jutta in this *vita*, and Guibert's expansiveness as his focus shifts towards Hildegard suggest that had he been able to pursue the project to the end it would have been a work of considerable length. Guibert says to Philip in Letter 15 that he had been forced to break off his own work in the middle due to an urgent recall to Gembloux, which he repeats in Letter 42 to Abbot Godfrey, adding that in his writing he had reached as far as Hildegard's move to Rupertsberg, but that due to the pressure of tasks subsequently assigned to him he had never been able to continue it. In that case, even what we have is not the full extent of his unfinished *vita*. The abrupt ending of manuscript B in mid-sentence and mid-page points to a very early loss of text, perhaps of a folio or a quire, because the loss seems to have been already evident in the source copy.

Did Guibert have access to the *VJ* or not? His portrayal in Ep. 38, VI of Jutta's vigorous, indeed fierce, resolve for celibacy, and especially his use of 'viriliter' is entirely of a piece with her portrayal in the *VJ*. Most noteworthy—indeed, almost a give-away—is the agreement between Ep. 38, VII and *VJ* III that Jutta was enclosed with just *two* others, not the *three* as mentioned in *AD* 1136, and much later, Trithemius. There is also agreement that Abbot Burchard presided at the actual ceremony of enclosure, not a bishop as might have been expected. Guibert concurs with the *VJ* and *AD* in giving Jutta's death at 24 years after her enclosure (Ep. 38, VIIII), though the implications for dating Hildegard's enclosure do not seem to have occurred to him, for he says she was enclosed in her eighth year (Ep. 38, VII). On the other hand, in view of my comments in the introduction to the *VJ* about Godfrey's possible use of the *VJ* in *VH* I and II, Guibert may have also been observing some kind of later 'canon' about Hildegard's early life, whose source was herself, so that he discreetly elides over discrepancies.

Guibert, however, had access to Jutta material other than that preserved in the *VJ*. There is a glaring inconsistency between *VJ* II, which says that

Jutta's father died when she was three years old, and Ep. 38, VI, where she persuades her father not to have any marriage contract drawn up for her; followed by other passing mentions of her father. Only Guibert tells of Jutta's attractive influence over young women and the opening up of her anchorhold to accommodate more disciples (VIII). Whereas at the end of *VJ* VIII there is only a brief and rather cryptic allusion to the place of Jutta's burial, the Ep. 38, VIIII lingers generously over the question. It almost seems as if Guibert took up the hint from the earlier document and set about researching the matter, for he assures us that he personally interviewed the brothers at Disibodenberg, and gives only sworn testimony of the events at Jutta's grave.

When, near the end of his life, Guibert received a copy of Theodoric's *VH* from Abbot Godfrey, his verdict was that it had been executed in better fashion than he could ever have done, though he went ahead and revised it anyway.[15] In one way we can quite agree with Guibert's assessment and not automatically assume he was resorting to another 'humility topos'. For Theodoric's bent was for including his source documents intact, whereas Guibert's approach, to judge from his treatment in XII of Hildegard's letter to himself, was to rework the source documents in his own cultivated style. That Theodoric's practice might have a particular value perhaps even Guibert might have had the intelligence and courtesy to concede.

Guibert's style and problems of translation

Guibert is a consummately skilled Latinist, a master rhetorician not loth to display his art. Translating his work into English has been a most exacting task.

Guibert's trademark is a very elaborate periodic style. He revels in it. He will weave a single sentence of paragraph length with subordinate and sub-subordinate clauses and phrases, holding the main verb at arm's length to the very end, while along the way acquitting himself perhaps of two concurrent story lines, or a story line and two or three parallel commentaries.

A good example may be found in section VII, where a single sentence

---

[15] See the introduction to *Guibert's Revision of the VH*.

leads from the fixed date of the induction, the gathering of the people, the liturgical ceremony with an excursus on its symbolism and quotations from scripture, the linking up of Jutta with Hildegard on whom there is an excursus, and a third member on whom there is a still longer excursus, all of which is finally sealed with a very emphatic main verb, 'she was interred'. It is an impressive example of form expressing meaning, provided one manages to steer successfully all the way to the end!

In the translation, lengthy sentences are occasionally divided into two for the sake of comprehensibility in English, such as the tightly packed passage in Ep. 38, V 'By the will ... days of her life' in which Guibert combines a running word-play on 'tenth' and 'tithe' with a narrative which moves from Hildegard's conception, with theological commentary, through to her oblation by her parents, all fortified with scriptural quotation. When dividing sentences it is sometimes necessary to bypass various colouring particles and the participial form of verbs serving an important hypotactic function. But I do so very reluctantly, only as a last resort.

There are frequent minor word-plays such as the staged triple object of the verb *colunt* ('cultivate') in Ep. 38, III, or minor rhymes like *pungerent quam ungeret* in XI, or there are major syntactical intricacies such as the amazing passage in Ep. 38, VIIII 'Because the atmosphere ... ineffable sweetness', which is all in fact one sentence, with a variety of sub-plots and sub-sub-plots. It seemed advisable to divide it into two. Even within this sentence, long pondering and consultation was needed in order to unravel the subtle verbal structure and insertion into the whole sentence of what is translated as '... Christ made known more clearly how greatly he valued both the holiness of the one buried, and the performance of the office which was being conducted ...'.

The structure of Guibert's letter

To provide some structure of reference the Letter to Bovo is here divided into sections as numbered and captioned below. The form of the document as finally edited by Guibert is respected, and no attempt is made to reconstitute the unfinished Life of Hildegard.

I   Salutation and circumstances of the writing of the letter.
II   How Guibert came to Hildegard's monastery.
III   Eyewitness account of the way of life at Rupertsberg.

GUIBERT'S LETTER TO BOVO

I

TO HIS VERY DEAR Bovo, brother Guibert, who has turned from the broad ways of the world which lead to death, to the path of a stricter way of life, by which, with God's help, he may be led to the courts of heaven.

Some of my friends have asked me if I might write back to them through this man[16] about the events which withdrew me from them, and about the character of the lady who together with the community over which she presides, invited me. But since it is you I embrace with special affection above my other friends who dwell with you, I address myself first of all to you. I then take the opportunity to address through you all who are kind enough to love me and be interested in how I am, in what my circumstances are, and what the virtue might be of the venerable mother Hildegard and the sisters who serve the Lord under her direction.

II

YOU WILL SURELY PERCEIVE that it is no wheel of fortune or fickleness that has driven me uselessly here and there, but rather that the loving kindness of Jesus Christ the Almighty One to whom I have entrusted myself with all my heart, has attended my pilgrimage with such great favour that I seem to have been transferred from the servitude of *bleary-eyed Leah*, with whom I have been worn out through heavy labour, to the delightful embraces of *comely Rachel* (cf. Gen. 29:17). When I look back and recognize how I have been guided from my previous way of life, where I dwelt far too long as in *a salty land deserted and arid* (cf. Jer. 17:8), *into a land flowing with milk and honey* (cf. Num. 16:13), I could leap for joy and sing: *The Lord has directed me, there is nothing I shall lack, he has*

---

[16] *per hominem istum*: perhaps a courier who brought the request, through whom a reply by 'return post' is expected.

set me down in a place of pasture. He has led me to refreshing water, he has revived my soul (Ps. 22:1–3), and the rest that follows up to the end of the same psalm.

Truly, *a people that has not known me obeys me* (Ps. 17:45), and rejoices at my presence. An undeserved honour has been paid to me; it has been heaped on my head and like a weighty burden weighs down upon me. The esteem entertained for me here is too much for my strength—it is a source of anxiety no less than embarrassment to my vulnerable conscience.

Summoned in a letter from the venerable lady and mother Hildegard, and as I believe, prospered by her prayers, at length I reached her. I have been graciously received here not only by her but also by all those under her. Now I dwell with her in the beauty of peace and of all delight and pleasantness. I am guided by her counsels, propped up by her prayers, brightened by her merits, sustained by her kindnesses and daily refreshed by conversation with her.

Insofar as she looks on external things, nothing would please her more to see than, for the time being, *that I stay* here *all the days of* her *life, and dwell in the house of the Lord* (Ps. 26:4) which she rules, and undertake the spiritual service of herself and her daughters and examine the books she has written. On this matter, when she is with me she uses what promises and prayers she can; on this matter she has approached me through others with many appeals. But on account of the greatness of her holiness, which I fear to offend, I have never completely accepted or refused, even though I would much rather abide in some disciplined monastery,[17] because I know there are some who rely on my counsel and are waiting on me for this purpose who would take it badly if I were to stay here.

III

THERE IS IN THIS place a marvellous contest in the virtues to be seen,

---

[17] *in aliquo regulari claustro commorari desiderem.* Guibert is in serious conflict with the 'irregularities' at Gembloux and has received invitations from other monasteries. In a pointed contrast with the life at Gembloux, Guibert goes on to describe the *regularis,* disciplined life at Rupertsberg in glowing terms; in view of his concerns over simony in his own monastery, he finds their economic independence in particular, *miraculum.*

where the mother embraces her daughters with such affection, and the daughters submit themselves to their mother with such reverence that it is hard to decide whether the mother surpasses the daughters in this eagerness or the daughters their mother.

With one accord these holy handmaids of God so cultivate God through lively devotion and themselves by self-command and one another with honour and obedience, that in them you can literally behold the delightful spectacle of the weaker sex triumphing with Christ's help over itself, the world, and the devil. For, mindful of the Lord's invitation: *Desist! and see that I am God* (Ps. 45:11) they refrain from work on holidays, and sit in composed silence in the cloister applying themselves to holy reading[18] and to learning the chant. On ordinary days they obey the Apostle who says *Whoever will not work shall not eat* (2 Thess. 3:10), and apply themselves in well-fitted workshops to the writing of books, the weaving of robes or other manual crafts.

So, by giving themselves to holy reading they acquire the light of divine knowledge and the grace of compunction, and by their engagement in exterior works they banish the idleness which is poison to the soul,[19] and curb the levity so apt to arise at idle gatherings from the multiplicity of words.

Besides this there is another marvel to consider here: that though this monastery was founded but recently—a short space of time ago, that is twenty seven years[20]—not by any of the emperors or bishops or the powerful or the rich of any region, but by a woman who was poor, a stranger, and sick; yet it has made such progress in its religious character[21] and in its resources that it is skilfully laid out, not with grand but with commodious and dignified buildings most suitable for a religious community, with running water distributed through all the workshops. Furthermore, not counting guests whom we are never without,[22] and the administrators of the house of which they have several, the monastery provides enough for the expenses of food and clothing of fifty sisters

---

[18] *sedentes lectioni.* This prayerful kind of 'reading' is the *lectio divina,* as prescribed in *RB* 48, 22.

[19] Cf. *RB* 48, 1.

[20] The year 1150. Guibert is writing, in this part of the letter, late in 1177.

[21] *in tantum religione et censu profecit*; for similar phrasing see *RB* Prologue 48.

[22] Cf. *RB* 53, 16.

without any shortfall.

The mother herself, the leader of so great a company[23] crushes the vice of inflation, so often born of prestigious position, with the profound gravity of humility. In her charity she pours herself out on all, giving the counsels required of her, solving the most difficult questions put to her, writing books, instructing her sisters, putting fresh heart into the sinners who approach her. She is wholly taken up with it all. Though she is weighed down both by age and infirmity, she is so mighty in the exercise of all the virtues that many are the things she could say with the Apostle such as: *I have become all things to all, that I might save all* (cf. 1 Cor. 1:22); and this: *I may be unskilled in speaking, but not in knowledge* (2 Cor. 2:6); and this also: *Gladly will I glory in my weaknesses, that the power of Christ may dwell with me; for when I am weak, then I am stronger and more powerful* (cf. 2 Cor. 12:9–10), and many sayings of this kind.

But at this point enough of these things.[24]

IIII

SINCE ON THE OCCASION of sending you news of my situation there was mention of the venerable mother in Christ Hildegard, and many have asked me often and insistently either to give an account in ordinary speech to those present, or to send something in writing to those absent[25]—in whatever style—concerning the origin, the way of life and the death of the lady who is today celebrated far and wide by so great a proclamation of her fame, I earnestly beg divine support for this task.

---

[23] *dux tanti agminis*: *agmen* has military connotations. It could be translated 'captain of such a column (of soldiers)'.

[24] This sentence marks the suture between the original *Letter to Bovo* and Guibert's *vita*, appended much later. It is clear that, from this point on in the account, Hildegard is no longer alive.

[25] *ut vel presentibus communi sermone narrarem, vel absentibus qualicumque stilo exarata transmitterem*. 'Those present' may mean the nuns of Rupertsberg, keen to have a *vita* of their foundress, with whom Guibert would use either a less formal Latin or a spoken vernacular, i.e. a form of medieval German. Guibert's vernacular, as a Walloon, would have been a form of language related to modern Dutch. His letters testify that he also spoke French. *Absentibus* may mean either Hildegard's network at large, or Guibert's monastic confreres at Gembloux and Villers.

I think it a matter of duty, and to the benefit of many, not to report everything concerning her, which would be impossible, but to report at least a few of the main points, and of these only those in which absolutely no injury to the truth would occur by my doing so. For the things I am going to say are as consistent with the confidence of my mind as if I were looking on them with my physical eyes, since some of these things I have learned from her own mouth, and much of the remainder from the report of those who had been present and declared what they knew with complete assurance. But so that the wordiness of this preface may not induce boredom, let the course of the narrative we are attempting begin here.

V

HILDEGARD THE CHOSEN VIRGIN and spouse of Christ was born in the town of ... in the vicinity of the city of Mainz, which is situated in the nearer parts of Germany, in about the eleventh hundred year of the Lord's incarnation. Her parents, of whom one was called ... the other ... ,[26] were of the highest rank according to the nobility of this world, enjoyed an abundance of earthly wealth, and were distinguished in popular acclaim. But what is better than all this, they were fervent toward God with holy dispositions and deeds. Theirs was *a great name, equal to the name of the great ones of the earth* (1 Chr. 17:8).

By the will of God who in the generation or bringing forth of children wonderfully ordains all things, she arrived as the tenth child of her father and mother. Making the most fitting provision they could, they set her apart through their mutual decision and free offering as their own tithe to the same God who commanded that tithes be offered him in the law, in order that she *might serve him in holiness and justice all the days of her life* (Lk. 1:74–75).

And she was in very truth completely set apart, since from her infancy she made herself a stranger to all the cares and all the children of the world.[27] Her heavenly spouse *desired her* comeliness and *beauty* (Ps.

---

[26] Their names, according to *VH* I were Hildebert and Mechtild. In his last years Guibert still asks the names of Hildegard's parents and her place of birth in his first letter to Abbot Godfrey of Trier (Ep. 40, Derolez, p. 385).

[27] *ab omnibus et curis et filiis seculi ab infantia alienam se reddens*. If the text read *filis*, it

44:12) which he had both placed in her by nature and would confer on her by grace. By way of response she set herself to long for him and to embrace him with all the expanse of her heart. To him who called her by means of an inner anointing, saying to her: *Hearken O daughter and see, and incline your ear and forget your people and your father's house* (Ps. 44:11), she replied with the devotion of a prompt and lively spirit: *Draw me after you*, she said, *and we shall run in the fragrance of your ointments* (Cant. 2:14).

Her *father and mother* had separated her from their other offspring; in a way they had *abandoned her* (cf. Ps. 26:10) to hope in God's mercy alone, so that she was casting herself totally on him not only in her thoughts but with her whole self. Consequently, he himself *in whom the prince of this world has no part whatever* (cf. Jn 14:30) *received her* (cf. Ps. 26:10), and she likewise sought to bear no part of the world with her, into the wide embrace of his loyal love. There he cherished her and nourished her, and, for as long a season as was suitable, hid her *in the shelter of his presence far from the plotting of people* (Ps. 30:21) *in the cleft of the rock and in a hollow of the wall* (Cant. 2:14), to be protected from the heat, the storm and the rain.

VI

THERE WAS AT THAT time a daughter of the count of Sponheim called Jutta. Though young in age, she was, by the maturity of her mind, an old woman surpassing those of advanced age. She had many suitors because of her outward beauty and the vast extent of her father's wealth. But she had been headed off by the divine choice and she spurned them all, using words like those the blessed Agnes is said to have used against the youth who was all on fire with love of her.[28] In this way *she kept herself unspotted from the world* (Jam. 1:27). Since God sustained her with his protection, she triumphed over all that would entice and divert her and clasped celibacy vigorously; she wrenched it from her heart,[29] so that she

---

would perhaps yield a more satisfactory meaning, i.e. 'threads/cords/ties of the world', but the text is *filiis*.

[28] Cf. Pseudo-Ambrose, *Passio S. Agnetis*, ed. by F. Jubaru, in *Bibliotheca Hagiographica Latina Antiquae et Mediae Aetatis* (1898–1901; supplement 1911), vol. 3, p. 358.

[29] *celibatum amplectens viriliter, ab animo extorsit; viriliter*—manfully, courageously,

might not dally in any way about it.

Her father[30] had set aside a great wealth for her in outward things, but she won him over so that no marriage contract should ever be written for her. Mindful of that text: *Evil speech corrupts good behaviour* (1 Cor. 15:33), she put up an unflinching resistance to all the base-minded who told her unseemly stories and who stood in the way of her vow, crying out in imprecation to them, 'Get away from me, you detestable purveyors of an *oil which shall never anoint my head!'* (Ps. 140:5) and, *to cleave to God is my happiness, to place my hope in the Lord my God* (Ps. 72:28). To this she directed herself with all the alacrity of her heart and put it into effect. Not only did she keep the most clear eye of her heart from going abroad, but she even withdrew her very body into a kind of work-house,[31]

---

staunchly: i.e. she forced herself. Jutta's moral 'virility', is a common theme of Ep. 38 and *VJ*.

[30] According to *VJ* II Jutta's father died when she was three, i.e. 1095, and her mother sometime about 1110. The historiographical sources for the counts of Sponheim are listed in Naumann-Humbeck, *Studien*, pp. 51–147; the evidence is also examined in J. Mötsch, 'Genealogie'. The *VJ* is not noted as a source by either author. According to the not always trustworthy Trithemius, *Chron. Sponh.*, p. 237, Count Stephan II died in 1118, and Meinhard, Jutta's brother, succeeded him. This dating is very doubtful. In fact, the last possible documentary attestation of Count Stephan (II?) is for the year 1111 (Naumann-Humbeck, p. 63, Mötsch, p. 72). *VJ* III, however, is quite clear that after Sophia's death it was Jutta's brother Meinhard, as if he were responsible, who worked to head off Jutta's idea of pilgrimage. In surviving documents of 1110 and 1112 a Meinhard appears as a witness among the free nobility, but not yet with the title of count. He is linked in 1110 with an Adalbert, the name of Meinhard's father-in-law, and in 1112 with a Godfrey, the name of Meinhard's eldest son, which suggests identification of Meinhard von Sponheim, cf. Naumann-Humbeck, p. 62, no. 38 and p. 63 no. 40, and p. 215. His name, this time as Lord and Count, appears in two charters of the Archbishop Adalbert in 1123, and in the charter for the foundation of Sponheim in 1124. He also appears in Archbishop Adalbert's charter of 1128 which records Meinhard's offering to Disibodenberg in recognition of his sister's vow, the township of Nunkirchen, inherited from his mother. I record Julie Hotchin's hypothesis that Meinhard had an elder brother Stephan who died young without issue. This is slightly supported by the fact that Stephan is a name of the father's family, and Meinhard a name of the mother's family. In that case, there could have been a Stephan III who died c. 1111, which would help explain a few anomalies. A suggestion of Constant Mews is that if Meinhard was born as late as 1095/6, he would only have assumed the title of Count when he came of age, perhaps the 1118 of Trithemius's dating. This means that Sophia as widow presided over the family for many years. See the Appendices for family trees of the Sponheim and Formbach families.

[31] *in aliquod ergastulum*; 'penitentiary' or work-house for slaves in the classical period.

where she could live in security, hidden away from all the turbulence of the world. Thus enticing no one by the sight of her beauty, she, *all of whose glory was from within* (cf. Ps. 44:14), would please him alone, being ever placed in view of the one who contemplated her within.[32]

After looking around various monasteries, it was the site of the monastery of Mount Saint Disibod the Bishop which lingered in her mind above all, both because it was renowned far and wide for the fervour of its piety, and because its round of worship was maintained away from the disturbance of a noisy crowd. She was delighted with it and drawn by the sweet odour of its good repute, so she betook herself there, and had an anchorhold built in which she might be secluded.[33] By dwelling there and spending the whole span of her life in meditation on the divine law, she would be free for God, and come to experience, at least by a foretaste, the sweetness of his peace in the measure that it is poured down from heaven, till at length, freed from the flesh and appearing in his sight, *she would be satisfied* in full, being destined to enjoy *his manifest glory* (cf. Ps. 16:15) forever.

In this way, she so provided herself with a haven of seclusion that she would not hinder the monks either by her own presence or by any of the visitors who approached her, or herself be hindered by anyone. On the other hand, far from the clamour of the crowd, she had free access by day and by night to the offices of the monks at their psalmody nearby.

She chose and predetermined that day, that is, the glorious solemnity of All Saints everywhere celebrated, on which she would enter her tomb, in order that, while she imitated those *kings and counsellors* in Job *who built solitudes for themselves* (cf. Job 3:14), she might be *sheltered* for a season *in this tent from those disputing tongues* (Ps. 30:21) which by their guile would dissuade her from the good, and that she might *lie down in peace in that very place and take her rest* (Ps. 4:9), in the hope that *under the shadow of God's wings* (Ps. 16:8) she might come through all the danger of the temptations and perils of this life and attain to that one thing she was seeking: that, once proven and made perfect, she might

---

[32] *in interni comtemplatoris respectu semper posita.* For God as the 'contemplator within', see *VJ* VI; a similar theme can be traced in the Rule of St Benedict, e.g. *RB* 4, 49; 7, 13.

[33] *in quo recluderetur*—i.e. formal *reclusion*, in which this particular kind of hermit called anchorite/anchoress was publicly dedicated to stability in an anchorhold, usually, though it seems not in Jutta's case, by the bishop, cf. Flanagan, *Hildegard of Bingen, 1098-1179: A Visionary Life*, pp. 28-31.

dwell in that *house* of God *not made with hands* (cf. Heb. 9:11), the eternal house, in heaven without end.

VII

WHEN THROUGH SPREADING REPORT the holy virgin's enterprise became widely known, the lady Hildegard's parents heard about it and were overwhelmed with a feeling of great joy, because they understood that God was offering them an opportunity and providing a place where they might bring his tithe-offering for safe-keeping. For they were afraid, and the sting of this fear caused them no slight worry that if this tithe-offering of the Lord were to remain out in the open, it might be preyed upon by *the birds of the air*, which eat *the seed falling by the wayside* (Mat. 13:4), or by *the beasts* of the field *which prowl about at night seeking their food* (cf. Ps. 103:20–21).

So they both came in their longing to the venerable servant of the Lord, and begged her earnestly to be so generous as to take to herself their daughter whom they had set apart for holy celibacy and divine service, so that she might stay with her always. Just as they had not hesitated to make their petition, so there was nothing to delay their obtaining what they sought, for it seemed she embraced the companionship of the girl as a consolation sent her from heaven.

What more? The fixed date of their induction came,[34] and many persons of both high and low degree came to be in attendance. According to the ritual of those laid to rest in the most solemn funeral liturgy, with burning tapers—which warned her to go out *with lamps alight* to meet *the bridegroom* at his midnight coming (cf. Mat. 25:6)—she was interred by the Abbot and brothers of the place as one literally dead to the world, together with her spiritual daughter Hildegard then in her eighth year of age,[35] and another handmaid of Christ of the same name, but of lower birth, her niece who was to minister to them. Crying out with all the longing of her heart she said: *This is my resting place forever, here shall I*

---

[34] 1 November 1112.

[35] Guibert is incorrect here. Hildegard was in her fifteenth year. Inconsistently, Ep. 38, VIIII correctly implies that the enclosure ceremony was twenty-four years before Jutta's death in 1136, i.e. 1112. Dating problems connected with Jutta and Hildegard's early religious life and their enclosure are discussed in the Introduction to the *VJ*.

dwell, for I have chosen it (Ps. 131:14), and again: *I shall go up into the place of the wonderful tabernacle* (Ps. 41:5), and this too: *Let us enter the house of the Lord with rejoicing* (Ps. 121:1).

She did not, however, *enter her burial-place* lifeless and barren, but as the scripture says, *in abundance* (Job 5:26). So, like a crop of wheat harvested in due season, an immense yield of produce eventually sprung from the root of her planting, which, cultivated by the heavenly Father, has clearly revealed itself up to this very hour. Surely there has also been fulfilled in her what the Lord says about himself in the Gospel: *Unless a grain of wheat falls into the ground and dies, it remains alone; but if it dies, it yields a great harvest* (Jn 12:24–25). For Jutta, having died to the world and withdrawn from it, was more fruitful in her one spiritual heir and daughter Hildegard, as can be seen today, than if she had been given in marriage and had brought forth a greater number of offspring through generation of the flesh.

VIII

AND SO WITH PSALMS and spiritual canticles the three of them were enclosed in the name of the most high Trinity. After the assembly had withdrawn, there they were left in the hand of the Lord. Except for a rather small window through which visitors could speak at certain hours and necessary provisions be passed across, all access was blocked off, not with wood but with stones solidly cemented in.

They earnestly inclined themselves to God with prayers and holy meditations, checking the urges of the flesh with constant fasts and vigils, vigorously[36] engaging themselves *in the contest of the struggle against all the spiritual forces of evil in the heavens* (Eph. 6:12). They considered that since *no-one born of woman ever remains in the same state* (cf. Job 14:1–2), and they were *carrying their treasure in vessels of clay* (2 Cor. 4:7) while running a course slippery with uncertainty, and were bereft of all human succour, like wards far removed from their father and mother, then why should they not fear, why should they not be passionately concerned on their own behalf? *They perceived that their tabernacle was beset all round by a countless host* (cf. Job 19:12), and they realized their inadequacy—so why would they not take refuge in the heavenly Father?

---

[36] *viriliter*, manfully, courageously, staunchly.

Why would they not implore unceasingly to be taken up and protected by him, and for *the armour of the Spirit* (cf. Eph. 6:13, 17) to be bestowed on them, that they might be defended from *the arrows* (cf. Eph. 6:16) of the hostile *powers of the air?* (cf. Eph. 2:2)

Through her wholly *honouring the Father* (Jn 5:23)[37] the blessed mother Jutta strengthened herself by ascetic endeavour even while she taught the disciples who were her daughters. By her resplendent examples of virtue she invited not only them but all who longed for a disciplined life to go forward.

Like the mighty heroine Judith,[38] to whom she harks back by her very name, with the *sword of the word of God* (cf. Eph. 6:17) she cut off the head of the intellectual Holofernes (cf. Jdt. 13:10–11), that is, that dominating vice of the devil by which he corrupts almost the whole human race, that vice of which the Lord said to blessed Job, *His power is in his loins, and his strength is in the navel of his belly* (Job 40:11). Resplendent in her victory, the female leader of so great a deed shone far and wide with the glory of her great renown.[39]

By the diffusion of the perfume of her sweetness, that is to say of her name, she not only fired many young women to the love and awe of God, as we mentioned before, but also attracted some of them to her presence in person. For indeed noble men and women began to flock to her, offering their daughters to her that they might take up the habit of holy religion and the life of professed virginity, and for their support they contributed vineyards, properties and estates.

These petitions and requests of theirs she handed on to the Abbot and the brothers of more mature age. With their counsel and permission, she agreed to receive the maidens and the gifts offered with them. When the entrance to her tomb was opened up, she brought inside with her the girls who were to be nurtured under the guidance of her disciplined guardianship.[40] It was on this occasion that what was formerly a sepulchre

---

[37] *hoc se venerando maxime*; the *hoc* refers back to the *supernum Patrem*, 'the heavenly Father', the object of the previous sentence.

[38] *instar Iudith viraginis fortissime*; for *virago*, see Gen. 2:23.

[39] *... dux tanti femina facti late resplenduit*—cf. Virgil, *Aeneid*, I, 364.

[40] This significant step eventually led by an inner logic to the development of a cenobitic community under Hildegard (X), and so on after that to Rupertsberg. St Aelred of Rievaulx, in his *De Institutione Inclusarum*, written for his sister, an anchoress, warns against the teaching of children, which, he says, 'would turn the cell into a school', cf.

became a kind of monastery, but in such a way that she did not give up the enclosure of the sepulchre, even as she obtained the concourse[41] of a monastery.

VIIII

HAVING KEPT UNSWERVINGLY TO her course—and with greater tenacity than I could say, for it is not about her deeds I had meant to write at this time—the blessed virgin Jutta, twenty-four years after her conversion, having vanquished *the prince of this world* (Jn 14:30), and so reaching the goal[42] of her mortal life, passed over through the exodus of her life-giving and *precious death* (cf. Ps. 115:15) to the embraces of the prince of heaven, Jesus Christ her spouse, whom she had loved and sought with all the affection of her heart.

The abbots and leaders of the region flocked to her funeral as did a vast crowd of both sexes. She was brought out of her prison, and, by a unanimous decision of all the brothers, was assigned for her burial-place, the middle of the chapter house. Because the atmosphere of silence and quiet had to be kept there,[43] the sick were not permitted any access to her grave. So her merits had to be made known in another way, just as I have heard they were from those same brothers under solemn witness of the truth.

When, according to the instruction of the Lord who said *If I your Lord and master have washed your feet, then you also ought to wash each other's feet; for I have given you an example that you also may do likewise* (Jn 13:14–15), the brothers, as I was saying, were carrying this

---

Aelred of Rievaulx, *Opera omnia*, ed. by A. Hoste and C.H. Talbot, CCCM, 1 (Turnhout: Brepols, 1971), p. 637. S. Flanagan discusses the institution of reclusion in her *Hildegard of Bingen, 1098–1179: A Visionary Life*, pp. 28–40. She is of the opinion that Aelred 'would also have disapproved of Jutta's reception and education of Hildegard in the cell at Disibodenberg' (p. 34).

[41] *frequentiam*—the numbers and the 'to-ing and fro-ing' to be expected in a community.

[42] *metam vite mortalis attingens*; a *meta* was a turning post in the circus or stadium.

[43] The chapter house was a place of special dignity, like the refectory (cf. *RB* 38, 5) and was reserved for the meetings of the 'chapter', i.e. the solemnly professed members of the community.

out in the solemn rite of the Sabbath,[44] then, as I said before, in order that Christ might make known more clearly how greatly he valued both the holiness of the one buried and the performance of the ceremony then being conducted, while all those present were looking on, they were struck with amazement yet at the same time gladdened when *a shaft of smoke* (cf. Cant. 3:6) *spreading a fragrance like cinnamon and balsam* (Eccli 24:20) billowed up from her tomb and filled the hearts of all with the delight of its ineffable sweetness.

But the brothers, from fear, would not suffer the dignity of so great a miracle to take place beneath their feet. So when the priests of the neighbourhood had been gathered together, they took up the holy body from its place in awe and reverence, and interred it honourably before the altar in the chapel of our Lady Queen of Heaven.[45]

X

NOW THAT THEIR *MAGISTRA* had been taken from their midst and received into peace, and since no one in her school[46] was found more outstanding in merit and holiness than Hildegard, so no one was judged more worthy to succeed her in the honour of teaching.[47] Accordingly, with the unanimous consent of the sisters—for they were secure concerning her discernment and self-control—she was chosen to exercise the supervision of discipline over them.

Though she resisted it with all her strength, she was constrained to assume the office of prioress[48] by the command of the Abbot and at the

---

[44] Cf. *RB* 35, 7 for the washing of the feet at the changeover of the weekly servers on Saturday (the Sabbath). There is, of course, the annual 'mandatum' ceremony during Holy Week, but the proper day for this is Holy ('Maundy') Thursday, not Saturday.

[45] *AD* reports that Archbishop Henry dedicated the 'Chapel of the holy Virgin Mary' in the new church on 1st November 1146. Guibert's reference to Mary as 'our Lady' is quite contemporary. St Bernard of Clairvaux and the Cistercians popularized this title, deriving from the culture of chivalry. Similarly, Guibert often refers to Hildegard as 'my lady'.

[46] *in scola eius*; cf. *RB* Prologue 45.

[47] *que ei in honore magisterii succederet*; Hildegard now succeeds Jutta as *magistra* of her school.

[48] *officium prioratus subire compellitur*. Hildegard immediately implements an ethos of *cenobitic* (community life) virtues, with an emphasis on discernment and moderation, contrasting with Jutta's emphasis on individual, anchoretic and penitential virtues. With

insistence of her sisters. She undertook it and, aware that the middle way is the safest way,[49] since virtue is a mean between the vices, she turned aside from the path of piety neither in this direction nor that. Instead, God ever kept his eyes upon her to direct her along this way, so that she *ran the* arduous *course* of this life without stumbling *till she received the reward of her crown* (cf. 1 Cor. 9:24–25).

XI

SHE UNDERSTOOD WELL THAT rigour toward vices was no less necessary than compassion toward our nature, for in no way was she lenient with herself, but spiritually trained herself to bring the stubborn beast of burden that was her body under the yoke. Only towards herself was she austere, whereas towards others she adapted and conformed herself as seemed appropriate,[50] practising nothing less than, and nothing more than, a prudent mean. In this way she neither cozened anyone through being easy-going, nor goaded anyone through being severe. Because of her discretion and sobriety, she appeared to all not only as irreproachable, but as both pleasing and worthy of emulation.

Thus, by the grace of God at work in her, though her government was quite strict, it did not seem oppressive or insupportable. Instead, just as

---

this move, what was once Jutta's anchorhold became formally a cenobitic monastery, so that there was at Disibodenberg a somewhat unequal double monastery, with an abbot as the ultimate superior over all, a prior for the main body of monks and a prioress for the small adjunct group of nuns. Hildegard became and always remained prioress, technically subject to the Abbot of Disibodenberg. So she was never an abbess. Most documents call her *magistra.*; Popes Eugene (Ep. 4, Van Acker, p. 10) and Adrian (Ep. III, PL 197, 153B) address her honourably as *praeposita*, the feminine form of 'provost'; in 1173, Pope Alexander calls her 'Prioress' (Ep. 10r, Van Acker, p. 25). The Charter of Frederick I (1163), translated in this volume, is the only contemporary document to address her as 'Abbess', almost certainly with a political purpose. Archbishop Hartwig, brother of Richardis von Stade, makes a distinction between his sister's title as *abbatissa*, and Hildegard's title as mere *magistra* even in his otherwise apologetic and sorrowful letter about his sister's death. Cf. Ep. 13, Van Acker, p. 29; Baird and Ehrman, pp. 50–51. In *VH* II, 4, Hildegard avoids even naming Richardis's 'higher title', i.e. *abbess*, using a generic *mater* instead; similarly with Guibert in Ep. 38, II–III.

[49] *sciens mediam viam esse tutissimam*; cf. Ovid *Metamorphoses* 2, 137: *Medio tutissimus ibis*.

[50] Cf. *RB* 2, 32.

salt when sprinkled in suitable measure tempers the acrid taste of any-thing it seasons, and just as an excellent wine exhilarates its drinkers by its natural dryness rather than repels them, so whenever this consummately prudent virgin was associated with anyone through friendship or conversation, she did not less stimulate her hearers than soothe them by her words and her writings fitted to the occasion, for she had a vivid quality, devoid of flattery.[51] Thus, as I say, she caused the minds of all who came into contact with her to ferment with the leaven of divine righteousness.[52]

When there were rebels in the community she did not immediately reproach them sharply or cut them off. Instead she used to overlook, warn, put up with, and patiently bide the time, until through a revelation from God she received counsel as to what she should do about them. This was her most vigilant practice, not only when she was still at Disibodenberg living with a few, but specially here, that is, in Bingen, where it has become a great assembly.[53]

XII

BUT LET ME RETURN to what I was saying earlier. Some years after the falling asleep of the lady Jutta, while she was still living in the place of her conversion, she was raised, despite her reluctance, to the service of holy leadership.[54] God was clearly determined to make her merits widely known, to manifest her to the world and to magnify her as an example for the praise of his name and for the correction of many. So the word of the Lord came to her not *in a vision by night*, but *openly* (cf. Num. 12:18), in

---

[51] *Cum vivida esset et sine adulatione, neque minus verbis et scriptis suis pro causarum ratione auditores suos pungeret quam ungeret.* There are points of comparison between Ep. 38 XI and the sketch of Jutta's character as counsellor in *VJ* V.

[52] Cf. *RB* 2, 5.

[53] At this point *G* (Klaes: G¹) the older manuscript ends.

[54] *ad sancte prelationis officium, licet renitens, assumitur*; this can hardly refer to Hildegard's office in her own community as *magistra* and prioress to which she succeeded after Jutta's death in 1136 (see X). The subsequent narrative indicates that Guibert is speaking of her visionary call several years later, in 1141, to *prophetic* leadership, in the wider arena of the Church at large.

the striking manner of her illumination,[55] commanding her to proclaim by means of the pen the things divinely revealed to her, and to hand them over to the Church to be read.

As you would know, she discourses extensively on the mode of her illumination in the first chapter of her book *Scivias*,[56] in many other passages in her writings, and particularly in that letter which she sent to me before I came to her,[57] after I had queried her concerning this by letter. Whoever reads these may well be struck speechless with awe at this strange manner, unknown to the world till now, of illumining the human mind. For these sources say that her soul was irradiated from her infancy with a certain light which she heard called *the shadow of the living light*, and that by means of it her soul ascended on high to the height of the vault in accord with the shifting patterns of the variable air and is spread over the various peoples however far away. They say that this same light was unlocalized and she was unable to observe any space in it, but that in it she discerned and from it she derived, by application of her mind alone and not of the senses at all, all that she presents.

She asserts that she does not see these visions in a sleeping state, but awake, so that in all this she never suffers the unconsciousness of ecstasy, and that in describing these visions she uses no other words than those she has heard. She bears witness moreover that she was worthy of something even more amazing, which is that from time to time she sees in this light we have spoken of, another light, which was named to her as *the living Light*. She is incapable of describing in words how she sees it. While she is actually contemplating it all sadness and anxiety is taken from her, so much so that it seems to her that she has at that time the age and health of a young girl and not of the old and sick woman she really is.

When did the world ever see and hear the like?

There are still many other things worth telling about her, things almost beyond belief which might well be inserted here. However, since they are

---

[55] *in aperta illustratione sue offensione*; *offensio* suggests something 'striking' or 'tripping' or 'confronting'.

[56] Cf. *Hildegardis Bingensis Scivias*, ed. by Führkötter, CCCM 43, Protestificatio, p. 4, lines 43–48.

[57] Ep. 103r, Van Acker 2, pp. 258–65. Other editions are: Hildegardis *Epistola de modo visionis suae* (Pitra, pp. 331–34), which gives the longer (and probably older) text in R. Dronke edits a version in *Women Writers*, pp. 250–56. See also *VH* 1, 8. Here Guibert summarizes the letter.

available to be read in her books and her letters, I have decided to omit them to avoid redundance.

Since therefore, as I was beginning to say, she was urged by divine command to write down and to publish the things revealed and that were going to be revealed to her, for a long time she was utterly terrified. She put off obeying, not from presumption but through fear, for she dreaded that if she attempted what was beyond her knowledge or capacity, what would come of it was not so much instruction for others as derision for herself. For indeed she was unlearned as far as training in the art of grammar goes, so that, as she herself freely confesses, while she had the skill to read the scriptures simply, like women who have only learnt the writings of the psalter, she was incapable of probing their meaning with sharpened insight unless illumined and helped by the force of interior inspiration.

XIII

MEANWHILE, SHE SHRANK FROM the embarrassment and was slow to obey. Moreover, apart from that slow and continuous ailment by which she had been oppressed almost from her infancy *in case she be puffed up through the greatness of revelation* (cf. 2 Cor. 12:7), she grew worse, not simply by chance but because she was laid low by an illness sent from God. So she lay prostrate on her bed, tossed about by her long-standing distress. She was *like one dumb who could not open her mouth* (Ps. 37:14), but held back her speech within her. She came very near to dying. She endured the mounting attack on the house of God not only with patience but also with thanksgiving, imitating that proven servant of God of whom it is written: *In all these things Job neither sinned with his lips nor uttered any folly against God* (Job 1:22).

For what cause, what enterprise, what strength is able to contend against God? She received an answer that she would never be free from the continuing scourge of this added sickness unless she obtained its removal by the interceding power of obedience, and that she should not doubt that this would be the eventual result, since she had as her leader and commander him *to whom nothing shall be impossible* (cf. Lk. 1:37). This is he who *blows* as he wills and *where he wills* (Jn 3:8), who *teaches man knowledge* (Ps. 94:10), and orders him to do nothing according to self-will, but *according to God's good pleasure* (Cf. Eph. 1:9). What difficulty could prevent her being instructed or obeying?

Another point was this: so that she could not plead the inadequacy of herself alone, and since like seeks like, there became known to her a monk in that same monastery who was sober, chaste, and learned in the wisdom of both heart and word.[58] As soon as he was informed about these things, he willingly consented to her entreaties. Exercising the restraint of his editorial work he clothed her words—however bare and unpolished—in a more presentable dress.

Worn out by the long ordeal and, knowing that *it is hard to kick against the goad*, and specially a goad from God (cf. Acts 9:5), she finally repented, and rounded on herself for her want of faith and her *smallness of spirit* (Ps. 54:9), for *that which is impossible with human beings is possible with God* (Lk. 18:27). She recalled that when Moses, *who used to speak with God as a man does with his friend* (Ex. 33:11), described himself as *uncircumcised in lips and lacking in eloquence* (Ex. 6:12,30) God himself gave him his brother Aaron to assist him in giving speech; and she recalled that when Jeremiah said, *Behold, I do not know how to speak, for I am only a child*, the answer was given, *Do not say 'I am a child', since to all to whom I send you, you shall go, and all that I command you, you shall speak* (Jer. 1:6–7). Turning it over in her mind nevertheless that, *out of the mouths of babes and those at the breast*, God *has brought forth praise for himself* (cf. Ps. 8:3), and that *Wisdom* not only *opens the mouths of the dumb, and made the tongues of infants to speak* (Wis. 10:21) but also, in what is most unusual, once corrected the folly of an insensible prophet by means of a dumb beast of burden (cf. Num. 22:28). *Pondering*, I say, *all these things in her heart* (Lk. 2:19), she finally girded herself to carry out what she was ordered to do.

XIIII

BUT SO THAT IN doing good she might do it well and irreproachably—for she was not unaware that he loses the virtue of the good work who in carrying it out abandons the line of due order—fearing this, she was herself most anxious that she should not sin by rightly making her offering and then not rightly portioning it out afterward, and thus by

---

[58] *sobrius, castus et eruditus corde et verbo in sapientia*; i.e. Volmar, the priest-monk of Disibodenberg who had already been Hildegard's *magister*, and was to become her secretary, accompanying her to Rupertsberg and ministering to her nuns. It was his death in 1173 which created the vacuum which Guibert eventually came to fill.

neglecting one matter, lose the other too. For this reason there is the example of Moses already mentioned, that great man who conversed with God. Though all that he had to do was revealed to him from heaven, he did not disdain to take helpful advice even from a man who was a gentile.[59]

So in this as in other matters she likewise decided what to do with the advice and sanction of her superior, so that, however the matter might turn out, provided she could not be faulted for presumption, she would not have to repent of it afterwards. For consider what happened to Moses himself, who undertook to lead the people not by his own decision but by the Spirit of God. Contrary to what he would otherwise have expected, it came about through God, that he himself and Aaron and those whom he had led forth from Egypt to take possession of the promised land, all excepting Joshua and Caleb and the priest Eleazar, were laid low in the desert through various forms of death.

Whereupon the Abbot was fetched to whom she was subject and on whose approval she waited in all things. She revealed to him the divine command given to her concerning the writing down of her visions. She confessed that she was suffering the weakness of the body through which she had been brought low for so long, because up to that point she had been so reluctant to obey, and that on account of this she wanted to hear his counsel concerning these matters and to obtain his permission, should he think it warranted, to fulfill the order; and that she also humbly begged him for the monk who had been pointed out to her, that he might critically receive her words and correct them.[60]

The Abbot was struck with wonder at the account of such a great novelty, and yet did not lose power over himself in sudden astonishment. Not being confident of directing an uncertain matter, and thinking over many issues in his mind, he answered that he did not dare freely express a verdict on so surprising a matter, and that he ... so subtle a ...[61]

---

[59] I.e. Jethro, priest of Midian, his father-in-law. Cf. Ex. 18:24.

[60] *monachum quoque in suffragium excipiende et corrigendi verba sua sibi designatum humiliter expetere*, i.e. Volmar.

[61] The text breaks off abruptly at this point, on folio 190^v of G^2, with a third of the column remaining empty. Since space was available for further copy there may have been a loss of text already in the source document. The next page, folio 191^r, was originally empty but was filled by a later hand with a letter of Hildegard to the clergy of Cologne, PL 197, 269b–71d. On the next page after that, folio 191^v, Guibert's revision of Theodoric's *vita* begins.

THE LIFE OF HILDEGARD

INTRODUCTION

Manuscripts and critical edition

The Life of Holy Hildegard is translated here from the critical edition by Monika Klaes, *Vita Sanctae Hildegardis*, CCCM, 126 (Turnhout: Brepols, 1993). The edited text, *Vita Sanctae Hildegardis Virginis*, is on pp. 1–71; Klaes reports her research into the document on pp. 60–145*. The source manuscripts are examined on pp. 157–73*, from which the following list of manuscripts is drawn:

T   MS 624 of the Österreichische Nationalbibliothek, Vienna, from the late twelfth century. There is a notice on the first page that it once belonged to the Carthusian monastery in Mainz. T contains eighty quarto-sized folios of eight quires comprising the *VH* alone. The last folio was already missing in the fifteenth century. On pp. 158–64* Klaes carries out a detailed palaeographic comparison of T with the *Liber Aureus* from Echternach,[1] and establishes beyond doubt that T is an autograph 'fair-copy' of the *VH* made by Theodoric of Echternach himself.

R   MS 2 of the Hessische Landesbibliothek, Wiesbaden, the 'Riesenkodex', i.e. the 'giant' codex, of 481 folio-sized sheets, arranged in double columns, containing the 'collected works' of Hildegard. It was written out by five different hands at Rupertsberg between 1180–1190.

R was once regarded as the oldest witness of the *VH*, and was used as such for the PL edition, but comparisons with T and internal evidence reveal the errors in spelling and placing of words in R. There is disarray in the chapter-numbering of Book III. The replacement of *domina* with

---

[1] Gotha Forschungs Bibliothek, MS Memb I 71. Printed edition in Weiland, MGH SS, 23, pp. 20–72.

mater in III, 20 indicates its production in St Hildegard's own community.

B   MS 674 of the Staatsbibliothek zu Berlin Kulturbesitz. This consists of three sections, later bound together as one. The first and third part contain writings of Hildegard, written out in the early thirteenth century by the same careful hand that also wrote out the Lucca manuscript of the *Liber Divinorum Operum*, while the second part is a collection of apocalyptic works, written out in the fourteenth century by a Guillelmus de Valle. The *VH* is found on fols 1–24. The oldest notice indicates it belonged to the monastery of St Mary in Pfalzel, Trier.

Apart from its variant readings, B shows other peculiarities. The captions describing the content of the chapters are inserted appropriately into the continuous text rather than listed together and prefaced to each book as Theodoric had arranged them. Secondly, the missing exorcism text of *VH* III, is written in the margin of fol. 21^r of this text. Finally, there is on fol. 57^v, unconnected with the text, a diagram of the acrostic from the incident of the guilty priest (*VH* III, 16), and a not very enlightening pastiche of Hildegard's interpretation of it.[2]

P   MS 4919 of the Österreichische Nationalbibliothek, Vienna, of 208 sheets, early fifteenth century. The oldest notice indicates it belonged to the monastery of St Pantaleon, Cologne. P comprises a variety of edifying religious works not all connected with Hildegard; one of them is a *Letter on the future dangers of the Church from the sayings of holy Hildegard* by Heinrich von Langenstein.[3] The *VH* is on fols 20^r–60^v. It was copied from T: the numbering of pages is identical, and the same hand also appears in later additions to T itself.

Bt   MS 835 of the Staatsbibliothek zu Berlin Kulturbesitz, dating from c. 1490, and clearly copied from T, if with many mistakes. It features several other important texts of Hildegard.

L   Additional MS 15102, British Library, of 246 sheets. Trithemius,

---

[2] A translation is included in the notes on the episode in *VH* III, 16.

[3] See G. Sommerfeld, 'Die Prophetien der hl. Hildegard in einem Schreiben des Meisters Heinrich von Langenstein', *Historisches Jahrbuch,* 30 (1909), pp. 43–61, 297–307.

Abbot of Sponheim tells in his foreword how he commissioned this as a direct copy of R in 1487.[4] The *VH* appears as the last document, on fols 224^r–45^r. It once belonged to the monastery of St James in Würzburg.

G1 G2 These are the manuscripts containing Guibert's revision of the *VH*. See the Introduction to that document for fuller information. Variations from the text of Theodoric's *VH* are found in the footnotes of this translation under 'Guibert'.

Theodoric of Echternach, the Endredactor

The final editor of the *VH* is the monk Theodoric of Echternach (d. 10 May 1192), whose best known other work is the *Chronicles of Echternach*.[5] Echternach was an ancient monastery in the diocese of Trier, founded, according to the *Chronicles*, by Pippin. Theodoric had a high reputation as *scholasticus* or *magister*, i.e. a teacher and director of studies for his monastery. While he and his community had close relations with St Eucharius in Trier (and also with St Maximin), he was never actually a monk there, but entered his own monastery at a young age, possibly as a child oblate, sometime in the first half of the twelfth century.[6]

---

[4] 'All these writings are contained in a certain great and very precious volume; the common opinion is that it was written by the hand of Saint Hildegard. I have seen the great book, or as I said volume, in the aforesaid monastery of St Rupert. All the letters which follow were written out from it, although with haste, in the year of the Lord fourteen hundred and eighty seven, by a certain monk of Saint Benedict of the monastery of Sponheim at my orders, who am however unworthy, Abbot of the same monastery.' From the Latin text in Klaes, p. 172*.

[5] *Chronicon Epternacense*, ed. by Ludwig Weiland, MGH SS 23, pp. 38–39. On Theodoric see Herwegen, 'Collaborateurs', p. 11.

[6] Theodoric introduces himself in the prologue of the *Chronicon* as *Theodoricus eiusdem aecclesiae humilis alumpnis:* 'Theodoric, humble foster-son of the same community'. He also characterizes himself in the *Libellus de libertate*, MGH SS 23, p. 67: 'There was at that time Theodoric, one of the disciples of that community, brought up in the monastic discipline from the time he was a child even to advanced age. So he had heard, seen and read many things, and knew very well the state of the community and its affairs from the beginning.' These texts seem to rule out Führkötter's assertion in 'Hildegard von Bingen und ihre Beziehungen zu Trier', *Kurtrierisches Jahrbuch*, 25 (1985), p. 70, that he had earlier been a monk of St Eucharius in Trier. Cf. Klaes, pp. 62–63*.

A passing statement in the *Acta Inquisitionis* and a note added to the *Book of Divine Works* has been taken to suggest that Abbot Ludwig of St Eucharius arranged for Theodoric as well as Godfrey of Disibodenberg to stay at Rupertsberg at some stage after the death of Volmar.[7] Klaes however demonstrates that this is unlikely. On pp. 67–78* she engages in a close palaeographic analysis of T, i.e. Theodoric's autograph copy, the Echternach Necrology and the *Liber aureus* of the *Chronicles*, tracking Theodoric's personal hand chronologically, and shows that it was precisely in Hildegard's last decade, the 1170s, that Theodoric was at his busiest at Echternach. He was holding down two jobs so to speak, not only as the *Magister scholarum*, but also the *Armarius*, or keeper of books and documents. Klaes emphasizes, p. 75*, that his work on the *VH* in the early 1180s was not motivated from any personal interest in Hildegard, but was carried out solely at the initiative of Abbots Ludwig and Godfrey, her friends, as he himself asserts in his three prologues. So the *VH* really was a 'labour of obedience' (*RB* Prologue 2).

Due to his historical and documentary expertise, Theodoric was in his last years the one most in a position to champion his abbot and community in a three-way legal strife between themselves, the emperor, and their bishop. He drew up the *Libellus de libertate Epternacensi*, in which he successfully defended the royally guaranteed independence and tax-free status of his community, against Henry VI's attempt to assign it to Archbishop John of Trier in exchange for the town of Nassau (p. 64*). What is so complicating is that Godfrey was simultaneously Abbot of St Eucharius, which community *was* directly under the Archbishop (p. 65*).

Theodoric's work on the *VH* can be dated fairly closely: 1181 was the year Godfrey took over the office of Abbot of Echternach from Ludwig, which gives us a *terminus a quo* for the composition of the *VH*. Ludwig, Abbot of Echternach *and* also of St Eucharius from 1168 died in 1187,

---

[7] *Godfrido et Dietrico, qui cum beata virgine morabantur:* 'Godfrey and Dietrich (Theodoric?), who stayed with the blessed virgin', *Acta Inq.*, p. 124. This should be compared with a note inserted later in the *Book of Divine Works* in R recording Hildegard's reaction to the death of Volmar: 'Then that most reverend and wise man before God and before men Ludwig, Abbot of St Eucharius in Trier, was moved with great compassion for my sorrow, and on his own account and that of other wise people faithfully provided me with steady constant help, since he had known this blessed man well, and me and my visions, while I, in my tearful sighs rejoiced over him [Volmar] as one taken up by God.' Cf. Klaes, p. 60*, n. (2) and Dronke, *Women Writers*, pp. 195, 313.

which is our *terminus ante quem.* So Theodoric received his commission from the abbots and carried it out between 1181–1187, during a period when there were *two* Abbots in tandem, one for either monastery. Only in 1190, after the solving of Echternach's political difficulties, largely through Theodoric's services, did Godfrey, Abbot of St Eucharius, officially take over also as Abbot of Echternach till his death in 1210.[8]

Theodoric's sources

When Theodoric commenced his work of compiling and editing a *vita* of Hildegard, perhaps some time in 1182, he had available to him the stock of sources assembled and left behind at Rupertsberg by Guibert in 1180. These are the sources:

• The autobiographical passages. Because they are of such special interest, these will be treated at greater length in the following section.

• Godfrey of Disibodenberg's *Libellus* ('Little Book').
   In his Letter 15 to Archbishop Philip, Guibert says that after Hildegard's death when at the urge of Philip and many others he undertook to write a *Vita*, the nuns produced, out of hiding as it were, a *libellus vite eius* 'a little book of her life'. This *libellus* of Godfrey is largely to be identified with *VH* I. According to Klaes's analysis (pp. 90–95*) it ends with chapter 7, while the remaining chapters, 8 and 9, were written by Theodoric, who despite the opening comment of 8 does not really add anything to the biographical narrative of Hildegard's life.
   After Volmar's death in 1173, Hildegard had great difficulties in obtaining a replacement from Disibodenberg.[9] In the end, Godfrey, of whom we know very little, was sent from Disibodenberg as supervisor of external affairs, though not as Hildegard's personal assistant and editor. So Klaes concludes from the internal evidence (pp. 104–05*). From Abbot Godfrey's letter to Guibert (Derolez, Ep. 41) and Guibert's Letter

---

[8] For more on the dating of the two Abbots' terms of office, cf. Klaes, p. 78*; the dates given in the index, pp. 196*, 202*, seem to be presented inconsistently.

[9] See the letter of Hildegard to Pope Alexander III, Ep. 10, Van Acker, pp. 23–24 and the letter of Pope Alexander to Wezelin, provost of St Andrews in Cologne, Ep. 10r, Van Acker, p. 25, Baird and Ehrman, p. 46.

19, we know Godfrey died in 1176.[10]

Despite pages of exhaustive analysis, Klaes does not really go into the question of just who it was that instigated Godfrey's work on a *vita* of Hildegard. It may be best to take our cue from the first prologue of the *VH*, and from letters of Abbot Godfrey to Guibert and assume that it was Hildegard's friend Abbot Ludwig.

In his *libellus* Godfrey of Disibodenberg shows a preference for concrete, visible and particular events, which becomes clear when his account is compared with the parallel accounts in the autobiographical passages. Godfrey, for example, depicts the growing numbers of noble young women who were joining Hildegard and the consequent constriction of space (*VH* I, 5) as sufficient motive for the move from Disibodenberg, whereas the autobiographical account begins immediately with a divine commission, Hildegard's resistance, and heaven-sent sickness (*VH* II, 2).

Consistent with the fact that he was dealing with his own community, Godfrey somewhat tones down the degree of strife that continued for years between Rupertsberg and Disibodenberg over the terms of their separation and continuing relationship.[11] He stresses more than the autobiography the significant role of the abbot of Disibodenberg in Hildegard's advancement. His literary style is essentially simpler than Theodoric's, meriting Guibert's description of the *libellus* as *simplici sermone descriptus* and its *stilus humilis.*[12]

Did Godfrey have the *VJ* as one of *his* sources? In 'Aus Kindheit', pp. 62–63, Staab hints at points of literary contact between the *VJ* and *VH* I, and we might add for further investigation, *VH* II. Some preliminary investigation of this is carried out in the Introduction to the *VJ*.

• The Miracle reports.

Guibert also says in his letter to Philip that the nuns had continued

---

[10] See Ep. 18, Derolez, p. 238, and Ep. 41, p. 388. In a later editing of his letters Guibert changed the name of Godfrey to that of Volmar, thus giving the impression that he directly succeeded Volmar. See Klaes, p. 86*, n. (107).

[11] Klaes examines the process of estrangement on pp. 103–08*. Other documents pertaining to this separation are the charters of Archbishop Arnold in 1158, and Hildegard's letter to Volmar which prefaces her *Explanation of the Athanasian Creed*, PL 197, 1065B–7A. In the latter her tone against the Disibodenberg monks hardens considerably.

[12] Ep. 15 to Archbishop Philip, Derolez, p. 214.

Godfrey's *libellus* with an account of some miracles. This is the source of the miracle reports presented by Theodoric in Book III. They may be divided into several sections.

The first section is from chapters 1–19, whose origin with the nuns at Rupertsberg is clear enough. The linguistic style is simple, almost formulaic; they speak of Hildegard as *pia mater* rather than the more formal *sancta virgo*; they are largely concerned with events in the neighbourhood of Bingen. Most reports refer to events in Hildegard's lifetime, but some, such as the healings wrought through the rope of Hildegard's hair sent by the nuns, may refer to posthumous events.

Chapters 14–16 are different, for they deal not with cases of healing but with apparitions of Hildegard at a distance to those in need (14 and 15) plus the incident of the guilty priest in 16. Their content and style is more complex, indicating the hand of Theodoric. There is a clear echo of the *Flores Epitaphii Sanctorum*,[13] by Thiofrid of Echternach, an earlier abbot of Theodoric's own community. In Book III, chapter 1 (col. 370B) Thiofrid describes how sometimes saints can appear, even in their lifetime, without being physically present to those who call on their help, sometimes to forewarn of danger and avert the attack of enemies.

Chapters 20–22 are distinguished for the very generous account of the exorcism of Sigewize, the highly dramatic climax of the entire book. This series of incidents in the year 1169 involving the demoniac Sigewize, seem to have marked the apogee of Hildegard's fame in her lifetime.

Chapters 26–27 culminate in an account of Hildegard's death. Theodoric expressly cites his sources: the nuns of Rupertsberg. The style is generally simple and unadorned, short on concrete information, such as names, and formulaic in its presentation of miracles. Here too, Hildegard is called *mater*. The death report largely comprises the spectacular atmospheric wonders taken to illustrate Hildegard's holiness. Guibert also mentions in his Letter 15 to Philip, that he has available to him an account of Hildegard's death, but this is almost certainly the same document of the nuns which Theodoric included in *VH* III, 27. None of this account compares with the far more personal quality of Jutta's death scene in *VJ* VIII. Would that Guibert had left behind an eyewitness account! Jutta was well served by Volmar in this.

---

[13] PL 157, 297–404.

• Hildegard's letter to Guibert, *De modo visionis suae*, a copy of which he left among the stock of sources at his departure from Rupertsberg. It is cited in *VH* I, 8, which indicates this section of *VH* I was not written by Godfrey of Disibodenberg, as he died before the letter was written.

• Theodoric's own contributions to the *VH*.

Theodoric's role in the *VH* is that of compiler/arranger of source documents, supplementary commentator, and overall architect of the finished product. In the prologues to the three books he clearly states his own structural purpose, and consistently carries it out. He adds almost no new biographical information about Hildegard apart from what is verifiable in the material available to him, and presented—and so in most cases preserved—by him.

His own contributions are most clearly distinguishable from his sources in *VH* II, where he typically introduces a section from Hildegard's autobiography, then follows it up with his own reflections on what has just been presented. His concern is to relate her life to scriptural models, using patristic modes of spiritual interpretation native to a monk, and in harmony with ideals of holiness prevalent in the milieu of monastic reform. Of special interest is Theodoric's interpretation, indeed his 'theology' of her role as woman and prophetess in *VH* II, 6.

Mention was made above of Theodoric's use of works by Thiofrid of Echternach, an earlier abbot of his community. Klaes traces echoes of other works by Abbot Thiofrid, some as actual quotations, some as possible allusions. References to them are supplied in the footnotes.

Finally, Theodoric is proclaimed by his Latin style. Whereas Guibert is a master of architectonic paragraph-length sentences, Theodoric's propensity is for turning out gems of intricately patterned word plays.[14] His entire style is pervaded with this technique of *Reimprosa* (rhyme-prose) as Klaes calls it, which she examines on pp. 80–82*.

---

[14] A good example of this feature occurs in *VH* II, 8 which reaches its climax with a beautifully sonorous:

> *gratiam in terris / gloriam in cellis*
> *gratiam sublimium meritorum / gloriam ineffabilium premiorum.*

The autobiographical passages

The *VH* is remarkable among *vitae* for its preservation of lengthy autobiographical[15] passages of its subject. Newman would see this feature as not less than the watershed of a new trend in hagiographical literature.[16] Theodoric inserts most of these passages under the heading of 'Visions'. More of them appear in *VH* II, though there are also some in *VH* III. Twelve or thirteen of these passages can be discerned according to content and character, rather more than Theodoric's express tally of 'Visions'. These are the passages as discerned by Klaes:

1. *VH* II, 2 *First Vision*, which is in two parts.

a.   (Lines 6–33) The five tones of righteousness marking the stages of salvation, from the time of Abel, through Noah, Moses, the Incarnation and so to the world's end.

b.   (Lines 34–102) Hildegard tells of her life from her birth and earliest visionary experience up to the recognition of her calling in Trier by the Pope.

2. *VH* II, 5 (Lines 13–101) *Second Vision*

The events surrounding the move to Rupertsberg, including the early hardships; the completion of *Scivias*.

3. *VH* II, 7 (Lines 2–24) *Third Vision*

The separation from Disibodenberg and confirmation of this in a document.

---

[15] Klaes, with her critical severity, does not easily concede the description 'autobiographical passages'. She speaks of (p. 17*) '... einige von ihm als Visionen Hildegards vorgestellte Text ... da sie aus der Perspektive Hildegards über ihr eigenes Leben berichten, meist als Autobiographie zitiert.'—'some texts presented by him as Hildegard's Visions ... usually cited as autobiography since they give information from Hildegard's perspective about her own life'; and (p. 109*) 'die in der Ich-Form von Hildegards Leben berichten'—'accounts of Hildegard's life in the first person singular'.

[16] 'Whether or not he [Theodoric] was consciously innovating, his editorial technique turned the *Vita Hildegardis* into the earliest known instance of a new literary genre, a *Zwischenform* midway between hagiography 'proper' (a male-dominated genre) and the literature of visions and revelations (a genre that would become increasingly female-dominated). Peter Dinzelbacher has characterized this intermediate genre as *Gnadenleben*: a species of hagiography that privileges the inner life so far as to slight external events, dwelling instead on 'special graces' and citing as its authority the subject's own confession.' Barbara Newman, 'Three-Part Invention: The *Vita Hildegardis* and Mystical Hagiography', in *Hildegard of Bingen: The Context of Her Thought and Art*, ed. by Charles Burnett and Peter Dronke (London: Warburg Institute, 1998), p. 186.

4. *VH* II, 9 (Line 2)—*VH* II, 10 (Line 23) *Fourth Vision*

Her thirty-day sickness when she nearly died, followed by an illness lasting three years. During this time she journeys to Disibodenberg and other monasteries.

5. *VH* II, 12 (Lines 9–40), not numbered by Theodoric.

The philosopher who first despised then supported them; resentment in Hildegard's community against her monastic discipline; She finishes *The Book of Life's Merits.*

6. *VH* II, 14 (Lines 2–90) *Fifth Vision*

Considerations on the human condition, seen as a struggle between *flesh* and *spirit*, which Hildegard explains with examples from Scripture; how she has acquitted herself in this struggle.

7. *VH* II, 15 (Lines 10–14) *Sixth Vision*

Wisdom reveals certain secrets to her in the form of a vision of three towers, in each of which there are three dwellings. No interpretation is offered.

8. *VH* II, 16 (Lines 2–26) *Seventh Vision*

She has a tremendous vision in which there is an explanation of the beginning of the Gospel of John. This is the beginning of her book *On the Divine Works.*

9. *VH* III, 20 (Lines 5–65) not numbered by Theodoric.

A year's illness, during which she became involved in the healing of an obsessed woman. She considers the nature of demons and their influence on human beings.

10. *VH* III, 22 (Lines 10–63) not numbered by Theodoric.

How the possessed woman was brought to Rupertsberg, and finally healed through an exorcism at the Easter vigil, carried out according to her instructions.

11. *VH* III, 23 (Lines 11–30) not numbered by Theodoric.

A forty-day illness from which she nearly dies. She journeys to other monasteries.

12. *VH* III, 24 (Line 5)–*VH* III, 25 (Line 11) *Eighth Vision*

She is healed of her illness by the vision of a very beautiful man; she composes the *Life of S. Disibod*, and the *Book on Divine Works.*

Klaes is satisfied that apart from minor editorial work Theodoric has left intact the substance of these texts as he received them. To him they were a source of wonder and awe as testimonies of the prophetic charism conferred on Hildegard. In several statements through the *VJ* he betrays that he himself is not overly familiar with her writings anyway.[17]

So the autobiographical texts are overwhelmingly authentic. That their simple yet striking style is consistent with Hildegard's other works also supports their integrity.[18] It is not so certain however, that the texts had not been edited, perhaps by Guibert as Klaes suggests (p. 113*), i.e. even *before* they came into Theodoric's hands. In such a case, they would have passed through Guibert's hands before he left Rupertsberg in 1180, as they certainly did in his own revision of the *VH* near the end of his life, in 1209.

In this revision of the *VH* we may have something of a 'control' for probing the autobiographical texts. If, amid the host of Guibert's stylistic refinements, some original Hildegard material is discernible, they yield the evidence that Theodoric added nothing to Hildegard's actual text, but at the most, omitted a phrase or two here, a sentence there. At the end of II, 11 he appears to have skipped over his available text by lightly paraphrasing it.

In his essay on Hildegard in *Women Writers* (pp. 144–65), Dronke treats these autobiographical passages as a continuous text, although he makes certain ommissions.[19] He argues for the composition of the whole in the years 1173–74, since the last work mentioned in them is the *Book of Divine Works*. Klaes (p. 112*) on the other hand is less inclined to regard them as an originally single document. She differentiates accounts according to the events they report concerning Hildegard's own life or the foundation of Rupertsberg, her illnesses, the tensions in the community, the way she coped with her difficulties. Sections 1a and 6 are visions concerned with salvation history, 6 relating it to the different kinds of moral behaviours of human beings. Sections 9 and 10 deal with the same

---

[17] See e.g. II, 15, where he says that it would be a good to explore the 'obscurity' of her subtle words but he must hurry on to the next task. Instead of giving himself to the exertion needed for understanding, he seems relieved at the end of book II that he has finally finished writing out the last cited text, grateful to have safely navigated 'so vast a sea of her visions'.

[18] On this subject see Marianna Schrader and Adelgundis Führkötter, *Die Echtheit des Schrifttums der heiligen Hildegard von Bingen*, Beihefte zum Archiv für Kulturgeschichte, 6 (Cologne: Böhlau, 1956), especially p. 14.

[19] From his edition on pp. 231–41, Dronke omits sections 1a, 3, most of 4, a large part of 5, 6; cf. Klaes, p. 111*, n. (200).

episode, 7 is a vision corresponding to the structure of the *Book of Divine Works*, though no interpretation is offered. Section 8 immediately follows describing the circumstances of a very special vision which inaugurates the same book. Klaes (p. 114*) would group together 1–6; she sees them as bracketed between two passages intended to give a 'heilsgeschichte' (salvation-history) perspective to all the reported events of her life. She places the composition of this group before 1163, after the completion of the *Book of Life's Merits*.

Within the second group of texts, the exorcism of Sigewize in 9 and 10 can be dated accurately to the year 1169.[20] This is consistent with the fact that after the end of 8, the *Book of Divine Works* is in an advanced state of planning but not yet written.

To sum up Klaes's analysis, the substance of Hildegard's 'auto-biography' was completed during Volmar's life-time, but in two phases, one ending in 1163 and the other in about 1170. Klaes observes (p. 116*) that the first six sections often have something of the *apologia* about them, as if Hildegard felt she had to account for herself, whereas in the remaining sections she is more self-possessed and authoritative, befitting the later phase of her life.[21]

Observations on translating terms in the *VH*

After 'living' with these documents over a period of time, the translator may be allowed to offer some observations on translating some of the terms used in the *VH* and in the other Hildegard documents.

In the *VH* the single word *visio* refers on the one hand to particular instances of what is seen (or even heard) in a para-normal manner, as in *a* vision, a 'revelation', and on the other hand, to the visionary gift itself, which seems to have been a generic mode of consciousness which could be tapped almost at will, a kind of waking clairvoyance. In this translation I allow this double meaning of *visio* to stand under the single English

---

[20] Hildegard speaks of this episode in two letters, one to Arnold, her nephew, just elected Archbishop of Trier (1169), Ep. 27r, Van Acker, pp. 90–91, and one to the dean of Cologne cathedral (PL 197, 258B–9C). Cf. Klaes, p. 115*, n. (211).

[21] Newman is not at all convinced by Klaes's conclusions, and argues instead that the whole text probably dates from 1170 and was written or dictated at Volmar's request. See her 'Three-Part Invention', p. 192.

word 'vision'.

The word *virgo* is here translated literally as 'virgin' rather than in my earlier translation, 'maiden'. *Virgo*, particularly in this religious setting, signifies a publicly recognized sacral role. Its formal sense is usually emphasized in the *VH* with adjectives like 'blessed', 'holy', 'godly' etc. It is rather the Latin word *puella* which covers senses such as 'girl', 'unmarried woman' (or 'newly married woman') and 'maiden'. The *VH* uses *puella* most often for the nuns of Hildegard's monastery. It is generally translated here as 'young woman'. The term *matrona* (e.g. II, 10) I translate as 'married woman'.[22] In sum, the anthropological/religious perspective seems to be that a *puella* (girl) might graduate as a *mulier* (woman) or *femina* (female person) to the *dignitas* (public standing) of either a *matrona* (married woman) with its derivative a *vidua* (widow), or of a *virgo* (virgin).

Surprisingly, the word *mulier* appears rarely—the preferred generic term for 'woman' is *femina*, and even this does not appear so often. Likewise, *vir* is a rare occurrence. When it does occur, especially in Hildegard's own discourse, we may assume the usage is quite deliberate, and to be given full weight. Hence the translation 'strong men' in *VH* III, 22.

A term which does appear often is *homo*. Hildegard is particularly given to the use of *homo*, and specially with reference to herself as an object of divine revelation. I speculate that during the early days when she was in her thirties and Volmar was her *magister*, she surely studied, perhaps in preparation of the liturgy, the terms used in the creation account of Gen. 1:27. Perhaps they discussed the famous incident in St Gregory of Tours's *History of the Franks* when at the council of Mâcon in 505 there was a bishop whose Latin was not too good, *qui dicebat mulierem hominem non posse vocitari*, 'who maintained that a woman could not be called "man"'. He had to be set straight by brother bishops more learned in Latin, doctrine, and the scriptures.[23]

---

[22] In Roman law the *matrona* was the fully legal wife in the sense of marriage proper, the mistress of her husband's household entrusted with the keys; it was a role with a distinctive *dignitas*, which it more than retained in its Christian transposition; indeed it gained in sacral ambience since, unlike the grades of 'sub'-marriage regulated for in Roman law, e.g. concubinage, from the outset there was but one form of marriage for practising Christians, the full version, and sacramental at that.

[23] Gregory of Tours, *Historia Francorum*, PL 71, Book VIII, 20. They adduced Gen. 5:1–

The approach to translating *homo* and its forms here is this:

Since Hildegard goes so far as to use *homo* when *vir* might have been more appropriate, e.g. 'that one man to whom she revealed all her secrets' (end of *VH* II, 4) or to use *homo* when *mulier* might have done: 'that *person* who spoke from the Holy Spirit' (end of *VH* II, 5), in such cases I usually translate *homo* as 'person' or 'man' or 'woman' according to the occasion. Plural instances of this vague general sense, i.e. *homines* are usually translated as 'people' or 'persons'.

But when *homo* is brought into juxtaposition with God, angels, or devils, even implicitly, then such broad translations are patently inadequate. Here the distinctly *human* character of 'homo' must be brought out, in contradistinction to the other categories just mentioned which, after all, refer to intelligent subsistences which are *personal* in nature but not *human*. In such cases, standard English is followed here and the singular *homo* is translated as the generic (i.e. inclusive) 'man' without article. When *homo* is used of a particular person, then in the case of a woman, notably Hildegard, I translate it as 'human being' or in one particularly hieratic situation (*VH* II, 2) 'human creature', and in the case of *a* man, 'man'. The plural *homines* in this sense I usually translate as 'human beings'.

Magistra is retained in this translation in its Latin form, italicized. Its

---

2, *in principio Deo hominem creante, ait 'Masculem et feminam creavit eos, vocavitque nomen eorum Adam,' quod est homo terrenus* ('in the beginning when God created man, 'he created them male and female and called their name Adam', which is earthly man'); they also explained to him: *Dominus Jesus Christus ob hoc vocitatur filius hominis, quod est filius virginis, id est mulieris* ('the Lord Jesus Christ therefore is called Son of Man, because he is the son of the Virgin, that is to say, of a woman'). In the introduction to the *VJ* a number of similarities were pointed out between Jutta and the Monegond whose life Gregory of Tours recounts in his *Vita Patrum*. There is no reason why the works of Gregory would not have been available at Disibodenberg. In a report for the year 1137 Trithemius says that much copying of manuscripts was carried out at both Sponheim and Disibodenberg, *Chron. Sponh.*, pp. 248, 256. Apart from the considerable library at St James, Mainz, they would also have had the resources of the great library of St Maximin at Trier to draw upon. Trithemius, op. cit., p. 250, reports that in 1143 Abbot Gerhard of St Maximin took refuge at Disibodenberg during strife with Archbishop Albero. The Chronicler reports in his 1094 entry, that he himself has travelled through France and stayed at the monastery of Bec, whose culture of monastic humanism he extols. Cf. Constant J. Mews, 'Hildegard and the Schools', forthcoming in *Hildegard of Bingen: The Context of Her Thought and Art*, ed. by Charles Burnett and Peter Dronke (London: Warburg Institute, 1998).

basic meaning is 'teacher', but whereas the male *magister* was clearly just that in the context of a male monastery or school, and Hildegard did, through her prophetic role and her writings, achieve a certain parity with, if not superiority to, the 'Masters' of the schools, *magistra* in these documents usually implies a complex role of prioress, administrator and spiritual mother of the women. Thus its tonality is richer than 'teacher' would allow through. It is worth noting that whereas Klaes uses *Meisterin* to translate *magistra* she uses never *Lehrerin*.[24]

Virtus is also a Latin word used in a complex way in these documents. Its root meaning is 'strength' as in *vir*, but it covers a variety of kinds of 'strength', 'power', 'force', 'potency'. It is particularly important to be aware of this in *VH* III, subtitled: *de miraculis eius et virtutibus*, for its subject is not really so much about Hildegard's 'virtues' in the sense of proven strengths of character, as about instances of her charismatic powers of healing, prophecy, and exorcism. The way Theodoric uses *virtus* in the opening lines of *VH* III 23 shows he is consciously including different nuances under the one word. The translation here follows his example, so that the multi-valence of *virtus* is allowed to stand under the single English word 'virtue'.

Sapientia or 'Wisdom' I spell with a capital if it seems to refer to the personified 'Wisdom' of the Old Testament 'sapiental' books, and I use a feminine pronoun for it. This is to respect the importance of this motif in Hildegard's religious repertoire. Otherwise I leave the word in lower case: wisdom.

In translating Hildegard's demonology, as in *VH* III, 20–22, it is well to keep in mind what she says in *VH* III, 20. She seems to say that there is in a demoniac an inalienable core untouched by the devil, a domain where some kind of faithfulness can still go on and over which God keeps guard. Thus I respect the original Latin *obsessa* by translating it as 'obsessed' rather than 'possessed'. There seems a subtle difference between what is suggested by 'obsessed'—i.e. beset, blockaded, besieged, cut off, and on the other hand, 'possessed', which, at least in popular English usage, suggests the entire diabolic 'ownership' of the demoniac.

I wavered about how to translate Hildegard's description of Volmar in *VH* II, 2 as *diligentis intentionis*. An initial translation was 'earnest', but

---

[24] On the other hand, Staab consistently uses *Lehrerin* in his German introduction to and translation of the *VJ*.

in the end I conceded, particularly to Constant Mews, that the most authentic translation was 'loving'. Hildegard uses the same adjective of Richardis in *VH* II, 5 when she speaks of her 'loving' friendship. There is no reason to doubt that Hildegard and Volmar enjoyed an affectionate yet deeply religious and chaste *amicitia*/friendship, lasting for decades, from the time when they were both relatively young in the 1130s till Volmar died in 1173.[25]

Finally, there is the vocabulary used for dealing with monastic life and the Church. For one coming to the Hildegard documents from study of the *Regula Basili*, as is the present translator, there are some curious resonances, for example, *frater* (brother) is a far more common term than 'monk', *soror* than 'nun' (*monialis/monacha*), which scarcely ever appears, and *cenobium* than *monasterium*, which also rarely appears. *Cenobium* however, I usually translate here as 'monastery'. The title 'abbot' appears often enough, but, no doubt because Hildegard was never an abbess, the feminine form never occurs, nor for that matter does the

---

[25] Still, one might be permitted to marvel at this long-lived chaste friendship, which seems to have moved from a female disciple-male magister modality to that of mother-son. There are several testimonies in Hildegard's writings to her mingled reverence and affection for Volmar. In Volmar's one surviving letter to Hildegard, he expresses that mix of reverence (*venerari*) and affection/love (*diligere*) we might expect in such a relationship. Nevertheless, maturity in chastity never came by default, and there is a passage in *VJ* VI, where Volmar speaks of a certain *fidelis* struggling for chastity (for that is surely what it is about), which, of the three examples itemized in that context, seems most likely one he knows *experimento*, 'by experience'. And one might be permitted to wonder about Hildegard's tears in *VH* III, 9, which do not appear in the *Acta Inq.* VI version. Hildegard was nothing if not realistic and unsqeamish about what was involved in the struggle for chastity, or indeed for any other virtue, in whatever form of life. This appears in many texts throughout the *Scivias*. Concerning the fight required of virgins she says: 'she who desires my Son ... sets at naught the burning she endures, for the sake of his love, but perseveres in chastity, choosing not to be consumed by the fire ...' (Book II, Vision III, 23; Hart and Bishop, p. 178).

The proximity of men and women in the same monastic foundation, however well intentioned, regulated, and successfully lived, did at different times lead to trouble. Trithemius reports (*Chron. Sponh.*, pp. 243, 248, 253, 261, 267) on the *cella* for nuns attached to the monastery of Sponheim, which was eventually disbanded, and how in 1206 the Abbot asserted that it was dangerous for the souls of monks to have women living alongside the monastery. For another example of ambivalence about the proximity of monks and nuns, see S. Flanagan *Hildegard of Bingen 1098–1179: A Visionary Life*, p. 34. See also Trithemius's treatment of this question in the selection from the Chronicles of Sponheim translated in this volume.

later medieval term 'abbey'. Reminiscent of the alternation of *qui praeest*, 'he who presides', and *qui praesunt*, 'those who preside' in the *Regula Basili* is the fact that references to an abbot, even an archbishop, are often balanced with, sometimes even replaced with, plural forms such as 'the elders', 'the senior brothers', 'the brothers of wise counsel' or 'the prelates', 'the superiors'. The terms 'laity' and 'lay' scarcely ever appear; far more usual are *fidelis*, 'faithful', or *Christi fidelis*, 'Christ's faithful'. Characteristic of the time is the use of *Domnus* (lord) and *Domna* (lady) as customary titles of respect for those of higher rank. A very common term is *ecclesia*, i.e. literally 'church'. Thus in *VH* II, 5 Richardis is named the 'mother' (Hildegard avoids 'abbess') of *cuiusdam sublimis ecclesie*, literally 'of a certain *church*'. I translate *ecclesia* as 'community' when it concerns a monastic or religious house as in Richardis's case, and 'church' when referring to a diocese, a perhaps unfortunate distinction.

THE LIFE OF HOLY HILDEGARD

HERE BEGINS THE PROLOGUE TO THE LIFE OF THE HOLY VIRGIN HILDEGARD.

TO THE VENERABLE LORD Abbots, Ludwig and Godfrey, Theodoric, humble servant of the servants of God, greetings with devoted prayers.

Your authority has given me a command to assemble into order the life of the holy and God-beloved virgin Hildegard which Godfrey, a man of splendid talent, began in commendable style but did not finish, and, as if weaving a garland with sweet-scented flowers,[26] to edit her visions interwoven with her deeds[27] in the form of a single work divided into books.

It seemed to me that this task was much too hard for my capacities, and that it would even be an embarrassment if I, if you please, were to sit as some sort of judge and hold the power of sentence over another's work. But then it dawned in my diffident and anxious mind,[28] that the tasks a lack of skill might refuse, charity might undertake, and that it would be better to put up with the ridicule of others in shame than incur the danger of disobedience.

So I have obeyed with these provisions, that since the book of the man above mentioned occupies the position of first place, it should sustain no loss of its rank; next, that the second book should contain a very beautiful and wonderful tapestry of the visions of the holy virgin, the third a written account of the miracles which God wonderfully decreed to work through her which we have sifted, portioned out, and arranged. Thus the

---

[26] For this phrase cf. Thiofrid, *Flores Epitaphii*, 4, 7; PL 157, 399A; cf. Theodoric, *Chronicon Epternacense*, MGH SS 23, p. 47, line 37.

[27] *In ordinem colligere ... in unius formam redigere:* cf. Theodoric, *Chronicon Epternacense*, MGH SS 23, p. 38, line 22; p. 47, line 44.

[28] Cf. Theodoric, *Chronicon Epternacense*, MGH SS 23, p. 38, line 20.

honour of the earlier writer will not be diminished, and the attention of readers will be spurred on to true wisdom, heavenly vision, and divine virtue.[29]

For what good person will not be greatly touched and all the more roused to yearn after eternal life through a way of life that is holy, devout, and honourable, when he sees this jewel[30] resplendent in the setting of so many virtues, especially of virginity, patience, and teaching?[31] Therefore we have taken pains that *the shining lamp* of Christ[32] *should not be* put away in a secret place *under a bushel*, as though to hide it, *but that it be placed on a lampstand to shine for all in the house of God* (cf. Mat. 5:15) with sparkling examples of her history, her words, and her way of life for our imitation.

But if, through the ignorant rashness of the one obeying, there be anything that fails to satisfy, may the loving-kindness of the lords who gave the order overlook it. Let any defect be attributed to us who imagined in our earnestness that we could carry out so weighty a task, despite our real weakness, by dint of sheer hard work.

In order that the character of this same work might be more clearly evident, we write out this letter before it and append to it the chapter headings so that the reader may know more quickly what he ought to find there.

HERE ENDS THE PROLOGUE

HERE BEGIN THE CHAPTER HEADINGS OF THE FIRST BOOK

I   On the birth, oblation, and education of the holy virgin, and how

---

[29] Cf. Sulpicius Severus, *Vita S. Martini*, 1, 6, ed. by J. Fontaine, p. 252.

[30] The imagery of jewels is characteristic of Hildegard, e.g., in her *Symphonia Virginum*, where she expresses the longing of virgins to follow the Beloved: 'Yet we trust in you and in your desire to seek a jewel amid the dust.' cf. Flanagan, *Hildegard of Bingen, 1098-1179: A Visionary Life*, p. 119.

[31] *doctrin(a)e*; or learning, wisdom, understanding communicated; *virtutum* includes miraculous powers.

[32] This Gospel image, much expanded here, was also used by St Bernard about Hildegard before Pope Eugene. Cf. *VH* I, 4, Gregory, *Dialogues*, 2, 1 and Thiofrid, *Sermo de sanctorum reliquiis* (PL 157, 404A).

from the brightness of the divine light, she received illumination to write.[33]

II   How she made progress in monastic profession under the holy veil, although she had to endure the continual pains of her illnesses.

III   How she became ill when she hesitated about writing down the things revealed to her in spirit, but when she wrote at the urging of her Abbot, she recovered her health.

IIII   How Pope Eugene visited her with messengers and his own letter from Trier, and urged her to write down what she saw in spirit.

V   How she languished in sickness when she was held back from going with her young women to that place shown her from heaven.

VI   How she laboured under ill health whenever she hung back from performing the orders of the heavenly vision.

VII   How she acquired the place through purchase and exchange with the owners, and how she chose the Bishop of Mainz as her protector, and how, having been admonished,[34] she went and separated it from the community of Disibodenberg.

VIII   How she assumed the labour of the active life, yet preferred the better portion of the contemplative life, and how she wrote about the manner of her vision to Guibert, a monk of Gembloux.[35]

VIIII   How she had a marvellous and extremely rare kind of visionary seeing, and how she applied herself, at one time to the active mode, at another to the contemplative.

---

[33] Cf. Thiofrid, *Vita S. Willibrordi*, 2, ed. by J. Schmitz (Luxembourg: Beffort, 1898), p. 3.

[34] Guibert adds: 'by sickness'.

[35] Guibert expands: 'to the venerable Guibert, beloved in Christ, a monk of the community of Gembloux'.

BOOK ONE

HERE BEGINS THE FIRST BOOK OF THE LIFE OF SAINT HILDEGARD THE VIRGIN BELOVED OF GOD

I

WHEN HENRY, THE FOURTH Emperor[36] of this name, ruled the Roman Empire, a virgin was born in the nearer parts of Gaul,[37] as illustrious for her high birth as for her holiness, whose name was Hildegard. Her father, Hildebert, and her mother, Mechtild,[38] though much involved in worldly cares and renowned for their wealth, were not ungrateful for the gifts of the Creator, and set aside their daughter for the service of God.

Because of this, even in her earliest years a precocious purity seemed to very much withdraw her from all the normal ways of the worldly.[39] For as soon as she was able to attempt her first words she would describe to those around her, both in words and gestures, the shape of her hidden visions. In contrast to the common way of looking at things outside oneself, it was by an unusual kind of seeing that she gazed on these

---

[36] *In Romana re publica regnante Henrico nominis huius quarto augusto.* Henry IV, 1056–1106, was always 'king' but not always acknowledged by the Church as Emperor, being several times excommunicated. Hence the original *augusto* in T was recognized as a mistake and erased; it is missing in R, L.

[37] *In Galliae citerioris partibus.* This refers to the borders of Roman Gaul established by the Emperor Vespasian in 74 AD, which were west, or in this particular stretch, south of the Rhine. Mainz or *Castrum Moguntiacum* was the Romans' main frontier camp against the Germans in the area and Bingen itself was another of the Roman border towns. In the medieval German empire this area was called the Rhine Palatinate, situated in western Franconia. Swabia lay to the south, Saxony and Thuringia to the north and east, and lower Lotharingia (Lorraine) to the west and north. *VJ* II also speaks of Jutta's 'Gallic stock'. See Staab, 'Aus Kindheit', pp. 62–63, for the suggestion of points of contact between *VJ* and *VH* I–II.

[38] These names were originally missing in T and inserted by a later hand; they are also missing in Ep. 38. For other documentary evidence of Hildebert's existence, and Hildegard's place of origin, see *Documents of Sponheim* in this volume.

[39] *prematura sinceritas ab omni carnalium habitudine multum dissentire videretur.*

visions.[40]

When she was about eight years of age, she was enclosed at Disibodenberg with Jutta, a devout woman consecrated to God,[41] so that, by *being buried with Christ* (Rom. 6:3), she might rise with him to the glory of eternal life. Jutta carefully fitted her for a garment of humility and innocence, and, instructing her in the songs of David, showed her how to play on the ten-stringed psaltery.[42] For the rest, except for some simple psalm notation, Hildegard received no other teaching in the arts of literature or of music from a human source—although there exist now not a few of her own writings, and indeed several books of no mean size. As she says in the introduction of her own book *Scivias:*

> When I was forty-two years and seven months old, the heaven opened, and a fiery light of the greatest brilliance came forth and suffused my whole brain and my whole heart and breast with a flame. Yet it enkindled in a way that did not burn but warmed, just as the sun does when it warms anything on which it pours out its rays. And suddenly I savoured the meaning and interpretation of books, that is, the Psalter, the Gospel, and other Catholic books of both the Old and New Testament. All this came about even though I did not know how to analyze the syntax of the words,

---

[40] It seems about here that we would place the episode of the five-year-old Hildegard and the unborn calf, reported in *Acta Inq.* VIII, and apparently excluded from Theodoric's definitive 'fair-copy' of the *VH*.

[41] Guibert reads: '... with a virgin dedicated to God, the daughter of the count of Sponheim, Juttha by name'.

[42] *et carminibus tantum Daviticis instruens in psalterio dechacordo iubilare premonstrabat.* It is not quite clear whether the reference is to the actual playing of an instrument, or whether Godfrey is using the familiar allegory from Augustine's commentary on Psalm 150, where the 'ten-stringed psaltery' signifies the ten commandments. On this question see Barbara Newman, *Symphonia: A Critical Edition of the 'Symphonia armonie celestium revelationum'* (Ithaca: Cornell University Press, 1988), pp. 22–23. To 'play' (*iubilare*) an instrument at the time often involved skills of extemporization, by which individual notes were extended in melismatic cadences. A. Blaise, in *Lexicon Latinitatis Medii Aevi,* CCCM (Turnhout: Brepols, 1975), p. 513, quotes the twelfth-century author, Honorius Augustodunensis, who says in his *Gemma animae sive de divinis officiis,* 1, 14, *longam neumam cum organis jubilant, qui jubilum vocatur,* and *pneuma quod dicitur jubilum.* On Honorius, who may have been at some time a canon of Mainz, see V.I.J. Flint, *Honorius Augustodunensis of Regensberg,* Authors of the Middle Ages, 2, no. 6 (London: Variorum, 1995), and on Hildegard's possible contact with Honorius see Constant J. Mews, 'Hildegard and the Schools'.

or to divide their syllables[43] or had any knowledge of their cases or tenses.[44]

II

BUT TO RETURN TO my purpose. The virgin of Christ, once she had made her vow of monastic profession and attained to the blessing of the holy veil,[45] continued to make ever more progress, *advancing from virtue to virtue* (Ps. 83:8). And her venerable mother mentioned above, took pains over her and rejoiced in her progress as she began to perceive with wonder that from a disciple she too was becoming a *magistra* and a path-finder in the ways of excellence. So it came about that the benevolence of charity glowed in her breast, a benevolence which shut out no-one from its embrace. The rampart of her humility defended the tower (cf. Cant. 8:9–10) of her virginity. Likewise, she backed up her frugality of food and drink with meanness of clothing. So too, she showed the guarded tranquillity of her heart by her silence and fewness of words. Among all these *jewels* of the holy virtues which adorned the spouse of Christ, *fashioned by the most high Maker* (Cant. 7:1), the guardian that watched over them all was patience.[46]

But just as *a furnace tests the potter's vessel* (Eccli 27:6), and *virtue is made perfect in weakness* (2 Cor. 12:9), even so she did not lack, almost from her very infancy, the frequent and almost continual pains of weaknesses—so much so that she would have to force her very feet to walk. At times the life in her body flickered very low, and she then became, as it were, the image of the *death which is precious* (Ps. 115:15). But *as she weakened in the outer man, so did she grow stronger in the inner man* (cf. 2 Cor. 4:16) with the spirit of knowledge and fortitude. For even as her body away, the fervour of her spirit was wonderfully enkindled.

---

[43] A medieval Latin idiom for 'to spell'.

[44] Hildegard, *Scivias*, ed. by Führkötter, CCCM 43, Protestificatio, pp. 3–4, lines 25–35.

[45] *sacri velaminis benedictione provecta* (*b. perfecta*) *crescebat ...*

[46] *que omnia sanctarum monilia virtutum, summi fabricata manu artificis patientia custos in sponsa Christi exornando servabat.* I accommodate this ungrammatical sentence by reading the gerundive *exornanda* as in PL 197, 93. The list of virtues here parallels Sulpicius Severus, *Vita S. Martini*, 2, 7, ed. by J. Fontaine; cf. Klaes, pp. 96–97*

III

WHEN SHE HAD MATURED in her holy way of life for many years[47] and all her concern was to please God alone,[48] at last the time drew near for her life and teaching to be displayed for the benefit of many. She was divinely warned through a voice which came to her, that she should not delay to write down whatever she saw or heard. But she, from feminine bashfulness, shrank from becoming the butt of common gossip and the rash judgments of others. Even so, she was constrained by a still sharper goad to make haste and reveal the heavenly secrets shown her. Finally, having lain in a wasting illness a long time, in fear and humility she laid bare the cause of her scourge, firstly to a certain monk[49] whom she had chosen earlier as her *magister*, and through him, to the Abbot.[50]

Though the Abbot was perplexed for his part at the strangeness and the novelty of the matter, he was also aware that *nothing is impossible to God* (cf. Lk. 1:37, 18:27). So he conferred with the more prudent among his community, and decided that what he had heard should be tested. Having examined a number of points both from her writings and from her visions, he gave orders that she should make public what God had bestowed. As soon as she applied herself to the task of writing, which she had not learnt, she quickly recovered her usual measure of strength, and rose from her sick-bed. The Abbot was persuaded by this strange event and, not content with his own favourable judgment, saw to it that the matter should be brought to public notice. He went to Mainz, the metropolitan See, and before the venerable Archbishop Henry[51] and the cathedral chapter, made known what he had learned and showed them the writings which the blessed virgin had lately produced.

---

[47] Cf. Theodoric, *Chronicon Epternacense*, MGH SS 23, p. 50, line 6.

[48] Gregory, *Dialogues* 2, Prol., ed. by Adalbert de Vogüé, Sources Chrétiennes, 260 (Paris: Cerf, 1978), p. 126.

[49] Guibert adds: 'a man of chaste and religious life'.

[50] Conon or Cuno, Abbot of Disibodenberg 1136–1155.

[51] Archbishop Henry of Mainz 1142–1153. See the biographical note below.

IIII

NOW SHORTLY BEFORE THIS, the High Priest of the holy Roman See, Eugene of happy memory,[52] had solemnly concluded the universal Council at Rheims,[53] after which he had been invited by Adalbert the Archbishop of Trier, and so was staying at Trier. The prelate of Mainz and his senior clergy thereupon decided that they should journey to Trier and seek an apostolic judgment so that it could be ascertained by his authority what ought to be upheld and what rejected.[54]

---

[52] Bl. Eugene III (Bernardo Pignatelli of Pisa) 1145–1153, was among those sent from Clairvaux to make the first Cistercian foundation in Rome at Tre Fontane and became its first Abbot. As Pope he remained very much a dedicated and prayerful monk, vitally concerned with Church reform. St Bernard's *De consideratione* is addressed to him. Eugene was remarkable for his equanimity in the midst of the intense political chicanery that swirled about him. Taken aback at the loss of life in the failed second Crusade, he would not support St Bernard or Abbot Suger in their hopes of having it revived. The picture we have of him in *VH* I, 4 compares with a character sketch by Bl. Peter of Cluny: 'Never have I known a truer friend, a more trustworthy brother, a kinder father. His ear is ever ready to listen, and his tongue is quick and able in speech. And he carries himself not as one's superior, but rather as an equal or even as an inferior. There is no arrogance, no domineering, no regality: justice, reason and humility claim the whole man.' (cf. Alban Butler, *Lives of the Saints*, ed. by Herbert Thurston and Donald Attwater (New York: P.J. Kennedy & Sons, 1956), vol. 3, p. 45).

[53] Godfrey has confused councils here. Pope Eugene was in Trier because in fact the council was held there from 30 November 1147 to February 1148. It had been preceded by a preparatory council in Paris at Easter 1147, and was shortly followed by another at Rheims 21 March–7 April 1148. The council of Trier promoted church reforms, issuing canons implementing the decrees of the Lateran Council of 1139 and reorganized schools of philosophy and theology. In the subsequent council of Rheims, St Bernard would play a major role in having the Bishop of Poitiers, Gilbert de la Porrée, ordered to amend some of his theological propositions.

[54] The pro-monastic Archbishop Henry undertook Hildegard's cause at a time of acute tension between traditional (monastic) and modern (scholastic) tendencies in the Church. By helping to secure her recognition by the Pope, Henry was buttressing the monastic cause at a time when the news from the second Crusade was not good, and St Bernard's prophetic authority was under fire, especially from the Roman cardinals, some of whom were also supporters of Gilbert de la Porrée. Henry's successful action would have reinforced his own prestige as regent while Conrad III was on crusade. Later, Henry was almost alone in opposing the election of Frederick I (4 March 1152), who within a year (March 1153) engineered Henry's deposition from office. Hildegard took up his cause in a letter to Pope Eugene at the time (Ep. 5, Van Acker, pp. 11–13). Henry retired as a Cistercian monk—probably at Eberbach near Mainz, with which Hildegard had much

Now the Pope, who was possessed of great discretion, was astonished to hear of such a novelty. But since he too knew that *all things are possible to God* (cf. Lk. 1:37, 18:27) he was keen to investigate the matter more thoroughly. So he sent the venerable Bishop of Verdun, Albero[55] and with him his secretary Adalbert,[56] and other suitable persons, to the monastery where Hildegard had lived enclosed these many years. They were to find out[57] from her own person what it was about without any commotion or intrusive curiosity. So they put her at her ease as they made their enquiries, and she revealed without fear the facts concerning herself. They then returned to the Pope and reported what they had heard to him and all his attendants, who had been waiting most expectantly. Once the Pope had accepted the report, he gave orders that the blessed Hildegard's writings be presented publicly, for they had been brought from the monastery above mentioned and given to him. Holding them in his own hands and himself taking the part of reader, he publicly read them out to the Archbishop,[58] the Cardinals and all of the clergy present. Then, announcing the findings of the men he had sent to investigate these things, he roused the minds and voices of all to give praise and thanks to the Creator.

The Abbot of Clairvaux, Bernard of holy memory,[59] was also present on that occasion. While the others were much exercised over the matter

---

contact. Henry did not enjoy his monastic retirement for long, but, evidently exhausted, died late in that same year. Consequently, Hildegard gained her recognition through two Cistercians and a Cistercian to be. On the ideological and political context of the Council of Trier and its bearing on Hildegard's recognition, see Constant J. Mews, 'Hildegard and the Schools'.

[55] There is a lacuna at this point in T but the name of Albero II of Verdun can be supplied from other sources.

[56] Adalbert (Albert) I, who succeeded Albero as Bishop of Verdun in 1156.

[57] Guibert adds: 'reverently'.

[58] Presumably Archbishop Albero (or Adalbero) of Trier, no great friend of the monastic cause. At the time he was locked in conflict with the monks of St Maximin at Trier. See *AD* 1143, and Constant J. Mews, 'Hildegard and the Schools'.

[59] Guibert adds: 'a man of consummate piety and illustrious reputation'. St Bernard (1084–1153) was canonized by Pope Alexander III in 1174, which was fresh news at the time of Godfrey's *libellus*. For the surviving correspondence between St Bernard and St Hildegard see Ep. 1 and Ep. 1r, Van Acker, pp. 3–7; Baird and Ehrman, pp. 27–32. This exchange predates the Council of Trier by one or two years, which illustrates that to some extent Hildegard's name was not unknown even at that early stage.

he intervened and warned the supreme Pontiff not to allow *so luminous a lamp to be covered up* through silence (cf. Mat. 5:15), but that if the Lord wanted to manifest at this time so great a charism, it ought to be confirmed by his authority. At this, the reverend Father of Fathers gave an assent as kindly as it was wise, and visited the blessed virgin with a letter of greeting[60] in which under Christ and in the name of blessed Peter, he granted her permission to make known whatever she learnt through the Holy Spirit and encouraged her to put it into writing.[61] He honoured the place which had nurtured her, sending a letter of most generous congratulations to the Abbot and the brothers of the monastery, in his own name.[62]

V

SO WITH THE MOST humble assurance blessed Hildegard opened up and dispersed far and wide the fair fragrance of a holy reputation through the words which she had received neither from nor through any human source. Not a few wealthy daughters of the nobility began to flock to her to be initiated into religious life according to a rule. Since an anchoress's single small dwelling could scarcely house them all, she was soon engaged in a quest for more spacious quarters to which they might transfer.

She was shown by the Spirit a place where the river Nahe flows into the Rhine, a hill dedicated in days of old to the name of St Rupert the Confessor, which he had once inherited by right of patrimony, and where he happily spent his life in the work and service of God, along with his blessed mother, whose name was Bertha, and the holy confessor Guibert.

---

[60] This letter is not extant. For the surviving correspondence between Pope Eugene and Hildegard see Ep. 2–6, Van Acker, pp. 7–16; translated in Baird and Ehrman, pp. 27–32. In her Letter 2, the earliest to survive, Hildegard speaks of the embassy sent her from Trier and the Pope's letter of approval and encouragement subsequently sent her.

[61] *...litteris salutatoriis beatam virginem visitavit, in quibus concessa sub Christi et beati Petri nomine licentia proferendi, quecumque per Spiritum sanctum cognovisset, eam ad scribendum animavit.*

[62] Only Godfrey offers this information, which illustrates well the Disibodenberg perspective of his reportage. In the charter of Pope Eugene III, dated Metz, 18 February 1148 as it survives, there is no mention of Hildegard or of any congratulations to Abbot Cuno and the monks.

From his tomb and relics there, St Rupert's name had become attached to the vicinity.

When the virgin of God learned of the place they were to move to—not with the eyes of the body but with inward vision—she made it known to her abbot and the brothers. But they were unenthusiastic; indeed, they could scarcely tolerate the thought of her going at all. Thereupon Hildegard fell into a long illness, much like the one before, and did not rise from her bed till the abbot and the others acknowledged that it was by divine command they were being urged to give their consent. They then ceased to oppose her, and indeed strove to help her as much as they could.

There was one of them, Arnold, a layman turned monk[63] who resisted the project most obstinately, and seemed to be stirring up the others to opposition. But when visiting a property of the monastery, the Weiler estate,[64] he was suddenly struck by so great a distress of body that he despaired of life itself. His tongue swelled up so grossly that he could not close his mouth over it. But he asked by signs, as best he could, to be carried to the church of St Rupert. As soon as he vowed there that he would not stand in the way any longer but would strive to help all he could, he immediately recovered his health. He began to be of assistance[65] to those preparing the quarters, and with his own hands cleared the vineyards around the site where the houses suitable for receiving the nuns were being built.

Because of the delays in carrying out the divine command, she for whose migration these dwellings were being prepared lay sick and utterly paralyzed, like a pile of heavy stones. No one could budge her from the bed on which she had collapsed. The Abbot found it hard to believe those who told him of it, and went in to see for himself. He tried with all his strength to raise her head, or to move her with a lever onto her side, but for all his efforts he accomplished nothing. He was so astonished at the strange phenomenon, that he concluded this was no ordinary human illness, but rather a divine chastisement. From then on, he would not offer

---

[63] *ex laico monachus.* The common term at the time for a 'lay-brother' is *conversus*, and for a lay-person *fidelis.*

[64] Weiler bei Bingerbrück, a property near Bingen given to the Disibodenberg monks by a *domina Bertha* and her son *Engelboldt.* See the 1128 charter of Adalbert, the 1148 charter of Eugene III, and Klaes, p. 99*, n. 169.

[65] Cf. Gregory, *Dialogues* 2, 3, ed. by A. de Vogüé, p. 150.

any more opposition to the divine decree, lest he himself incur something worse.

Since the above mentioned site belonged partly to the canons of the church of Mainz, and the estate with the oratory of St Rupert was the possession of Count Bernard of Hildesheim,[66] an embassy of loyal retainers acted between them, and the virgin of God, having foreknown[67] it, obtained authorization for herself and her sisters to take up residence there.

VI

AND SO, AFTER HER long inability to walk, at last both parties considered that she and her sisters should be sent out to the place which she had already foreseen in spirit. The Abbot came in to her as she lay there in her affliction and told her in the Lord's name to rise up and go forth to the dwelling place prepared for her by heaven. At this she rose up very sprightly as if she had not at all been disabled for so long a time. Amazement and wonder seized all who were present.

And not undeservedly, for the circumstances which had attended her sick-bed were no less amazing. For from the time that the Saint received the heavenly command to change her place of dwelling, whenever the project seemed to move toward fulfilment, she would experience alleviation of her bodily suffering, while on the other hand, whenever she observed that the business was quashed through the blocking tactics of its opponents, she would suffer all the more severely. Sometimes she would suddenly rise from her bed and walk round all the corners and rooms of the anchorhold, all the while unable to speak.[68] Then with faltering step

---

[66] Bernard (1110–1155) died during Frederick I's first trip to Italy. Though he is called 'Count' both here and in the Rupertsberg Inventory of 1200, in the first charter of Arnold of Mainz (1158) he is called *vicedomnus* 'deputy' or 'steward'. J. Hotchin refers to him as Jutta's nephew in 'Images and Their Places: Hildegard of Bingen and Her Communities', *Tjurunga*, 49 (1996), p. 29, n. 17.

[67] Guibert adds: 'what was going to happen in these matters she was concerned about'.

[68] Hildegard reveals her acute personal distress at this time in her letter 74r to Abbot Cuno: 'I know for a fact that God moved me from that place for his own inscrutable purposes, because my soul was so agitated by his words and miracles that I believe I would have died before more time if I had remained there.' Ep. 74r, Van Acker, p. 162; Baird and Ehrman, p. 163.

she would return to her bed, and at once be able to speak as before. She laboured under this kind of illness not only at that time, but, as often as she hung back in feminine alarm or doubted that the purposes of the divine will would be achieved, she drew on these alternations as an argument in her own person of the assured outcome.[69]

VII

AT LAST, THE HANDMAID of God left the place of their original dwelling together with eighteen young women consecrated to God. And if her legacy to those she was leaving was one of sadness and tears, to the district she was now entering she brought joy and exultation. For ahead of her in the town of Bingen and nearby villages, there were many of distinguished rank as well as no small number of common folk, all of whom went out to welcome her, with much dancing and singing of the divine praises. When she and her, or rather Christ's, little flock entered the place prepared for them, in the spontaneous devotion of her heart she glorified the divine Wisdom who disposes all things. She nurtured the virgin nuns committed to her charge with motherly affection, and never ceased to instruct them wisely in the rules of the order.[70]

So that it might not seem that she had taken over and occupied what properly belonged to another, she secured her new abode from its former owners partly by purchase and partly by an exchange of property, using the offerings of the faithful which the fame of her reputation had attracted. Once she had obtained it freehold, she made sure it would always remain freehold; since it was subject to the protection of the church of Mainz, she would have no other defender than one from the Bishop's See itself. Otherwise, if she were to take on a lay advocate, she might seem be to be hiring a wolf in sheep's clothing. It was in just this way that many churches in Christendom had been afflicted and laid waste as by a common plague.

She maintained herself and her daughters in this much deference

---

[69] *quotiensque feminea trepidatione tardasset vel dubitasset superne voluntatis peragere negotia hoc certitudinis in se capiebat argumentum.*

[70] Cf. *Regula S. Benedicti juxta S. Hildegardim explicata,* PL 197, 1053–66, and Feiss (tr.), *Explanation of the Rule of St Benedict by Hildegard of Bingen,* (Toronto: Peregrina, 1990).

towards the authorities of the monastery from which they had come: that they would look to them rather than elsewhere[71] for their spiritual needs, that is, concerning the character of holy order or the profession of monastic life. And as circumstances and times required it, they would receive priests from the monastery whom they themselves had asked for by name according to their individual and free choice.[72] These were to support them as much through the care of souls and the celebration of the holy liturgy as through the administration of temporal goods.

The venerable Henry[73] and Arnold,[74] Metropolitans of Mainz not only gave their permission and counsel to these provisions but decreed and ratified them in writing with the consent of abbots, so that by the authority of privileges[75] the community of St Disibod was precluded from usurping a right over the estates of St Rupert, or to put it more accurately, was forbidden to do so by the Divine power on high.

The virgin herself, realizing by inward revelation that such serious negotiations required her to go to back to the monastery itself, hung back at first through alarm like the prophet Jonah. But she was struck by the whip of divine reproof and became sick almost to the point of death. So, being chastised under this lash she had herself conveyed to the oratory and there vowed to go wherever God might order her to go, if only his blows might cease. She then asked that she be placed on a horse and supported by hands be led off. As soon as she had been led a very little way along the road she recovered her strength and went gladly on her way.

When she reached Disibodenberg, she explained why she was compelled to come, and, while there, separated the place of her new

---

[71] *que de spiritualibus, hoc est de ordinis tenore et de monachatus professione querenda essent, ab eis potius quam aliunde susciperent.*

[72] These arrangements were confirmed in a letter from Pope Alexander III (1159–1181) to Wezelin, Hildegard's nephew and Abbot of St Andrew in Cologne, through whom Godfrey of Disibodenberg the present author was eventually sent to Rupertsberg. Ep. 10r, Van Acker, pp. 25–26; Baird and Ehrman, pp. 46–47.

[73] See in *Documents of Rupertsberg* the 1152 Charter of Henry, Archbishop of Mainz (1142–1153), who gave Hildegard personally and her foundation at Rupertsberg much moral and practical support.

[74] See the two charters of Arnold, Archbishop of Mainz (1153–1160) dated 22 May 1158.

[75] *privilegiorum* refers to a technical legal transaction conferring rights, such as exemption, and duties on named parties.

monastery along with some other properties belonging to her community, from the brothers of that monastery, but left to them the larger portion of possessions which had been given to it when the sisters had been first received, and in addition left them a not inconsiderable sum of money so that there might remain no just cause for complaint.[76]

VIII

BUT LET ME TAKE up again what the sequence of her story requires. Although the blessed Hildegard often suffered in herself the *throbbing birth-pangs* of Leah, nonetheless she feasted with the *bright eyes* of *fair Rachel* on the light of an inward visionary seeing (cf. Gen. 29). Whatever she saw interiorly, she spread abroad in speech and writing as far as she knew how to do so.

Now as to the nature of her vision, or the mode of her seeing, it is known to have been very rare, and even unique among even the greatest saints while in the shadow of this mortal life. Therefore it is fitting that something more be said about it. Let us inform ourselves chiefly by means of her own words, insofar as she was able to make it public. She speaks in this way in a letter which she wrote to Guibert, a monk[77] of Gembloux, who had enquired about the truth of the reports he had heard about her. She said:

---

[76] Hildegard's brief and sharp Letter 75 to Abbot Cuno suggests that this visit to Disibodenberg was more tumultuous and acrimonious than Godfrey presents here, though it does reveal she had a party of supporters among the monks. See Ep. 75, Van Acker, pp. 162–63; Baird and Ehrman, pp. 162–63. The cause of the financial tension between the monks and the nuns was the property which had passed to Disibodenberg when the sisters were received there. Hildegard is telling the monks that she gives them back these possessions in large part and then effectively buys out the rest so that they could not complain again.

[77] Guibert adds: 'afterwards Abbot of the same community'. Guibert or Wibert was a Walloon monk, whose own monastic situation being rather desperate, and, consumed with curiosity about what he had heard of her, wrote Hildegard several questioning letters. He edited them into a collection at the end of his life: see Ep. 16–22, Derolez, pp. 216–50. The following quotation is taken from her first, long reply to him, *Epistola ad Guiberti de modo visionis sue*, Ep. 103r, Van Acker 2, pp. 258–65. Subsequently, he succeeded in a scheme to emigrate to Rupertsberg and spent the last two years of her life as Hildegard's faithful companion and friend. See the introductions to Ep. 38 and to Guibert's revision of *VH* in this volume.

God works wherever he wills, for the glory of his own name and not that of earthly man. For my own part, I am always in trembling fear, because I derive no assurance from any capacity in me. Instead *I stretch out my hands to God* (cf. Ps. 142:5) that I might be sustained by him, just as a feather lacking all force of its own strength flies upon the wind. What I behold in vision I cannot fully understand as long as I am in the condition of the body and in an invisible soul, since in these two a human being is weak.

Still, I have always seen this vision in my soul, even from my infancy, when my bones and nerves and veins had not yet grown strong, up to the present time, though I am now more than seventy years of age. And in this vision my soul, as God wills it, ascends to the height of the vault and the shifting patterns of the variable air, and spreads itself out over the various peoples, though they are in distant regions and places far away from me. And because I see these things in my soul in such a way, I survey them according to the changing form of the clouds and other created things. Moreover, I do not see these things with my outward eyes or hear them with my outward ears or perceive them with the thoughts of my heart or through any contribution of the five senses, but only in my soul, for my outward eyes remain open, and I do not undergo the unconsciousness of ecstasy, but see them wide awake, by day and by night.

VIIII

FROM THE PRECEDING WORDS we can gather how truly wonderful and very rare was this holy virgin's mode of visionary seeing. To use the image of those sacred beasts that Ezechiel saw, she was like *the winged animal, that moved forward and did not turn back; and then again, it moved forward and did turn back* (Ezech. 1:9, 14).[78] So Hildegard herself would not turn back from the active life, which she knew well, to anything of a baser nature. On the other hand, she could not remain absorbed in the contemplative life, for she was still bound to the body. So we can say that from the contemplative life to the active life, she *did* turn back.[79] It is as if God were saying to her concerning the mode of the

---

[78] Cf. Thiofrid, *Vita S. Liutwini* 2, p. 9, and 10, p. 27, ed. by W. Lampen, Collectanea franciscana neerlandica, 3/6 ('s Hertogenbosch: Teulings, 1936); *Vita S. Willibrordi*, 29, ed. by J. Schmitz, p. 35.

[79] Gregory the Great's *Homilies on Ezechiel* 1:5, 12 (*Corp. Christ. Ser. Lat.* 142, pp. 63–

active life: *I will not leave you or abandon you* (Heb. 13:5), that is, he did not allow her to turn back from her worthy way of life, while on the other hand, it was as if he were saying to her concerning the mode of contemplative life: *turn aside your eyes, for they cause me to fly away* (Cant. 5:5), that is, he allowed her to turn back from gazing on his incomprehensible majesty, to the labour of her everyday life. '*Turn aside your eyes*', he asks 'from the contemplation of me, *for they cause me to fly away*, because in this life they are not capable of perfectly knowing me.' On this point the psalmist also has something to say: *A man comes to his deep heart, and God shall be exalted* (Ps. 63:7–8). For what is found deeper than a pure heart, what more sublime than that the incomprehensible should be comprehended?[80] In this way while the blessed virgin was still in the flesh she both laboured in the active life, and in the contemplative life gazed with all her desires on the very light inaccessible of the Divinity.

Now as we make an ending of this first book, let us bless the Lord who looked upon his chosen handmaid from the very beginning when she was born, and raised her, his beloved one, even to the brightness of his vision.

HERE ENDS THE FIRST BOOK OF THE LIFE OF THE VIRGIN SAINT HILDEGARD

---

64 and PL 96, 826B).

[80] Bede, *On the Canticle of Canticles* 4, 6, 4 (*Corp. Christ. Ser. Lat.* 119B, p. 303).

BOOK TWO

HERE BEGINS THE PROLOGUE OF THE SECOND BOOK

SMALL TALENTS, SURELY, ARE insufficient for great enterprises,[81] yet the love and obedience by which I declare I am always and wholly bound to you Ludwig and Godfrey, most worthy of abbots, raise my mind from impossibilities to attempt what is possible. Therefore, though unsupported by any talent of my own, I have obeyed your behests in the love of Christ, and taken over arranging and completing, as God may prosper it, the second book on the Life of the blessed virgin Hildegard, a book bestrewn with secret and mysterious visions as with pleasant flowers. I begin at that place where Godfrey of worthy memory finished the preceding book.

In this book, the words of the God-beloved virgin herself radiate such a light of prophecy that she seems to have received no less a grace than did the Fathers of long ago. For example, just as we read that Moses *tarried in the Tent of Meeting* (cf. Ex. 24:18, 32:1, 34:34), she also lingered in the bower of heavenly visions, in order that she, like him, might learn something from God to impart to her hearers. For was she not delayed in the heavenly tabernacle, and did she not transcend the cloud of all worldliness when the Spirit of Truth taught her the text and the words of the Gospel of John: *In the beginning was the Word*, etc.? (Jn 1:1) For this same Holy Spirit who flowed into the heart of John when he sucked this profoundest of revelations from the breast of Jesus, desired, through the manifold[82] grace of his majesty to teach *her* what John was worthy to announce.

But let us leave off speaking of these things for the time being, and deal with what we have proposed to do, as this same Spirit shall inspire.

May the reader not take it amiss if some things already written down in the preceding book of the Life are repeated in the following work on her visions. In order to preserve the proper order in the telling of her history, we thought it fitting that in the description of her visions we should not

---

[81] Thiofrid, *Vita S. Liutwini*, Prol., ed. by W. Lampen, p. 1.

[82] *divisivam* 'divided, allocated'; *divinam* 'divine' Bt, corrected afterwards to *divinam* in T. For the same form of word cf. Rupert of Deutz, *In Ez.* 1:9, CCCM 23, p. 1654, line 431.

tamper in any way with the authority and integrity of her own words, brought forth as they were by the Holy Spirit.

We first of all preface the chapter headings to this book as well, so that the subjects which follow may be found more easily in their proper places.[83]

HERE ENDS THE PROLOGUE

HERE BEGIN THE CHAPTER HEADINGS OF THE SECOND BOOK

---

[83] Cf. Theodoric, *Chronicon Epternacense*, MGH SS 23, p. 47, line 48.

BOOK TWO

HERE BEGINS THE SECOND BOOK IN WHICH THE VISIONS OF THE HOLY
VIRGIN ARE INSERTED

I

ONCE THE BLESSED VIRGIN had moved to that place to which she had
been divinely ordered, she finished the book of her visions[84] which she
had begun at Disibodenberg. Moved by the spirit of prophecy, she also
composed certain books on the nature of man, the elements and the
variety of created things, and how human beings might derive help from
this knowledge, and many other secrets.

Anyone who would ponder deeply the character of her words brought
forth from divine revelation, can clearly see with what discretion she
replied to the letters sent her from various regions. These letters, it might
be added, both her own and those sent to her, have been gathered into a
single volume.

Moreover, who would not marvel that she composed chant of the
sweetest melody with a wonderful harmony, or that she produced an
alphabet not seen before and a language never heard before? Besides
these she explained some of the Gospels and composed other allegorical
commentaries. The *Key of David, who opens and none shall shut, who
closes and none shall open* (cf. Apoc. 3:7) had opened to her all these
things, giving her soul cause to be glad and to sing that the King had *led
her into his cellar* (Cant. 1:3 Vulg.) to be *inebriated with the riches of his
house*, and to *drink from the torrent of his delight* (Ps. 35:9).[85] And so
she, as it is written, *conceiving* of the fear of the Lord gave birth and
made the spirit of salvation to be upon the earth (cf. Is. 26:18).

How great a thing it is and worthy of admiration that whatever she saw
or heard in spirit, with the same sense and in the same words, and with a
careful and pure mind, she wrote down in her own hand, or orally dictated

---

[84] This was her first major theological work, *Scivias*, composed between 1141–1151.

[85] Cf. Thiofrid, *Vita S. Liutwini* 1, ed. by W. Lampen, p. 7.

their content to one faithful male collaborator,[86] who then rendered their cases, tenses, and conjugations according to the exactness of the grammatical art which she did not know,[87] while he presumed neither to add nor subtract anything to their sense or meaning.

Concerning this matter she even wrote to Pope Adrian[88] that in a heavenly vision she heard the following said to her:

> Whenever something is shown to you from on high in familiar human form, you shall not publish it in the Latin language yourself, for this familiarity is not given to you. Rather, let him who has a file[89] not neglect to finish it off in a form pleasing to the human ear.

II

IT SEEMS FITTING TO insert at this point some of the writings from her

---

[86] *et ore edidit uno solo fideli viro symmista contenta*; i.e. Volmar, a monk of Disibodenberg, Hildegard's secretary and *magister*. Klaes, pp. 128–29*, examines the use of *symmista*, tracing it back from Theodoric through Thiofrid of Echternach's *Vita S. Willibrordi* Ch. 7, to Letters 58 and 66 of St Jerome. It appears in the greeting formula of a letter from Volmar to Hildegard (Ep. 195, Van Acker 2, p. 443; Pitra, p. 346) 'To the reverend Domna Hildegard, most sweet mother, most holy magistra and co-worker of God (*symmistae Dei*)...'

[87] There are grounds for not accepting Hildegard's presentation of her 'ignorance' entirely at face value. Klaes on p. 130*, n. 262 gives Herwegen's assessment (I translate from the French): 'We are rather of the opinion that when Hildegard began to write, she had only a very basic knowledge of Latin, but through constant practice acquired a more than adequate knowledge of it' ('Collaborateurs', p. 95). Dronke (*Women Writers*, p. 194) assesses Hildegard's Latin in a letter written to Abbot Ludwig in the mid 1170s: 'It is an elaborate letter in thought and language. Here, late in life, we see how Hildegard had acquired the power to construct complex, fluent and fluid sentences, apparently quite unaided: she was just then without a secretary, and the text shows no trace of reworking by another hand.' See Führkötter's summary (translated from the German) of scholarly analysis of Hildegard's authorship and Volmar's editorship, in *The Life of the Holy Hildegard*, trans. by James McGrath (Collegeville, Minnesota: Liturgical Press, 1995), n. 30.

[88] Ep. 8 *Hildegardis ad Anastasium papam*, Van Acker, pp. 19–22; Baird and Ehrman, pp. 41–43. The nomination of Pope Adrian as the addressee is an error. It seems Theodoric has 'clarified' the passage by adding the words 'in the Latin language', which are not found in the independent transmission of the letter.

[89] I.e. of literary 'polish'.

visions. Then we shall see how appropriately that line from the Song of Songs may be applied to her: *My Beloved sent forth his hand through the key-hole, and my entrails trembled at his touch* (Cant. 5:4). These writings of hers are as follows. She says:

FIRST VISION

In mystical vision and in the light of love, I both heard and saw these words concerning Wisdom which shall never fail:[90]

The five tones of righteousness resound, sent forth to the human race from God, in which are established the salvation and redemption of believers. These five tones transcend all human works, for all human works are themselves nourished by them; for there are those who do not heed the sounds, yet it is with the help of these tones that all the works of man are brought to fruition in the five senses of his body. And their sequence is like this:

The first tone was accomplished through the sacrifice of faithful Abel which he immolated to God.

The second was when Noah built an ark at God's command.

The third was through Moses when the Law was given to him, which was sealed in the circumcision that came from Abraham.

But in the fourth tone, the Word of the most high Father descended into the womb of the Virgin and put on flesh, for this was the same Word who had combined clay with water and thus fashioned man. Therefore, every created thing has cried out through man to the same Word who made it, so that for man's sake God has carried all things in Himself. Indeed at one time He created man, and at another time He carried him, so that he might attract to Himself all whom the serpent's guile had caused to be lost.

The fifth tone shall be accomplished when every error and provocation is brought to an end. Then human beings shall see and understand that no-one can do anything against the Lord.

In such a way the Old and New Testaments shall be brought to fruition in the five tones sent forth from God, and the marvellous number of human beings shall be filled up. And after these five tones a certain season of brilliant light shall be granted by the Son of God, such that he shall be acknowledged openly by all flesh.

After this, the Divinity shall be at work in itself, for as long as it wills.

---

[90] Cf. Hildegard, Ep. 16r (To Archbishop Philip of Cologne), Van Acker, pp. 49–51; Baird and Ehrman, pp. 66–67.

Wisdom teaches me in the light of love, and bids me tell how I was established in this vision. It is not I who tell these words about myself but rather true Wisdom who tells them about me, and this is how she[91] spoke to me: 'Listen O human creature[92] to these words and tell them not according to yourself but according to me; taught by me, you shall speak about yourself like this:'

When I was first fashioned, when in my mother's womb God raised me up with the breath of life, he impressed this vision in my soul.[93] For by the one thousand and one hundredth year after the Incarnation of Christ, the teaching of the Apostles and the burning righteousness which he had established in Christians and in the spiritual,[94] began to slacken and turn to wavering. It was in those times I was born, and my parents, with sighs[95] promised me to God. In my third year of age I saw so great a light that my soul trembled,[96] but, because I was still an infant, I could not convey anything about it.

In my eighth year I was offered to God for a spiritual way of life, and until my fifteenth year I used to see many things and often spoke about them in my simplicity, so that those who heard them wondered where they might be coming from or from whom. Then I too wondered at it in myself, that while I beheld these things inwardly in my soul, I yet had my outward sight as well, and I did not hear this of anyone else. So I concealed the

---

[91] One of the important motifs of Hildegard's theology is the feminine image of personified Wisdom as found in the Old Testament sapiential books, esp. Proverbs 8–9, Wisdom 7–9, Sirach 24. The orthodox medieval mind well knew how to play a full-blooded allegory which engaged all the emotions (consider St Francis's 'Lady Poverty'), without slipping the moorings of revealed faith into a gnostic rip-current, and supposing that the imaged persona of the virtue or quality had a hypostatic existence. However, what makes personified Wisdom a special case in the history of Christian theology is that it is one of the scriptural antecedents of the Logos of Jn 1:1–3; Newman touches on some of the issues in *Sister of Wisdom: St Hildegard's Theology of the Feminine* (Berkeley: University of California Press, 1987), esp. pp. 42–46.

[92] *audi O homo.*

[93] Cf. the beginning of Hildegard's letter to the prelates of Mainz, Ep. 23, Van Acker, pp. 61–66; Baird and Ehrman, p. 76.

[94] Guibert puts it: '... in the Christian people and in spiritual persons (*hominibus*)'; see Hildegard, *LDO* 3, 5, 7, CCCM 92, p. 416 (3, 10, 7, PL 197, 1005B/C), where she speaks of the times degenerating into 'womanly weakness' (*muliebri debilitate*).

[95] *suspiriis me vovebant.* Note that the verb is in the imperfect. According to Ep. 38, V and VI, her parents thought of offering their tenth child to God as a tithe, but they took some time to decide on a suitable way of doing it.

[96] Guibert adds: 'in my entrails'.

vision I saw in my soul for as long as I could, and was ignorant of many outward events because of a recurring ailment I have suffered from my mother's milk until now, which wore out my flesh and sapped my strength.

I was quite exhausted by these things and asked my nurse if she could see anything apart from outward objects. 'Nothing' she then replied, because she saw none of them. Then, seized by a great fear, I did not dare to tell about these things to anyone—although in my conversations and my lessons I used to announce many things about the future. And on occasions when I was completely inundated by this vision, I would say many things which were strange to my hearers, and I behaved more like an infant than one of my years. But when the force of the vision ebbed somewhat, I blushed profusely and often wept, and often would have gladly kept silent if I had been allowed. But because of my fear of people at the time, I did not dare to tell of the manner in which I saw. Nevertheless, a certain noblewoman to whom I had been entrusted for instruction, observed these things and laid them before a certain monk known to her.[97]

God poured out his grace in this woman like a river of many waters, so that she granted her body no respite from vigils, fastings, and other good deeds, until she completed this present life with a worthy end. God showed her merits afterwards by certain beautiful signs.[98] After her death, I continued seeing as before,[99] till my fortieth year of age.

Then in this same vision I was constrained by the great pressure of my pains to reveal openly what I had seen and heard. But I was very afraid, and blushed at the thought of proclaiming what I had kept silent about for so long. Nevertheless, from then on my veins and my marrow were filled with the strength which I had lacked from my infancy and youth. I told these things to a certain monk, my *magister*, who was of a worthy way of life[100] and a loving disposition, and a stranger, as it were, to the prying ways of many people, so that he listened generously to these strange tales. He marvelled at them, and ordered me to discreetly write them out until he

---

[97] *et cuidam sibi monacho noto monacho aperuit.*

[98] See Ep. 38, VIII for the events subsequent to Jutta's burial. Perhaps the most remarkable of these signs is Hildegard's own vision of the journey of Jutta's soul to heaven; see *VJ* IX. Hildegard has no need to dwell at length on Jutta since she had already instigated a memorial to her *magistra* in the writing of the Life of Jutta. See the introduction to the *VJ*, Genesis and Authorship.

[99] *Ita permansi videns.*

[100] *qui bone conversationis*; *conversatio* (='way of life') refers to the character of his monastic life. See *RB* 58, 17 for the monk's vow of *conversatio morum*.

could see what they were and where they came from. But as soon as he concluded that they were from God, he made them known to his Abbot, and from then on was very keen to work with me in these things.

In this vision I understood without any human instruction the writings of the prophets, of the Gospels, and of other saints and[101] of certain philosophers, and I expounded a number of their texts, although I had scarcely any knowledge of literature, since the woman who taught me was not a scholar. Then I also composed and sang chant with melody, to the praise of God and his saints, without being taught by anyone, since I had never studied neumes or any chant at all.

When these things had been brought to the hearing of the church of Mainz and discussed, they all declared that they were from God and from the prophecy which[102] the prophets of old had prophesied. Then my writings were taken to Pope Eugene while he was staying in Trier. He was pleased to have them read publicly before many, and read them out himself. Putting great trust in God's grace, he sent his blessing along with a letter, and ordered[103] me to carefully commit to writing whatever I saw or heard in vision.

III

WE CAN GATHER CLEARLY from this very beautiful vision of the blessed virgin, from her account of the fear that seized her at the approach of the Holy Spirit, and also from the apostolic blessing and her commission to write down what she had received, that it was truly her *beloved* heavenly spouse, Jesus Christ, who *sent forth his hand* (Cant. 5:4) that is, the operation and inspiration of the Holy Spirit, *through the key-hole*, that is, through his secret grace, and *her entrails*, by which is meant her mind, *trembled at his touch*, that is, at the infusion of his grace, because of the unexpected vitality of the Spirit and the force of it, which she felt

---

[101] This significant 'and' is missing from R and the PL text, where the sense is 'and of certain other holy philosophers'.

[102] *quam ... prophetaverant*. This accusative relative pronoun may be an instance of Hildegard's Latin which escaped her editor's attention. Guibert corrects it to an ablative *qua ... prophetaverant*, 'with which ...'

[103] *Precepit*. In Godfrey's account (*VH* I, 4), Pope Eugene simply grants her a *licentia* ('permission'), and then personally encourages her (*animavit*) to write.

within.[104] What text is more apt, what more fitting? Just as the *gentle whisper of a breeze* (1 Kg. 19:12) came to Elijah as the sign of a more intimate visitation of God, so also whenever she was rapt in the heights of contemplation, her mind savoured the sweetness of the Divine Spirit.

And what did she do? *I arose*, she says, *that I might open to my Beloved* (Cant. 5:5). O virgin truly blessed, of whom as it is written that, because *she loved purity of heart, grace was on her lips, and so she has for a friend the King* (Prov. 22:11, cf. Ps. 44:2–3,11), that is Christ, from whom she received so great a gift! Since the Holy Spirit *breathes where he wills* (Jn 3:8) and *distributes to each as he wills* (1 Cor. 12:11), and since he was willing to endow her so abundantly, how could she not *rise up to open to her Beloved*? To refuse she was not able. Therefore *she opens the latch of her door to her Beloved*, and now with her voice, now by her writing, proclaims abroad what she has heard within. And what did she hear within? *Let your fountains be dispersed abroad, and in the streets distribute your waters* (Prov. 5:16).

IIII

ACCORDINGLY, WHEN SHE BEGAN to abound with overflowing streams of good works as with the rivers of Paradise, crowds of people of both sexes came flocking to her,[105] not only from the whole neighbourhood, but from

---

[104] *et venter eius, scilicet mens sua, ad tactum eius, hoc est ad infusionem gratie sue, intremuit ob insolitum vigorem Spiritus et pondus, quod interius sensit.* Theodoric applies to Hildegard the interpretation of this verse coming from Abbot Rupert of Deutz, for whom the 'key-hole' text suggests a divine gift enabling one to expound the word of Scripture to others due to a knowing inwardly infused by God in contemplative prayer. This is a sense of the text not commonly found in other medieval writers. See Rupert of Deutz, *Comm. In Canticum Canticorum* 5, and *Comm. Super Mattheum* 12 (PL 168, 914a, 1611c). For Theodoric's use of Rupert, see Klaes, p. 131*, and Barbara Newman, 'Hildegard and Her Hagiographers', in *Gendered Voices: Medieval Saints and Their Interpreters*, ed. by Catherine M. Mooney (Philadelphia: University of Pennsylvania Press, forthcoming 1999).

[105] *utriusque sexus populorum*, Thiofrid, *Flores Epitaphii* 4, 6 (PL 157, 398C).

every part of threefold Gaul[106] and from Germany. Through the grace of God she adapted her exhortations to the circumstances of each person's life. For the health of their souls she put questions to them from the Holy Scriptures and answered them.[107] Many received advice from her concerning the sicknesses of the body from which they were suffering, and not a few were relieved of their infirmities through her blessings.

Because of the true prophetic spirit that was in her, she could *discern the thoughts* (cf. Lk. 5:22) and intentions *of human beings*, and so she rebuffed those who approached her in a perverse and frivolous cast of mind—as if to try her out. When they could not resist the spirit by which she spoke, they stood chastened and corrected and were compelled to give up their unworthy venture. There were Jews too who came to cross-examine her, and she would convict them out of their own Law, urging them on to faith in Christ with words of devout warning.[108]

Like the Apostles *she made herself all things to all* (cf. 1 Cor. 9:22).[109] When strangers arrived, she spoke kindly and gently as seemed appropriate to each one, even if they were of doubtful character. Whenever there arose the rancour of some dispute among the young women with her, or the grief of worldly sadness, or despondency, or carelessness, Hildegard would chastise them with a disposition of much love and motherly sweetness. In time she was able to see through their desires, motives and thoughts—so much so, that in the Divine Office she answered them with blessings fitting according to the character of each one's heart.[110]

---

[106] This refers to the division of *Gallia Comata* or Greater Gaul—roughly what is beyond Provence—after the time of Julius Caesar, into three administrative districts: *Aquitania*, centred on Bordeaux, *Lugdunensis* on Lyons, and *Belgica* on Trier. Cf. Thiofrid, *Vita S. Willibrordi*, 12, ed. by J. Schmitz, p. 16.

[107] Cf. Sulpicius Severus, *Vita S. Martini* 25, 6; ed. by J. Fontaine, p. 310.

[108] Throughout the tenth to twelfth centuries, Mainz had the largest Jewish community and rabbinical school in Europe. See *AD* 1097.

[109] Cf. Thiofrid, *Vita S. Liutwini* 10, ed. by W. Lampen, p. 28.

[110] *in officiis etiam divinis secundum qualitatem cordis sui propriis benedictionibus eis respondebat*. One occasion this might have taken place was when a reader, before approaching the lectern, inclined to the prioress and asked for a blessing: *Jube Domne benedicere*—'command O Lady a blessing'. Did Hildegard take the opportunity to enlarge on the blessing? St Bernard read the inner dispositions of each monk when all were at psalmody, cf. *Exordium Magnum* 3,5 (PL 185, 417C).

She saw in spirit the past life and conduct of people, and in the case of some, she could even foresee the way their present life would end, and, according to the character of their conduct and merits, their soul's glory or punishment. These great mysteries, however, she would reveal to no-one except that one person, to whom as we have said earlier, she disclosed all her secrets. For example, at a time of silence, she would know about what and where, to whom and why, in what manner and for how long they were speaking. At the same time, she kept guard over these gifts with the highest of all virtues, humility. And knowing that *God resists the proud, but gives grace to the humble* (Prov. 3:34, 1 Pet. 5:5), she always gave the praise to the all-mighty benevolence of divine grace.

V

THOUGH IT PLEASED HER heavenly Bridegroom to visit his beloved spouse frequently, and though she was adorned with a dowry of gifts so great and of such a kind, yet in order that, as it is written, *the greater she became, the more she humbled herself in all things* (Eccli 3:20), he allowed her to be tried often by the numerous sufferings of her illnesses. We can make this clearer if we insert at this point a text from her visions so that *her virtue, made perfect in weakness* (cf. 2 Cor. 12:9), might not remain hidden, and the reader's flagging interest also be revived by providing some pleasing variety.

Do you wish to know what she endured because she did not make known the heavenly vision shown to her, concerning her move from the place where she was at the time, to another? Listen to her as she writes about it:

SECOND VISION

At one time, I could not see any light because of a clouding over of my eyes, and I was so pressed down by the weight of my body that I could not raise myself. So I lay there, overwhelmed by intense pains. Why I suffered like this was because I did not make known the vision in which it was shown to me that I must move with my young women from the place where I had been offered to God, to another place. And so I endured these pains continually until I named the place where I am now. As soon as I recovered my sight, I was somewhat alleviated, though I was not yet fully freed from the illness.

Now when my Abbot and the brothers, and the people of that district realized the nature of the proposed change, that we were wanting to go from a lushness of fields and vineyards and from the beauty of that place to an arid place with no conveniences, they were shocked, and conspired among themselves to block us so that it should not come about. They were even saying that I was deceived by some kind of vain imagination. When I heard this, *my heart was crushed* (Jer. 23:9) *and my flesh and my veins withered* (cf. Job 30:30, Ps. 101:4). So I lay in bed many days when I heard a loud voice forbidding me to proclaim or write down anything more of this vision in that place.

Then a certain noble marchioness we knew[111] approached the Archbishop of Mainz and put the whole story before him and other wise people. They replied that no *place is made holy* (cf. 2 Mach. 2:8) except by good works and therefore it seemed reasonable for this proposal to go forward. Thus, with the Archbishop's permission and in reverence for God we came to that place with a great escort of our neighbours and other visitors.[112]

Then the ancient deceiver put me to the proof with many mockeries. For example, many were saying: 'What is this? So many *mysteries are revealed* (cf. 2 Esdr. 10:6) to this foolish and unlearned woman when there are so many strong and wise men? It will come to nothing for sure!' For indeed many wondered about the revelation, whether it was from God, or from some withering influence of the spirits of the air who lead many astray.

When I began to dwell in that place with twenty noble young women of wealthy parents, we found no dwelling or inhabitant there except for an ex-soldier and his wife and children. Such was the distress of trials and the pressure of work which fell on me, it was as if storm-clouds were blocking the sun, so that amid deep sighs and overflowing tears I said: 'Oh, Oh, *God does not confound anyone who trusts in him!*' (cf. Ps. 21:6, 24:2) But God favoured me again—just as the sun shines forth through the breaking clouds, or as a mother offers milk to her crying baby, and he is comforted from crying.

Then I saw in true vision, that the trials which had come upon me were

---

[111] Richardis (d. 1151), of the powerful von Stade family, was born Sponheim-Lavantall, and so was distantly related to Jutta of Disibodenberg. One daughter, mother of the Adelheid who entered monastic life at Rupertsberg, was at one time Queen consort of Denmark. Another daughter, Richardis, also entered at Rupertsberg, and was very close to Hildegard but was to occasion her one of the most keenly felt sorrows of her life, as she goes on to describe. See Führkötter's note translated in *The Life of the Holy Hildegard*, n. 38.

[112] This last sentence is missing in PL.

after the pattern of Moses. For when he led the children of Israel out of
Egypt across the Red Sea into the desert, they murmured against God and
greatly distressed Moses too, although God had lit up their way with so
many wonderful signs. Likewise, God allowed me to be afflicted in some
measure by the common people, by my kinsfolk, and by some of those
living with me when they lacked necessities—although, by God's grace a
certain amount was given to us in alms. For just as the children of Israel
distressed Moses, so *they* also *shook their heads at me* and said (cf. Job
42:11): 'What is the good of this, that noble and wealthy young women
should leave a place where they lacked nothing to be reduced to such
beggary?' But truly, we were awaiting the grace of God to come to our
help, for it was he who had shown us this place.

After the distress of this ordeal, God showered down his grace upon us.
For many who at first jeered at us and called it an arid and useless place,
came to us from all sides offering us help and filling us with blessings.
Many wealthy families gave their dead an honourable burial with us; many
others, recognizing this vision as worthy of trust, came to us most eagerly,
just as the prophet says: *They will all come to you those who despised you*
(cf. Is. 60:14). Then my spirit revived and I, who had earlier wept for
sorrow, now wept for joy[113] that God had not led me into oblivion since he
confirmed everything by raising up this place and by multiplying many
useful items and buildings.

It was not his will, however, that I remain completely free of anxiety.
Such has been his way in all my affairs since my infancy, to allow me no
unruffled joy in this life, through which my mind could become inflated.
For while I was writing the book *Scivias* I bore a deep love for a certain
noble young woman, daughter of the above mentioned marchioness,[114] just
as Paul loved Timothy. She joined herself to me in loving friendship in
everything, and comforted me in all my trials, until at length I finished that
book. But after this, because of the high station of her family, she inclined
after the dignity of a higher title, so that she was named the mother[115] of a
certain very eminent community. She did not seek this however, according

---

[113] Cf. Gregory, *Dialogues* 3, 3, ed. by A. de Vogüé, p. 268.

[114] *quandam nobilem puellam, supradicte marchionisse filiam, in plena karitate habebam;*
i.e. Richardis, daughter of Richardis von Stade.

[115] I.e. 'abbess'. Hildegard flinches at the 'higher title' she does not have, and purposely
avoids even naming it. See Ep. 38, X and note. Dronke, in supplying 'abbess' instead of
the original 'mother' (*Women Writers*, p. 151), misses something of Hildegard's wry
irony, born of grief now calmed, if not forgotten. Note that Guibert also studiously avoids
'abbess', using a generic 'mother' instead, in Ep. 38, II–III.

to God, but according to this world's honour. After she withdrew from me, in a region[116] far away from us, she soon lost this present life, and along with it the title of her new dignity.

There were also other noble young women who acted likewise and separated themselves from me. Some of them afterwards lived so negligently that many said their works showed that they had sinned against the Holy Spirit and against that person who spoke from the Holy Spirit. I and those who loved me wondered why such great persecution came upon me, and why God did not grant me consolation, since I did not wish to continue in my sins, but rather desired to bring good works to fruition with God's help. Amidst these circumstances I completed the book *Scivias* as God willed.

VI

FROM THE PRECEDING ACCOUNT of her vision and of all that the blessed virgin endured, it is clear that *God himself had chosen* and foreordained *as her inheritance* (Ps. 32:12) the site which he indicated to her, over which he chastised her with blindness because of her delay. He chose it so that his holy name might be all the more glorified there,[117] on the one hand because of the merits of Saint Rupert and those resting in Christ with him there, and on the other, for the advancement of the blessed virgin and those who accompanied her there.

In all this a story from the distant past comes to mind. A beautiful comparison suggests itself to us between Deborah the prophetess and the place where she presided (Jg. 4:4), and our prophetess and her chosen abode. Thus Origen says:

Deborah furnishes no small consolation to the sex of women. She challenges them, in case they lose hope over the weakness of their sex, that they can become capable even of the prophetic charism, but they should understand and believe that what merits this charism is purity of mind and not any distinction of sex.

---

[116] Richardis departed for the abbey of Bassum far to the north in the archdiocese of Bremen, of which her brother Hartwig was Archbishop. It was he who wrote to Hildegard telling of his sister's unexpected death on 29 October 1152 and that before she had died she expressed in tears her longing and regret for Hildegard's monastery. Cf. Ep. 13, Van Acker, p. 29; Baird and Ehrman, pp. 50–51.

[117] Cf. Thiofrid, *Vita S. Liutwini*, 3, ed. by W. Lampen, p. 11.

So Deborah, which means *bees*, assumed the role of prophecy.[118] For indeed every prophecy blends the pleasant honey-combs of heavenly teaching with the sweet honey of the Divine Word, as David says: *Your words are sweeter to my throat than honey in my mouth* (Ps. 118:103).[119]

She is said to have *taken her seat of prophecy between Ramah and Bethel;* (Jg. 4:5) which means, *Ramah*—high place, and *Bethel*—house of God. Nothing lowly therefore, nothing cast down ought to be found at the prophetic seat. So it was in Solomon, the seat of Wisdom stands firm in the gates of the city, or dwells on the ramparts of the city walls, or acts freely on the towers.[120]

Thus we can say that prophecy dwelt in blessed Hildegard *between the house of God and the high place*, for though it was seen manifest in a particular place yet it was to be received in a spiritual manner. It teaches you O holy soul, whoever you are that dwell there, to spurn the things of earth, and to *seek the things which are in the high places of heaven where Christ is, seated at the right hand of God* (Col. 3:1–2). There his prophetic gift urges you to ascend, there it strives to draw all its hearers. *Blessed indeed is the glory of the Lord that emanates from his place* (Ezech. 3:12). The blessed virgin who foresaw it in spirit, speaks of securing the freehold title to it, in her own writing:

VII

THIRD VISION

I SAW IN VISION, and was taught and compelled to make known to my superiors, that our place with all that belonged to it, should be separated from that place where I had been offered to God, and that we would owe

---

[118] *in prophetie forma versatur.*

[119] Origen (Rufinus's translation) *In Lib. Iud.—On the Book of Judges*, Jg. 5:2. ed. by W.A. Baehrens, *Origenes Werke, 7: Homilien zum Hexateuch in Rufins Übersetzung* (Leipzig: 1927), p. 492, line 24–p. 493, line 6 (PG 12, 970C).

[120] Origen, *loc. cit.* Jg. 5:3, p. 493, lines 14–35 (PG 12, 970D). Of the ease with which monks had recourse to Origen it has been said: 'the monks were less afraid of him than were the accredited Theologians', O. Lottin, quoted in *The Spirituality of the Middle Ages*, ed. by J. Leclercq et al. (London: Burns and Oates, 1968), p. 184. It may be worth noting that women were among Origen's students in the catechetical school at Alexandria, and assisted him as tachygraphers, amanuenses and calligraphers. See Eusebius, *Church History*, Book 6, Ch. 23.

deference and obedience to the servants of God there, only as long as we found good faith in them towards us. I confided these things to my Abbot, but he was racked with illness so that he could do nothing about it. Indeed he finished his life only a few days later. But when these proposals reached the succeeding Abbot and the Archbishop of Mainz and the authorities of the church there, they upheld them in faith and charity, confirming their provisions in a document affixed with a seal.[121]

While all this was going on I endured many attacks from certain quarters, just like Joshua, whose enemies tried to bring him to confusion because he was the conqueror of others (cf. Josh. 7–11). But just as God helped him, so he freed both myself and my daughters. Likewise, just as Joseph's own brothers[122] were envious of him (cf. Gen. 37) because he was loved by their father more than the others, with the result that they sold him and took back his torn robe to their father saying that a wild beast had devoured him, so also certain evil-willed people tried to tear from us the garment of the Lord's' grace and praise. But God came to our help, just as he also restored Joseph to honour.

Although we were under great pressure, by God's grace we were enlarged, just like the children of Israel, who, *the more they were oppressed the more they increased* (Ex. 1:12). And so, in the joy of my heart I looked to God, and because he had stood by me in my trials, I willingly cast aside care.

VIII

WE MIGHT PAUSE HERE to consider how the blessed virgin, though sorely weighed down by the attrition of bodily infirmity and by the persecutions of both diabolic and human hostility, yet ever merited to be strengthened and confirmed by divine consolation. For, since the Holy Spirit wished to store *his grace destined for many* (cf. 2 Cor. 4:15) in *his chosen vessel* (Acts 9:15), he was intent on scouring all the stains of dregs in her with the lime of correction, so that by means of chastisement she might make progress, search out more intensely the will of the Lord, and order the whole course of her life to his purpose, *rendering* to God, according to

---

[121] See the first and second charters of Arnold Archbishop of Mainz dated 22 May 1158 in Documents of Rupertsberg.

[122] *fratres sui*; the reference is clearly to Hildegard's 'brothers' of Disibodenberg and their political manoeuvrings with their common 'father', the Archbishop, to undermine Hildegard's good name with him, and the success of her objectives with them.

the apostle, a *spiritual service* (Rom. 12:1). As was fitting! For God freely illumined her with substantial gifts of nature and grace,[123] and at the same time prepared grace and glory for her in great abundance. He gave her grace on earth, glory in heaven, grace of the sublimest merits, glory of ineffable rewards. It was in view of all this that she was chastened by earthly contradictions, as it is written: *The Lord disciplines every child of his that he accepts* (Heb. 12:6), so that in her, merits upon merits might be increased. This is made clear in the following vision which she describes thus:

VIIII

FOURTH VISION

AT ONE TIME[124] GOD laid me low on a bed of illness, and allowed excruciating airs to course through my whole body. The blood in my veins, the fluid[125] in my body, even the marrow in my bones dried up so much it was as if my soul must be released from the body. I remained in that strife for thirty days such that my abdomen burned with the heat of a fiery air. Some reckoned that this sickness was a punishment. Even the strength of my spirit implanted in my flesh gave way, and though I did not pass out of this life, I was not fully in it either. My inert body was laid out over a haircloth[126] on the ground, but my end was not yet in sight, though my superiors, my daughters and my neighbours came in great mourning to watch at my passing.

But from time to time during those days I beheld in true vision a battle-line of angels, of a number beyond all human reckoning. The *angels* of that army *were fighting with Michael against the dragon* (Apoc. 12:7) and they were prevailing; God was ordaining what was to be done about me. Then *a mighty one from among them cried out* to me (cf. Apoc. 5:2, 10:1, 3) and

---

[123] Cf. Thiofrid, *Flores Epitaphii* 2, 3 (PL 157, 345C).

[124] Guibert adds: 'suddenly'.

[125] *caro cum liuore.* The text in PL 197, 109 reads, *caro cum liquore.* The critical reading, *liuore*, i.e. blue-black colouring, bruising, or envy, spite, ill-will, could easily occur through the omission of a single consonant, 'q'. Still, Hildegard does use the term *liuor* in her medicine to refer to two of the four bodily humours. See also Hildegard, *Explanatio Symboli S. Athanasii*, PL 197, 1070C.

[126] *super cilicium.* This was the monastic custom followed by Jutta when she was dying. See *VJ* VIII.

said, 'Ah, Ah, eagle, why do you sleep on in your knowledge? Rise up from your hesitancy! You shall be known! O jewel of splendour, all eagles shall look upon you while the world will groan. Eternal life shall rejoice! And so, rise up O dawning light, to the sun![127] Rise up, *rise up, eat and drink!* (1 Kg. 18:41)' And soon the whole battle-line resounded in solemn chorus: '*O voice of joy!* (Jer. 33:11) The heralds have fallen silent, for *the time* of your passing *has not yet come!* (cf. Jn 7:6) Therefore *girl, rise up!*' (Mk 5:41) Immediately my body and my senses were turned back to this present life. When my daughters who had been weeping for me perceived the change, they lifted me from the ground and placed me back in bed, and so I regained my former strength.

The suffering of this illness had not quite left me, but the spirit within me grew stronger day by day, more than ever before. It was the most *evil spirits of the air* (cf. Eph. 2:2, 6:12), to whom are committed all the punishing tortures of human beings, who administered me this punishment, since God allowed them to bring it against me. And so these spirits became my tormentors, the same ones who applied live coals to the blessed Laurence and other martyrs.[128] These came hurrying to me, crying out in a loud voice: 'Let us seduce this woman, so that she has second thoughts about God, and rails at him for overwhelming her with such sufferings.' For just as it happened to Job when by God's permission Satan so struck his body that he crawled with vermin (cf. Job 2:7–8) so, in my case, it was a fiery air that entered in and consumed my flesh. This also happened to *Jeremiah, who lamented his sorrow in tears* (Lam.: prol.). But the Devil could not persuade Job to rail against God.

But I, soft in flesh, timid in mind, was completely terrified of these sufferings. Yet God strengthened me to bear them with patience, and in my spirit I said: 'O, O, Lord God, all the ways in which you wound me I know are good, because all your works are good and holy, and because I have deserved all this from my infancy; and besides, I trust that you will not permit my soul to be tortured like this in the life that is to come.'[129]

---

[127] For the eagle and the dawn see Hildegard, *LDO* 3, 2, 10, CCCM 92, p (3, 7, 10, PL 197, 972A). She particularly uses images of jewel, eagle, and especially the dawn for the Blessed Virgin in her Hymns 10, 11, 15, 21 and 22 (Newman, *Symphonia*). Very early in her career she addresses Bernard of Clairvaux, 'you indeed are an eagle gazing on the sun': Ep. 1, Van Acker, p. 5.

[128] Cf. Thiofrid, *Flores Epitaphii*, 4, 6 (PL 157, 397B).

[129] Cf. Origen (Jerome's translation), *In Ezechiel*, Hom. 1, 1, ed. by W.A. Baehrens, *Origenes Werke*, 7: *Homilien zum Hexateuch in Rufins Übersetzung* (Leipzig: 1927), p. 319.

X

WHILE I WAS STILL labouring in these pains, I was warned in true vision to go to the place where I had been offered to God, and announce the words which God would show me. So I did this and returned in the same pain to my daughters. I also made haste to travel to communities in other places, and reveal there the words which God ordered me. Through all this, the vessel of my body was *being baked* as it were *in an oven* (cf. Lev. 7:9)[130]—just as God has put many to the test whom he has ordered to announce his words, and praise to him for it!

But he did provide me with much help in two of my daughters and in others, who tended me unwearyingly in my sufferings. And so with a sigh I gave thanks to God that my fellow human beings did not tire of me. Indeed, so great was the pressure of pains in my flesh that if they were not from God, I could not have survived for long. However racked I was by these things, still, I continued dictating, singing, and writing through the heavenly vision whatever the Holy Spirit wished to announce through me.

When three years had gone by in these ailments, I saw a cherub in a blazing fire, in which is a likeness of the mysteries of God. And this cherub was pursuing with a fiery sword the spirits of the air who were torturing me, so that they fled from me crying: 'Ach, Ach! Woe, woe! Surely that woman is not escaping us? That means we shall not be able to carry her off!' And soon my spirit within me fully revived and my body was renewed in its veins and marrow, so that I completely recovered my health.

XI

CONSIDER HOW ON TWO fronts, whether racked by the pains of her weaknesses, or plagued by the terrors of the demons, the holy virgin was not only not vanquished, but was even glorified with a multiple victory by means of an angelic defence.

Firstly, while she laboured in her weakness, this woman of wonderful innocence armed herself with the virtue of patience, as if the divine Word were consoling her in her distress, saying: *My grace is enough for you; for virtue is made perfect in weakness*, she *gladly gloried in her weaknesses, that the power of Christ might dwell in her* (2 Cor. 12:9). And so she grew confident that she was loved by him whom she merited

---

[130] See Hildegard, *LDO* Prol., CCCM 92, p. 45 (PL 197, 741B).

to have take up her cause.

Secondly, when she was being provoked by the trickery of the demons, this outstanding woman of war[131] armed herself with the safeguard of apostolic teaching. How? *Take up the helmet of salvation*, it says, *and the sword of the spirit, which is the word of God* (Eph. 6:17), and again, *put on the armour of God, that you may be able to stand up to the tactics of the devil, for our struggle is not against flesh and blood, but against the lords and rulers of this darkness* (Eph. 6:11–12). Thus with great skill in warfare, and with such weapons as these, our protagonist waged battle unconquered. Though still confined in the flesh and earthbound, she yet contended with the *spiritual powers of wickedness in the heavens* (Eph. 6:12).

These very princes of darkness shuddered when they saw advancing against them a woman trained in tactics like these and armed *with the panoply of the strong* (Cant. 4:4). They shuddered I say, and crying out with woe, they fled in confusion, for fear and trembling had come upon them when they saw a *cherub* (cf. Ezech. 28:14), *terrible as a phalanx in battle-array* (Cant. 6:3,9),[132] covering the handmaid of God, while pursuing them with a flaming spear in case they troubled her. Thus *they were astonished, bewildered, in a turmoil; a trembling seized them* (Ps. 47:6,7), so that they too said: *This is the war-camp of God* (Gen. 32:2), *let us flee from Israel!* (Ex. 14:25) And they fled immediately. Thus whenever the athlete of God[133] wrestled between the spirits above and the spirits below, she put her enemies to rout and was always glorified with a glad victory.

We cannot pass over in silence how at a certain point when she was hard-pressed by fever, she saw a number of saints who were saying:

'Avenge O Lord, *the blood of your saints!*' (Apoc. 19:2) And others were saying to her: 'You must bear the pain you suffer with a good will.' And still other saints were conferring among themselves: 'Is she to come with us or not?' And others replied: 'Things past, present and future do not yet allow her. But when her task is finished, we shall take her with us.' Then all cried together: 'O happy, O most determined soul, *rise up* (cf. Eph. 5:16), *rise up* like the eagle! For the Sun has led you forth, though you do

---

[131] *bellatrix egregia.*

[132] Cf. Thiofrid, *Vita S. Liutwini*, 10, ed. by W. Lampen, p. 28.

[133] *adleta Dei:* cf. Thiofrid, *Flores Epitaphii*, 1, 4 (PL 157, 327C).

not know it.'

And from that moment she recovered her health.

XII

BUT HILDEGARD INCURRED NOT only the troubles of her own frail health and the fury of the demons, but also attacks from other people—and in this God was with her also, bringing the hearts of her enemies around to the better. She describes this herself when she speaks of the conversion of a philosopher who was against her, or rather God, to begin with. But as time passed *a change* was worked in him *by the right hand of the Most High* (Ps. 76:11).[134] And when through the guile of Satan vain thoughts of pride began to arise in the hearts of her young women, she put an end to them with the exhortations of the holy Scriptures. This is what she says of these cases:

> A certain philosopher, reputed for his wealth, had long cast doubt on the things I saw, but in the end he came round to our cause, and generously endowed our place with buildings and properties and other necessities. My soul was overjoyed that God had not brought us into oblivion. With sharp but wise scrutiny, he examined what the written accounts of this vision were and where they came from, until at length he gave full credit to their divine inspiration. Thus God quenched the injustice of his heart, just as he sank Pharaoh beneath the Red Sea who had wanted to take the children of Israel captive (cf. Ex. 14), and this man who had previously spurned us with venomous words, turned toward us with many blessings. Many were astonished at the change in him and became much more ready to believe, so that by means of that wise man God poured out his blessing on us, *like oil which descends upon the beard, upon Aaron's beard* (Ps. 132:2). Because of this, we all claimed that philosopher as our father and he who was so eminent in his own right, petitioned to be allowed burial with us, and so it came about.[135]
> At that I was much confirmed in my mind. I took care of my daughters' necessities whether of body or of soul, just as I had been appointed to do by my superiors.[136] And so I was most concerned when I beheld in true

---

[134] Cf. Theodoric, *Libellus de libertate*, MGH SS 23, p. 64, line 36; p. 72, line 1.

[135] Cf. Theodoric, *Chronicon Epternacense*, MGH SS 23, p. 42, line 43.

[136] *sicut a magistris mihi erat statutum.*

vision that the spirits of the air were fighting against us, and saw moreover, that these same spirits had entangled some of my noble-born daughters as in a net with an array of vain thoughts.

So, through the revelation of God, I made this known to them and fenced them about and armed them with the words of Holy Scripture and with the discipline of the Rule and with a sound monastic life. But several of them, darting at me with glowering eyes, tore me to pieces with words behind my back, saying that they could not endure it, this insufferable hammering away of mine at the discipline of the Rule, by which I wanted to curb them.

But God also comforted me with other good and wise sisters, who stood by me in all my sufferings. Thus God dealt with me as he did with Susanna, whom he freed from false witnesses through Daniel (cf. Dan. 13). Though I was often worn out with trials of this kind, yet by the grace of God, I finally brought to an end the Book of Life's Merits, divinely revealed to me.

XIII

THUS, BETWEEN SETBACKS AND successes, this virgin devoted to God so conducted herself that she was neither inflated by the successes nor disheartened by the setbacks. Rather, she maintained the same vigour in either circumstance, neither being disturbed by blame nor seduced by praise. She kept her soul as taut and ready as a stretched bow with every discipline. Thus, her authority never grew slack as she governed both herself and her nuns—at one time exercising severity, at another time kindness. Her dignity was seasoned by courtesy, and from her tongue flowed a pleasantness of speech sweeter than honey. Indeed, in all things she was possessed of sound teaching, whether she writes about human nature, the conflict between flesh and spirit, or the counsels of the holy Fathers, which she understood through divine revelation. She says:

XIIII

FIFTH VISION

IN TRUE VISION I saw the form of man. Though it is of twofold nature, that is, of soul and of body, yet it is a single composition, just as when someone puts together a house out of stone, and covers it with ashy material, and strengthens it in case it collapses and comes apart. For indeed man is the work of God[137] and so is with every creature, as every creature is with him. But the work of man, since it has no life, is unlike the work of God, which is life, just as a potter's jar is unlike a smith's handiwork. For the nature of the soul looks out upon infinite life, whereas the body clings to perishable life—they are not in accord, for however much they are associated in man, yet they are distinctly two.

Consequently, when God sends his spirit upon a person by means of prophecy and wisdom and even miracles, he often afflicts his flesh with pains, so that the Holy Spirit can dwell there. For if he does not constrain it with pain, it easily becomes enmeshed in worldly behaviour—as happened to Samson and Solomon and others, in whom the sighs of the spirit grew fainter and fainter as they inclined themselves to gratifying the flesh.

Now prophecy, wisdom, and miracles ought to be a source of glad delight. But when, at the prompting of the devil, a person wastes the time cultivating the pleasure of the flesh, he says again and again 'O what a foul stench! How I have rotted in my impurities!'[138]

Why is it that the spirit afflicts the flesh?[139] It is because the spirit itself instinctively holds the mere whiff of sin in disgust. When however, on account of frequent pleasure, the flesh undermines the desires of the soul, the flesh wallows in the stench of sin. So it is when the spirit is harassed like this and can no longer sigh upwards, that the flesh afflicts the spirit. Thus by the grace of God, this affliction cuts both ways.

This conflict which we have spoken of in relation to man, began with Abel, who was hated by his own brother; it continued with Noah, who bore insult from his own son; and with Abraham, who incurred abuse from his friends;[140] and with Jacob who became a fugitive from his brother; and with Moses, who was afflicted by his friends when they sided with his enemies.

This conflict was to be found even among the disciples of Christ, when the flesh suffocated the spirit in one of them due to his hardened want of faith. Yet there were others whose spirit strove against their flesh. Zaccheus in the Gospel, for example, also strove with the spirit against the flesh. But the young man in the Gospel who spoke with Christ did not have a spirit that strove against the flesh, and so turned away from the Son of

---

[137] *Homo enim opus Dei est*; see Hildegard, *LDO* 1, 4, 100, CCCM 92, p. 243 (PL 197, 885B and 888C).

[138] *Ach immundo fetore fecis feteo*. Cf. Thiofrid, *Flores Epitaphii*, 1, 5 (PL 157, 328D/329A).

[139] Ibid 1, 2 (322A).

[140] Guibert reads: 'specially from his friends'.

God. At first Saul crushed his spirit with unbelief, but God cleared away this evil from him, just as he cast Satan from Heaven into the abyss, and so he made a Paul out of Saul.

Abel, who in the overflowing desire of his soul offered sacrifice, was sanctified whereas Cain was rejected, because the flesh suffocated his spirit through hatred. Again, Noah was justified because he sacrificed to God, whereas his son answered to the baseness of the flesh by his sly treatment of his father, and so he was deprived of liberty, and being unworthy of the name of son, was called a servant.

Abraham, however, was given increase, because, being obedient to God, he strove with all his might against the clamourings of the flesh. This man was changed into a new people, while the liberty of his sons and his friends who opposed him vanished when they were cast out from the freeborn children of Israel. And Jacob too was dear to God, because in his soul's desire, he ever drank in righteousness, and he continued in the blessings of God to the end. Esau his brother, however, was deprived of God's blessing, on account of the hatred he bore Jacob. Moses the servant and friend of God, whom he knew and served in mysteries and miracles, restrained the impulse of the flesh in himself. And so, those who bore hatred for him perished, and did not reach the land of promise.

The apostles restrained their flesh. But Judas was completely blind in the desire of his soul, for he followed Christ more for the acclaim of the people than for faith in him. Just so, those disciples who did not sustain the desire of the soul in fullness, listened willingly enough to the teaching of Christ,[141] but because they were of a lukewarm spirit, withdrew from him, that they might not have to endure the full measure of righteousness.

Even in the exuberance of the flesh Zaccheus did have a spirit that strove against the flesh, so that he became disgusted with all his works. Therefore, because he was righteous, when he heard tell of the Son of God he ran to meet him there and put his faith in him—for he had already been mourning his sins in spirit (cf. Lk. 19:1–10).

On the other hand we find in the Gospel the young man burdened with riches who listened willingly enough to the reports of what was happening, and did go to the Son of God and ask what he should do; but when he obtained the full and perfect answer, he yielded to despondency and withdrew from Christ, because the flesh suffocated the spirit. Saul, too, feeling no compunction whatever in his hardened heart, raised high the horns of his pride against the faith of Christ. But God laid him low, and mortified the will of the flesh in him, and brought him round to the good.

---

[141] See Hildegard, *LDO* 3, 5, 9, CCCM 92, p. 421 (3, 10, 9, PL 197, 1010D).

And I, poor little creature that I am, have especially loved and called upon those who have striven against the flesh with their spirit, and have turned away from all who have hardened themselves against the spirit, and have suffocated it.[142] I have never taken my rest—rather I have been worn out by many trials, till at length God rained down the dew of His grace upon me, just as he spoke to his friend: *I will be an enemy to your enemies, and those who afflict you, I will afflict, and my angel shall go before you* (Ex. 23:22–23), and again: *I have conferred great honour on my servant, and all his enemies I have humbled* (cf. 1 Chr. 17:10).

For God so constrained me by many harsh experiences, that I scarcely dared think how great was the benevolence of his grace towards me. But then I saw what great difficulties would confront all who resisted the truth of God. And because of the trials and sufferings I endured from the heat of the air, my body was trampled down like clay earth that becomes like glue when mixed with water.[143]

XV

IT WOULD BE OF great benefit no doubt, to explore the obscurity of such subtle utterances, if our task were not rather to inscribe in writing the text of the holy virgin's visions, and to unfold the story of her life in further words. Let our mind go to work, so that through exertion it might be enlarged, and what we cannot grasp in an offhand manner we may grasp through earnest application. But since we must now hasten on to other topics—with poised pen let us write out a select number of her visions. She says:

SIXTH VISION

IN VISION I GAZED at three towers, by means of which Wisdom showed me certain secrets.

The first tower had three chambers. In the first of the chambers there were noble young women and certain others, who were listening with burning love to the words of God from my mouth—and indeed they had a kind of unceasing hunger for this. In the second chamber there were certain other steadfast and wise women, who embraced the truth of God in their

---

[142] See Theodoric, *Chronicon Epternacense*, MGH SS, 23, p. 49, lines 26 ff.

[143] See Hildegard, *Causae et curae* 2, ed. by Paul Kaiser (Leipzig: Teubner, 1903), p. 42, line 10.

hearts, saying: 'O how long shall we continue to have the benefit of these things?' And they did not weary of it. In the third chamber, there were strong armed men of the common people, who had been led to wonder at the miracles above mentioned, and came rushing impetuously towards us, longing for them eagerly. And they kept doing this, just as the common people do when they seek protection in the secure and strong tower of some prince in order to be fortified against their enemies.

In the second tower there were three chambers also, two of which had become parched with dryness. This dryness appeared like a thick cloud. And the inhabitants of these two chambers were of one mind, saying: 'What are these things the woman announces as if from God and where do they come from? It is hard for us to live in a way different from those who went before us or those living now. Therefore let us go back to those who know us, for we cannot put up with other ways.' And so they went back to the common people mentioned above. Those in this chamber or in the first were no good whatever. And in true vision I heard a voice speaking to them: *Every kingdom divided against itself shall be laid waste, and every house pitted against itself shall fall* (Lk. 11:17). But in the third chamber of the same tower there were the common people. In different ways, they loved the words of God that I brought forth from true vision, and stood by me in my trials, just like the publicans who clung to Christ.

Upon the third tower there were three ramparts, the first of wood, the second adorned with resplendent precious stones, and the third made of hedge.[144]

But another structure was hidden from me in my vision, so that I cannot at this stage learn the words of it[145]—yet in the true light I heard that what I shall put down in writing in the future concerning it will be stronger and more excellent than the writings which have preceded it.[146]

---

[144] See Hildegard, *LDO* 1, 2, 22, CCCM 92, p. 82 (PL 197, 767B/C).

[145] Guibert adds: 'at all, since it must be revealed at another time, as God wills it'.

[146] Hildegard uncharacteristically offers no interpretation of this vision, and Theodoric does not enlarge on it. We might hazard some guesses, and I thank Barbara Newman for a lead here: The first two chambers of the first tower seem to hold her faithful followers among the nuns at Rupertsberg and at Eibingen, both noble-born and others. The third chamber is specifically a class of men among the common people devoted to her, perhaps even parish clergy. In the first two chambers of the second tower are the malcontents in her communities and those who have abandoned monastic life and gone back to the world, while the third chamber holds the ordinary people in the world who have been loyal to her and helped her when needed. The third tower, so briefly adumbrated, is perhaps not referring to classes of people at all. The last image of the hidden structure seems to represent her culminating theological work, the *Liber Divinorum Operum*, still at a very

XVI

SEVENTH VISION

SOME TIME LATER I saw an extraordinary mystical vision, at which all my inward parts trembled, and my body lost all capacity of feeling—for my knowing was changed into another mode in which, as it were, I did not know myself.[147] It was as if the inspiration of God were sprinkling drops of sweet rain into my soul's knowing, the very same with which the Spirit instructed John the Evangelist when he drank in from the breast of Jesus the most profound of revelations.[148] His senses at that time were so touched by the sacred Divinity that he revealed hidden mysteries and works, saying *In the beginning was the Word* ... (Jn 1:1) etc.

For it was the Word, which before all created things had no beginning, and after them shall have no end, which summoned all created things into being.[149] He brought his work into being like a smith causing his work to shower sparks.[150] In this way, what was predestined by him before ever the world was, appeared in visible form. Therefore man is the work of God along with every creature.[151] But man is also said to be the worker of the Divinity and a shadow of his mysteries, and should in all things reveal the Holy Trinity,[152] for *God made him in his image and likeness* (Gen. 1:26). So, just as Lucifer for all his malice could not bring God to naught, so too, he shall not succeed in destroying the human race, however much he tried to with the first man.

And thus the vision mentioned above taught me and allowed me to expound the words of this Gospel and everything it speaks of, which from the beginning is the work of God. And I saw that this same explanation would have to be the beginning of another writing which had not yet been revealed, in which many questions about the creations of the divine mystery would need to be considered.

---

early stage of its conception. Except for agreement on the last point, Dronke offers a substantially different interpretation in *Women Writers*, pp. 160–62.

[147] See Hildegard, *LDO* 3, 2, 14, CCCM 92, p. 374 (3, 7, 14, PL 197, 976C).

[148] See Hildegard, *Explanatio Symboli S. Athanasii*, PL 197, 1069D.

[149] See Hildegard, *LDO* 1, 4, 105, CCCM 92, p. 251 (PL 197, 890D).

[150] See Hildegard, *Scivias*, ed. by Führkötter, CCCM 43A, Book Three, Second Vision, Ch. 5, p. 353, lines 190–92.

[151] *homo opus Dei cum omni creatura*: Hildegard, *LDO* 1, 1, 14, CCCM 92, p. 57 (PL 197, 749C).

[152] See Hildegard, *LDO* 1, 1, 3, CCCM 92, p. 50 (PL 197, 744C).

XVII

YOU CAN SEE THAT, however far we go with our writing, we always have an ever more abundant stock of prophetic visions, deeds, and words of the blessed virgin. These overflow with such teaching and truth of the highest grace, that only a stubborn mind would be so rash as not to make every effort to comprehend her and strive to honour her. Who indeed but the Divine Spirit, the all-good bestower of graces, caused her to drink from so overflowing a fountain of saving wisdom that a flood of spiritual teaching, like a *river of living water* (Apoc. 22:1, cf. Jn 7:38), flowed from her heart so copiously.

In short, she flew on the feather of inward contemplation, hidden within herself, to the very secrets of heavenly vision, and there obtained knowledge of the Gospel of John. Is there a wise person who could doubt that this holy woman was a seat of eternal Wisdom, since to her God revealed so great a *treasure of interior knowledge?* (Col. 2:3)[153] Surely, the genuineness of that moral discipline which was habitual to her, set in order the natural emotions of her soul in such a way that the love of divine contemplation brought her with unerring progress to the heavenly realms, where she delighted to cry out to Christ her spouse in the joyous song of her heart: *Draw me after you, we shall run in the odour of your perfumes* (Cant. 1:3), and where too, as one of those *holding harps in their hands*, she *intoned the song of Moses the servant of God, and the song of the Lamb* (Apoc. 15:2–3), which is to say the song of the Law and the Gospel.

Now as we fix here the end of the second book, let us also sing a song of praise to the Lord that we have navigated so vast a sea of the holy virgin's visions. Meanwhile, let us draw breath, and if the Spirit is favourable, let us prepare the sails of our ship for the next book in which we shall describe her miracles.

HERE ENDS THE SECOND BOOK

---

[153] See Thiofrid, *Vita S. Liutwini* 23, ed. by W. Lampen, p. 45.

BOOK THREE

HERE BEGINS THE PROLOGUE OF THE THIRD BOOK ON THE MIRACLES OF
THE HOLY VIRGIN

NOW THAT WE HAVE traversed the above two books concerning the life
and the visions of the blessed virgin Hildegard, it is no burden for me,
and for you moreover a necessity, Ludwig and Godfrey, most illustrious
abbots, that I continue with my writing and add a sequel on her miracles
and virtues. I approach the task of arranging this third book, not in any
assurance of my ability to finish it, but in the confidence of obeying your
instruction.[154]

But why do you consider this a necessity? Surely that holy love with
which you cherished her in this life is reason enough. But when she died,
you in your loyal affection did not intend to be separated from her
either.[155] Thus, moved by this holy love, you thought it necessary that by
means of me, your deputy, her deeds be brought to the notice of future
generations, so that they might glorify the Lord. For he who *is wonderful
in his saints* (Ps. 67:36) was most wonderfully at work in her, so that in
all her good deeds she might be worthy of imitation.[156]

Indeed whatever can be said about her, it is all joyful and lovable, all
of it right, worthy and honourable, for she is remarkable, not only for the
entire holiness of her conduct, or for her inward contemplation of the
mysteries of God, but also for the working of extraordinary miracles as
well, whose number so exceeds all measure, that even an outstanding
talent could scarcely find the words to praise her.

Nevertheless, if, through your prayers, the Lord graciously sends us the
favourable breeze of his Spirit as we are *launched out on the deep* (cf. Lk.
5:4),[157] we do have a few things to tell out of many, and hope through the

---

[154] Thiofrid, *Vita S. Willibrordi*, Prologue, ed. by J. Schmitz , p. 3.

[155] See Thiofrid, *Vita S. Liutwini* 23, ed. by W. Lampen, p. 44.

[156] *immitabilis* in R, *immutabilis* (unchanging) in L, which gives a sense of 'so that she
persevered in all good deeds'.

[157] See Thiofrid, *Flores Epitaphii*, 4, 1 (PL 157, 383C).

prosperous course of our narrative to enter the harbour of salvation. A prosperous journey!

HERE ENDS THE PROLOGUE

HERE BEGIN THE CHAPTER HEADINGS OF THE THIRD BOOK ON THE VIRTUES OF THE HOLY VIRGIN

---

[158] *septem mensium.* In the actual text of *VH* III, 5, the baby is said to have been seven weeks, not months, old.

HERE END THE CHAPTER HEADINGS

BOOK THREE

HERE BEGINS THE THIRD BOOK ON THE MIRACLES OF SAINT HILDEGARD

I

SO POWERFUL A CHARISM of healings shone out in the blessed virgin, that scarcely anyone approached her sick who did not immediately regain good health. This will be abundantly clear from the following examples.[159]

A certain noble young woman, Hildegard, had left parents, home, and the world, and devoutly clung to the authority of holy Hildegard her loving mother.[160] At one time she was beset by a recurring fever[161] but was not cured by any remedy. Only one course of action occurred to her, that she should implore the help of the holy virgin. In accordance with the word of the Lord: *they shall lay their hands on the sick and they will become well again* (Mk 16:18), she placed her hand on her and by her blessing and prayers cast out the fever and healed her.

II

SOME TIME LATER, A certain brother Roric, who lived in the same cell,[162] wore the monastic habit, and lived by a religious rule, was racked by a similar recurring fever. When he heard of the miracle worked for the

---

[159] For much of this paragraph cf. Sulpicius Severus, *Vita S. Martini*, 16, 1, ed. by J. Fontaine, p. 286.

[160] *sancte Hildegardis pie matris magisterio devote adheresat.*

[161] *cum tercianis febribus.* 'Tertian' fever was a fever, like malaria, held to recur every 'three days'.

[162] *qui in eadem cella ... coversabatur.* A *cella* was either an individual monk's 'cell', or a branch or daughter house of a monastery in it's early stages. Is it possible that here is a kind of male anchorite attached to the nuns' monastery? There is a 'Roric, priest' at Rupertsberg in the late 1220s/early 1230s, who is one of the witnesses interviewed in *Acta Inq.* II and VIIII.

above-mentioned sister, he devoutly and humbly besought Hildegard and obtained her blessing with the sign of the Cross, whereupon the fever immediately vanished[163] and the sick man was cured.

III

IN THE SAME MONASTERY there was a domestic, Bertha, who used to serve the sisters faithfully. But a tumour on her neck and chest began to choke her aggressively. The affliction had so far advanced, that she could neither take food nor drink, nor even swallow her saliva. When she was brought to the servant of God, she begged with signs rather than words a remedy for the disease which was already well-nigh fatal. Feeling compassion for her, especially in view of her unstinting good service to them, she traced the sign of the holy Cross over the affected parts and restored her to the best of health.

IIII

A CERTAIN SWABIAN FROM the village of Thalfingen had swollen up through his whole body. When he heard of her reputation, he traversed the great distance and came to her and was not disappointed of his hope. In her kindness she kept him with her a number of days. At length, she traced over the weak man with her hands and blessed him, and through the grace of God restored him to his former sound health.

V

THERE WAS A BABY at Rüdesheim, Symon by name, only seven weeks born,[164] who was convulsed through all his limbs with a pitiful tremor. He was brought along by his wet-nurse, and at Hildegard's prayers God granted the favour and he was healed.

---

[163] Sulpicius Severus, *Vita S. Martini*, 19, 1, ed. by J. Fontaine, p. 292.

[164] *septem hebdomadas natus*. In the chapter headings he is reported as seven months, not weeks, old.

VI

SHE CAME TO THE help not only of those nearby, but also of those far away.

A certain Arnold of Wackerneim, whom she had long known, experienced such pain in his throat that he could draw breath only with difficulty. Since his own efforts were fruitless, he devoutly sought the advocacy of her prayers. So she, placing her trust in the mercy of God, blessed some water and sent it to her friend. After he had sipped some, by the gift of God the pain left him.

VII

IN BINGEN, THE DAUGHTER of a woman called Hazecha fell ill, and for three days was unable to speak. When her mother ran and sought the help of the holy virgin for her daughter, she received from her only blessed water. But when her daughter sipped some of it, she immediately recovered her voice and her strength.

VIII

IN THE SAME WALLED town there was a youth beset by so severe an illness that he was thought to be already near the end. The woman just mentioned, whose daughter had been healed, gave him some water to drink which she still had left over and then bathed his face with it. At that he recovered his strength and was healed.

VIIII

IN THE DIOCESE OF Trier a certain noble young lady called Lutgard, was pining away, passionately in love with a certain physically attractive young man,[165] for, being well guarded, she was unable to have the opportunity of quenching her lust. Her parents knew the reason for this kind of debility, and in faith they besought the counsel and help of the

---

[165] *cum adolescentuli cuiusdam ad carnem speciosi vehementi amore deperiret.*

holy virgin by means of a messenger, and because of their heartfelt appeal, they merited a favourable hearing. She first prayed to God, and, pouring out her tears, blessed bread from her own table[166] and sent it to the girl. When they gave it to her to eat, it promptly cooled the fire of that ardour in her.

X

SYBIL, A MARRIED WOMAN from the city of Lausanne across the Alps implored her aid by means of a messenger. By sending her the following letter she freed her from a haemorrhage. She said:

> In the name of him who disposes all things rightly, place these words next to your heart and your navel: 'In the blood of Adam, death arose; in the blood of Christ, death was extinguished. Through the same blood of Christ I order you, O blood, to check your flow!'[167]

As we have said this was how the married woman above mentioned was set free.

XI

LET US NOT FAIL to note that whenever a small portion of her hair or clothing were applied to any of the sick, they were restored to their former health.

For example, the wife of the mayor of Bingen had continued too long in the labour of childbirth and was already despairing of life, when a messenger ran swiftly to the monastery of the virgin of God, asking if in some way she could come to the help of one in such excessive labour. Her young women offered a plait of her hair which they had kept for some time, and gave instructions that this should be girded round her naked body. When this was done, she happily went forward with the birth, and was freed from death.

---

[166] Two of the sisters present at table with Hildegard on this occasion, Odilia and Hedwig, testify in *Acta Inq.* VI.

[167] Hildegard, *Epistola ad Sibillam*, in Pitra, p. 521. Cf. Klaes, p. 51.

XII

TWO OTHER MARRIED WOMEN were freed from similar pains of childbirth by means of the same plait of hair.

XIII

IT WAS OF NO less profit to two women of Staudernheim. Because of their disturbance of mind their parents had led them round the places of the saints, but to no avail. When they were eventually girded with the same plait of hair sent them by the young women, from that moment they regained their health of mind and body.

XIIII

WHO WOULD BELIEVE THAT the same blessed virgin could forearm even by means of a vision the needy whom she had commended in her prayers?

Rudolph, a young man from Ederich, was staying overnight at a small country estate. When all grew quiet and he was lying down to sleep, he invoked the protection of the blessed virgin. Then—O wonderful thing!— Hildegard herself appeared to him in a vision, in the same appearance and habit as she had in the body. She revealed to him that, if he did not leave quickly, he would be in peril of his life from adversaries who were lying in wait for him. So he immediately left the place along with some of his companions. But others who stayed behind were beset in the early morning by the band of enemies. They then knew how beggared of sense they had been, not to have heeded the vision and departed while there had still been time.[168]

XV

HOWEVER MIRACULOUS IT MAY seem, yet it is a fact that it was possible

---

[168] Guibert puts the sentence: 'When they were taken they then knew for themselves how beggared of sense they had been not to have heeded the vision of the virgin of Christ along with their friends, and left while there had still been time.'

for the holy virgin to bestow benefits on people in spirit while she was still dwelling in the flesh, for Christ himself, in order to make known her merit, deigned to reveal[169] to her through the Spirit the desires of those absent as well as those present.

In Andernach there was a certain knight lying on his death bed, whose friends were visiting him and talking over his affairs, when at length the hour came and the bell for church sounded. At this, they left one of the women to watch over him while they hurried off to the church.

Now that he had obtained some silence at last, with deep sighs he called upon God with his whole heart. Piteously he implored that by the merits of this holy virgin God might bestow healing on him. No sooner had he finished his prayer, when he deserved to be refreshed by means of a great vision: it seemed to him that the venerable virgin appeared to him and approached him, gently inquiring if he wanted to be healed. When he replied that he very much desired it, she placed her hand upon the man's head and responded: 'In the name of him who said: *they will lay their hands upon the sick and they will become well again* (Mk 16:18), let this infirmity depart from you, and you be healed!' When she had spoken these words, the vision disappeared, and the sick man, to the wonder of all who had assembled, rose up from his bed quite recovered.

XVI

IT SEEMS NOT FAR from our purpose to tell of what happened in the case of a certain priest, because in this tale the virtues of the holy virgin are demonstrated, and a miraculous incident is rightly impressed on the memory as a warning[170] through which anyone living negligently might, please God, turn to the better. This incident took place in a village of Swabia called Rüdesheim.

The day was over and the night was coming on when the priest of a certain village entered the church in order to light the lamps for the sanctuary. Then, to his surprise, he saw that there were two candles on the altar still alight and burning. Now a young scholar had come with him, who used to regularly and attentively assist him in the divine liturgy.

---

[169] Guibert qualifies it: 'often reveal'.

[170] Sulpicius Severus, *Vita S. Martini* 22, 6, ed. by J. Fontaine, p. 302.

When the priest asked him 'Why did you neglect to put out the candles?' the young man replied 'I did put them out.' Whereupon the priest approached to perform the task himself, but discovered an unfolded altar cloth, of the kind that is unrolled for the Divine Mysteries.

While he was standing there at a loss, the young man collapsed on the ground, and entirely beside himself, shouted: '*The sword of the Lord* (Is. 34:6) has struck us!' The priest thought he had been knocked down, and hurried to raise him from the ground. But the young man was unharmed, and made this pronouncement: 'If we see the letters on the altar cloth, we shall not die!' The priest was thinking that the youth was foolishly shouting like this from fright, not knowing what he said; nevertheless he went up to the altar again, and in the place where the holy rites are carried out, he found on the cloth five letters in the form of a cross, not written with human hand. They were, horizontally, A.P.H.; and vertically, K.P.D.[171]

When the priest had seen and carefully noted this, the young man recovered his strength and got up, while the priest, having folded the altar cloth and put out the candles, went home none the wiser. The letters lasted for seven days, but from the eighth day onwards they disappeared.

Being perplexed in himself he made known what had happened to certain devout and wise persons, but none of them could explain what it might mean, until after sixteen years had passed, when news was spreading through the whole world that the blessed Hildegard was illumined by the Holy Spirit, so he came to her and was able to understand the meaning of so strange a portent in accordance with what she herself taught him through the Holy Spirit.

Just as Daniel of old read what appeared on the wall (cf. Dan. 5), so Hildegard read what was written on the cloth, explaining the letters in this way: K—*Kyrium*, P—*presbyter*, D—*derisit*, A—*ascendat*, P—*poenitens*,

---

[171]
$$K$$
$$A \ P \ H$$
$$D$$

There is a diagram of this acrostic among Hildegard's letters on sheet 57^v of B and a strange version of the meaning of the letters. I translate (from Klaes, p. 121*): 'The Lord is lacking a priest / he first mocked Christ / he laments to Christ about the charge / the altar has a cup / go up O pupil to drink / the priest has wings' (!). Cf. Klaes, pp. 121–22*, 166.

H—*homo*.[172] When he heard this the priest was seized with fear and confronted his sinful conscience.[173] So, after he had corrected himself he became a monk, and strove by means of penance to amend the negligence of his past life. Thus, in just the way that the holy virgin had explained the letters, he rose to a higher and stricter life, and showed himself a perfect servant of God by a holy way of life.

XVII

AMIDST ALL THIS IT is remarkable of her that she, not so much led as driven by the Divine Spirit, came to Cologne, Trier, Metz, Würzburg and Bamberg to announce to the clergy and the people what God wanted of them.[174] She also made known whatever was for the benefit of souls, as God had revealed it to her, in Disibodenberg, Siegberg, Eberbach, Hirsau, Zwiefalten, Maulbronn, Rothenkirchen, Kitzinger, Krauftal, Herde,[175] Hönningen, Werden, Andernach, Marienberg, Elsen,[176] and Winkel.

---

[172] I.e. *Kyrium presbiter derisit*: 'the priest has mocked the Lord', and *ascendat poenitens homo*: 'let him rise/go up (to the altar?) a repentant man'.

[173] *peccatricem accusat conscientiam*; the perspective is Hildegard's strong monastic bent and her promotion of the Gregorian reforms of the Church, particularly the restoration of celibacy for priests and the extirpation of simony. She reckoned that on a criterion of holiness the monastic lifestyle was higher than that of the diocesan clergy. E.g. *Scivias*, book II, vision 5, chapters 3 and 4 (trans. by Hart and Bishop, p. 204). Thus the priest had probably not been living in celibacy, or was involved in simoniac practices, or both.

[174] See *VH* II, 10 and III, 23 where Hildegard mentions her journeys. There are also references to her journeys in her letters. In her translation of the *VH* into German, *Das Leben der Heiligen Hildegard*, pp. 143–46, Führkötter accounts for four journeys between 1158 and 1177: Hildegard's journey along the Main river (between 1158 and 1161), a Rhineland Lotharingia journey (1160), a Rhine journey (between 1161 and 1163) and a journey into Swabia (1170–1171).

[175] Führkötter (op. cit., p. 110) identifies the *Herde* of the text with Hördt in Bayern. Klaes (p. 122*, n. 234) suggests rather the Premonstratensian monastery of Herde in the diocese of Trier. Rothenkirchen and Elsen were also Premonstratensian. Eberbach and Maulbronn were Cistercian, while Hönningen, Andernach and Gottesthal were foundations of Augustinian canons, the rest were Benedictine (either monks or nuns).

[176] Führkötter (op. cit., p. 111) on the basis of close textual analyses refers the *Clusin* of the text to Klause, the monastery of St George at Rheingau. On the other hand, Klaes (p. 122*, n. 235) points out that in 1145 a Norbertine (Premonstratensian) monastery called *Elsun* was founded on the Lahn in the diocese of Cologne.

XVIII

AT ONE TIME, CLOSE to the town of Rüdesheim, where she used to ford the currents of the Rhine and put in at a spot near the nuns' monastery,[177] a certain woman approached her boat, carrying a little child[178] in the crook of her arms. She besought Hildegard in tears to lay her holy hands on the child. Being deeply moved, and remembering him who said: *Go to the pool of Siloe, and wash* (Jn 9:7), she drew water from the river with her left hand, and blessed it with her right. When she sprinkled it into the child's eyes, through the favour of God's grace it gained its sight.

XVIIII

ON ANOTHER OCCASION THERE was a man who used to suffer acute attacks of epilepsy.[179] In his anxiety he implored the venerable virgin to come to his aid. She made the sign of the Cross over him with a healing blessing and from that day forward he was never burdened with this affliction again. When he announced back at home that a miracle had been worked in him,[180] many hastened to her for a remedy of the same affliction, and when she blessed them with the sign of the Cross, they were set free.[181]

---

[177] In 1165 Hildegard founded a second monastery of nuns just across the Rhine at Eibingen, using the remains of an Augustinian double foundation destroyed by Emperor Frederick (J. Hotchin, 'Saintly Expectations and Earthly Networks: The Construction of Hildegard's Sanctity' (unpublished MA thesis, Department of History, Monash University, 1997), ch. 3). Here she settled her nuns who were not nobly born, and twice a week used to visit them. Thus she could be readily found by those seeking her help while she was travelling between the two houses. Eibingen still flourishes today as the Benediktinerinnenabtei St Hildegard.

[178] *puerulum*, and likewise further on, *puer*. However, this is not a little boy but a little girl. Her name was Mechtild and she appears years later as a witness in *Acta Inq.* III and VII.

[179] *Caducum morbum acriter patiebatur.*

[180] The text in PL seems to depart from R (and T) by finishing the sentence, rather lamely, with 'all those of his household rejoiced and gave thanks to God'.

[181] *per benedictionis sue liberati sunt signaculum.* The *signaculum* was the Sign of the Cross.

XX

AMONG OTHER SIGNS OF her virtues, the Lord gave the holy virgin a charism of casting out demons from the bodies of the obsessed.[182] The venerable lady[183] herself tells the story of what happened to a certain noblewoman still of tender years. She says:

> After the vision had instructed me in the text and the words of the Gospel of John, I fell back into my bed sick, and from the weight of it I could in no way lift myself up. This illness was blown into me by a blast of the south wind, whereby my body was ground down by such sufferings that my soul could scarcely bear it. For half a year the blast so went through my body that I was in as great an agony as if my soul were about to quit this life.[184] Then there came another blast of moist wind which mingled itself with this heat in such a way that my flesh was somewhat cooled, otherwise it would have been utterly burnt up. Thus I was afflicted for the space of a whole year, though I saw in true vision that my life had not yet done with its earthly course, but was to be prolonged for some time yet.
>
> In the meantime it was reported to me that far from us in the regions of the lower Rhine, a certain noblewoman had been obsessed by a devil. Indeed, messengers came to me about this woman[185] again and again. But I, in a true vision, saw that God had permitted her to be obsessed and overshadowed by a kind of blackness and smoke of a diabolical fog, which oppressed all the senses of her rational soul and did not allow her to hope by raising her intellect on high. It was as when the shadow of a person or some other object, or a smoke covers and envelops whatever is in its path. So this woman lost the right use of her senses and actions, and was

---

[182] For analysis of the following events concerning Hildegard and Sigewize, see Newman, 'Three-Part Invention', pp. 199–205. Newman concludes that Sigewize (p. 202) was 'afflicted with a preaching devil'. She notes (p. 203) that Hildegard's long-remembered sermon against the Cathars in 1163 was at Cologne, Sigewize's home town, not long after the demon began to plague her. 'Whatever else this narrative may be, it is the story of a relationship between women—of Sigewize's unusual response to Hildegard ... and Hildegard's reciprocal response to her "fan" (p. 202).' Newman remarks (p. 203) Hildegard's great empathy for Sigewize in her whole account of the affair.

[183] T *domina*; R and PL: *mater.* This use of 'mater' in the Riesenkodex reflects its copying by the nuns at Rupertsberg.

[184] See Theodoric, *Chronicon Epternacense*, MGH SS 23, p. 50, line 7.

[185] *de hac (femina).* Re could also be implied. Here it is taken as a grammatical reference to the *nobilis femina* just mentioned, hence 'woman' is supplied. For a contrast, cf. the parallel passage in Guibert's revision of the *VH.*

constantly shouting out and doing unseemly things.[186] But when by the command of God this evil was lessened in her, she was no longer so weighed down.

While I was thinking this over and wanting to understand how a diabolic form enters a human being, I saw and heard the answer—that a devil does not actually enter a human being in its own form; rather with the shadow and smoke of his blackness, he overshadows and covers him over. If he really could enter a human being in his own form, all the person's members would disintegrate more quickly than chaff scattered by the wind.[187] Therefore, God does not allow him to enter a human being in his own form, but as we said above, he envelops his victim, and warps him into insanity and unseemly ways, and snarls through him as through a window, and moves his limbs outwardly. Yet the demon is not within him in his own form, rather it is as if the soul of a person is in a stupefied sleep, and does not know what the flesh of the body is doing.

Then I saw that there is a swarm of malevolent spirits who with their clever ways at corrupting things go through all the world seeking, wherever they may find them, those through whom they can contrive discords and moral aberrations. It was these demons who at the very beginning when they were created, spurned God in the presence of the most righteous angels saying: 'Who is *he* to have such authority over us?' (cf. Lk. 20:2, Mk 11:28) They said this from envy, disgust and derision, and they have continued till now in the same, and these are the motives of all they do, for indeed they began it all with the false step of their primal mockery.

But since God wants his people to be purified by means of these demons, by his permission and mandate they stir up a stupor in the air, and by means of a foam of the air they vomit[188] up plague, and cause floods and dangers in the waters, provoke wars and spawn adversities and evils.[189] God allows these things to happen, because in their arrogance human beings wallow in crimes and murders. But when God has purified his people in this way, he reduces the same spirits to confusion, as happened to the woman mentioned above.

Indeed when, by God's permission, the vile spirit had long confused many through her on account of the wanton behaviour and the sins to which he had swayed them, still some were struck with terror and because

---

[186] See Hildegard, *LDO* 3, 2, 9, CCCM 92, p. 365, lines 60–61 (3, 7, 9, PL 197, 970A).

[187] See Hildegard, *Vita S. Disibodi*, PL 197, 1101C.

[188] Cf. Hildegard, *Scivias*, ed. by Führkötter, CCCM 43A, Book Three, Ninth Vision, Ch. 2, p. 520, line 189.

[189] See Hildegard, *LDO* 1, 4, 4, CCCM 92, p. 139 (PL 197, 809A).

of this repented, and thus the malevolent spirit himself was confounded. For God allows his friends to be afflicted by setbacks and illnesses so that they might be cleansed from evils. Hence his enemies are confounded when his chosen ones are refashioned by their purification into resplendent jewels before God.

After the woman had been led around to the saints in many places, the spirit that was oppressing her was conquered by the merits of the saints and the prayers of the people, and bellowed out that there was a little old hag[190] in the regions of the Rhine, through whose counsel he would need to be cast out. When her friends understood this, they led her to us in the eighth year of her torment, just as the Lord wished.

XXI

BEFORE WE CONTINUE WITH the words of the virgin of Christ, it would be well worth inserting at this point the letters which the Abbot of Brauweiler resolved to send to Hildegard concerning this demoniac woman, and the one she sent in reply to him. By means of these, the malice of the demon may be more clearly understood, and the judgments of God be more fully praised, which, though inscrutable, were ever just.

After seven years this woman was led to Brauweiler, that she might be set free there by the merits of Saint Nicholas. When the foul spirit had been summoned, it declared that it would not leave its little tenancy except that they had the counsel and help of a little old hag in the regions of the upper Rhine, as she herself said above. The demon toyed with her name and mockingly called her Scrumpilgard.[191] And so they sought her counsel, and sent her the letter of petition which follows:

> To the venerable lady and mother Hildegard, to the spouse of Christ who embraces him with all her inward being, to the daughter of the most high King, Gedolf the overseer, such as he is, of the monastery of Brauweiler, together with his brothers detained in this valley of tears, pledge the devoted loyalty of their affection, with all the prayers of which they are capable.
>
> O most lovable lady, though your face is not known to us, the fame of your virtues is much celebrated among us, and *though we may be absent in*

---

[190] *vetula*; here, this diminutive of 'old woman' has a mocking sense: 'hag', 'witch', 'biddy'.

[191] In English the meaning would be something like 'Wrinklegard'.

body, yet in spirit we are ever present to you (cf. 1 Cor. 5:3);[192] the Lord who knows all things knows how strong is the affection of our love for you. Accordingly, the news has been heard in our land and it has spread abroad in popular talk what the Lord has brought about in your regard, namely, *he who is mighty has done great things through you, and holy is his name* (Lk. 1:49). Already, both the clergy and the people know with what great miracles the fountain of the living light has shone out in you, and the outcome of events declares it too. For a work shines in you not of human origin, but of divine, proceeding from a charism, a pre-eminent gift, which human reason does not dictate but which proceeds from the most luminous fountain.

But why do we delay? 'It would be better to weep than to speak'.[193] Therefore, the sweetness of your holiness, O most devout lady, will not think it rash of us if we presume in the simplicity of our hearts, compelled as we are by very great need, to lay before you what has given rise to this need,[194] for we have no doubt that from you we shall receive good counsel.

For a certain noble woman, obsessed for some years by a malevolent spirit, was led to us by the hands of her friends so that by the help of blessed Nicholas, under whose patronage we are placed, she might be set free from the menacing enemy. But the cunning and wickedness of this most crafty and wickedest of enemies has drawn so many people—perhaps even thousands—into error and doubt, that we fear the greatest harm may be done to holy Church. For all of us, together with the throng of people, have been labouring already for three months in every way to set this woman free, and—we cannot say it without grief—because of our sins which press upon us, we have made no headway at all.

Because of this, all our hope is, after God, in you. For this demon, being summoned one day of late, has finally made known to us that the obsessed woman can be set free only by the virtue of your contemplation and the liberality of divine revelation.

For does not God intend great things through her liberation? Assuredly! Thus shall the overflowing kindness of our Redeemer condescend through you to bring the labour of our toil and our grief to abundant fruition in gladness and exultation, when he brings to nothing all the error and infidelity of men and sets free this obsessed handmaid of God. So shall we be able to say with the prophet: *This was the Lord's doing, and it is marvellous in our eyes* (Ps. 127:23), and, *the snare is broken, and we have*

---

[192] Throughout this letter Hildegard is addressed in the formal plural second person.

[193] Gregory, *Dialogues* 3, 1, ed. by A. de Vogüé, p. 264.

[194] Cf. Theodoric *Libellus de libertate*, MGH SS 23, p. 67, lines 20–23.

been set free! (Ps. 123:7)

Therefore may your holiness be very sure to let us know in a letter whatever God may inspire or reveal in vision to you about this matter. This we urgently and humbly implore you. Farewell![195]

When the blessed Hildegard had received this letter and had carefully gone through it, she was tenderly sympathetic to those making the request and instructed her sisters to humbly apply themselves to both public and private prayers for the above mentioned need. She, having offered prayer, raised the eyes of her mind to the Lord, and wrote back this reply, just as she saw and heard it in true vision, dictated from no other source than that of inexhaustible Wisdom itself:

To Gedolf, Abbot of the community of Brauweiler, Hildegard.

Though I have been confined by the scourges of God in a protracted and severe illness, I have done the best I could to respond quickly to your request. What I have to say is not from me, but from *him who is* (Ex. 3:14).

There are various kinds of malevolent spirits. But this demon you are asking about has crafty ways which are assimilated to human behaviour through the vices;[196] therefore he likes to lurk about with human beings, and will ignore and mock even the cross of the Lord and relics of the saints and other things which pertain to the service of God; he does not fear them much. True, he does not love these things, but he only puts on a show of fleeing them, just as a stupid and careless person attaches little importance to the words and the warnings brought him by the wise. He is therefore more difficult to expel than other demons. For *he shall not be cast out without fasts*, scourgings, *prayers*, almsgivings and by the express command of God (cf. Mk 9:29, Mat. 17:20).

Listen then to the reply not of man, but of *him who lives* (Apoc. 1:18).

Choose seven priests of known good character, who are commended by their worthy way of life, in the name and order of Abel, Noah, Abraham, Melchizedek, Jacob and Aaron who offered sacrifice to the living God, and the seventh in the name of Christ who on the Cross offered his own self to God the Father.

After fasts, scourgings, prayers, almsgivings and celebrations of Masses, they shall then, with humble disposition and in priestly vestments

---

[195] Van Acker did not include the three letters in this chapter in his critical edition of Hildegard's letter but refers the reader (p. 152) to Klaes's forthcoming edition of the *VH*. For another English translation see Letter 68, Baird and Ehrman, pp. 147–48, Letter 68r (Hildegard to Abbot Gedolphus), pp. 148–49 and Letter 69, pp. 151–52.

[196] Cf. Hildegard, *Causae et curae*, ed. by P. Kaiser, p. 58.

and stoles approach the sufferer. As they stand around her, let each of them take in his hand a rod in the likeness of that rod with which Moses struck Egypt, the Red Sea and the rock by the order of God (cf. Ex. 7:8–10:23), so that, just as God manifested miracles there through the rod,[197] so he also might glorify himself when this vilest enemy is cast out by the rods.

There shall be seven priests, in the likeness of the seven gifts of the Holy Spirit, so that *the Spirit of God* who in the beginning *hovered over the waters* (Gen. 1:2) and *who breathed into the face* of man *the breath of life* (Gen. 2:7), might blow out the unclean spirit from this exhausted human being.

Let the first one who is in the name of Abel hold the rod in his hand and say: 'Hear this you malevolent and foolish spirit, whoever you are inhabiting this human being, hear these words not thought out beforehand by man,[198] but made manifest by *him who is* (Ex. 3:14) and *who lives* (Apoc. 1:18).[199] When at his command you are crushed, then be off with you! Listen to him who is who says: I who am without a beginning, but from whom all beginnings came forth, I who am the ancient of days say this: I am by my own self the Day, who never came forth from the sun, but the one from whom the sun caught alight. I am Reason,[200] which was not uttered from another, but that from which breathes forth all rationality. I have therefore made mirrors of my face to be contemplated, in which I survey all the wonders of my timelessness, which shall never fail. I have established these same mirrors in a symphony of praises, for mine is a

---

[197] Cf. Thiofrid, *Flores Epitaphii*, 3, 2 (PL 157, 373A).

[198] Hildegard, *LDO* Prol., CCCM 92, p. 45, line 23 (PL 197, 742A).

[199] In all manuscripts the exorcism rite suddenly breaks off here with the words *et cetera*. What is translated from here to the end of the letter is found in B where it was written in the margin by a later hand (B[1]) with a sign indicating it was to be inserted at this point. Cf. Klaes, pp. 115–16*. Although T attests that this insertion was not part of Theodoric's final version of the *VH*, it was part of the material used by him, and he expressly alludes to it and assumes it is available to the reader. That it had an independent existence as an exorcism ritual-text is proved by its survival among Hildegard's letters in the Vienna codex 1016 (Wa), for a description of which see Van Acker, pp. XLIV–XLV. When B was rebound in the 18th century, some of the margin was lost and the text is somewhat problematical. Cf. Peter Dronke, 'Problemata Hildegardiana', *Mittellateinisches Jahrbuch*, 16 (1981), pp. 127–29.

[200] *ratio*; i.e. the *Logos* of Jn 1:1, the Hebrew *Dabhar*, the *Word* which has power to effect what it expresses. The derivatives of the Greek *logos* were often translated into Latin by the word *ratio* and its field, e.g. the Vulgate of Rom. 12:1 *rationabile* (λογικὴν) *obsequium*. Jn 1:1–3 was of intense interest to Hildegard, who made it the subject of her *Liber Divinorum Operum*, with which there are close links throughout this text.

voice like thunder, by which I set in motion the whole orb of the earth with the living sounds of all created things.'[201]

And then let this priest and the other six priests mentioned above who are standing by, strike her with rods—not too hard—upon the head and upon the back, upon the chest and upon the navel and upon the kidneys, upon the knees, upon the feet,[202] and let them say:

Now then, O Satan, you malevolent spirit who wear out and oppress this human being and the form of this woman,[203] through him who lives and who brings forth and speaks these words by means of a simple person unversed in human learning:[204] you are commanded, and he himself now commands you that through his own name you depart from this human being here whom you have long been wearing out, and in whom you have continued till now. And so, by this rod, at the command of the true Beginning, that is, by the Beginning himself,[205] you are never more to do her[206] harm.

---

[201] For the section from 'I who am without ...' see Hildegard, *LDO* 1, 4, 105 CCCM 92, p. 248 (PL 197, 888D–9A). From this Klaes restores the text 'I have ... the wonders', whereas Dronke only has *abissos* followed by a question mark.

[202] Note that in the nominated parts of the body, the number seven figures again.

[203] *hunc hominem et formam mulieris huius.*

[204] *hec verba per simplicem et humana doctrina indoctum hominem protulit*; i.e. Hildegard herself. Cf. Hildegard *LDO* 3, 10, 38, CCCM 92, p. 462 (PL 197, 1038B).

[205] *in precepto veri principii, scilicet in ipso principio*; this continues the reference to the Vulgate text of Jn 1:1–2.

[206] *eum*; i.e. not 'him' but 'her', for this is referring to the woman as *hominem*. The understanding of the obsessed woman as generic *homo*, and Hildegard herself as *homo*, is a feature of this passage. There are other shifts of grammatical gender in these passages, as when *eum* refers not to Sigewize as *homo*, but to the diabolical spirit, in which case it is translated as 'him'. The use of language here, and other aspects of these texts, such as the role of priests, are weighted with significance in terms of theological anthropology. There can be few more powerful texts in the Christian tradition than *VH* III, 20–22 for illustrating the teaching of John-Paul II in *Mulieris Dignitatem* (Australian edition: Homebush, St Paul Publications, 1988), 'From this point of view, the "woman" is the representative and the archetype of the whole human race: she represents the humanity which belongs to all human beings, both men and women (no. 4, p. 15) ... We can also see that the struggle with evil and with the Evil One marks the biblical exemplar of the "woman" from the beginning to the end of human history. Is not the Bible trying to tell us that it is precisely in the "woman"—Eve/Mary—that history witnesses a dramatic struggle for every human being, the struggle for his or her fundamental "yes" or "no" to God (no. 30, p. 106)?'

You are summoned and vanquished through the sacrifice and prayers and help of Abel, in whose name we strike you!

And again let them strike her as above: You are summoned and vanquished through the sacrifice and prayers and help of Noah, in whose name we strike you!

And again let them strike: You are summoned and vanquished through the sacrifice and prayers and help of Abraham, in whose name we strike you!

And let them strike her as above: You are summoned and vanquished through the sacrifice and prayers and help of Melchizedek, in whose name we strike you!

And again let them strike her as above: You are summoned and vanquished through the sacrifice and prayers and help of Jacob, in whose name we strike you!

And let them strike her as above: You are summoned and vanquished through the sacrifice and prayers and help of Aaron, in whose name we strike you!

And let them strike her as above: You are summoned and vanquished through the sacrifice and prayers and help of the great High Priest, the Son of God, for whom all true priests have sacrificed and do offer sacrifice,[207] in whose name and power we strike you!

And again let them strike her saying: By that confusion with which you at your first appearance[208] *fell* like lead *from heaven* (cf. Lk. 10:18), you are to depart, confounded, from this human being and never again do her harm!

But let that height which no height has ever attained, and that depth which no depth has ever fathomed, and that breadth which no breadth has ever encompassed set her free from your strength, your stupid malice and all your crafty tricks, so that you depart from her confounded, and in such a way that she may neither sense nor know you. Just as you were cut off from heaven, so may the Holy Spirit cut you off from her; and just as you are a stranger to all happiness, so may you be a stranger to her; and just as you never longed for God, so may you never long to come near her again.

Therefore, be off, be off, be off from her O devil, and all the malevolent spirits of the air with you! You are summoned by the force of the Eternal who created all things and who made man, and by the kindness of the humanity of our Saviour, who himself set man free, and who by fiery love

---

[207] *adiutorio summi sacerdotis, filii Dei, cui omnes veri sacerdotes sacrificaverant et sacrificium offerunt.*

[208] *in prima apparitione*, i.e. attendance at the heavenly court.

established man in unfailing life.

Vanquished as you are by the Passion which was through the wood of the holy Cross, and by the Resurrection of life, and by that power which cast forth the devil from heaven into hell, on account of which you at your first appearance *fell* like lead *from heaven* (cf. Lk. 10:18), depart then in confusion from this human being, and never again harm her in her soul or in any of the limbs of her body. You are commanded by the Almighty One who made her and created her. Amen.

If it has not yet been expelled, let the second priest along with the other priests standing by him follow the same sequence until God comes to his help.

When the holy virgin had finished this letter revealed by the Holy Spirit, she sent it by the hand of that man whom she had discreetly sought out, as she tells in the book *Scivias*,[209] to the monastery where the woman was held, so that it might be humbly recited over her. The reader came to the place where it is written at the end:

And I, unlearned and poor little feminine form that I am, O blaspheming spirit of mockery, speak to you in the name of that Truth in which I, poor little and unlearned form that I am, by the light of Wisdom, have seen and heard these things; I command you by that same Wisdom to depart from this human being, leaving her in a stable condition, and not in the turbulence of your instability.

At that point the foul spirit gave out an almighty roar, and with an extraordinary caterwauling and a frightful din he came out of her screeching, to the utter fright of the bystanders. For the space of about half an hour he had kept up his frenzy, until, when it pleased God, the demon forsook the vessel he had so long occupied.[210]

When she realized she had been set free, the woman reached out her hands to the bystanders, so that they could help her up, for she had no strength left. She then prostrated herself before the high altar of Saint Nicholas and gave thanks to God for her liberation.

But when the people saw this, they made a din the way that crowds do,

---

[209] I.e. Volmar. The reference is to Hildegard's preface to *Scivias.*

[210] Cf. Rupert of Deutz, *Vita Heriberti*, 17, ed. by Peter Dinter, Veröffentlichungen des Historischen Vereins für den Niederrhein, insbesondere das Alte Erzbistum Köln, 13 (Bonn: Röhrscheid, 1976), p. 60.

noisily expressing their thanks and praise to God with loud clapping and stomping, while the brothers were intoning the hymn *Te Deum laudamus*. Then alas, sad to say, the same ancient enemy, by the inscrutable judgment of God, came back and sought out again the vessel he had just abandoned. And so the woman began to quake all over, and with a hissing and a shouting, raised herself up and took to raving more wildly than before. At this, the bystanders were terrified and, overwhelmed with disappointment, asked the foul spirit why he had dared return to God's creature. He replied: 'I was terrified of the sign of the crucified, and so I fled. But when I did not know where to go, I sought out again my empty vessel which was not sealed.'[211]

When the letter and the adjurations of the holy virgin were used in order to force it out again, he snarled and shouted out that he would not leave except in the presence of the little old crone herself.[212] Then, those who were of sounder judgment persuaded the friends and guardians of the woman to lead her to the blessed virgin. They received a blessing from the Abbot and brothers and a letter of commendation, and so set out for the place. The letter is as follows:

> To the venerable lady Hildegard, worthy of every act of thanks, Gedolf the unworthy Abbot of Brauweiler, and all his brothers, wish you life, progress, the world under your feet, and whatever of a higher order it is possible to wish for a handmaid of Christ.
>
> By now the whole world knows that the Lord has looked on you[213] and poured out his grace in you. Whereas up to this time we have spoken with your holiness only through our messengers and letters about the pressing need of the woman obsessed by a malevolent spirit, now at the last we speak to you by means of her own person, who is now led to you in great hope. We express again the plea of her pressing need and devoutly add prayers to our prayers, that the nearer to you she is in body, the more benefit you may be to her in spirit.
>
> For by means of the letter you sent us, dictated by the Holy Spirit, we summoned the demon and he did relinquish for a brief time the vessel he had occupied. But alas, by whatever judgment of God we do not know, he returned and again invaded his abandoned vessel which he now exhausts more cruelly than he did before. When we summoned him again even more

---

[211] Cf. Gregory, *Dialogues* 3, 7, ed. by A. de Vogüé, p. 282.

[212] Cf. Theodoric, *Libellus de libertate*, MGH SS 23, p. 71, line 27.

[213] This letter also addresses Hildegard in the formal plural second person.

strongly and insistently, he finally replied that he would not leave that vessel except in your presence.

For her sake, we send her to your holiness so that what we did not deserve, because of our sins which press upon us, the Lord may accomplish through you, and so that he who is powerful over all things may be glorified in you when he casts out the ancient enemy. May your maternal love prevail!

XXII

IT SEEMS APPROPRIATE TO pick up again the thread of our discourse from which we had digressed a little by including these letters, that all might see how it was to glorify his holy virgin that God so prolonged the liberation of this woman. It would have been easy for the Almighty to fulfil what was sought on behalf of the obsessed, by means of other saints, to all of whom the woman had been led around these many years. But God assigned the glory of this miracle to the holy virgin, since he wished to reveal more clearly to all, in her own life-time, the character of her merits. It will be easier to understand how it happened from her own words:

> At the arrival of this woman we were quite terrified as to how we might cope with seeing and hearing her, by whom so many people had been disturbed for so long a time. But God rained down the dew of his sweetness upon us, and without shrinking back or trembling or any help from strong men, we found a place for her in the living quarters of the sisters. From then on, neither on account of the dread or confusion with which the demon troubled all those who came near on account of their sins, nor on account of the mocking and foul words with which he wanted to defeat us, nor on account of his disgusting blasts of air, did we give her up at any time.
>
> I saw that the demon suffered three tortures in this woman: the first when she was led from one place to another of the saints, the second when the common folk gave alms for her, the third when he was compelled to depart through the prayers of the spiritual by the grace of God.
>
> And so, from the Purification of Holy Mary until the Sabbath of the Pasch,[214] we and our neighbours of both sexes, laboured on her account

---

[214] I.e. from 2 February to Holy Saturday, on which day the Easter Vigil was celebrated. Thus the exorcism closely followed the inner logic of the Liturgy, covering the

with fasts and prayers, with almsgiving and penances of our bodies.

In the meantime, by the power of God, the unclean spirit was forced, however unwillingly, to utter many things before the people about saving Baptism, the sacrament of the Body of Christ, the peril of the excommunicated, the ruin of the Cathars,[215] and other such things. All this was to his own confusion and to the glory of Christ, and many were made stronger in faith thereby, and many more prompt to amend their sins. But whenever I saw in true vision that he was bringing forth lies, straightaway I refuted him, whereupon he would fall silent and grind his teeth at me. Yet I did not forbid him to speak before the people when he uttered what was true.

At length the day of the Holy Sabbath[216] came, when the priest hallows the baptismal font with his breath when he sends it into the font, along with those words which the Holy Spirit has infused into the rationality of man and the doctors of the Church. For in the first creation the Spirit of the Lord stirred the waters, as it is written: *The Spirit of the Lord hovered over the waters* (Gen. 1:2).

The woman who was present there[217] was seized by a great fear and began to tremble. Since she was stomping at the earth with her feet, and because of the dreadful spirit which was assailing her, she emitted frequent

---

Septuagesima period (pre-Lent), which in the Office commences by revisiting the fall of Adam and Eve, through Lent, during which great figures in subsequent salvation history are presented in the readings, the progressive exorcisms of baptismal candidates are carried out, and the contest of the faithful with sin is intensified in personal penance. It all culminates in the Paschal vigil which is marked by its baptismal character, including the renewal of baptismal promises by the faithful who once again abjure the Devil and all his deceits and works.

[215] 'It is even said in another source that Sigewize reported the whereabouts of certain Cathars in Mainz, leading to their interrogation and ultimate conversion,' Newman, 'Three-Part Invention', p. 203 and n. 62. Catharism was a neo-gnostic movement, first noticed in the tenth century in Bulgaria (the 'Bogomils'), and reaching its peak in the West in the late twelfth and thirteenth centuries. They flourished in the Rhineland, precisely in the latter half of Hildegard's lifetime. In 1163, six years before the present incident, four men and one *iuvencula* were burnt as Cathars at Cologne, cf. *Chronica Regia Coloniensis*, ed. by G. Waitz, Scriptores rerum germanicorum in usum scholarum (Hannover: Hahn, 1880), p. 114. Shortly before the burning, Hildegard had preached before the clergy of Cologne about the Cathars, acknowledging their criticisms of morally corrupt clergy, but vigorously repudiating their doctrine and motivation; see Ep. 15r, Van Acker, pp. 34–47; Baird and Ehrman, pp. 54–56; and Constant J. Mews, 'Hildegard and the Schools'.

[216] Guibert adds: 'of the Pasch, when there were about three thousand people present'.

[217] Guibert adds: 'with me'.

blasts of air.[218] Immediately I saw and heard in true vision, that *the power of the Most High*, which once *overshadowed* (Lk. 1:35) and ever overshadows Holy Baptism, spoke to the diabolical fog by which the woman was being worn out: 'Go forth, Satan, from the tabernacle of this woman's body; yield place in her to the Holy Spirit!' Then the unclean spirit withdrew from her in a horrible way with a discharge from the woman's private parts,[219] and she was set free. From then on, she continued in her right senses, both of soul and body as long as she lived.[220] When this was revealed to the people, all of them proclaimed with songs of praise and words of prayer 'Glory to you, O Lord!'

In just such a way God allowed Job's whole body to be infested with the horror and putrefaction of worms, since Satan was thinking that through his scheme to impugn God's honour, he might prevail against Job. But God kept guard over Job's soul and did not allow Satan to touch it, because through his faith Job did not abandon God. Thus Satan was confounded and left him, and it was God who had the victory over him—so Satan might understand that no one can prevail against God. Just so,[221] though this woman was handed over to be troubled by the malevolent spirit, God did not allow her soul to fail in good faith. Therefore the Devil was confounded in her, because he could not turn her aside from God's righteousness.

XXIII

WITH WORDS SUCH AS these the virgin of God celebrated the works of divine mercy accomplished because of her and through her. Yet she gives her account gently, sweetly, modestly and humbly, attributing nothing to herself, for she held that to flee the vaunting of one's virtues was itself a

---

[218] *Sufflatum sepe emisit.* The *sufflatum* emitted by the woman reflects the 'blowing-*out*' on the part of the spirit of evil, the opposite of the 'breathing-*into*' which characterizes the Spirit of God; similarly the 'overshadowing' of the Spirit opposes the 'fog', the choking obfuscation of the devil. Whether the woman emits wind through the mouth in a kind of belching or even hyperventilation, or from the rear, of which something is said shortly, is unclear.

[219] *Tunc immundus spiritus per verecunda loca femine cum egestione horribiliter egressus est.* Cf. Sulpicius Severus, *Vita S. Martini* 17, 7; ed. by J. Fontaine, p. 290.

[220] Sigewize lived on as a sister at Rupertsberg (*Acta Inq.* II). Hildegard's account is at the most a very few years after the incident, and implies that she has already died.

[221] Guibert follows with: 'it happened to this woman, since she was handed over ...'.

mark of virtue.[222]

After so humble an account of this virtue, in which she arrogates nothing to herself, as if she were saying with the Apostle: *Lest the greatness of these revelations should exalt me, there was given to me a sting of my flesh, an angel of Satan to beat me* (2 Cor. 12:7), she immediately adds an account of the weakening of her whole flesh which followed as though it were in truth a sting against pride. She says:

> It is no wonder that, after this woman's liberation, a severe ailment assailed me again, withering the very blood in my veins and the very marrow in my bones,[223] and setting all my entrails below in a turmoil. My whole body languished, just as plant life loses its viridity in winter. And I saw that the wicked spirits were then laughing at me raucously: 'Aha! She's going to die, and all her friends who helped her rebuff us are going to cry!' But I knew that my soul's departure was not yet near. Nonetheless I endured that infirmity for over forty days and nights.
>
> In the meantime it was shown to me in a true vision that I was to visit certain communities of spiritual people, both of men and of women,[224] and candidly lay before them the words that God would show me. When I eventually tried to do this, though I had no strength of body, my infirmity somewhat lightened. So I put God's command into effect, and I calmed the dissensions that had been going on among certain people.
>
> When, for fear of the people, I neglected these courses of action which God had commanded me, the sufferings of my body increased, and they did not cease until I obeyed, just as it happened to Jonah, who was afflicted severely till he inclined himself again to obedience.

XXIIII

FOLLOWING THIS THE SPOUSE of Christ merited an exalted visitation in which she received so great a consolation, that from the delight of it she said she had been filled with a rapture of immeasurable joy:[225]

---

[222] *quia virtutum iactantiam fugere virtutis loco ducebat.*

[223] See Hildegard, *LDO* 1, 3, 15, CCCM 92, p. 131 (PL 197, 803D).

[224] *quasdam congregationes spiritualium hominum, virorum ac mulierum.*

[225] *ut eius delectacione diceret se repletam fuisse inestimabilis gaudii exultacione.*

EIGHTH VISION

A most beautiful and most loving man[226] appeared to me in a vision of the truth. He brought with him so great a consolation that the sight of him perfused all my inward parts as with a fragrant balm, and I soared with a vast and immeasurable joy, while I longed to gaze on him forevermore.

And he commanded those who were afflicting me to depart, saying: 'Be off with you! for I will not have you torment her any longer.' And with a great howling they shouted as they left: 'Ach! Why did we ever come here, since now we have to leave confounded?'

Immediately, the illness which had been disquieting me like waters scudded into waves by stormy winds, left me at the man's words, and I recovered my strength just as travellers do when they return to their homeland and resume their familiar round. I felt renewed to the very blood in my veins and the marrow in my bones, as if I had been brought back from the dead. But *in patience I held my peace, and in meekness kept silent. Such words as I spoke* after my distress, *were like those of a mother after her labour* (cf. Is. 42:14).[227]

XXV

AFTER THIS, WITH MOST humble insistence and devotion, my Abbot and the brothers urged me to write, as God should will, the Life of St Disibod to whom I had previously been offered, since, they said, they had no worthwhile records from that time. So I first prayed and called on the Holy Spirit, and, warned in a true vision, I looked to true Wisdom and as it taught me concerning the life and merits of the saint, so I wrote them down.

I then wrote *Liber Divinorum Operum*, in which, as almighty God inspired me, I saw the height and the depth and the breadth of the vault, and how the sun and the moon and the stars, and the other objects were arranged in it.

XXVI

THE HOLY VIRGIN COMPOSED many other written works and remarkable

---

[226] *Pulcherrimus inquit et amantissimus vir.*

[227] Hildegard, *LDO* 2, 1, 31, CCCM 92, p. 302 (2, 5, 31, PL 197, 928A).

proofs of her prophetic charism, as we have said above. In them we have discovered sure signs of the learning her soul acquired from the Holy Spirit, wholly given over as it was to divine instructions. Those who pursue the love of doctrine and knowledge can find much profit in them, for the things ordained by God were revealed to human beings through her in whom the Wisdom of God was seated with highest authority as on a throne of power, and through her, performed wonders and wisely judged all things.

Now that we have edited everything as far as the capacity of our limited talent allows, let us turn our pen to the words of her holy daughters, who have written worthily of her memory.[228] With the help of the Lord let us append to this work faithfully and truthfully what they saw and heard, especially concerning her blessed passage from this life, which they have written down with their own hands. They say:

> There was a certain woman cruelly troubled by a dumb spirit, over whom the brothers of Maria Laach had laboured much. When the men had conveyed her with much effort to them on a pallet, Hildegard firmly opposed the impudence and arrogance of the demon with words revealed from the Holy Spirit. She did not leave off her prayers and blessings until, by the grace of God, she set the woman free from the malevolent enemy.
>
> Similarly there was another woman who, on account of the wild fury of her raving, was bound with strong chains. When this woman was led to her, she ordered her unchained. Immediately, to the amazement of everyone present, she recovered her health of mind and body, and giving thanks returned to her own.
>
> Again, at the cloister of Aschaffenburg, the devil, pretending to be an angel of light, urged on a certain sister to good works, prayers, vigils, and fasts, and even to participation in the sacraments. He strove to bring her to ruin by having her confess crimes to which she had never succumbed. At the same time he afflicted her in this way: that the names and the sight of certain persons and animals caused her such horror that whenever she saw or heard them she emitted a terrifying cry for sometime afterward. So she was sent with a letter by her prior and community to the holy virgin, who comforted her and set her free from the delusion of the devil.
>
> With the same virtue she set free two other women beset by a demon. One of these was a poor little thing and blind, and, through pity, was received into the monastery, where she happily lived out her life in the habit of the spiritual.

---

[228] Cf. Theodoric, *Chronicon Epternacense*, MGH SS 23, p. 38, line 22; p. 38, line 15.

XXVII

HAVING THUS SET FORTH these things, we fast approach the end of this work; so let us see also the end of the life of the holy virgin and the signs with which God illuminated it, as the sisters we mentioned above have described it. They say:

> When the blessed mother had devotedly waged battle for the Lord with many difficult struggles, she felt the weariness of this present life and daily *yearned to be dissolved and to be with Christ* (Phil. 1:23). God graciously heeded her longing, and as it had been her wish, by the spirit of prophecy revealed to her end, which she foretold to her sisters.
>
> She had laboured in illness for some time, when in the eighty-second[229] year of her life, on the fifteenth day before the Kalends of October [17 September], she departed with a happy passage to her heavenly spouse. Her daughters, to whom she had been all joy and solace, wept bitterly as they took part in the funeral rites of their beloved mother. For though they did not doubt her reward or the favours that would be conferred on them through her, yet they felt the most intense grief of heart over the departure of her by whom they had ever been consoled.
>
> But God showed clearly in her passing what standing she had before him. For in the early dusk on Sunday, two arcs of brilliant and varied colour appeared in the sky over the room in which the holy virgin gave up her happy soul to God. They widened to the size of broad highways and reached to the four corners of the earth, one going from north to south, the other from east to west. But at the apex where the two arcs intersected, there emerged a bright light in the form of a full moon. It extended itself widely and seemed to dispel the darkness of night from that dwelling.
>
> Within this light a glowing red cross became visible, at first small, but later increasing to an immense size. And all around it were countless circles of varied colour, in which, one by one, small crosses took shape, likewise glowing red, each with circles around it, though these crosses and circles were noticeably smaller than the first. And when they spread themselves over the sky, their width inclined more to the east, and they seemed to bend toward the earth where the dwelling was in which the holy virgin had passed away, and so cast a brilliant light upon the whole mountain.
>
> It is worthy of belief that by this sign God was showing how bright was the splendour with which he was illumining his beloved one in heaven.

---

[229] eightieth: B.

Marvellous indications of her merits were not lacking before she was buried. For two men, who, with fervent hope, made bold to touch her holy body, recovered from a severe illness. Her funeral rites were reverently celebrated by venerable men, and in a venerable place she was interred,[230] where, through her merits, her many benefits are available to all who come seeking them with devout heart. Furthermore, the fragrance of a wonderful sweetness[231] diffused about her tomb and its sweet scent filled the nostrils and lungs of many.[232]

We hope, and most firmly believe, that her memory before God is everlasting, for on her he had conferred even in this life a specially privileged share of his gifts.

To God be praise and honour unto ages of ages! Amen.

HERE ENDS THE THIRD BOOK ON THE MIRACLES OF THE HOLY VIRGIN HILDEGARD

---

[230] Trithemius, *De Luminaribus sive de Illustribus Viris Germaniae*, in *Johannis Trithemii Opera Historica*, vol. 1, ed. Marquand Freher (Frankfurt: 1601; repr. Frankfurt/Main: Minerva, 1966), p. 138, says that Hildegard *sepulta in medio chori iam dicti monasterii Sancti Ruperti, ante maius altare*—'was buried in the midst of the choir of the aforesaid monastery of Rupertsberg, before the main altar'. *Chron. Sponh.:* an entry under the year 1498 (p. 410) says, 'in the same year the tomb of the holy Virgin Hildegard at Rupertsberg was opened in the presence of the entire community there, and others present for the occasion, one of whom was our Abbot John Trithemius, who by his prayers obtained an arm of the holy Virgin from the *magistra* and community, for whom she had worked many benefits in the time of their tribulations. These relics were enclosed with others in a certain stone slab.' What survives of Hildegard's relics today are to be found at Rüdesheim/ Eibingen on the Rhine. Her heart and tongue are preserved in a golden reliquary in the parish church on Eibingerstrasse.

[231] Guibert adds: 'in the manner of lilies and the most precious scents'.

[232] Guibert: 'of all those standing by'. Cf. Thiofrid, *Flores Epitaphii*, 1, 5 (PL 157, 328D); id., *Sermo de sanctorum reliquiis*, PL 157, 328D; id., *Vita S. Willibrordi*, 24, ed. by J. Schmitz (Luxembourg: 1898), p. 29.

EIGHT READINGS

INTRODUCTION

Octo lectiones in festo sancte Hildegardis legende survives in only one early thirteenth-century manuscript, MS 5527-34 in the Bibliothèque Royale in Brussels (Klaes's siglum: G^2), containing also the longer version of Guibert's Letter to Bovo, which it directly follows. *Eight Readings* is here translated from the edition by Monika Klaes in *Vita Sanctae Hildegardis*, CCCM, 126 (Turnhout: Brepols, 1993), pp. 75–80. She analyses the work on pp. 146–52*.

Since it is included in the collected works of Guibert, he would seem to be the obvious candidate for the author of *Eight Readings*, but the internal evidence is against it. Not only are the literary style and techniques not his, but the fact that in section VIII the wrong year is given for Hildegard's death, indicating that the author did not know Hildegard personally, definitely rules out Guibert's authorship. Klaes is entirely persuaded that the author is Theodoric of Echternach himself. Given that *Eight Readings* is largely derivative of the *VH*, Theodoric would have composed it in the later part of the period 1182–1187, after completing the *VH*.

The first section functions as a prologue. It is presented in a sonorous periodic style laced with scriptural quotations, quite consistent with Theodoric's style in his own passages of reflection in the *VH*. Thereafter the author shows himself intimately cognizant with the text of *VH*, from which he nimbly selects here and there, in order to stitch together a single narrative sequence. He will typically select from the autobiographical passages of Hildegard herself and insert them at just the right narrative point, converted into the third person. That trademark of Theodoric's style, *Reimprosa*, appears even in passages not deriving from the *VH*.

In making use of the *VH*, the author often changes or adds a word or phrase to sharpen up the expression. An apt example may be found in IIII, where he adds to an autobiographical passage from *VH* II, 2 on the editorial work of Volmar, a clause 'used a file on her work' and replaces 'finishing' with the word 'polishing', or the author will expand and give a little more colouring to the original expression of the *VH*, e.g. the rather formulaic 'neither disturbed by blame nor seduced by praise' (*VH* II, 13) he renders as 'neither disturbed by it when she was scorned nor seduced by the experience of being praised' in VII. At the end of this Reading he states it was 'the Lord Jesus Christ' who appeared to Hildegard (*VH* III, 24) which is more explicit than Hildegard's actual text.

Eight Readings II tells us what the *VH* and Ep. 38 do not: that Hildegard received the veil at the hands of the Bishop of Bamberg. This connects directly with the account of Jutta and Hildegard's enclosure in *VJ* III, and answers questions about Hildegard's age at the time. But where did the author come across this uniquely attested item of information? Similarly, in *Eight Readings* VII we learn that Hildegard's philosopher in *VH* II, 12 came from Mainz. Presumably these details were to be had in material Theodoric did not include in his final draft of the *VH*, but had ready in mind as he was composing *Eight Readings*.

There is a curious presentation of the Jutta-Volmar-Hildegard connection in Section III, giving the impression that Hildegard confided in Volmar, received the Abbot's approval and Volmar's collaboration and began the writing down of her visionary work, all while Jutta was still alive. This is probably due to a mistaken conflation of information, i.e. from Godfrey in *VH* I, 3 and from Hildegard in *VH* II, 2, for it is contradicted in the next section IV, which tells of the divine commission to write, following the report of Jutta's death.

Section II gives 1100 as the year of Hildegard's birth, and section VIII mistakenly gives 1181 as the year of Hildegard's death. This is easily accounted for. To the year 1100, the year of her birth as given approximately in *VH* II, 2, the author added eighty-one years in accordance with the 'eighty-second year' of her death as reported in *VH* III, 27. It is clear at any rate that the author was relying solely on his literary sources, and did not know Hildegard personally. It is also consistent with the fact that in *VH* I, 1 Theodoric, or Godfrey his source, does not give the year of Hildegard's birth.

EIGHT READINGS

TO BE READ ON THE FEAST OF SAINT HILDEGARD

I

IT IS A GREAT encouragement toward the grace of the virtues when the merits and virtues of the good are proclaimed to the praise of God in holy Church, so that the minds of the faithful are more ardently inflamed thereby to their imitation. Therefore it is right that we, with cheerful hearts and festival praises, remember on *this day* (Acts 20:26) the annual commemoration in honour of holy Hildegard, the Virgin beloved of God, and it is fitting that *young men and maidens, the old together with children* (Ps. 148:12) should eagerly praise and magnify the splendour and glory of the Lord. For Jesus *Christ* himself *who is the Power and the Wisdom of God* (1 Cor. 1:24), clearly shows his *great Power* and *Wisdom, which is without measure* (Ps. 146:5) when through the Holy Spirit he so ardently inspires the frail feminine sex to declare the *power of his awesome deeds* (Ps. 144:6).[1] *He came to meet* holy Hildegard, of whom we speak, *with the blessings of his sweetness* (Ps. 20:4), when he quickened her in her mother's womb with the breath of life.[2] He wished to illumine her with the light of his brilliance, and in his mercy generously bestowed on her a many-sided charism that she might come to the help of a world that was perishing.

II

IN THE ONE THOUSAND one hundredth year of the incarnation of the

---

[1] *cum femineum sexum fragilem ... per Spiritum Sanctum tam vehementer accendit.*

[2] *cum spiraculo vite animaretur in utero matris.*

Saviour, which was the forty-fifth year of Henry, the fourth of this name as King and the third as Emperor,[3] when the Christian people had almost fallen away from the apostolic teaching and was already wavering in the divine law, there arose a noble scion in the nearer parts of Gaul, the blessed virgin, who as we have said was divinely illumined by means of the vision implanted in her soul in her mother's womb.[4]

In her third year of age she saw so bright a light above her that she trembled in her entire being; but, being an infant, she was unable to convey anything about it.

When she was in her eighth year her parents offered her to the Lord, because they saw in her the dispositions of a certain heavenly mystery. She was at first enclosed with a holy woman at Disibodenberg and later received the holy veil at the hands of the venerable Bishop of Bamberg.[5] As time went by she made progress both in the simple reading of the Psalter and in the many-sided understanding of monastic life.[6] The holy woman mentioned above took pains over her and rejoiced at her progress; she advanced from virtue to virtue, with which she was carefully adorned as with precious ornaments for the love of her heavenly spouse.

III

SHE GLOWED WITH AN overflowing benevolence of mind. So that her marvellous charity might shut out no-one from its embrace, the rampart of her humility defended the tower of her virginity. Hence she sustained her

---

[3] This historical accuracy about Henry contrasts with the original (Godfrey's) opening sentence of the *VH* in T.

[4] The foregoing section of the paragraph is virtually identical with the opening of the revised version of the *VH* in the collection of Guibert's letters; Klaes (p. 150*) argues that it is the reviser of the *VH* who is dependent on the *Eight Readings*.

[5] Otto, Bishop of Bamberg 1103–1139. This links Hildegard's profession with that of Jutta's on 1 Nov 1112. Perhaps by the use of 'later', the author is attempting to collate information that is obscure to him, i.e. the 'eight years old' of Hildegard's own account (*VH* II, 2), and the known enclosure of Jutta and Hildegard (*VJ* III and Ep. 38, VIII) in 1112, or he simply realized Hildegard could not have made monastic profession at the age of eight. See the discussion of Jutta's and Hildegard's early religious life and enclosure in the introduction to the *VJ*.

[6] *ita demum nunc psalterii simplici lectione, nunc monastice vite multiplici proficiebat erudicione.* Very elegant *Reimprosa*.

young body with frugality of food and drink, and her tranquillity of heart with fewness of words. The lustre of obedience lit up these shining jewels of the holy virtues.

Although up to her fifteenth year she used to see many things and often speak of them, arousing the wonder of many, thereafter, from her fear of the public and her maidenly reserve, she did not dare to speak of the vision implanted in her soul.

However the woman with whom she was living observed this and made it known to a certain devout monk. Since the matter was so remarkable, he reported it to his abbot, at whose command he collaborated with her from then on most diligently. When that devout woman departed in a *death which is precious in the sight of the Lord* (Ps. 115:15), the holy virgin continued to see visions by the divine will up to her fortieth year of age.

IIII

AFTER THIS, JUST AS she herself bears witness in her visions, the heaven opened and a fiery light of the greatest brilliance came forth and irradiated her brain and enkindled her whole heart and breast with a flame, which however, did not burn but warmed. From then on she savoured the meaning of the Old and New Testaments, though she did not obtain analysis of the words or knowledge of cases and tenses. For, as she wrote to Pope Adrian, she did not hear it given to her in the heavenly vision.[7] Rather, the monk above mentioned used a file on her work, and polished her visions and writings into a form pleasing to the human ear.

As *the potter's vessel is tried in the fire* (Eccli 27:6) and *virtue is made perfect in weakness* (2 Cor. 12:9) she often suffered from the prolonged pains of her illnesses, but from this she was, like the Apostle, made stronger and more capable. When the time drew near for God to display her life and teaching for the benefit of many, a voice divinely came to her warning her not to delay to write down whatever she might see or hear. But she delayed over it from bashfulness,[8] and so was chastened by infirmity. However, when at the urging of her abbot she put her hand to

---

[7] The author darts from a reference to *Scivias* in *VH* I, 1 to a reference to her letter to Pope Anastasius excerpted in *VH* II, 1.

[8] The author deletes the 'feminine' qualifying 'bashfulness' in *VH* I, 3.

writing, she recovered her health.

Who could easily recount what she saw, what she wrote, and what she taught? Indeed, that vast sea of her writings, that is the book called *Scivias*, and the one called *Vitae Meritorum* and the one called *Divinorum Operum* are prodigious monuments and proofs of her prophetic charism, proofs that in her the Wisdom of God was seated with the very highest authority as on a throne of power and through her discerned the truth of things wisely.[9]

V

BESIDES ALL THIS, WE can scarcely marvel at it enough that though she did not have knowledge of literary art, she composed an account of an alphabet not seen before, and a language never heard before, and what is more, a chant of sweet melody in a harmony of the musical art.[10] When all these things were related to the authorities of the church of Mainz, they held a discussion and could not find that they were anything other than ordained by God. Over and above these, the lord Pope Eugene when he was at Trier, welcomed this marvel in faith and visited her with his messengers and a letter, and by his own authority urged her to write down whatever she saw in spirit.

After this she laboured under a severe illness until with her young women she moved to that place shown her from heaven. This place had been neglected for a very long time; though it was at that time only intermittently inhabited by a tenant, among all the thorn bushes and vines it still held the church of Saint Rupert and his mother, hallowed through their lying in rest there. There the virgin of God and her twenty young women were tried for some time under very great distresses, from which she was relieved after a time when God gave consolation.

VI

MEANWHILE SHE EXHORTED THE crowds who flocked to her and revealed

---

[9] This paragraph borrows from *VH* II, 17 and *VH* III, 26, which are certainly Theodoric's contributions to the *VH*.

[10] *Et suavem cantus melodiam ad musice artis simphoniam.*

the secrets of their minds, while through her labours, she alleviated the bodily needs of some and the infirmities of others.[11] She foresaw in spirit the past life and conduct of people, and in the case of some, she could even foresee the way their present life would end, and, according to the character of their merits, their soul's glory or punishment. She even had this special gift that in the Divine Office she answered her young women with blessings fitted according to the disposition of each one's heart.[12]

She was urged by vision to work for the freehold possession[13] of their place. After a grave illness she caused this freehold to be secured in all charity by having it confirmed through the authority of a letter under the seal of the Archbishop of Mainz.

She often used to see both good and bad angels. Once, when she had been sick for a period of three years, she beheld a Cherub repelling the corrupt spirits from her with a fiery sword. So, when she was racked by weakness and the terror of the demons, she was not only not vanquished, but was glorified by means of an angelic defence. In short, whenever the athlete of God wrestled between spirits above and spirits below, she put her enemies to rout and was always glorified with a glad victory. At a certain point when she was hard-pressed by fever, she saw some saints who chanted in a great voice: 'Avenge O Lord *the blood of your saints* which has been poured out!' (Apoc. 19:2) When they had said this to her, then, because she bore what she suffered with a good will, she recovered from her infirmity.

VII

A PHILOSOPHER OF MAINZ[14] gives proof that the Lord came to her help

---

[11] In this and the following section, the author borrows text from the chapter headings to *VH* II and III.

[12] *in divinis officiis iuxta habitudinem cordis sui respondebat benedictionibus propriis;* See *VH* II, 4 and note.

[13] *ut laboraret circa loci sui emancipacionem.* The background of these terms in Roman law is the distinction between *possessio* (a using, occupying, holding, or seizing) and *mancipium* (the legal title, dominion, formal possession gained only through public transfer before witnesses).

[14] That the philosopher came from Mainz we know only from *Eight Readings.* The impression given here is that he had even more of a role to play in the building of the new monastery than the report suggests at *VH* II, 12.

when people attacked her. At first he scorned her, sharply opposing her in what she said and wrote; but after *the right hand of the Most High* had *changed* him (Ps. 76:11), he changed and praised the Lord in her and co-operated with her in the building of the monastery and asked to be buried there when he died. And he was not defrauded of his desire, because afterward he was honourably buried in that very place.

In all this the holy virgin was neither inflated by successes nor downcast by setbacks, but in the one same vigour of mind she was neither shaken by blame nor seduced by the experience of being praised. She was always possessed of sound teaching in all things, as she discerned it through divine revelation. Thus she often chastised her young women for the vain thoughts which the demons insinuated among them, while she revealed to them privately the secrets of their hearts.

Beyond this, who would doubt that she was a seat of eternal Wisdom, to whom God willed to manifest so great a treasure of inward knowledge that she learned in true vision the Gospel of John: *In the beginning was the Word and the Word was with God* (Jn 1:1). In short, she flew up on the feather of inward contemplation to the very secrets of heavenly vision.

Moreover, on a certain occasion when she was sick she merited to be visited by our Lord Jesus Christ himself. She received so great a consolation from this that she was overwhelmed in a rapture of immeasurable joy and thereafter had no more of the infestation of demons.

VIII

WITH ALL THESE AND other gifts of grace the heavenly Spouse, who *is* ever *wonderful in his saints* (Ps. 67:36), wonderfully glorified his spouse, so that in all her good deeds she might be ever worthy of imitation. He made her remarkable not only for all the holiness of her conduct, or for her inward contemplation of the mysteries of God, but also for her working of extraordinary miracles as well, whose number so exceeds all measure that they could scarcely all be described.

How she restored the sick to health, how she powerfully curbed the shameless goings-on of the spirits of illusion and cast them forth from the bodies they obsessed, how she came to the help not only of those who were present but also of those who were absent, and how she did many similar things—*are these* things *not all* written down in the monuments of her history and *sealed in the treasures* (Deut. 32:34) of her memory? Because she did not love her own glory but rather God's, *which remains forever* (cf. Ps. 88:37), *the Lord has caused his wonders* in her *to be remembered* forever (Ps. 110:4).

She knew of her death long beforehand and foretold it to her sisters. In the year one thousand one hundred and eighty-one of the Incarnation of the Lord, on the fifteenth day before the Kalends of October [17 September 1181] she departed with a happy passage to her heavenly Spouse. But God showed clearly in her passing what standing she had before him by an immense and shimmering light which was poured out over her dwelling throughout the night. There were also the two men who with fervent hope made bold to touch the holy body. They recovered there and then from the illnesses they had so long suffered. Furthermore, in the place where she had been reverently buried by venerable men, through her merits, her many benefits are available to all who come seeking them with devout heart, to the praise and glory of our Lord Jesus Christ, who with God the Father and the Holy Spirit lives and reigns as God for ever and ever. Amen.

GUIBERT'S REVISION OF *VH*

INTRODUCTION

Guibert's Revision of the Vita S. Hildegardis is found in the two collections of his correspondence and other works, contained in MS 5387-96, i.e. G^1, and MS 5527-34, i.e. G^2, of the Bibliothèque Royale in Brussels. Monika Klaes has edited a selection of the more extensively revised sections of this document in *Vita Sanctae Hildegardis*, CCCM, 126 (Turnhout: Brepols, 1993), pp. 93–106, which are here translated. Other variations from the less revised sections may be found in the notes to the translation under *Guibert*. Klaes evaluates the document on pp. 146–52* and the manuscripts on pp. 173–78*.

The re-editing by Guibert is suggested by the transmission of this version of the *VH* in the collections of Guibert's works, also by the fact that whenever the name of Guibert appears it is augmented with a fuller description, and by certain characteristics of content and style, such as the elimination of some traces of Theodoric's *Reimprosa*. In particular, the circumstances of its provenance in the older of the two manuscripts, G^1, are suggestive, for here the revised *VH* appears written out in the same quire by the same hand, immediately following on the correspondence between Guibert and Abbot Godfrey of St Eucharius dated to 1209. Guibert writes to Godfrey in the context of revising his own letters and works.[1] Bearing in mind that we are reading his letters in the form he wants us to read them, Guibert asks Godfrey:

> I ask you, could you let me know through a letter the names of the father and the mother and the town of the lady Hildegard if you can recall them? For I have written a little something about her, and I would gladly insert the names if I could remember them.

Godfrey sends a reply accompanied by a copy of the *VH* and a request:

> Desiring to inform your dear self concerning the parents and the town of

---

[1] Ep. 40, Derolez, pp. 384–86.

the blessed Hildegard, I send you the Life of the same holy Hildegard, which at the instigation of myself and my predecessor, Abbot Ludwig of worthy memory, Magister Theodoric put together, following the copy of the provost Godfrey, who succeeded Fomar the first provost at that place ... We therefore ask you, dear brother, and very much beg you that if in the Life of holy Hildegard above mentioned there is anything omitted through the avoidance of a long text because of our decree and counsel, it may please you in your discretion to insert or correct, and bring them to our knowledge.[2]

What this does testify to is that Guibert felt entitled to make his insertions and emendations to a copy of the *VH*. Klaes (p. 156*) also refers to an authorization sent by Hildegard to Guibert to edit her text in the *Visio ad Guibertum missa*.[3]

In his revision Guibert adds brief descriptions to some persons mentioned in the *VH*, sometimes adding a little information. He makes innumerable relatively minor stylistic alterations, such as inversions of word order, small insertions, the 'improving' by substituting a more stylish form for a common form (e.g. *quemadmodum* for *sicut*) of pronouns, prepositions, conjunctions, or he fills out verbal forms with auxiliary verbs etc. He constantly tends to more explicit expressions, as with insertions of personal and demonstrative pronouns. Not all of these niceties can be replicated in an English translation.

He re-allocated *VH* I, 9 to the beginning of *VH* II, renumbered the chapters of the entire second book accordingly, and extensively rewrote the captions. However, I have presented all selections translated here under their corresponding section of the *VH*, which here always refers to Theodoric's version.

Guibert's interest was roused above all by the autobiographical passages. These he most strongly reworked and augmented. For this reason, they form the bulk of Klaes's selection, here translated. From having worked through these sections in close comparison with the *VH*, I as the translator am persuaded that Guibert may well have inserted here some original Hildegard material. What alerted me to this was to discover that some of the larger additions to the autobiographical material, i.e.

---

[2] Ep. 41, Derolez, pp. 387–89.

[3] Pitra, p. 432.

whole sentences and clauses, are in a simple Latin style, most unlike Guibert's style. Their linguistic level is sometimes on a par with Hildegard's, as allowed through after Volmar's editing, sometimes below it.

Therefore I conjecture that Guibert may have taken with him from Rupertsberg in 1180 a copy of Hildegard's autobiographical texts, such as they were before Theodoric came into their possession. Perhaps it served as a kind of talisman for himself of his revered *domna*, or he had a fond idea of finishing his own *vita* sometime. We know that in his retirement years he grafted his own incomplete *vita* onto his original letter to Bovo, so that by being included in the systematic collection of his letters its survival might be more assured. Similarly, in revising Theodoric's *VH* he may have calibrated the autobiographical sections against his own copy of them, not without a fair bit of minor tinkering besides. In that case, the version of Hildegard's autobiography we have here would represent the assured survival of Guibert's own copy, but such as he wished it presented.

Note: No references to scripture are included; *italics* are used here to indicate where Guibert's revision departs from the text of Theodoric's *VH*.

GUIBERT'S REVISION OF *VH*

(*VH* I, 1, 3–6)

In the one thousand one hundredth year of the Incarnation of the Saviour, which was the forty-fifth year of Henry, the fourth of this name *as king and the third* as Emperor, when the Christian people had almost fallen away from the apostolic teaching and was already wavering in the divine law,[4] a virgin was born in the nearer parts of Gaul *in a town in the territory of the city of Mainz*, who was as illustrious for her high birth as for her holiness. Her name was Hildegard, her father was Hildebert, her mother Mechtild.

(*VH* II, 1–17 renumbered in Guibert's revision as II, 2–18)

I   *How she had a marvellous and very rare kind of visionary seeing.*

II   *On him who* grammatically revised the things she expressed in writing, song, and in a strange language with letters.

III   *On* her first vision and on the blessing of Pope Eugene and his permission to write.

IIII   *How, according to* the Song of Songs, she was frequently *visited* by the Spirit.

V   How she used to *reveal the minds and the characters of those who flocked* to *her, and how in all this she preserved humility.*

VI   How she was blinded *from her second vision*, because she did not reveal it.

VII   How she may be compared to Deborah and her place which the Lord chose.

VIII   On the third vision, and *on* the freehold possession of her place,

---

[4] The foregoing section of the paragraph is verbally dependent on the opening of *Eight Readings* II. See Klaes, p. 150*. It is noteworthy, that while Guibert replicates the inaccurate dating of Hildegard's birth from *Eight Readings*, later, in III, 27, he does not replicate the false dating of Hildegard's death, which, of course, he very well knew about. He evidently did not notice the resultant inconsistency in his text.

and how God freed her from the distressing trial.

(*VH* II, 2, 58–102, renumbered 3, 1–58)

I was quite exhausted by *all* these things and asked a *certain good woman who used to nurse me* if she could see *with her eyes* anything apart from outward objects. 'Nothing' she replied *to this*, because she *was aware of* none of them. Then, seized by a great fear, I did not *anymore* dare to tell about these things to any *person*—although in my conversations and my lessons I used to *proclaim in my speech* more *and more* about the future. And on occasions when I *had been* completely inundated by this vision, I would say many things which were strange to my hearers, and I behaved more like an infant than one of my years. But when the force *itself* of *this same* vision ebbed somewhat, I blushed very much and often wept, and would often have gladly kept silent if *in this same vision* I had been allowed. But because of the fear of people I then had, I did not dare to tell of the manner in which I saw. Nevertheless, a certain woman *of very noble birth* to whom I had been entrusted for *discipline and* instruction, observed *all* these things and laid them before a certain monk *well* known to her.[5]

---

[5] *et cuidam monacho sibi familiari aperuit. familiari* is something more than the *noto* of

God *also* poured out his grace in this woman like a river of many waters, so that she granted her body no respite from vigils, *and from* fastings, *and from* other good deeds, until she *happily* completed this present life with a worthy end. God showed her merits afterwards by certain beautiful signs. After her death, I continued seeing as before up to my fortieth year of age.

Then in this same vision I was constrained by great pressure *and by many* pains *of my body* to reveal openly *those things* which I had seen and heard. But I was very afraid and blushed at the thought of proclaiming *these things* which I had kept silent about for so long. Nevertheless, from then on my veins and my marrow were filled with the strength which I had lacked from my infancy and youth. I told these things to a certain monk, *whom I had chosen earlier as my magister,*[6] who was of a worthy way of life and a loving disposition, and a stranger, as it were, to the prying ways of many *other* people, *on account of which* he listened generously to these strange tales. He, *being struck with fear* and wondering *what these things might be* ordered me to discreetly write down *what I saw and heard,* so that he could see *their beginning and end and so that he could consider* what they were and where they came from. But once he *saw and* concluded that they were from God, he made known *these things* to his Abbot, and from then on worked very keenly with me *day and night* in these things.

But I in this vision understood *and perceived* without any human instruction the writings of the prophets, of the Gospels, and *the precepts* of other saints and of certain philosophers, and I expounded a number of their texts, although I had scarcely any knowledge of literature, as the woman who taught me was not a scholar. Then *in the above mentioned vision* I also composed and sang chant with melody, to the praise of God and his saints, though I had never studied *human* chant, *and I did not know how to tell the neumes by myself.*

When *all* these things *were* brought to the hearing *of the prelates* of the church of Mainz and discussed *there,* they all declared that they were from God and from the prophecy *with* which the prophets of old had prophesied. Then *these same* writings *of mine* were taken to *the apostolic* Eugene while he was staying in Trier. He was pleased *to receive them* and had them read publicly before many *who were present,* and *indeed* read them out himself.

VH II, 2.

[6] This vital information does not appear in the autobiographical passage of *VH* II, 2 as it stands, but is reported almost verbatim in *VH* I, III, suggesting that Godfrey of Disibodenberg was relying on a copy of Hildegard's autobiographical documents containing the phrase now missing from Theodoric's edition.

Putting great trust *and confidence* in God's grace, he sent his blessing *to me* along with a letter, and ordered me to carefully commit to writing *those things which* I saw or heard in *the above mentioned* vision.

(*VH* II, 5, 14–38, renumbered 6, 1–32)

At one time, *my eyes were so afflicted with a clouding over* that I was unable to see any light, and I was pressed down by *so great a* weight of my body that I could not *be lifted up either by me or by any other person* . So I lay there, *all day and all night* overwhelmed by *these* intense pains. Why I suffered like this was because I did not make known *what I had seen before, that is, what had been* shown to me in *true* vision: that I must move with the young women *staying with me* from the place where I had been offered to God *by my parents*, to another place. And so I endured *this suffering* continually until I named the place where I am now. As soon as I recovered my *eye*sight, *I became lighter so that I was as before*, although I was not yet fully freed from *this same* illness.

Now when my Abbot *and the whole community who were under him*,[7] and *all* the people of that district realized, *they said, what was this*, that we were wanting to go from a lushness of fields and vineyards and from the beauty *of the buildings* of that place to an arid *place where we would have no pasture and no* conveniences—they were shocked and conspired among themselves to block us so that it should not come about. They were even saying that I was deceived by some kind of vain imagining. When I heard this, my heart was crushed and my flesh and my veins withered. So I lay *sick* in bed many days when I heard a loud voice *in the same vision* which forbad me to proclaim or write down anything more of this vision in that place.

Then a noble *woman, that is a* marchioness we knew *well*, approached the Archbishop of *the See* of Mainz *and other wise people* and put the whole story before *them. The same Archbishop along with other wise people said* that no place is made holy except by good works and therefore *these proposals could* reasonably go forward. And so, with the *same* Archbishop's permission and in reverence for God we came to that place with a great escort of our *local people* and other visitors.

(*VH* II, 5, 55–78, renumbered 6, 1–27)

Then I saw in true vision, that the trials which had come upon me were after the pattern of Moses. For when he *rescued* the children of Israel out

---

[7] This replaces 'and the brothers' of the *VH*. Several other emendations betray Guibert's consciousness of hierarchy.

of Egypt and led them across the Red Sea into the desert, they murmured against God and distressed Moses too *with many distresses*, although God had lit up their way *there* with so many wonderful signs. Likewise, *even* God allowed me to be afflicted in some measure, *that is*, by the common people, by my kinsfolk and *indeed* by some of those remaining with me when they lacked *daily* necessities—although, by God's grace a certain amount was given to us in alms. For just as the children of Israel distressed Moses, so they also shook their heads at me and said: 'What is the good of this, that noble and wealthy young women should leave a place where they lacked no *necessities* to be reduced to such beggary?' But truly, we *for our part* were waiting for the grace of God to come to our help, for it was *God* who had shown us this *same* place.

After the distress of this ordeal, God showered down his grace upon us, *so that* many who at first jeered at us and called it an arid and useless place, *flocked* to us *with much help* from all sides offering us help and filling us with blessings. *Indeed* many wealthy families gave their dead an honourable burial with us; *thus* many others, recognizing this vision as worthy of trust, came to us most eagerly, just as the prophet says: They will all come to you those who despised you. Then my spirit revived and I, who had earlier wept for sorrow, now wept for joy that God had not led me into oblivion since *God more and more* confirmed everything by raising up this place and by multiplying many useful items and buildings.

(*VH* II, 5, 97–101, renumbered 6, 1–7)

I and *others* who loved me wondered *very much* why such *harsh experiences* and so great a persecution came upon me, and why God did not grant me *the assurance of his* consolation, since I in *no way desired* to continue in my sins, but rather desired *as much as possible* to bring good works to fruition with God's help. *Amid all* these circumstances I completed the book *Scivias as God through his assistance gave me help for the task.*

(*VH* II, 7, 2–24, renumbered 8, 1–34)

In *the same* vision *which had been implanted in me from my infancy, I saw another in which I* was taught and compelled to make known to my superiors, *and to certain others* that our place *along with the allodial properties* that belonged to it *and our income*, should be separated from that place where I had been *previously* offered to God, *with the proviso* that we would owe the deference *of* obedience *and seek the care of our souls from the servants of God there* only as long as we found *the service of God faithfully carried out there and* a good *and holy* faith in them towards us.[8] I confided these things to my Abbot, but he was racked with illness so that he *was unable to* do anything about it, *for in the same illness* he finished *this present* life only a few days later. When *however* these *same* proposals reached the Abbot *who afterward succeeded the dead man,* and *were laid before* the Archbishop of *the See of* Mainz and the authorities of the *same* church, they upheld them in faith *and in most pure* charity, confirming their provisions in a document affixed with a seal.

While all this was going on I endured many attacks from certain people, just as Joshua *bore,* when his enemies tried to *capture him and* bring him to confusion because he appeared the conqueror of others *like them.* But just as God helped him, so, *after many trials* he freed both myself and my daughters. Likewise, just as Joseph's own brothers were envious of him *when they saw that* he was loved by their own father more than the others, with the result that *in their treachery* they sold him and took back his torn robe to their father saying that a *wicked* wild beast had devoured him, so also certain evil-willed people tried to tear from us the garment of the Lord's' grace and praise. But God came to our help, just as he also restored Joseph to *his* honour.

Moreover, though *I and my daughters who were with me* were under great pressure, by God's grace *from day to day* we were enlarged *in prosperity,* just like the children of Israel, who, the more they were *trampled on by their enemies* the more they increased. And so in the joy of my heart I looked to God, and because he had stood by me in *so many* trials, I *thereupon* willingly cast aside care.

(*VH* II, 9, 5–12, renumbered 10, 1–12)

I was in that strife *of death* for thirty days *and nights* such that *I was constantly on the brink of quitting the world, since a blast of painful airs coursed through all my entrails, for I was burning* with the heat of a fiery air, such that *from the same* heat my abdomen *and my whole body was in a fever. Because of this many were saying: 'we do not understand* that illness, *except that* we reckon it is a punishment. Even the strength of my spirit *which was* implanted in my flesh gave way, *such that I neither entirely* passed from this life nor was I fully in it either. My body was *so changed that I was* laid out over a hair-mat on the ground, but my end was not yet in sight, though my superiors, my daughters, and my neighbours

---

[8] This sentence restructures the *VH* considerably, re-using phrases in a different way. Possibly some of Guibert's own past griefs and concerns for monastic life are coming to bear in his editing. See the Introduction to Ep. 38.

came in great mourning to watch at my *end*.

(*VH* II, 9, 29–46, renumbered 10, 1–23)

It was the most evil spirits of the air, to whom are committed all the punishing tortures of human beings, who administered this punishment to me, since God allowed them to bring it against me. And so these spirits became my tormentors, the same ones who applied *burning* coals to the blessed Laurence and *many* other martyrs. *So these evil spirits* came hurrying to me *with their unsettling malice*, crying out in a loud voice: 'Let us seduce this woman, so that she has second thoughts about God and *hurls blasphemy against* him, *that is*, rails at him for overwhelming her with such sufferings.' *And* just as it happened to Job when by God's permission Satan so struck his body that he was *full of* vermin, so in my case, it was a fiery air that entered *my body* and consumed my flesh *as if to devour it*, as also happened to *the prophet* Jeremiah, who mourned his sorrow in *a voice of lamentation*. But the Devil could not persuade Job to rail against God.

But I, soft in flesh, timid in mind, was absolutely terrified of these sufferings. Yet God strengthened me *so that in patience I willingly bore these punishing weaknesses*, and in my spirit I said: 'O, O, Lord God, all the ways in which you wound me I know are good, because all your works are good and holy, and because I have deserved *these punishments* from my infancy *up to the present time*; and besides, I trust that you will not permit my soul to be tortured like this in the life that is to come.'

(*VH* II, 10, 1–16, renumbered 11, 1–24)

But although I was still labouring in these pains, *yet* I was warned in true vision to go to *that* place where I had been *originally* offered to God, and *there announce* the words which God would show me. So I did this and returned in the same pain to my daughters. *And in the same sufferings* I also made haste to travel *as God wanted* to communities *of the spiritual* in *certain* other places, and there reveal to them the words *of truth* which God *showed me and* ordered me *to announce. Thus* through all this, the vessel of my body was being baked as it were in an oven—just as God put many to the test whom he has ordered to announce his words, and praise to him for it!

But *God* did give me much help in two of my daughters *in particular* and *also* in *certain* others, *who being strong in wisdom and charity* tended me in my sufferings *and did not grow weary of them. They were always moved with compassion for me, for God inspired them so that they thirsted assiduously to help me.* And so with *sighs* I gave thanks to God that my fellow human beings did not tire of me *in my weaknesses*. Indeed, so great was the pressure of *fevers and other conditions* in my flesh that if they were not from God, *such were my punishments* that I could not have survived for long. However racked I was *by these unremitting pains*, still, I continued dictating, singing, and writing through the heavenly vision whatever the Holy Spirit wished to *reveal and* announce through me.

(*VH* II, 12, 9–40, renumbered 13, 1–46)

A certain *wealthy* philosopher, *much* reputed for his wealth, *who* had *previously* cast doubt on *all* the things I saw, came to us *in great keenness and God inspired him to* generously endow our place with buildings and properties and other necessities. *Then* my soul was *filled with joy again* that God had not *led* us into oblivion. *Certain writings composed by me from the divine vision were brought to this same philosopher,*[9] *which he* examined with sharp but wise scrutiny, *looking into* what the written accounts of this vision were, and where *or from whom* they came from, until at length he gave full credit to their divine inspiration, *and, sending up a sigh, said how right it was that he should* now turn toward us with greater blessings *in full piety*, who had previously spurned us with venomous words. *For indeed* God quenched in his heart *the ill-will and contradiction which he had been disposed to hurl against us*, just as he sank Pharaoh beneath the Red Sea who had wanted to take the children of Israel captive. Many were astonished at the change *for the good* in him and became much more ready to believe *him*, so that by means of that *same* wise man God poured out his blessing on us, like oil which descends upon the beard, upon Aaron's beard. Because of this, we all claimed that philosopher as our father. *Consequently* he who was so eminent in his own right, petitioned *that when his time here was over he might* be allowed burial with us, which is what happened.

At that I was much confirmed in my mind. I took care of the daughters *entrusted to me* in all their necessities whether of *their* bodies or of *their* souls, just as I had been appointed to do by my superiors. And so *for this reason* I was most concerned when I beheld in true vision that *malevolent* spirits of the air were fighting against us, and saw moreover, that these same spirits had entangled *certain ones* among my *more* noble-born daughters as in a net with an array of vain thoughts.

So I, through the revelation of God, made known *to these same young women how through the guile of malevolent spirits they had let into their heart an array of vain thoughts*[10] and *with God's help* I fenced them about

---

[9] The Latin of this addition is rather crude, far from Guibert's style, perhaps even from Hildegard's (edited) style.

[10] The Latin here seems a little confused; the reflexive and non-reflexive forms do not

and armed them *as much as I could* with the words of Holy Scripture and with the discipline of the Rule and with a sound monastic life. *Because of this* several of them, darting at me with glowering eyes, tore me to pieces with words behind my back, saying that they could not endure it, this insufferable hammering away of mine at the discipline of the Rule, *through* which I wanted to curb them *according to the imposition of my will*.

But God also comforted me with other good and *holy and* wise sisters, who stood by me *to console me* in all my sufferings *with which I had been overwhelmed*. Thus God dealt with me as he did with Susanna, whom she freed through Daniel *when she was hemmed in* by false witnesses. And though I was often worn out with trials of this kind, yet by the grace of God, I finally brought to an end the Book of Life's Merits, divinely revealed to me.

(*VH* II, 14, 44–82, renumbered 15, 1–51)

Abel, who in the overflowing desire of his soul *was the first to* offer sacrifice *to God*, was sanctified whereas Cain was rejected, because in the latter the flesh suffocated his spirit through hatred. Again, Noah was justified because he sacrificed to God, whereas his son answered to the baseness of *his*[11] flesh by his sly treatment of his father, and so he was deprived of *his* liberty, and *was* unworthy of the name of son, *but instead* was called a servant.

Abraham, however, was given increase, because *in his obedience* to God he strove with all his might against the demands of the flesh, *and so* he was changed into a new people, *wherefore* the liberty of his sons and his friends who *did not consent to his will* vanished when they were cast out from the freeborn children of Israel. And Jacob too was dear to God, because in his soul's desire, he ever drank in righteousness, and he continued in the blessings of God to the end. Esau his brother, however, on account of the *hateful mind* he bore toward Jacob was deprived of God's blessing. Moses the servant and *loving* friend of God, whom he knew *in his own mystery*[12] and *whom* he *also* served by miracles, *utterly* restrained *his will and* the impulse of the flesh in himself. And so, *many of his friends who hardened themselves against him and* who bore hatred for him perished, and did not reach the land of promise.

The apostles *of Christ also* restrained their flesh. But Judas *who had*

---

tally. I conclude the original author was trying to say something as I have translated it.

[11] *sue*, not *eius*, and similarly later in the sentence.

[12] *in mysterio suo*; there is a conscious parallel between Moses and Hildegard throughout this passage.

joined himself to them was completely blind in the desire of his soul, *and* he followed Christ more that *by this* he might have the acclaim of the people than for faith in him. *But there were other* disciples who did not hold in fullness the desire of the soul, who listened willingly enough to the teaching of Christ, but because they were of a lukewarm spirit, they could not endure the full measure of *his* righteousness, *and so* withdrew from him.

Moreover Zaccheus *while he lived fully* in the exuberance of the flesh did have *however* a spirit that strove against the flesh, so that he was *often* disgusted with all his works. Therefore, because he was righteous, when he heard *the report* of the Son of God he ran *quickly* to meet him there and put his faith in him—for he had already been mourning his sins in spirit.

On the other hand we find in the Gospel *that* young man burdened with riches who listened willingly enough to the reports of what was happening and *so* he went to the Son of God, and asked *him* what he should do; but when he obtained the full and perfect answer *from him*, he yielded to despondency and *so* he withdrew from Christ, because the flesh suffocated *his* spirit. Saul, too, *kept his heart hardened against God*, and *in overweening confidence of mind* raised high the horns of his pride *to fight* against the faith of Christ. But God laid him low, and mortified *all* the will of the flesh in him, and *thus* brought him round to the good.

And I, poor little creature that I am, have especially loved and called upon those who have striven with their spirit against the flesh, and have turned away *as much as I could* from all who have hardened *their flesh* against the spirit, *so that they* have suffocated *this same spirit of theirs in this way*. I have never taken my rest in freedom from care—rather *my spirit has* been worn out by many trials. But God rained down the dew of His grace upon me, just as he spoke to his friend *and servant*.

(*VH* III, 20, 5–65)

After the vision had instructed me in the text and the words of the Gospel of John, *I was weighed down by* so great a weight *of illness that* I fell back into my bed sick, and *lying there* I could in no way lift myself up. This *same* illness was blown into me by a blast of the south wind, so that *day by day* my body was ground down in this sickness by such sufferings that *even* my soul *within me* could scarcely bear it. *Thus* for half a year the blast of the wind above mentioned so went through my *whole* body that I was *constantly* in as great an agony as if my soul were about to quit the life *of the body*. Then in case my flesh utterly burnt up, there came another blast of moist wind, so that it was somewhat cooled. Thus I was in *that affliction* for the space of a whole year, yet I saw in true vision that *the end of my body was not yet at hand;* but *that the earthly course of* my life but was to be prolonged for some time beyond yet.

In the meantime, *that is, during the same affliction* it was reported to me *by certain persons* that *in another province* far from us, in the regions of the lower Rhine, a certain noblewoman had been obsessed by a devil. *Popular rumours* concerning this *matter frequently reached me, and people were asking questions, talking about it over and over again; and even* messengers *sent to make representation* to me about this *same evil* came time after time. But I, in a true vision, saw that God had permitted *this same woman* to be obsessed and overshadowed by a kind of darkness and dense fog of the devil, which oppressed all the senses of her rational soul and hindered her from lifting up her intellect in hope. It was as when the shadow of a person or *the shadow or smoke of* some other object covers and envelops whatever provides *an obstacle* in its path, *from which it cannot snatch itself away.* So this woman lost the right use of her senses and actions, and was constantly shouting out and doing things *which were* unseemly. But if by the command of God *this same blackness and smoke of diabolical fog* were *somewhat diminished* in her, she would no longer be so weighed down.

While I was thinking over this and wanting to understand how a diabolic form enters a human being, I saw *in true vision* and heard the answer—that a devil does not actually enter a human being in its own form; rather, *by overshadowing him* with the shadow and smoke of its blackness, he covers him *all around and envelops him, since,* if he really could enter a human being in his own form, all his members would disintegrate more quickly than chaff scattered by the wind. Therefore God does not allow *a malevolent spirit* to enter a human being in his own form, but he *douses* him *with his shadow and smoke,* and warps *and forces* him into insanity and unseemly ways, and snarls through him as through a window, and moves his limbs outwardly. Yet the demon is not within him in his own form, rather it is as if the soul of a person is in a stupefied sleep, and does not know what the flesh of the body is doing.

Then I saw that there is a *kind of* swarm of malevolent spirits who with their clever ways at corrupting things go through all the world *constantly* seeking, wherever they may find them, those *human beings* through whom they can contrive discords and moral aberrations, *since* it was these demons who at the very beginning when they were created, spurned God in the presence of the most righteous angels saying: Who is *he* that he has such authority over us? *And* they said this out of envy, hatred, and ridicule, and have continued up till now in the same, and these are the motives of all they do, because they began it all with the false step of their primal mockery.

Moreover since God wants his people to be purified by means of these demons, so *by* the permission and mandate *of God himself* they stir up a stupor in the air, and by means of a foam of the air they vomit up plague, and cause floods and dangers in the waters, *and indeed* provoke wars and spawn *many other* adversities and evils. God allows these things to happen, because through their *great* arrogance human beings wallow in *the most vile and shameful* crimes and murders. But *after* God has purified his people in this way, he reduces the same spirits to confusion, as happened to the woman mentioned above.

Indeed when, by God's permission, the vile spirit had long confused many through her, on account of *the extent* of *their* wanton behaviour and the *serious* sins to which he had swayed them, still many *of those present* were struck with terror and because of this *did penance,* and thus *in the end this same* malevolent spirit was itself *brought to confusion.* For God allows his friends to be overwhelmed by *many* setbacks and illnesses *in order* that, *as I said above,* they might be cleansed from *their* evils. *And thus man brings* his enemies *into great confusion since they see that* his chosen ones have, through this *very* purification been made into resplendent jewels before God.

After the *above mentioned* woman had been led around many places to the *relics of the* saints, the *malevolent* spirit that was oppressing her was *finally* conquered by the merits of the saints and the prayers of the people, and bellowed out that *there was* a little old hag in the upper regions of the Rhine through whose counsel it would need to be cast out. When her friends understood this, they led her to us in the eighth year of her torment, as *was the will of* the Lord.

(*VH* III, 21, 116–36)
But when the same woman realized she had been set free, she reached out her hands to the bystanders so that they could help her up, for she did not have the strength *to rise up. When they had helped her up*, she prostrated herself before the high altar of *blessed* Nicholas and gave thanks to God for her *deliverance*.

But when the people saw this, they made a *great* din the way crowds do, *and rushing in*, they noisily expressed their thanks and praise to God with loud clapping and stomping, while the brothers were intoning the hymn *Te Deum laudamus*. Then alas, sad to say, the same ancient enemy, by the inscrutable judgment of God, came back and sought out again the vessel he had just abandoned. And so the woman began quaking all over, and, with a *great* hissing and a shouting, raised herself up and took to raving more wildly than before. At this, the bystanders were terrified and, overwhelmed with disappointment, asked the foul spirit why he had dared return to God's creature, he replied: 'I was terrified of the sign of the

Crucified and fled. But when I *thought twice about* where *I ought* to go, I sought out again my empty vessel which was not sealed.'

When the letter and the adjurations of the *blessed Hildegard* were used in order to force him out again, with *savage snarls* he shouted out that he would *in no way* leave *its vessel* except in the presence of the little old hag *mentioned above*. Then, those who were of sounder judgment persuaded the friends and guardians of the woman to *put their efforts into* leading her to *the monastery of* the blessed Hildegard. They received a blessing from the Abbot and brothers and a letter of commendation, and so *hastened* to that place. The letter is *written down* as follows:

(*VH* III, 22, 10–34)

At the arrival of this woman we were quite terrified *and in fear* as to how we might cope with seeing and hearing her *by whose exhaustion* so many people had been disturbed for so long a time. But God *so* rained down the dew of his sweetness upon us, *that* without *any* shrinking back or trembling or any help from strong men, we found a place for her in the living quarters of *our* sisters, and from then on, neither on account of the *diabolic* dread or confusion with which the *same vile spirit* troubled the people who came near on account of their sins, nor on account of the mocking and *most* foul words with which he wanted to defeat us, nor on account of his disgusting blasts of air *which he constantly let out at us*, did we give her up in any way.

I saw that the demon suffered three tortures *of punishments* in this *same* woman: the first *torture, that is*, when she was led from one place to another *to the relics* of the saints, the second when the common folk *of the world* gave alms for her *liberation*, the third when through the *labours and* prayers of the spiritual by the grace of God it was compelled to depart.

And so, from the Purification of *the blessed virgin* Mary until the Sabbath of the Pasch, we and our neighbours, *both women and men*, laboured on her account with fasts and prayers, with almsgivings and the *wearing out* of our bodies.

In the meantime the *same* unclean spirit was forced by the *divine* power, however unwillingly, to utter many things before the people about saving Baptism, *and many things about* the sacrament of the Body of Christ, *and much also about* the peril of the excommunicated, *and indeed a great deal about* the ruin of the Cathars, and *many* other such things. All this was to his own confusion and to the glory of Christ, and by it many were made stronger in faith and many *indeed* readier to amend their sins. But whenever I saw in true vision that he was bringing forth lies, straightaway I refuted him, whereupon he would fall silent and grind his teeth at me, although I did not forbid him to speak before the people when he uttered what was true.

(*VH* III, 23, 23–30)

When I eventually tried to do this, though I had no strength of body *to carry it out*, my infirmity *became* somewhat lighter. So I put God's command into effect, and, *by God's grace,* calmed the dissensions that had been going on among certain people.

When, for fear of the people, I neglected *to carry out* courses of action *of this kind which were enjoined on me* by God's command, the sufferings of my body increased, and they did not cease until I obeyed, just as it happened to Jonah, who was afflicted severely till he inclined himself to obedience again.

(*VH* III, 25, 1–11)

After this with most humble insistence and devotion, my Abbot and the brothers urged me to write *something,* as God should will it, *concerning* the life *and the miracles of* St Disibod to whom I had *originally* been offered, since, they said, they had no worthwhile records from *his* time. So I first prayed and invoked the Holy Spirit, and, warned *also* in true vision, I looked to true Wisdom and as it taught *and announced to* me concerning the life and merits of the *same blessed father,* so I wrote them down.

Then almighty God inspired me,[13] *so that* I saw the height and the depth and the breadth of the vault, and how the sun and the moon, the stars and the other *lights* were arranged in it.

(*VH* III, 27, 4–17)

When the blessed mother had devoutly waged battle for the *King and Master of all things* with the many struggles of her labours *and sufferings,* she felt the weariness of this present life, and, *fainting for the joy of the most high blessedness,* daily yearned to be dissolved and to be with Christ. *Wherefore,* God, *being unwilling to put off the worthy desire of his beloved any longer,* by the spirit of prophecy revealed to her the end *of this mortal life as* she *had* wished *before him with sighs, which she repeatedly told her daughters would happen in a short while.*

And thus the blessed virgin had laboured in a *serious* illness for some time, when in the eighty-second year of her life, on the fifteenth day before the Kalends of October [17 September], she *was freed from the toilsome prison of this life and* went with a happy passage to her heavenly spouse,

---

[13] The reference to Hildegard's writing of the *Liber Divinorum Operum,* present in the *VH* text, is missing here.

whom she had longed for with her whole heart. Her daughters, to whom *after God* she had been all joy and *all* solace, wept bitterly as they took part in the funeral rites of their beloved mother. For though they did not doubt her reward and the favours that would be conferred on them *by God* through her, yet they *were afflicted with* the most intense grief of heart over her departure, *by which they seemed to lose the unique consolation of her through whom God had visited them.*[14] But God clearly showed *even* in her passing *through a manifest miracle how great* was the standing she had before him.

---

[14] The Latin in this sentence is poorer than in the *VH*. Reflexive and non-reflexive forms of possessive pronouns are confused in a way which does not appear in the *VH*.

DOCUMENTS OF RUPERTSBERG

CHARTER OF HENRY, ARCHBISHOP OF MAINZ

The following is a translation of Document 175 in *MUB* 2, pp. 326–28.
The source document is the original charter, stamped with Archbishop
Henry's seal, preserved in the Hauptstaatsarchiv, Munich, Urk. Nr. 3187.
Henry, who had sponsored Hildegard before Pope Eugene at the Council
of Trier, here records his consecration of the restored church on
Rupertsberg, where Hildegard and her nuns have established themselves
from Disibodenberg (1147–1151), his giving of the veil to some of the
nuns, and his transfer to them, for their upkeep, of the mill property
Mühlenwert by the Binger Loch on the Rhine.

Date: 1152 [before February 15].[1]

IN THE NAME OF the holy and undivided Trinity. Henry, by favour of the
grace of God, Archbishop of the diocese of Mainz.

Let all Christ's faithful both those alive now and those yet to come, know
that a certain chapel on mount St Rupert the Confessor, situated by the
river Nahe outside the walls of the city of Bingen and long neglected and
left derelict by its tenants, has in our time been repaired and restored to
the worship of God.

For certain faithful virgins, conquering the inducements of the flesh,
and refusing lawful marriage so that they might deserve to be joined
indissolubly with the Son of God, have extinguished in themselves all
natural heat by the shower of heavenly grace,[2] and have transferred from
another place to the above mentioned place, as revealed through the Holy
Spirit. Here, under their *magistra* Hildegard, who shines with many and

---

[1] The *terminus ad quem* since the document is dated in the reign of Emperor Conrad III,
who died on 15 February 1152.

[2] *in se omnem genuinum calorem ymbre celestis gratiẹ extinxerunt*; the *ad hoc* use of a 'y'
for 'i' or 'u' is a feature of the spelling in this document. Acht reads the 'y' as 'i' which
yields the ablative of *imber*, not the genitive *umbrae*.

wonderful virtues, and with many other virgins, they prefer fasting to the feasting of the flesh, and in prayers and vigils earnestly give effect to the work of virginal grace, so that they might enter through the door of the heavenly kingdom with Christ, the spouse of virgins, and, having been proved worthy, abide in his company forever.

We who were called to recommission that chapel, therefore dedicated it on the feast-day of the Apostles Philip and James,[3] to the honour of the blessed Mary Mother of God and the above mentioned apostles, and also of the holy confessors Martin and Rupert, and gave the holy veil to certain young women, and have made over as a means of income to the virgins serving God in that place—since they were labouring for the lack of a mill—a mill property called Mühlenwert, which was subject to our authority, located next to Loch on the Rhine, with all its catchment and the whole extent of its waters, with its roads and paths, with its area for halting, its exits and approaches.

We have made this transfer with the counsel of our friends using all the legal right of a solemn and episcopal transfer of possession, in the measure it was within the bishop's province to do, precisely so that, in those ways in which the same place previously belonged to us, so now and subsequently into the future it may serve the necessity and the benefit of the same sisters, with all their dependencies.

In enacting this, we implore in the Lord that the same assembly of virgins might be mindful of us in their prayers, and of all our successors and predecessors, that we might be reckoned among the number of the elect, and, when the burden of the flesh is set aside, may merit to enjoy eternal happiness.

Moreover, that this transfer of possession may remain valid and irreversible for all time, we have caused this charter to be written, and we have sealed it with the impression of our seal, and have confirmed its provisions under the sanction of our anathema, determining that if anyone is rash and profane enough to presume to usurp this transfer of the aforesaid church conveyed by our hand, or to alienate it in any other way, let him be liable to a well-merited excommunication, and let him feel both here and in the time to come the judgment of the divine rebuke.

---

[3] 1 May. Since the document is dated no later than February 1152, this yields the latest possible date for the consecration of the church of St Mary at Rupertsberg as 1 May 1151.

The following are the witnesses of this handing over of possession: Hartmann, the senior provost,[4] master[5] Willhelm, Hugo,[6] Abbot Cuno of Disibodenberg; the canons: Ruding, Giselbert, Conrad; the freeholders: Herman[7] Count Palatine and Henry his brother, Hugo[8] of Stein, Udalric of Braunshorn, Werner of Merxheim; the ministers: Embric count of the Rhine, Mengoz the deputy,[9] Regenbod and Frederick of Bingen; townsmen of Bingen: Lutfrid, Embrich, Volueric, Adalbero, Volcnant, Gernot, Godeschal and his brother Conrad, Gerlach, Vortuvin, Zacho and many others.

These things are given effect in the year of the Lord's incarnation MCLII, in the fourteenth indiction, during the reign of king Conrad, the fourth of this name.

FIRST CHARTER OF ARNOLD, ARCHBISHOP OF MAINZ

The following is a translation of Document 230 in *MUB* 2, pp. 413–16. The original charter, stamped with Archbishop Arnold's seal, is preserved in the Hauptstaatsarchiv, Koblenz, Urk. Kl. Rupertsberg Nr. 1. Archbishop Arnold of Mainz confirms as a freehold possession of Rupertsberg the gift of Herman count palatine of the Rhine and his wife Gertrude of their allodial property in Bingen, and confirms other transfers and purchases.

Date: 22 May 1158.

IN THE NAME OF the holy and undivided Trinity. Arnold, by favour of the divine goodwill, Archbishop of Mainz.

---

[4] I.e. the cathedral dean or administrator.

[5] *magister*, i.e. head and teacher in the cathedral school.

[6] Hildegard's brother, who appears as cathedral cantor or precentor in a later document (217), of 1156, not here translated, and in document 230, of 1158, a translation of which follows.

[7] Count Palatine of the Rhine 1142–1156.

[8] The text reads literally 'Hûog', a misprint surely. 'Hugo of Stein' appears also in the next document.

[9] Attested as the episcopal vicar, or chancellor of Mainz between 1145–1152/3.

Since it is right that we should with all devotion reverence and love the monasteries under our supervision, it is also just that we should take care, using every effort of mind and body, that donations given for the service of God to those living their lives according to the Rule in these same monasteries, should not through rapacity or neglect be unjustly wrested from them. In view of this, we bring it to the attention of all subsequent posterity that Herman, Count Palatine of the Rhine, with his wife Gertrude,[10] coming on a certain occasion to the place of the blessed confessor Rupert situated next to Bingen, for the welfare of his soul and with every right and in complete liberty made over the allodial property he possessed within the town and outside the town consisting in both fields and vineyards, for the use of the church of the same blessed Rupert, and of the sisters serving God in that spot.

When, after his death, we had come to Würzburg, the widow of the above mentioned Herman again renewed and confirmed this donation in our presence and in the presence of the lord Eberhard the venerable Bishop of Bamberg and of very many other people, without any dissent. That is to say, she handed over the aforementioned allodial property using her royal sanction to the freeman Hugo of Stein, in order that he should offer it as a righteous oblation for all time at the altar of the above mentioned church. What was done was observed and attested by many when we came afterwards to Bingen.

Moreover, these are other donations by which to our knowledge the same place was augmented: the marchioness Richardis[11] gave an allodial property she possessed in Ockenheim, to the same place. Our minister Marcward also contributed a house in Bergen and a vineyard in Büdesheim to the same place. Also Count Odalrich, that is, of Ahr, gave a half-share of a house in Bermersheim. In the same town Hugo, the Cathedral cantor and his brother Drutwin[12] and certain other faithful [gave] five houses and a half-share. Wendela too made over four houses in Weitersheim and a house in Harwesheim, by authority of his royal sanction, along with a sixth part of a tithe in Roxheim and twenty

---

[10] Hermann von Stahleck was Count Palatine from 1142–1156; Gertrude was sister of Emperor Conrad III.

[11] Richardis von Stade who died in 1152; she was a distant cousin of Jutta's.

[12] Hildegard's brothers. Drutwin appears in the 1127 Sponheim charter with his father. In 1176 Hugo briefly acted as provost at Rupertsberg. For remarks by Guibert on Hildegard's brothers, see Ep. 26, Derolez, p. 279.

servants. Guda of Geisenheim gave on behalf of his daughter Osbirna, a house and a half-share in Appenheim by the hand of his son Arnold, and Embrich count of the Rhine [gave] the allodial property he had in Welgesheim.

Now Herman the provost of Holy Cross[13] and the sons of his brother, that is, Bernard the deputy of Hildesheim possessed vineyards next to Bingen. The above mentioned sisters gave twenty marks before many witnesses and bought these vineyards from the sons of the above mentioned Bernard, the same Herman granting approval by authority of his royal sanction. Also, for fifteen marks they redeemed three houses in Bermersheim from a certain Godebert and his wife from Selzen, and this before many witnesses. And they came into the use of five houses in Appenheim and a house and a half-share in Langenlonsheim with no dissent.

So that all these transactions may remain valid and irreversible to all posterity for all time, we have caused the present page to be signed with the impression of our seal and corroborated by our authority, determining by the power of God the omnipotent Father, and by the authority of blessed Peter prince of Apostles and our own, that whoever attempts to challenge these provisions be subjected to everlasting anathemas unless he come to his senses.

The witnesses of what is written out here are: Hartman, senior provost, Arnold cathedral guardian, Sigelous the dean, Willhelm master of the Cathedral school, Hugo the cantor, Baldemar Abbot of St Alban, Godfrey Abbot of St James, Helenger Abbot of St Disibod, Anselm Abbot of St John in Johannisberg, Burchard provost of Jechaburg, Hetzekin provost of St Moritz, Baldwin Abbot of St John, Godfrey provost of Frankfurt, Conrad provost of St Gangolf; canons: Ruding, Dragebod, Gernot, Ortwin; Conrad count of Kyrburg and his brother Emich of Altenbamberg, Godfrey count of Sponheim, Berthold count of Nied, count Gerhard and his brother Rupert of Bernbach; freemen: Gerhard of Kälberau, Marcward of Bierstadt, Werner of Wallbach, Dammo of Badenheim; ministers: Helprich the deputy and his brother Herman, Peter, Wicnand, Embrich and his brother Meingott, Arnold, Dudo,

---

[13] Herman is attested as provost at the monastery of the Cross in Hildesheim from 1155–1163, and from 1162 as Bishop of Hildesheim.

Godebald the marshal, Werner, Reinbod, Dietrich, Hartrous, Fredrick and Embrich and many others.

These things are given effect in the year of the Lord's incarnation MCLVIII, in the sixth indiction, under Pope Adrian, during the reign of the most glorious Emperor Frederick the first of this name. Given at Mainz on the eleventh before the Kalends of June [22 May].

SECOND CHARTER OF ARNOLD, ARCHBISHOP OF MAINZ

The following is a translation of Document 231, *MUB* 2, pp. 416–18. The original charter, stamped with Archbishop Arnold's seal, is preserved in the Hauptstaatsarchiv, Koblenz, Urk. Kl. Rupertsberg Nr.2. This document covers much of the ground appropriate to a set of Constitutions for Rupertsberg. Archbishop Arnold confirms the economic independence of the nuns' monastery and of the possessions acquired at its foundation from its mother-house, Disibodenberg, assigns to the Abbot of Disibodenberg responsibility for the priestly ministry there and the prerogative of conducting monastic professions at Rupertsberg, affirms the nuns' right to a free election of a successor to their spiritual mother, takes their monastery under archdiocesan protection and keeps under his supervision the conduct of the office of provost.

Date: 22 May 1158.

IN THE NAME OF the holy and undivided Trinity. Arnold, by favour of the divine goodwill, Archbishop of Mainz.

Since, as the Apostle testifies, by the gracious goodwill of the Lord we must work as husbandmen in his field (cf. Mat. 9:38, 21:1–16), the duty of our office requires that we root out whatever weeds there are in the Lord's field, and replace them with the good (cf. Mat. 13:24–29). Therefore we have thought it right to bring to the notice of all the faithful, both those now living and those in time to come, that we who love tranquillity and concord desire that those who dwell under our rule should serve God with a greater care in the harmony of charity.

Because of this, we, desiring that the brothers of Disibodenberg and the sisters of Rupertsberg located at Bingen have no cause for grievance against each other, have decided that these sisters should have free-hold possession of both the place and their estates in independence of the brothers, and should incur no hindrance from them on any pretext whatever.

For the lady Hildegard came from Disibodenberg to Rupertsberg with certain young women dedicated with her to God, and, by a just exchange of property redeemed that place from several persons with vineyards contributed to her by certain of the faithful. Having entered into common counsel,[14] the aforesaid brothers through the lord Abbot Cuno then gave to them and those after them eight houses in various places, in perpetual exchange for the offerings which the same young women had contributed for themselves to the monastery of Disibodenberg.

Afterward the lord Abbot Helenger[15] confirmed this when, in our presence and in the presence of many others, his brothers having given assent without any dissent, he released the same place as a freehold possession just as we mentioned above. And we generously granted this for the service and need of the same sisters, decreeing that they should have possession of these things and whatever else in whatsoever offerings which have been given or shall be given to them, without any stipulations of the aforesaid Abbot or his successors.

However, that these sisters might not suffer neglect through uncertainty about priests, we judge that, whoever the Abbot of Disibodenberg may be, now and in the future, he should maintain the care of their souls, in that he shall provide priests for them, that is to say monks of worthy reputation, who shall care for them in all things according to their need and petition. Let him not remove them without the sisters' consent,[16] let him willingly concede them the blessing of monastic profession in accordance with the arrangement of blessed Benedict, and in all concerns to which they might call him, let him help them with a good will, as long as the monastic spirit flourishes in both of the above mentioned monasteries, and these requests can be honourably asked of them by the sisters and be granted them by the brothers.

We have also laid it down, that after the death of their spiritual mother,

---

[14] *inito communi consilio*; *inito* is improved to *initio* in one manuscript, yielding the sense 'in the beginning/originally', but *inito* is without doubt the original reading, being also used by Emperor Frederick in the following document.

[15] Helenger, Abbot of Disibodenberg 1155–1178.

[16] *nec iterum illos sine voluntate earum amoveat.*

the same sisters should, in a free election according to the Rule of blessed Benedict, choose another for themselves as spiritual mother, who is of benefit and suitable to their common and sound purpose in both internal and external matters. To her they shall all show a fitting obedience in all things, and to her they shall refer all matters that need to be decided upon in the place above mentioned.

Therefore we receive the same place with all that concerns it under the patronage of Saint Martin and under our protection and that of our successors. All the rights which the other monasteries under our rule have in all spiritual concerns, we also grant to this monastery and do not allow any other advocate to be appointed to it by our successors except ourselves and those who succeed us in our office.

Moreover, that this considered deed of ours may remain valid and irreversible before all posterity and all time, we have caused this present page to be sealed with the impression of our seal, and have decided to corroborate it with our authority by the power of God and the authority of blessed Peter and our own, so that whoever attempts to infringe it, let him be subjected to the penalty of everlasting anathema unless he comes to his senses.

The witnesses of this matter are: Hartman, senior provost of the church, Arnold guardian of the cathedral, Sigelous the dean, Willhelm the Cathedral scholar, Hugo the cantor, Baldemar Abbot of St Alban, Godfrey Abbot of St James, Helenger Abbot of St Disibod, Anselm Abbot of St John in Johannisberg, Burchard provost of Jechaburg, Hetzekin provost of St Moritz, Baldwin Abbot of St John, Godfrey provost of Frankfurt, Conrad provost of St Gangolf; canons: Ruding, Dragebod, Gernot, Ortwin; Godfrey count of Sponheim, Conrad count of Kyrburg and his brother Emich of Altenbamberg, Berthold count of Nied, count Gerhard and his brother Rupert of Bernbach; freemen: Gerhard of Kälberau, Marcward of Bierstadt, Werner of Wallbach, Dammo of Badenheim; ministers: Helprich[17] the vicar and his brother Herman, Peter, Wicnand, Embrich and his brother Meingott, Arnold, Dudo, Godebald, Reinbod, Dietrich, Fredrick and his brother Embrich, Hartrous, Inkelschal and many others.

---

[17] Helprich was the Archbishop's vicar for Mainz from 1155–1160 and his brother a mayor during the same years.

These things are given effect in the year of the Lord's incarnation MCLVIII, in the sixth indiction, under Pope Adrian, during the reign of our most glorious Emperor Frederick, the first of that name. Given at Mainz on the eleventh before the Kalends of June [22 May].

CHARTER OF EMPEROR FREDERICK I

The following is a translation of Document 274, *MUB* 2, pp. 484–86. The original charter, stamped with Emperor Frederick's seal, is preserved in the Hauptstaatsarchiv, Koblenz, Urk. Kl. Rupertsberg Nr.3 (A). Here the Emperor takes Rupertsberg and all its property under his protection, confirming its foundation and all the goods acquired at that time and its independence from the monastery of Disibodenberg, whose Abbot retains responsibility for the priestly ministry at Rupertsberg, as long as he respects their freedom to choose their abbess and their provost. Several passages are simply taken over from the second charter of Archbishop Arnold of Mainz. This is the only contemporary document which gives Hildegard the title of 'abbess': see the notes here and at Ep. 38, X.

   Date: 18 April 1163.

IN THE NAME OF the holy and undivided Trinity. Frederick, by favour of the divine goodwill, Holy Roman Emperor.[18]

In the judgment of God who sees all things, we believe there will be equal merit to benefactors and those who confirm their benefactions. We also believe that the responsibility of the whole government pertains to our imperial majesty, and specially that, in order to foster the well-being of all the holy communities[19] of God we ought with all haste to abolish all that hinders them, lest they deteriorate through serious obstruction, or, for whatever occasion that arises, dwindle in our time from their original culture and religious spirit. Therefore, while we faithfully carry through these provisions in both the fear and the love of God, may we receive an

---

[18] *Romanorum imperator augustus.*

[19] *sanctarum Dei ecclesiarum saluti. Ecclesia* in this context refers not to dioceses but to communities of monks or nuns.

equal share in the merits and the glory of those who have offered these contributions through their devout affection toward God.

Consequently, let it be known to both the present age, and the succeeding posterity of all Christ's faithful in our realm, that we, through the intervention and petition of the venerable abbess,[20] lady Hildegard, take under our protection the monastery of Rupertsberg located at Bingen and its nuns who serve God there, and their possessions both movable and immovable and their fields and all matters belonging to the aforesaid place, which they already have or by the gift of God are able to obtain in the future. With the protection of our unreserved corroboration we confirm the abovementioned place, the abbess, her sisters and all their possessions in accordance with the instrument of Arnold, by imperial privilege at one time the venerable archbishop of the See of Mainz.

We remember and commend to everlasting memory that the aforesaid lady abbess Hildegard moved from Disibodenberg to Rupertsberg with certain young women dedicated with her to God, and with a just exchange redeemed the same place as their own property from various people with vineyards contributed to them by certain of the faithful. Having entered into common counsel,[21] the aforesaid brothers through the lord Abbot Cuno[22] then gave to them and those after them eight houses in various places in perpetual exchange for the offerings which the same young women had contributed for themselves to the monastery of Disibodenberg.

Afterwards the lord Abbot Helenger[23] confirmed this and in the presence of the aforesaid Archbishop Arnold and of many others, his brothers having given assent without any opposition, released the same place as a freehold possession. This proviso was retained, that whoever

---

[20] Here and lower down are the only contemporary references to Hildegard as 'abbess'. See the note to Ep. 38, X. The use of this title seems to be flattery with a political purpose. Frederick had been in a state of schism since 1159, supporting an anti-pope Victor IV against Alexander III (1159–1181), who for his part addresses Hildegard in a letter as 'prioress' (Ep. 10, Van Acker, p. 25). When Victor died and Frederick compounded his contumacy by setting up a successor to him, he tasted Hildegard's prophetic wrath in full, see Ep. XXVII (PL 187, 186–87), and Barbara Newman in *Scivias*, trans. by Hart and Bishop, pp. 15–16.

[21] *inito communi consilio.*

[22] Cuno, Abbot of Disibodenberg, 1136–1155; the documentation has not survived.

[23] Helenger, Abbot of Disibodenberg, 1155–1178; the documentation has not survived.

might be the Abbot of Disibodenberg, now or in the future, should have the care of their souls, and provide according to their need and petition priest-monks of worthy reputation to dispense to them the divine things, and that he should not remove those who have been provided against the sisters' will, and in all matters to which they might call him, he should help them with a good will, as long as the monastic spirit flourishes in both of the above mentioned monasteries, and these requests can be honourably asked of them by the sisters and be granted them by the brothers.

Also we have laid it down that after the death of their spiritual mother, the same sisters should, in a free election according to the Rule of blessed Benedict, choose another for themselves as spiritual mother who is of benefit and suitable for their common and sound purpose in both internal and external matters. To her they shall all show a fitting obedience in all things, and they shall refer to her all matters which need to be decided upon in the place above mentioned.

Thus, receiving under our imperial protection the same place with its nuns and its possessions, we have decided, and have hallowed it by imperial edict that no one should usurp for himself the advocacy of this same place, but that through the imperial right hand and the help of the Archbishop of Mainz it should always continue free and secure from all attacks and injustices ...

CHARTER OF CHRISTIAN, ARCHBISHOP OF MAINZ

The following is a translation of Document 337, *MUB* 2, pp. 571–72. The original charter, stamped with Archbishop Christian's seal, is preserved in the Hauptstaatsarchiv, Koblenz, Urk. Kl. Rupertsberg Nr.4. Archbishop Christian exempts the properties and other possessions of the Benedictine nuns at Rupertsberg from the payment of an episcopal levy.

Date: 1171.

IN THE NAME OF the holy and undivided Trinity. Christian, by the grace of God, Archbishop of the See of Mainz, to all Christ's faithful, both now and in the future.

If we have contributed to the venerable places something for the provision of those serving God there of those things which are within our right, we hope that it would work towards the eternal salvation both of us and our successors to whom a commemoration of prayers is due.

Therefore let the faithful know, those of our own time and of future times to come that I, Christian, humble overseer of the metropolis of Mainz, for the honour of the holy Mother of God at her community located on the Rupertsberg at Bingen, have by our own hand, with the consent and encouragement of my senior counsellors, made over so great a use of our right that at our request, in the district of the Rhine and in all places which belong to our church, no episcopal levy shall be required by my stewards from the trusteeships and the possessions of the nuns serving God in the community of the above mentioned monastery; in accordance with the authority of our grant let all things which concerns them there be held by perpetual right entirely free of the debt of this levy.

And since from the resources of the principal church, bishops may come to the help of poorer communities, therefore, in order that our grant may remain irreversible in our time and in the time of our successors, we have confirmed the page which bears witness of this transaction with the impress of our seal.

We also note the witnesses in whose presence this has taken place. These are: Arnold the senior provost, Burchard provost of St Peter, Werner senior provost at St Marien im Felde, Berthold provost at Mariengreden, Henry the cantor,[24] Siegfried provost of St John, Conrad the provost,[25] Herman the provost,[26] Egeno,[27] Babo, Helet, Berengar the cellarer,[28] Conrad. And the layfolk witnesses: Gerlac count of Veldenz, Gerhard count of Nürings, Conrad count of Altenbamberg, Walter of Hausen, Hartman of Büdingen, Volmar of Metz, Werner of Bolanden, Dudo the chamberlain,[29] the Rhinegraf senior[30] and junior, Arnold Rufus,

---

[24] Attested as Cathedral cantor at Mainz from 1170–1171.

[25] Of St Gangolf.

[26] Of St Moritz.

[27] Those named from Egeno to Conrad are canons of the Cathedral.

[28] Attested as Cathedral 'cellarer' at Mainz from 1171–1177.

[29] The archbishop's chamberlain at Mainz.

[30] Embrich II, Rhinegraf from 1158.

Reimbot,[31] Conrad of Leihgestern, Herman, Conrad of Rüdesheim, Arnold of Geisenheim and his brother Meingott, and many others.

This act is given effect in the year of the Lord's incarnation MCLXXI, in the fourth indiction, during the reign of the most serene Emperor Frederick.

INVENTORY OF THE POSSESSIONS OF RUPERTSBERG

INTRODUCTION

The following is translated from Document 14, *Urkundenbuch zur Geschichte der mittelrheinischen Territorien*, vol. 1, pp. 365–91, and copied from a manuscript of 1210, presumably the original. This is a long inventory made by the nuns of Rupertsberg of the goods and possessions of their monastery. The headings under which the contents are arranged are: Introduction; Estate of Herman count palatine; Bermersheim; Okkenheim; Vineyards which the lady Gepa gave to our community; Isenheim; Longesheim; Genzingun; Volkesheim; Appenheim; Dolengesheim; Weitdersheim; Basenheim; Bunnenheim; Basenheim; Brunnenheim; Wilre; Haresheim; Weilengesheim; These are the vineyards we have in Bingen; Item vineyards which we have in Weilar; Vineyards which we have in Longesheim; Item vineyards in Okkenheim; Item vineyards in Drehtingeshausen; Vineyards in Bermersheim; Vineyards in Wellingsheim; Vineyards in Appenheim; Vineyards in Rüdesheim; Vineyards in Genzingun; These are the leases which are paid by us; Witnesses concerning the estate of Lufrid and Regelind; Witnesses of Dypurgis; Witnesses concerning Volkesheim; Witnesses; Witnesses. At this point there is an addition in another hand pertaining to the years 1210–1220, which partly uses German. It ends with a section headed 'Rüdesheim'.

Date: 1200.

INTRODUCTION
In the year of the Lord's incarnation one thousand, one hundred and

---

[31] Of Bingen.

forty-seven, through a revelation of the Holy Spirit to our blessed mother Hildegard, we moved from Disibodenberg to the place of our patron blessed Rupert. In this same place our blessed mother happily lived for thirty years. Although we had no possessions whatever at this spot, we bought the first foundation from the lord Bernard, count of Hildesheim[32] for twenty marks. However, of the things which we now possess, some we bought, others were contributed for the souls of the faithful ...

---

[32] A nephew of Jutta's, see *VH* I, 5, and Julie Hotchin, 'Images and Their Places': Hildegard of Bingen and Her Communities', *Tjurunga* 49 (1996), p. 29, n. 17.

ACTA INQUISITIONIS

INTRODUCTION

As an epilogue to this collection of documents the *Acta Inquisitionis de Virtutibus et Miraculis S. Hildegardis* ('Proceedings of the enquiry into the virtues and miracles of S. Hildegard') is here translated from the Latin text edited by Peter Bruder, a canon at Bingen on the Rhine, in *Analecta Bollandiana*, 2 (1883), 116–29. The document has sometimes also been referred to as *Protocollum Canonisationis* ('The protocol of canonization').

Bruder explains that when in 1632, during the Thirty Years' War, the monastery at Rupertsberg was burnt by the Swedes, the nuns took their collection of documents with them across the Rhine to the monastery at Eibingen, the daughter house founded by Hildegard. In 1814, he says, the government of Nassau dissolved this monastery too, and transferred its historical documents to the public archives in Wiesbaden. When in 1866 the duchy of Nassau was annexed by Prussia, all Rupertsberg documents were moved to the state archives in Koblenz.

While visiting the archives in Koblenz in 1882, Bruder had all these documents spread out before him, when he came across the original 'instrument' concerning Hildegard's miracles and virtues, as completed by three canons of Mainz on 16 December 1233. It consists of a single very large parchment sheet, 780 x 250 mm, with 97 full lines of script on the front of the sheet, and on the back 22 full lines and 42 'half-lines'. Three seals of the canons who drew up the document are attached by cords.

The three canons had sent this charter to Gregory IX (1227–1241) as part of the diocesan enquiry undertaken with a view to Hildegard's canonization. Pope Gregory however wrote back on 6 May 1237 that the depositions of witnesses had been taken down with insufficient attention to detail and form.[1] He charged the new commissioners:

---

[1] It is worth recalling that, 'even the petition for Bernard's canonization, which had never

You shall proceed steadily and thoroughly with the aforesaid enquiry according to the form given to the commissioners, and set out what you have found clearly and judiciously under your seals, preserving them faithfully for our approval.

It is something of a mystery that the canonization of Hildegard was not accomplished during the pontificate of Gregory IX, for although he had much to do with formalizing the procedures of canonization, few popes would seem to have been personally better disposed.[2]

Up to the pontificate of Innocent IV (1243–1254), no new document of Hildegard's cause had been sent back to Rome, for in a letter dated 24 November 1243, Pope Innocent refers to the fresh enquiry his predecessor had asked be made. He then goes on,

> if you have proceeded in this way, be sure to send the proceedings themselves under your seals to us ... But if not, make careful enquiry through witnesses worthy of credence concerning the above mentioned miracles, and any new ones she may be said to have worked, and

---

stood in doubt, was initially rejected by Alexander III, and passed muster only after his *vita* had been revised by its principal author.' Newman, 'Hildegard and her Hagiographers'.

[2] As Hugo(lino), he had been made Cardinal deacon by his uncle Innocent III in 1198, and served on legations to Germany where he had heard of Hildegard for himself (*Acta Inq.*). On the one hand, Pope Gregory showed a strong sense of ecclesial order when he formalized the procedures for papal canonization which were to be henceforth normative. As Cardinal he befriended the Spaniard Dominic Guzman, whose Order of Friar Preachers (the Dominicans) he later set up over the Roman Inquisition he founded when Pope to combat heresies, especially the Cathars. He cleared certain obstacles to the study of Aristotle at the University of Paris, therefore paving the way for the eventual approval of scholastic theology. On the other hand, Pope Gregory was possessed of a deeply felt, even mystical, religious fervour, and realized that the subjectivism of the heresies needed to be countered not only by solid doctrine, but also by the living witness of holiness in the Church. As Cardinal, he had been the supporter of Cistercians, Camaldolese and even of the followers of the apocalypticist, Abbot Joachim of Fiore (d. 1202). Most importantly he became the patron and friend of St Francis of Assisi, who loved him dearly. Francis died just a few months before Hugo became Pope, and on 16 July of the same year as the letter quoted in *Acta Inq.* (1228), was canonized by his friend at Assisi in a very solemn liturgy. Pope Gregory was also a friend of St Clare of Assisi, whose monastery at San Damiano he visited more than once before and after he became Pope. He respected her staunch opposition to any mitigation of her ideals, and granted her the sought-for *privilegium paupertatis*, thereby enfranchising her with the privation of all endowments and property.

concerning the truth about her life. Then have a careful record made of what these same witnesses have told you in a straightforward, honest and orderly fashion that they know of all we have mentioned above; whom you will have been sure to examine individually, not in the presence of the others as such. Then faithfully submit these reports to us again under the same seals.

From the surviving state of the charter it is clear the commissioners did revise the document. There are 53 additions made in the spaces between the lines clarifying the depositions, two sections struck out with ink, and 42 half lines added at the end of the original charter, with reports of miracles which took place since 1233. It seems reasonable to suppose that the commissioners would have made a fair copy of this emended version to send on to Rome. But if they did, no such copy has come to light. So it is uncertain whether Innocent IV ever received a second form of the report, and indeed there is no dating after the additions to the present document. There is no evidence that Innocent ever canonized Hildegard.

Moving to the next century, Trithemius says that Popes Clement V (1305–1314) and John XXII (1316–1334), instituted new commissions of enquiry into Hildegard's history, virtues, miracles, etc., and that in 1317 the necessary documents were sent to John XXII, who 'having carefully read over the testimonies sent to him, made no difficulty about canonizing the virgin, as I am assured by the apostolic writing, although this event, longed for by many, was not brought to pass'.[3]

Among the documents of Rupertsberg in the archives at Koblenz, Bruder also discovered a *Litterae Indulgentiarum* (Letter of Indulgences), dated at Avignon, 5 December 1324, in which twelve bishops each grant forty days' indulgence to all those faithful who go on certain prescribed feast days to the church at Rupertsberg and pour out their devout prayers in that place. The *festum S. Hildegardis* ('the Feast of Saint Hildegard') is one of the days specified. This document seems to indicate that, in the intervening few years from 1317, Pope John XXII either formally canonized St Hildegard, of which there is no other evidence, or more

---

[3] *Acta Inq.*, p. 129. The reference in Bruder's notes is *Annales Hirsaugiensis*, tom. II, page 142, edit. S. Gallia. 1690. Inspection of a photocopy of the page from this edition has failed to verify the reference. On the other hand, Trithemius gives a similar report about the early fourteenth-century attempt to have Hildegard canonized in *Chron. Sponh.*, p. 305. Here he says that it was Abbot Willicho of Sponheim who took up the matter with Pope John XXII.

likely gave public verbal approval of her cult.

Here we sketch a few of the subsequent indications of Hildegard's status. From the thirteenth century onwards Hildegard's feast day was celebrated at the monasteries she founded, and at Gembloux. It was taken up at a number of other Benedictine and Cistercian houses and other places as well. Her name appears in a number of local martyrologies up to the fifteenth century. In the later middle ages her reputation stood highest as a reformer and apocalypticist, a 'prophet of clerical chastisement'. In 1220 the Cistercian abbot, Gebeno of Eberbach, compiled an anthology of her texts on these themes called *Pentachronon seu Speculum Futurorum Tempororum*, which achieved far greater circulation than copies of her individual works.[4] 'It was chiefly through Gebeno that Hildegard had a readership at all in the late Middle Ages, and because of Gebeno's polemical interests, that readership was primarily male.'[5]

In the sixteenth century Cardinal Baronius included Hildegard's name in the Roman Martyrology for 17 September. This greatly helped establish her name on a broader ecclesial front. In the eighteenth century Pope Benedict XIV referred to 'Blessed' Hildegard's visions in his magisterial treatise on heroic virtue.[6]

Throughout the nineteenth century Hildegard's star rose steadily. When the monastery of Eibingen was suppressed from 1806–1904, her cult was continued locally at Bingen. When Abbot Guéranger restored Benedictine life in France after its collapse in the Revolution, he established her feast day at Solesmes, and in Germany, Beuron adopted it

---

[4] See Kathryn Kerby-Fulton, 'A Return to the "First Dawn of Justice": Hildegard's Visions of Clerical Reform and the Eremitical Life', *American Benedictine Review*, 40:4 (December 1989), esp. p. 390.

[5] Newman, 'Hildegard and Her Hagiographers: The Remaking of Female Sainthood', in *Gendered Voices: Medieval Saints and Their Interpreters* (Philadelphia: University of Pennsylvania Press, forthcoming 1999).

[6] 'What is to be said of those private revelations which the Apostolic See has approved of, those of the Blessed Hildegard, of St Bridget, and of St Catherine of Siena? We have already said that these revelations, although approved of, ought not to, and cannot, receive from us any assent of Catholic, but only of human faith, according to the rules of prudence, according to which the aforesaid revelations are probable, and piously to be believed in (*probabiles et pie credibiles*)', quoted by Benedict J. Groeschel, *A Still Small Voice: A Practical Guide on Reported Revelations* (San Francisco: Ignatius Press, 1993), p. 28.

following his lead. Also in the nineteenth century, J.-P. Migne dedicated a volume to her (PL 197) in his monumental series of the 'Fathers, Doctors and writers of the Church'. He had been helped by the Benedictine monk, Johannes Baptista Pitra, though Migne did not acknowledge this. Pitra, who eventually became a Cardinal, continued to be a great promoter of Hildegard, being greatly exercised over the theology of private revelations. In 1882 he edited and published at Monte Cassino a supplementary volume of works of hers not included in the PL volume.

At this point it should be remarked that the amorphous 'Benedictine Order' was an historically anomalous concept. It was only furnished with some apparatus of centralization during the pontificate of Leo XIII (1878–1903). In 1916, Hildegard's feast-day was inscribed officially in the general Benedictine calendar with the rank of a memoria, which it retained after the revision of the Benedictine calendar in 1961. Her feast was also celebrated in the Cistercian Order, and in the dioceses of Mainz, Trier, Limburg, and Speyer.[7]

It was only in 1930[8] that an historical section was instituted at Rome in the Congregation of Rites, as it was then called, with a brief to proceed with causes of saints unable to be investigated any longer on the basis of juridically drawn up depositions of eye-witnesses, but for which historical and literary documents were available. According to Klaes, in 1941, Hildegard's cult received approval along with a number of other historically and regionally venerated saints.[9]

So is Hildegard canonized or not? In the absence of any unambiguous evidence, it is perhaps safest to answer in the negative. And yet this 'still

---

[7] For information in the preceding three paragraphs, see Flanagan, *Hildegard of Bingen, 1098-1179: A Visionary Life*, pp. 12–13, and Rombaut Van Doren, 'Ildegard di Bingen', in *Bibliotheca Sanctorum* (Rome: Istituto Giovanni XXIII, Pontificia Università Lateranense, 1961-1970), vol. 7, cols 764–65.

[8] Cf. the *motu proprio* of Pius XI, 'Gia da qualche tempo', *Acta Apostolicae Sedis* 22 (1930), 87–88.

[9] 'Eine offizielle Kanonisation kam damals nicht zustande, erst 1941 wurde Hildegard in einem paschalen Verfahren zusammen mit weiteren regional vererhten Persönlichkeiten heiliggesprochen', Klaes, p. 19*. Examination of the *Acta Apostolicae Sedis* for 1941 did not yield any evidence of this as reported by Klaes, and correspondence with the Congregation for Saints' Causes failed to elicit any further information on the point.

uncanonized, neo-canonical saint'[10] is today honoured as 'saint' in the highest quarters. In 1979, on the occasion of the 800th anniversary of her death, Pope John-Paul II himself wrote of 'Saint Hildegard' to the Bishop of Mainz.

The Church has seen fit so far to accord to three women saints the title of 'Doctor of the Church'. It remains to be seen whether the character of Hildegard's doctrine will lend itself to having her also declared a Doctor of the Church.

In the following translation, all the additions made after 1233 in the main body of the document are included in (round brackets). The two passages which were struck out are included in [square brackets]. Occasionally 'Hildegard' has been inserted to help distinguish the feminine pronouns. I have instituted chapter divisions in this translation for purposes of reference. The entire last chapter, chapter X, consists of appendices made after 1233.

---

[10] Newman, her concluding words to 'Hildegard and her Hagiographers: The Remaking of Female Sainthood'.

ACTA INQUISITIONIS

I

TO THE MOST HOLY father and Lord, Gregory, most high Pontiff of the holy Roman Church, Gerbodo, provost of the greater church,[11] Walter, deacon[12] and Arnold, scholastic of Saint Peter at Mainz,[13] reverently kiss your feet, with as much devotion as duty. We received the mandate of your Holiness in the following form:

> Gregory, Bishop, servant of the servants of God, to his dear sons ... to the provost of the greater church, ... deacon and ... scholastic of Saint Peter at Mainz, greetings with our apostolic blessing.
>
> God *who is wonderful in his saints* (Ps. 67:36) confirms the holy life of *those who sowed in tears* (Ps. 125:5) with the virtue of miracles, as if indicating by *these signs following* (Mk 16:17) that for their merits he has granted to them eternal glory.
>
> Whereas our beloved daughters in Christ, the abbess and sisters of the monastery of St Rupert at Bingen in the diocese of Mainz have petitioned us that, since, by the merits of Hildegard of holy memory, abbess of the said monastery, God has deigned to work many miracles up till now, and still deigns to work them, and she who had only learnt to read the psalter composed many books through the revelation of the Holy Spirit, books which were worthy of being brought to the notice of the Roman Church, we, who heard of her praiseworthy and holy way of life while we were serving in a lesser office together with Leo of worthy memory, titular cardinal priest of Holy Cross, in a legation to the German regions, ought now to exalt her on earth whom the Lord has honoured in heaven, by canonizing her and inscribing her in the catalogue of the saints and by

---

[11] Attested as provost of the Cathedral of Mainz 1223–1235, cf. *Regesta archiepiscoporum Moguntiensium. Regesten zur Geschichte der Mainzer Erzbischöfe* 1–2, 742–1288, ed. by J.F. Böhmer and C. Will (Innsbruck: Wagner, 1877–86; repr. Aalen: Scientia, 1966), vol. 2, p. 273.

[12] Attested as deacon of St Peter, 1217–1245, cf. *Regesta archiepiscoporum Moguntiensium*, vol. 2, p. 495.

[13] Attested from 1216–1234, cf. *Regesta archiepiscoporum Moguntiensium*, vol. 2, p. 502.

conferring our authority on her books which we have ordered conveyed to us, in order that they be received by all. And that, just as the light should not lie hidden in the darkness, and *a city on a mountain should not be hidden* (Mt 5:14), so what God is working through her merits should be brought into the light.

Since she is said to have so shone with miracles that she is held by all in the above mentioned regions to be a saint, we have inclined to the petitions of the sisters above mentioned, who do not believe that what is made manifest by such great evidence should be ignored. Thus, through our apostolic letter we charge you to undertake on our behalf a diligent enquiry into the truth from witnesses worthy of credence, concerning her history, her way of life, her reputation, her merits, her miracles, and in general all her circumstances, and that what you shall learn, you shall set forth faithfully under your seals, and dispatch to us, together with the above mentioned books, by means of a faithful messenger. If you cannot all be involved in carrying out this task, then let two of you at least carry it out.

Dated at the Lateran, on the sixth day before the Kalends of February [27 January 1228],[14] in the first year of our pontificate.

Commanded therefore by this authority, we went personally to the monastery of Saint Rupert. There we received witnesses worthy of testimony according to this form, concerning the history, way of life, reputation, merits, signs, and other circumstances of the blessed Hildegard. We had to refuse some witnesses, not because there were not enough witnesses, but because there was not enough time to give to them all.

II

THE *MAGISTRA* OF SAINT Rupert in Bingen, Elysa by name, declared on oath concerning the miracles of blessed Hildegard, that she saw a demoniac Mechtild (by name, from the village of Laubenheim), set free at the tomb of blessed Hildegard. (In particular) she saw the noble women Reguwize and Seguwize, set free in the same way (in the presence of blessed Hildegard), who afterward served in the same monastery for the rest of their lives. She also saw many epileptics set free there (whose names

---

[14] On p. 119 Bruder notes the year as 1227, but Hugo became Pope only on 19 March 1227.

names and places of origin they did not note down, God knows). Those
suffering various kinds of recurring fevers were set free at her tomb when
they called on her name (whose names they no longer recall, it happened
so often).

The prioress Agnes on oath says the same; the sister of the *magistra* on
oath says the same thing. Beatrix the guardian,[15] Odilia the cellarer,
Hedwig the lay-sister, on oath, say they saw the same thing. Sophia the
chantress, on oath, says the same.

Roric the priest,[16] on oath, says the same, but he adds that when he
approached to summon that demoniac (Mechtild), but before he spoke to
her, she called him by his two names, saying *Henry! Roric!* which had not
been known in those parts before. Furthermore, he saw four crows sitting
in the windows below the church just then. When he asked the demoniac
who the crows were, he[17] replied, saying they were his companions who
were waiting for him to depart. When he had said this, she opened her
mouth wide and let out a very black smoke, and in this way the obsessed
woman was set free; but not all immediately agreed about this, though the
sounder part of the community, put on oath, were for it. He also added
that he saw eighteen demoniacs set free at her tomb when they called on
her name (whose names and places of origin they did not note down).
Daniel the priest, on oath, says the same. The provost of the same place,
on oath, says the same.

Concerning the time, the *magistra*, says, on oath, that all these things
took place over a space of less than 30 years.

III

BEATRIX THE GUARDIAN (FROM Koblenz) said, on oath, that when she
was twelve years old, she was offered to the same monastery and lived
with the blessed Hildegard for some time. She saw and heard the holy
Hildegard foretell the day of her death before everyone in chapter, and

---

[15] *custodissa*, 'novice mistress'?

[16] A 'Roric, monk' appears in *VH* III, 2 as a resident at Rupertsberg.

[17] I.e. the demon, by means of the demoniac. There is an unmarked transition from the
female demoniac to the 'masculine' demon; the 'crows' are waiting for their fellow
demon's exit from the demoniac. 'One frequent sign of possession in females was
speaking in a loud, raucous "masculine" voice', from a note to me by Barbara Newman.

that after her death she saw a blind woman Mechtild from the castle (of Pieletia) receive her sight who had called on the name of the same virgin (while she was alive). She also saw one out of his mind (whose name she forgets) restored to sanity. And she knew a serving woman Mezza (from Veche), who had carried away earth from her tomb and placed it in a not very honourable place. She was headed off and corrected by the blessed Hildegard and compelled to bring back the earth. When it had been replaced, and she was contrite over what she had done, she was immediately set free. She knew that her sister Clementia[18] (from the village of Trechtingshausen), who is now ... [19] had given hairs of the blessed Hildegard to her brother, and because of this was castigated by the same (blessed Hildegard) till she had brought the hair back. She saw a lay woman (whose name she forgets), in whose leg there was a bone which had protruded so abnormally that she could not walk. When the same bone was rubbed with the hairs of the blessed Hildegard, the bone immediately vanished, and she was healed immediately.

With these (last) contributed items the greater and sounder part of the chapter, when asked, agreed on oath. She also saw him (the knight, Herman of Mainz), who poked the blessed Hildegard with his foot in annoyance, lose his foot by the scourge of God.

The cellarer, who had lived with the blessed virgin six years and more, on oath said the same thing, adding that when a certain woman with recurring fever (whose name she does not know), begged her help, she had water conveyed in her shoe to the same woman, who sipped it and was immediately healed. She also added that when two young women (Richardis and Gertrud) were serving in the refectory, the blessed Hildegard said to them: 'Take great care over yourselves for fourteen days, and do penance', and when those days were at an end, they breathed their last. She also added that the same thing happened in a similar way to a certain cleric (Albert from the village Ebersheim). With this the lay-sister Hedwig agreed on oath.

Mechtild (from Rüdesheim), said on oath that, as she heard from her own mother, she had been born blind, but that when the blessed Hildegard was on a visit to the town (Eibingen) where another monastery

---

[18] I.e. Hildegard's blood sister.

[19] *quae nunc est*; grammatically it seems this can only refer to Clementia, but since she was older than Hildegard, she would have had to be impossibly old to be still alive in the late 1220s/early 1230s.

had been founded, her mother ran up to meet her, carrying her and begging the favour of the blessed virgin. The blessed virgin however, since she was still in a boat, took up water from the Rhine in her left hand, blessed it with her right and washed the blind eyes with it, so bestowing her with sight.[20]

[Henry, a canon of Bingen, said on oath, that when he applied hairs of the blessed Hildegard to two sick women, they were immediately set free from demons.[21]]

IIII

HEDWIG THE LAY-SISTER[22] SAID, on oath, that she had really witnessed this. She also added that there was a certain young woman (Gertrud by name), who had transformed herself into a scholar. But the blessed Hildegard called her by her real name, that is Gertrud, though she had never met her before. She said to her: 'Change back to a better state,[23] because for you I do not count any more years', as if she were saying, 'You are going to die within the year.' Now, on seeing the blessed Hildegard, she was cut to the heart and confessed that she was a woman. So she changed back and in the same year she died. With her the above witnesses (the first ones) concurred on oath. Because of her beauty the same young woman had blackened her face with a dark colour in case she should be loved by many, and as to this the entire neighbourhood proclaimed the same.

---

[20] Cf. the incident in VI below and in *VH* III, 9.

[21] *de daemoniacis*, literally, from demoniacs.

[22] It seems Hedwig was a widow, as she testifies shortly below to near fatal difficulties in labour.

[23] More fundamentally at issue here than male-female roles is the difference between scholastic/this-worldly and monastic/eschatological perspectives in the face of impending death. Hildegard's invitation to Gertrud, *convertere ad statum meliorem*, has a double nuance: Gertrud should quit being a 'scholar' and the playing with roles by which she pursued it, because even if there were anything in it, it is past all relevance for her now. She should 'return to herself' (Lk. 15:17), to what she really is: on one level, a woman, but above all, one who needs to prepare herself for imminent eternity. See Sabina Flanagan's remarks on this incident in *Hildegard of Bingen, 1098–1179: A Visionary Life*, p. 217, n. 8.

She also added that there was a certain married woman of Bingen who, having been suspected of the death of her husband, was assigned the ordeal of a red-hot iron. She ran to the blessed Hildegard and reported what had been done to her; but the blessed Hildegard blessed the red-hot iron, so that when she carried away the red-hot iron she remained unharmed. Public report in the town of Bingen agrees with this incident. She also said that when she (Hedwig) was twice in labour and near extremity, she called on the help of the same blessed Hildegard and was (immediately) set free. She also says that she witnessed, both while Hildegard was alive and after her death, many demoniacs and epileptics (whose names they do not know), set free.

Hedwig says the same thing (about Alceia), adding that the blessed Hildegard was constantly sick in bed from the scourge of God, except when she was irradiated by the Holy Spirit. Then she would walk about the monastery singing that sequence inspired by the Holy Spirit which begins: 'O sceptre and diadem!'[24] With this the cellarer and guardian agreed on oath. She said that she saw a burning candle upon her (the blessed Hildegard's) tomb when the Mass for the dead was being chanted. Though it had been put out, it caught alight by itself at the beginning of the Gospel, and this happened not once but often.

She also saw an insane man (whose name she does not know) who was a demoniac, tied up and forcibly restrained by others on her tomb. But he eventually escaped their hands and threw himself into the Nahe, which is at the foot of the hill. Many of those standing around believed that he was dead, but when they called on the virgin's favour, he was dragged out alive. After he had been set free from the demon he declared that he had been protected from the water by a great sleeve of the virgin's. Public report (in Bingen) agrees with this fact, as does also the greater part of the community on oath.

V

RAPOTO, HENRY AND HUMBERT, citizens of Bingen say on oath, that they saw the blessed Hildegard over many days, and that she cast out demons from all who came to her from their province and from elsewhere, cured

---

[24] *O Virga ac Diadema*; this was a Sequence for the Virgin Mary; see Newman, *Symphonia*, pp. 128–31.

epileptics (whose names they do not know), and worked many other signs, which they themselves saw, and that her holiness should not be doubted.

Hartado agrees on oath with what was just said, and adds this, that he saw four demoniacs and epileptics (unknown and whose names he does not know), set free by the merits of the same virgin.

Henry (who has now died), a canon of Bingen, said on oath that he applied hairs of the blessed virgin's to two sick women, and they were immediately set free. Concerning demoniacs he agreed with those mentioned above, that is, with Rapoto, Henry, Humbert, citizens, and with Hartado, canon of Bingen.

Conrad, canon of Bingen, from what he himself had witnessed, agreed with the above mentioned concerning the demoniacs.

VI

THE *MAGISTRA* ON OATH speaks of a certain report that she heard from those more worthy of credence and from the lady (Hedwig) herself from Dornbuc, that when on the anniversary of holy Hildegard she lit in honour of the same lady Hildegard a certain candle which was no longer than a hand and scarcely sufficient to last out the celebration of Mass, it lasted from the hour of Vespers to the hour of Mass on the following day. On her anniversary, the entire neighbourhood flocks and indeed it does flock (to her tomb).

Concerning the child born blind, she understood from the seniors of the monastery that Hildegard restored its sight by bathing its eyes with water from the Rhine, while she was on a boat between Rüdesheim and her own monastery at about a half a mile from her tomb. The woman herself in her old age confessed before us that it was so.[25]

She understood also from the seniors that Wilhelm, archdeacon of Trier, had been given hairs of Hildegard as a relic and had hidden them in a silken pouch which he had put in a wooden box and placed on the altar in the church of Dalevingen. When the church and all that was on the altar was burnt the silken pouch remained unharmed (the wooden box itself being entirely burnt up).

She also understood that a certain noble woman of Trier (whose name

---

[25] See the testimony of Mechtild in III above and the incident in *VH* III, 9.

she does not know), became disturbed in mind at the incantation of a certain young man, with the result that she was completely out of her mind. Her parents were grieving over this and fled to Hildegard, asking her favour. She took bread from her own table, blessed it and sent it to the sick woman. As soon as she had tasted some she was cured. Odilia the cellarer saw this miracle and Hedwig the lay-sister on oath, who at that time were at table with her (with the blessed Hildegard).

She also understood from the seniors of the monastery that the blessed Hildegard immediately corrected any sister whose mind strayed to vain things at the Divine Office, and that when they were reading the lessons, she would give them a blessing fitted to their inner disposition, expressing their own desires word for word. Some of them she knew afterward confessed (the same thing) in the Cistercian habit.[26]

When a certain man (whose name is not recalled) who had been unjustly excommunicated, was buried in her (the blessed Hildegard's) monastery, because of which the church of Mainz had suspended divine services there, and he had to be cast out, she (the blessed Hildegard) made the sign of the cross over his tomb with her staff, so that up to the present time, the tomb of the same man has not been able to be found.

A certain man (whose name is Henry from the village of Nierstein) had bound himself to the devil in homage, so that every year he sacrificed some animal to him: at first he offered animals, then his children, and finally his wife. When she perceived this, she fled to the blessed Hildegard and implored her help, telling her the sequence of what happened. Hildegard gave her a portion of her hair, which she then twisted into her own hair as she was commanded. Perceiving this, the demon said to the husband: 'You have deceived me! I have no right in her due to the incantations of Hildegard.' This husband then stripped his wife and put her in a bath, so that he could at length accomplish what he wanted.[27] But because the devil could not have her, he broke the neck of her husband instead.

When a certain Bishop of Mainz, Christian by name, was received at Bingen with the resounding of bells, he perceived that these bells were

---

[26] I.e. the sense, according to the later interpolation, is that some of them left Hildegard's monastery later for a monastery of Cistercian nuns, where they made this deposition.

[27] I.e. he wants to wash off any material invested with a prophylactic 'spell' from Hildegard which by remaining on his wife, might prevent him from carrying out his sacrifice.

resonating words like these: one was 'Pastor, mourn now!' and the other was 'While still safe, fly quickly!' These words seemed to be for the Bishop. There was a third word spoken in the person of the Bishop: 'I am going, and I leave the earth in confusion.' He told these words to the sisters who were present, when he was under inspiration.[28]

With this the prioress Agnes agrees, Odilia the guardian, Sophia and many others, all on oath.

VII

MECHTILD (OF EBERNBURG) ALSO says, on oath, that she had long been troubled by a demon, and says that through calling on the blessed Hildegard she was set free, and that the community had seen that she had been troubled and was set free, and they are there to this day. She also said that she saw other demoniacs and those suffering various kinds of recurring fever set free there (whose names she does not know).

Guta agrees with her on oath and adds that a certain boy (Otto of Sonnenburg) who was an epileptic, prayed earnestly on this account at the tomb of blessed Hildegard, and was (immediately) set free, and that there was a carpenter at the castle of his mother (Gisela of Boppard) who was mentally disturbed. When they called on the help of the blessed Hildegard, he was set free. With this the public report of the same place agrees.

Mechtild says on oath that she knew the blessed Hildegard, and that she had stayed with her continually. She also agrees with Mechtild, the one born blind. Also she agrees with the *magistra* about the blind woman who regained her sight after the death of Hildegard and about other matters.

VIII

BRUNO, GUARDIAN OF ST Peter in Strasbourg and priest, says on oath concerning the life of the blessed Hildegard that, according to what he

---

[28] Though the text nominates the bishop as Christian, the story would take on a wonderful relevance if it were referring to his predecessor, Arnold, murdered in the monastery of St James, Mainz, in 1160.

heard from public report, and according to what he read in the little book[29] which had been written about her life immediately after her passing by two religious, that is, Godfrey and Theodoric[30] who had stayed with the blessed virgin, the contents of which are in every way true: she took her origin from noble parents; when she was about five years old she saw a cow and said to her nurse: 'Look nurse! What a beautiful calf is in that cow, white and marked with all kinds of spots on the front and feet and back!' The nurse marvelled at this and immediately reported it to her mother. So the mother gave orders to the woman whose cow it was, that when the cow had calved, its offspring should be immediately shown to her. When this was done she realized that all the blessed girl Hildegard had foretold was true. So her parents wondered about her, and, perceiving that her ways were different from those of other people, made arrangements for her enclosure in a monastery. Entrusting her in her eighth year of age to a certain anchoress, Jutta by name, sister of the count of Sponheim, they offered her to serve the Lord under the Rule of blessed Benedict at Disibodenberg.

Concerning her way of life, he says that once her reputation for holiness had spread about far and wide, many noble young women flocked to her. But since the dwelling of a single anchoress was insufficient to accommodate them, she was warned by the Lord, or rather, compelled to transfer herself as leader to St Rupert's. When, through her confessor, she reported this to the Abbot, he was slow to accept it. The miracles by which she obtained the permission, and her move to the place divinely shown her, and how she built a new monastery in an unknown place, and set up the service of the Lord there with eighteen young women are found in more detail in the little book of her life. In this monastery she set up provisions for fifty nuns[31] and two priests, and

---

[29] *in libello*; Guibert refers to a *libellus*, 'little book' by Godfrey of Disibodenberg, afterward incorporated as *VH* I–VII.

[30] *Gotfrido et Dietrico*. A number of elements, each individually true, seem to have been mismatched. There *was* a *vita* initiated *immediately* after Hildegard's death, but by Guibert of Gembloux, who had indeed stayed with her. There *were* two authors, Godfrey of Disibodenberg, who had stayed with her and indeed wrote a 'little book', but died in 1176 three years *before* Hildegard's death, and Theodoric of Echternach, who had never stayed with her, the *endredactor* of the *VH* which is *not* a 'little book' and which he did not commence immediately after Hildegard's death but in 1182 at the earliest.

[31] *dominarum*; literally 'ladies', i.e. solemnly professed nuns, who also came from the nobility.

moreover for seven poor married women in honour of the Holy Spirit, and one in honour of blessed Mary. Furthermore, she founded another monastery across the river Rhine at half a league's distance, where she set up provisions for thirty nuns.

Concerning her reputation, he says that three bearers of the apostolic office, having heard her reputation, wrote to her, namely Eugene, Adrian and Anastasius, and she also wrote to them. In addition, the Archbishops of Mainz, Cologne and Magdeburg, the patriarch of Jerusalem, many bishops, the holy Abbot Bernard of Clairvaux and other abbots and provosts and prelates of other churches wrote to her, to whom she wrote back in reply. All of these are collected in the book of her letters.

Concerning her merits, he says that when Emperors Conrad and Frederick made enquiries about their end, they learned of their future, and thus she led them back to better ways: this is found in more detail in the book of her letters already mentioned. Every year on her anniversary many people both from the neighbourhood and from further away flock to her tomb, imploring her for the healing of mind and body. Moreover, though she had no earthly master, when she was forty-two years old she began to write not a few books through the revelation of the Holy Spirit, which is contained in more detail in the opening of her book *Scivias*, namely, the book *Scivias* which she finished after eleven years, *Book of Medicinal Remedies*, a *Book of Explanations of the Gospels*, a chant of heavenly harmony, an unknown language along with its own letters: which she completed after seven years; this is to be gathered in more detail from the introduction to the book of Life's Merits. Moreover, in the five years after that, she wrote *The Book of Life's Merits*: finally, she wrote *The Book of Divine Works* in seven years: which is explained in more detail in the introduction to this same book.

But concerning signs, he says he believes in every way that the signs which the Lord worked in her life through her, which are written down in the little book of her life, are true, and that the Lord worked more of them through her while she was alive and after she died than the human memory can retain.

Concerning her circumstances, he says that when he had transcribed her books from the originals in her monastery, that is, the book *Scivias*, the *Book of Life's Merits*, the *Book of Divine Works*, he had made arrangements to go on pilgrimage to blessed Martin, and took the books already mentioned with him to Paris. So that he could be more assured in studying them, through many labours and great difficulties he brought it about that the Bishop then presiding in that place summoned a meeting of all the masters reading in theology at the time and gave to each of them three quires of those books so that they could examine them, from the octave of Martin to the octave of Epiphany. When they had been examined they returned them to the Bishop, who assigned them to William of Auxerre his master for the time being. He returned them to the Bishop, confirming the judgments of the masters that the words in them were not human but divine.

He also says concerning her reputation, that his mother was in the village (called Lorch), two miles distant from the monastery which Hildegard had built, she, together with many other married women heard the report of Hildegard's holiness. She then took him with her, and humbly begged her to place the hand of her blessing upon her, and this she did.

Concerning the books which were examined, master Arnold, a scholastic of Saint Peter says the same as Bruno, for he was then studying theology in Paris.

Wilhelm, a canon of Saint James in Mainz, agreed on oath with Bruno except for the examination of the books and his coming to Hildegard. The greater part of the community agreed on oath with Bruno, except for his coming to blessed Hildegard.

Concerning the examination of the books, Master John, canon of Mainz and now provost of Bingen, agrees also with what was said above, for he was in Paris at that same time studying theology. He also says that there are few still alive who know the truth about holy Hildegard better than he does.

[When we asked the community why the blessed Hildegard was not working signs of late, they said that when the Lord showed so many miracles after her death there was so great a gathering of peoples at her tomb, and the monastic life and the divine office were so disrupted by the tumult of the people that it was reported to the lord Archbishop. So he came personally to the place and ordered her to stop the signs.[32]]

---

[32] St Bernard was also said to have been ordered by his successor at Clairvaux to stop working miracles because it was disturbing to the brothers' peace: Conrad of Eberbach, *Exordium Magnum Cisterciense*, ed. by Bruno Griesser, CCCM, 138 (Turnhout: Brepols, 1994), 2, 20. This work came from Eberbach not far from Rupertsberg, across the Rhine. Hildegard had had close links with the monks there, and, it seems likely, the nuns

VIIII

RORIC THE PRIEST (MENTIONED) above among the first witnesses said
also that when he summoned the obsessed woman Mechtild, the demon
appeared in her limbs in the form of a great nut and that when the hair of
blessed Hildegard was applied to this, he fled visibly from one limb to
another, leaving them darkened as with some black colour like coal.
Eventually when he had become exhausted, he departed in the form of a
most foul smoke, and neither he nor the crows appeared again.

The community confessed on oath that her writings really were her
own, that is the book *Scivias, The Book of Life's Merits, The Book of
Divine Works* which were examined in Paris by masters of theology.
These books together with *The Book of Explanations of Certain Gospels,
The Book of Epistles, The Book of Medicinal Remedies, the Book of
Compound Medicine*, her chant and her unknown language, along with
the little book of her *Life* were transcribed by the same Bruno the priest,
guardian at St Peter in Strasbourg, a faithful man of worthy reputation
and procurator of the above mentioned monastery. These we send to you
enclosed under our seals, imploring your holy Paternity on bended knees
that since so outstanding a light has till now as it were been *hidden under
a bushel*, you may be willing to *put it on a lampstand so that it might
shine for all who are in the house of God* (Mat. 5:15), by inserting her
name in the catalogue of the Saints and that you should instruct with your
commands certain suitable men that they may carry out this pious task to
its due fulfilment by reproving objectors with ecclesiastical censure.

These things are given effect at St Rupert in the year of the Lord 1233, on
the seventeenth day before the Kalends of January [16 December].

X

THE NOBLE BOY, OTTO by name, from (the castle of) Sonnenburg, who
suffered epilepsy every day, was put on the tomb of the blessed Hildegard
and when the help of the blessed Hildegard was invoked on his behalf, he
was immediately set free.

The carpenter of the castle of the noble woman Gisela of (the city) of

---

maintained the association after her death.

Boppard, who, being mentally disturbed, was immediately set free when the help of the blessed Hildegard was invoked: this is corroborated throughout Gotha and the public report of that place.

A married woman from the village of Büdesheim, long troubled by a demon, was lately set free by the merits of the blessed Hildegard at her tomb.

There was a certain man from the neighbourhood of the monastery, very much insane and tied up in a tub, who was brought to the tomb of blessed Hildegard. When the sisters applied hair of the blessed Hildegard to him, though he did not know what they were doing, he was immediately cured. In particular, this happened lately. It is attested on oath by Sophia the chantress and her sisters of the same monastery, who say that they were witnesses to this.

There was Albrad, from Daniel's parish, who was obsessed by a demon and very exhausted. She was set free at the tomb of blessed Hildegard when they called on her. It is corroborated by Daniel the priest and by Roric the priest who say that they witnessed this.

Eberhard of Sibeneich was obsessed by a demon was set free at the tomb of blessed Hildegard. This (took place) in fact just two years ago.

Conrad of Bingen was a boy who suffered dreadfully with epilepsy almost continually. He was placed on (the tomb) of the blessed Hildegard and by her merits was immediately set free. Afterwards, there was never a relapse. And this happened within the current year.

In addition, Adelaide, from the village of Cullenbach, who was obsessed by a demon, was set free at the tomb of the blessed Hildegard through her merits. This happened close to the Rogation days.

These three miracles are attested by the *magistra* of Saint Rupert, and the entire community of the same monastery, who say that they witnessed them.

That the blessed Hildegard wrote the book *Scivias*, the *Book of Life's Merits* and the *Book of Divine Works* without any earthly master but as the Holy Spirit dictated, and that these books were diligently examined at the behest of the Bishop of Paris by all the Parisian masters who read in theology, so that each of these masters had three quires for examination, and that their verdict was that the words in them were not human but divine: this is corroborated by Bruno, guardian at St Peter in Strasbourg (who swore ... the books at Paris),[33] Arnold scholastic at St Peter in

---

[33] There is apparently a missing word here: perhaps 'he saw'.

Mainz and currently a commissioner, Master John, scholastic at Mainz, provost of Bingen and currently a commissioner, who was then studying theology in Paris, and knew that the same books were examined in Paris.

APPENDICES

MAP 1

The Holy Roman Empire at this Period
(simplified)

MAP 2

Disbodenberg, Rupertsberg and Sponheim Abbeys

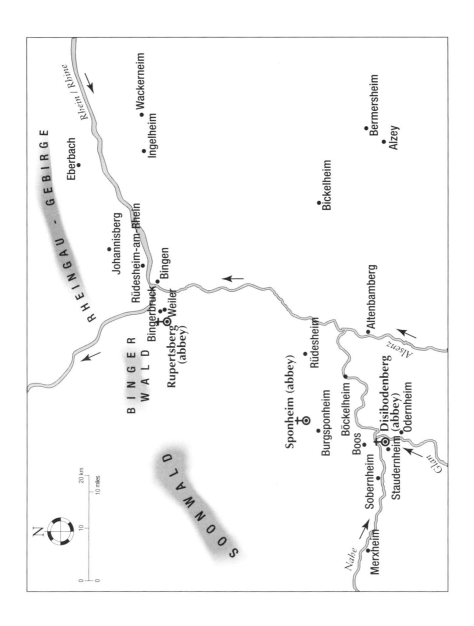

GROUND-PLAN OF DISIBODENBERG

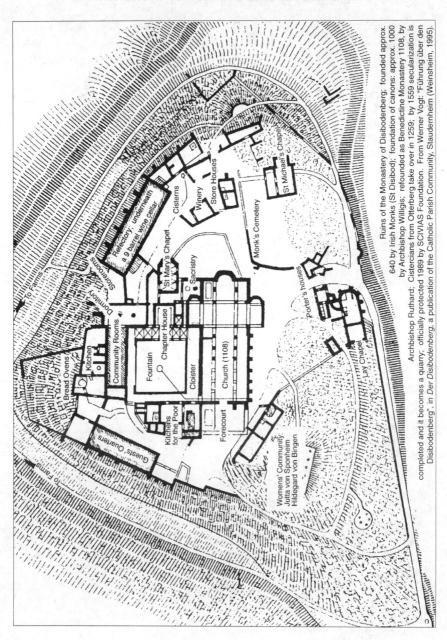

Ruins of the Monastery of Disibodenberg; founded approx. 640 by Irish Monks (St Disibod); foundation of canons: approx. 1000 by Archbishop Willigis; refounded as Benedictine Monastery 1108, by Archbishop Ruthard; Cistercians from Otterberg take over in 1259; by 1559 secularization is completed and it becomes a quarry; officially protected 1989 by SCIVIAS Foundation. From Werner Vogt: "Führung über den Disibodenberg", in *Der Disibodenberg*, a publication of the Catholic Parish Community, Staudernheim (Weinsheim, 1995).

Labels on plan:
Refectory: underneath a 9-barrel wine cellar
Cisterns
Winery
Store Houses
St Michael's Chapel
'St Mary's Chapel
Monk's Cemetery
Sacristy
Storerooms
Dormitory
To Farm
Porter's houses
Community Rooms
Chapter House
Fountain
Cloister
Church (1108)
Lay Chapel
Kitchen
Bread Ovens
Kitchens for the Poor
Forecourt
Guests' Quarters
Womens' Community:
Jutta von Sponheim
Hildegard von Bingen
To Farm

GROUND-PLAN OF THE RUINS OF RUPERTSBERG

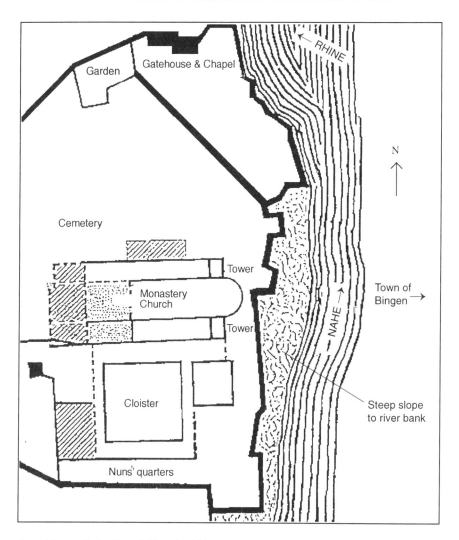

Rupertsberg: dedication of Church, 1 May 1151; destroyed by the Swedes in 1632, at which the nuns took refuge in the sister monastery of Eibingen. It remained a picturesque ruins overlooking the Nahe untill 1801, in the Napoleonic era, when it was sold off as state property. Throughout the 19th century nearly all traces of the ruins were progressively removed; private dwellings now cover the site; in 1857 stones from the Church were used in a railway embankment.

GENEALOGICAL TABLE I:

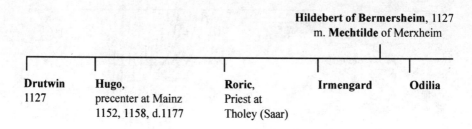

Hildebert of Bermersheim, 1127
m. **Mechtilde** of Merxheim

Drutwin	**Hugo,**		**Roric,**	**Irmengard**	**Odilia**
1127	precenter at Mainz		Priest at		
	1152, 1158, d.1177		Tholey (Saar)		

GENEALOGICAL TABLE II:

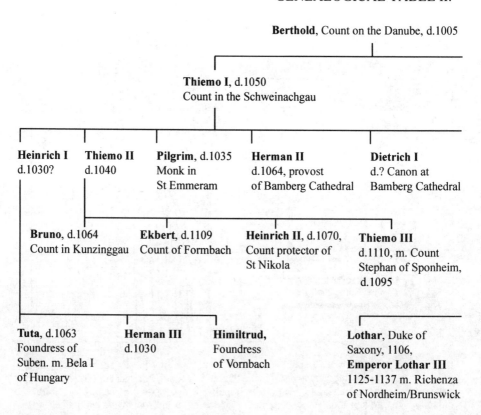

Berthold, Count on the Danube, d.1005

Thiemo I, d.1050
Count in the Schweinachgau

Heinrich I	**Thiemo II**	**Pilgrim**, d.1035	**Herman II**	**Dietrich I**
d.1030?	d.1040	Monk in	d.1064, provost	d.? Canon at
		St Emmeram	of Bamberg Cathedral	Bamberg Cathedral

Bruno, d.1064	**Ekbert**, d.1109	**Heinrich II**, d.1070,	**Thiemo III**
Count in Kunzinggau	Count of Formbach	Count protector of	d.1110, m. Count
		St Nikola	Stephan of Sponheim,
			d.1095

Tuta, d.1063	**Herman III**	**Himiltrud,**	**Lothar**, Duke of
Foundress of	d.1030	Foundress	Saxony, 1106,
Suben. m. Bela I		of Vornbach	**Emperor Lothar III**
of Hungary			1125-1137 m. Richenza
			of Nordheim/Brunswick

HILDEGARD OF BINGEN

| Jutta | Clementia
Nun at
Rupertsberg | Name ? | Name ? | Hildegard
1098-1179
September 17 |

FORMBACH FAMILY AND CONNECTIONS

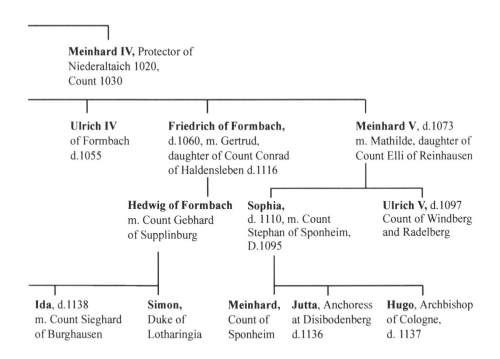

Meinhard IV, Protector of
Niederaltaich 1020,
Count 1030

Ulrich IV
of Formbach
d.1055

Friedrich of Formbach,
d.1060, m. Gertrud,
daughter of Count Conrad
of Haldensleben d.1116

Meinhard V, d.1073
m. Mathilde, daughter of
Count Elli of Reinhausen

Hedwig of Formbach
m. Count Gebhard
of Supplinburg

Sophia,
d. 1110, m. Count
Stephan of Sponheim,
D.1095

Ulrich V, d.1097
Count of Windberg
and Radelberg

Ida, d.1138
m. Count Sieghard
of Burghausen

Simon,
Duke of
Lotharingia

Meinhard,
Count of
Sponheim

Jutta, Anchoress
at Disibodenberg
d.1136

Hugo, Archbishop
of Cologne,
d. 1137

GENEALOGICAL TABLE III:

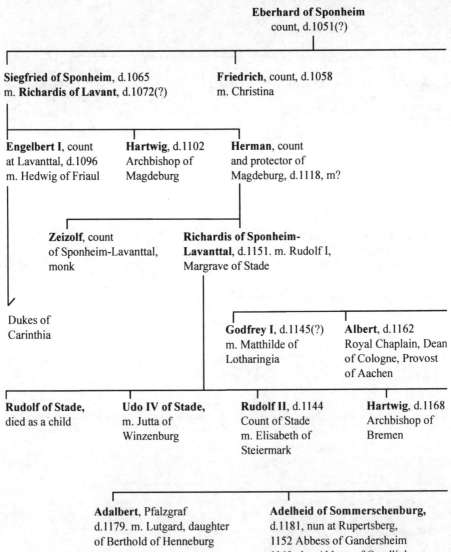

Eberhard of Sponheim
count, d.1051(?)

Siegfried of Sponheim, d.1065
m. **Richardis of Lavant**, d.1072(?)

Friedrich, count, d.1058
m. Christina

Engelbert I, count
at Lavanttal, d.1096
m. Hedwig of Friaul

Hartwig, d.1102
Archbishop of
Magdeburg

Herman, count
and protector of
Magdeburg, d.1118, m?

Zeizolf, count
of Sponheim-Lavanttal,
monk

**Richardis of Sponheim-
Lavanttal**, d.1151. m. Rudolf I,
Margrave of Stade

Dukes of
Carinthia

Godfrey I, d.1145(?)
m. Matthilde of
Lotharingia

Albert, d.1162
Royal Chaplain, Dean
of Cologne, Provost
of Aachen

Rudolf of Stade,
died as a child

Udo IV of Stade,
m. Jutta of
Winzenburg

Rudolf II, d.1144
Count of Stade
m. Elisabeth of
Steiermark

Hartwig, d.1168
Archbishop of
Bremen

Adalbert, Pfalzgraf
d.1179. m. Lutgard, daughter
of Berthold of Henneburg

Adelheid of Sommerschenburg,
d.1181, nun at Rupertsberg,
1152 Abbess of Gandersheim
1160 also Abbess of Quedlinburg

SPONHEIM FAMILY AND CONNECTIONS

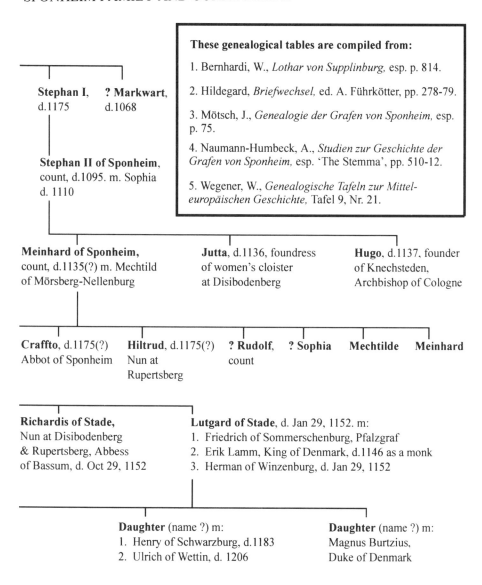

These genealogical tables are compiled from:

1. Bernhardi, W., *Lothar von Supplinburg,* esp. p. 814.

2. Hildegard, *Briefwechsel,* ed. A. Führkötter, pp. 278-79.

3. Mötsch, J., *Genealogie der Grafen von Sponheim,* esp. p. 75.

4. Naumann-Humbeck, A., *Studien zur Geschichte der Grafen von Sponheim,* esp. 'The Stemma', pp. 510-12.

5. Wegener, W., *Genealogische Tafeln zur Mitteleuropäischen Geschichte,* Tafel 9, Nr. 21.

Stephan I, d.1175   **? Markwart,** d.1068

Stephan II of Sponheim, count, d.1095. m. Sophia d. 1110

Meinhard of Sponheim, count, d.1135(?) m. Mechtild of Mörsberg-Nellenburg

Jutta, d.1136, foundress of women's cloister at Disibodenberg

Hugo, d.1137, founder of Knechsteden, Archbishop of Cologne

Craffto, d.1175(?) Abbot of Sponheim

Hiltrud, d.1175(?) Nun at Rupertsberg

? Rudolf, count

? Sophia   **Mechtilde**   **Meinhard**

Richardis of Stade, Nun at Disibodenberg & Rupertsberg, Abbess of Bassum, d. Oct 29, 1152

Lutgard of Stade, d. Jan 29, 1152. m:
1. Friedrich of Sommerschenburg, Pfalzgraf
2. Erik Lamm, King of Denmark, d.1146 as a monk
3. Herman of Winzenburg, d. Jan 29, 1152

Daughter (name ?) m:
1. Henry of Schwarzburg, d.1183
2. Ulrich of Wettin, d. 1206

Daughter (name ?) m:
Magnus Burtzius, Duke of Denmark

BIBLIOGRAPHY

See Abbreviations on pp. xxv–xxvii.

PRIMARY SOURCES

Acta Inquisitionis de virtutibus et miraculis S. Hildegardis, magistrae sororum ord. S. Benedicti in Monte S. Ruperti iuxta Bingium ad Rhenum, ed. by Petrus Bruder, in *Analecta Bollandiana*, 2 (1883), 116–29, sometimes called *Protocollum Canonisationis*, 'The Protocol of Canonisation'.

AELRED OF RIVAULX, *Opera omnia*, ed. by A. Hoste and C.H. Talbot, CCCM, 1 (Turnhout: Brepols, 1971).

PSEUDO-AMBROSE, *Passio S. Agnetis*, ed. F. Jubaru, in *Bibliotheca Hagiographica Latina Antiquae et Mediae Aetatis* (Brussels: Socii Bollandiani, 1898–1901; supplement 1911), vol. 3, p. 358.

Annales Sancti Disibodi, ed. by G.W. Waitz, in MGH SS, 17 (Hannover: 1861; repr. Stuttgart: Anton Hierseman, 1963), pp. 4–30.

Chronica Regia Coloniensis, ed. G. Waitz, Scriptores rerum germanicarum in usum scholarum (Hannover: Hahn, 1880).

CONRAD OF EBERBACH, *Exordium Magnum Cisterciense*, ed. by Bruno Griesser, CCCM, 138 (Turnhout: Brepols, 1994).

Decrees of the Ecumenical Councils, vol. I (Nicaea I–Lateran V), ed. by Norman P. Tanner (London: Sheed & Ward, 1990).

EBBO, *Vita Ottonis Episcopi Babenbergensis*, in MGH SS, 12, ed. by Rudolf Köpke.

FORTUNATUS, Venantius (*Vita I*) and BAUDONIVIA (*Vita II*), *Vita S. Radegundis*, ed. by B. Krusch, MGH SS rer. Mer., 2 (Hannover: 1888), pp. 358–95. *Vita I*: pp. 364–77; *Vita II*: pp. 377–95.

GREGORY, SAINT, *Dialogues*, ed. by Adalbert de Vogüé, Sources Chrétiennes, 260 (Paris: Cerf, 1978).

GUIBERT OF GEMBLOUX, *Guiberti Gemblacensis Epistolae*, ed. by Albert Derolez, CCCM, 66–66A (Turnhout: Brepols, 1988-89). The Letter to Bovo: *Epistola* 38, vol. 66A, pp. 366–79.

GUIBERT OF NOGENT, *Autobiographie*, ed. and trans. by Edmond-René Labarde (Paris: Les Belles Lettres, 1981).

HILDEGARD, SAINT (1098–1079), *Causae et curae*, ed. by Paul Kaiser (Leipzig: Teubner, 1903).

———, *Hildegardis Bingensis Epistolarium*, ed. by Lieven van Acker, CCCM, 91–91A (Turnhout: Brepols, 1991-93).

———, *Hildegardis Bingensis Liber Divinorum Operum*, ed. by A. Derolez and P. Dronke, CCCM, 92 (Turnhout: Brepols, 1996).

———, *Hildegardis Bingensis Liber Vite Meritorum*, ed. by Angela Carlevaris, CCCM, 90 (Turnhout: Brepols, 1995).

———, *Hildegardis Bingensis Scivias*, ed. by Adelgundis Führkötter and Angela Carlevaris, CCCM, 43–43A (Turnhout: Brepols, 1978).

———, *Symphonia: A Critical Edition of the 'Symphonia armonie celestium revelationum'* (Symphony of the harmony of celestial revelations), ed. and trans. by Barbara Newman (Ithaca: Cornell University Press, 1988).

———, *Lieder/Hildegard von Bingen*, ed. by Pudentiana Barth, M. Immaculata Ritscher and Joseph Schmidt-Georg (Salzburg: O. Muller, 1969).

———, *Analecta Sanctae Hildegardis Opera Spicilegio Solesmensi Parata*, ed. by Johannes Baptista Card. Pitra, in *Analecta Sacra*, vol. 8 (Monte Cassino: 1882; repr. Farnborough: Gregg Press, 1966).

Mainzer Urkundenbuch, vol. 1, *Die Urkunden bis zum Tode Erzbischof Adalberts I (1137)*, ed. by M. Stimming, Arbeiten der Historischen Kommission für den Volkstaat Hessen (Darmstadt: Verlag des historischen Vereins für Hessen, 1932; repr. 1972).

Mainzer Urkundenbuch, vol. 2, 1–2, *Die Urkunden seit dem Tode Erzbischof Adalberts (1137) bis zum Tode Erzbischof Konrads (1200)*, ed. by Peter Acht (Darmstadt: Selbstverlag der Hessischen Historischen Kommission, 1968–71).

The Monastic Constitutions of Lanfranc, ed. and trans. by David Knowles, Mediaeval Classics (London: Thomas Nelson and Sons, 1951).

RB 1980: The Rule of St Benedict in Latin and English with Notes, ed. by Timothy Fry (Collegeville, Minnesota: Liturgical Press, 1981).

Regesta archiepiscoporum Moguntinensium. Regesten zur Geschichte der Mainzer Erzbischöfe 1–2, 742–1288, ed. by J.F. Böhmer and C. Will (Innsbruck: Wagner, 1877–86; repr. Aalen: Scientia, 1966).

RUPERT OF DEUTZ, *Vita Heriberti*, ed. by Peter Dinter, Veröffentlichungen des Historischen Vereins für den Niederrhein, insbesondere das Alte Erzbistum Köln, 13 (Bonn: Röhrscheid, 1976).

STAAB, Franz, 'Reform and Reformgruppen im Erzbistum Mainz. Vom "Libellus de Willigisi consuetudinibus" zur "Vita domnae Juttae inclusae"', in *Reformidee und Reformpolitik im Spätsalisch-Frühstaufischen Reich. Vorträge der Tagung der Gesellschaft für Mittelrheinische Kirchengeschichte vom 11. bis 13. September 1991 in Trier*, ed. by Stefan Weinfurter, Quellen und Abhandlungen zur Mittelrheinische Geschichte, 68 (Mainz: Selbstverlag der Gesellschaft für Mittelrheinische Kirchengeschichte, 1992), pp. 119–87. Appendix II: *Vita domnae Juttae inclusae* (edited text), pp. 172–87.

SULPICIUS SEVERUS, *Vita S. Martini*, ed. by Jacques Fontaine, Sources Chrétiennes, 133 (Paris: Cerf, 1967).

THEODORIC OF ECHTERNACH, *Chronicon Epternacense*, in MGH SS 23.

———, *Vita Sanctae Hildegardis*, ed. by Monika Klaes, CCCM, 126 (Turnhout: Brepols, 1993). *Vita S. Hildegardis Virginis* (edited text), pp. 1–71.

THIOFRID, *Vita S. Liutwini*, ed. by W. Lampen, Collectanea franciscana neerlandica, 3/6 ('s Hertogenbosch: Teulings, 1936).

———, *Vita S. Willibrordi*, ed. by J. Schmitz (Luxembourg: Beffort, 1898).

TRITHEMIUS, Johannes (1462–1517), *De Luminaribus sive de Illustribus Viris Germaniae*, in *Johannis Trithemii Opera Historica*, ed. Marquand Freher (Frankfurt: 1601; repr. Frankfurt/Main: Minerva, 1966), vol. 1, pp. 123–183.

———, *Chronica Insignis Monasterii Hirsaugiensis*, ibid., vol. 2, pp. 1–235.

———, *Chronicon Monasterii Sponheimensis*, ibid., vol. 2, pp. 236–435.

Urkundenbuch zur Geschichte der mittelrheinischen Territorien, Vol. 1, *Von den ältesten Zeiten bis zum Jahre 1169*, ed. by Heinrich Beyer, Leopold Eltester, and Adam Goerz (Koblenz: 1860; repr. Hildesheim: Georg Olms, 1974).

TRANSLATIONS

GODFREY OF DISIBODENBERG AND THEODERIC OF ECHTERNACH, *Das Leben der Heiligen Hildegard von Bingen. Ein Bericht aus dem 12. Jahrhundert*, trans. by Adelgundis Führkötter, 3rd edn (Salzburg: Otto Müller, 1980).

GREGORY OF NYSSA, *Ascetical Works*, trans. by V.W. Callahan (Washington: Catholic University of America, 1967).

GREGORY OF TOURS, *History of the Franks*, trans. by Lewis Thorpe (Harmondsworth: Penguin Books, 1974).

———, *The History of the Franks*, trans. by D.M. Dalton, 2 vols (Oxford: OUP, 1927).

———, *Vita Patrum: The Life of the Fathers by St Gregory of Tours*, trans. by Seraphim Rose and Paul Bartlett (Platina, California: St Herman of Alaska Brotherhood, 1988). The Life of Monegond, pp. 278–85.

Handmaids of the Lord, Contemporary Descriptions of Feminine Asceticism in the First Six Christian Centuries, ed. and trans. by Joan M. Petersen (Kalamazoo, Michigan: Cistercian Publications, 1996). The Life (*Vita A* and *Vita B*) of St Radegund, pp. 363–432.

HILDEGARD, *Briefwechsel*, ed. by Adelgundis Führkötter, 2nd edn (Salzburg: Otto Müller, 1990).

———, *Explanation of the Rule of St. Benedict by Hildegard of Bingen*, trans. Hugh Feiss (Toronto: Peregrina, 1990).

———, *Letters of Hildegard of Bingen*, vol. 1, Letters 1–90, trans. by J.L. Baird and R.K. Ehrman (Oxford: OUP, 1994).

———, *Scivias*, trans. by Columba Hart and Jane Bishop, with introduction by Barbara Newman and preface by Caroline Walker Bynum, The Classics of Western Spirituality (New York: Paulist Press, 1989).

The Jews and the Crusaders: The Hebrew Chronicles of the First and Second Crusades, ed. and trans. by Schlomo Eidelberg (Madison: University of Wisconsin, 1977).

The Life of the Holy Hildegard, trans. by James McGrath, from the German translation of the *VH* and commentary by Adelgundis Führkötter OSB, English text ed. by Mary Palmquist, with assistance of John Kulas OSB (Collegeville, Minnesota: Liturgical Press, 1995).

The Life of the Saintly Hildegard, trans. by Hugh Feiss (Toronto: Peregrina, 1996).

SILVAS, Anna, 'Saint Hildegard of Bingen and the *Vita Sanctae Hildegardis*', *Tjurunga*, 29 (1985), 4–25; 30 (1986), 63–73; 31 (1986), 32–41; 32 (1987), 46–59.

STAAB, Franz, 'Aus Kindheit und Lehrzeit Hildegards: Mit einer Übersetzung der Vita ihrer Lehrerin Jutta von Sponheim', in *Hildegard von Bingen: Prophetin durch die Zeiten, zum 900 Geburtstag*, ed. by Abbess Edeltrude Forster and the Community of St Hildegard's Abbey, Eibingen (Freiburg: Herder, 1997).

DICTIONARIES

BLAISE, Albert, *Lexicon latinitatis medii aevi, praesertim ad res ecclesiasticas investigandas pertinens*, CCCM (Brepols: Turnhout, 1975).

DU CANGE, Charles du Fresne, *Glossarium mediae et infimae latinitatis, conditum a Carolo duFresne, Domino du Cange, auctum a monachis ordinis S. Benedicti; cum supplementis integris D.P. Carpentarii*, ed. by Léopold Favre, 5 vols (Niort: 1883–87; repr. Graz: Akademische Druck- u. Verlagsanstatt, 1954).

LATHAM, R.E., *Revised Medieval Latin Word List, from British and Irish Sources* (London: OUP for the British Academy, 1965).

LEWIS, Charleton T., and Charles SHORT, *A Latin Dictionary* (Oxford: Clarendon Press, 1879).

MAIGNE D'ARMIS, W-H., *Lexicon manuale ad scriptores mediae et infimae latinitatis* (Paris: J.-P. Migne, 1858).

NIERMEYER, J.F., *Mediae latinitas lexicon minus: A Medieval Latin/French/English Dictionary* (Leiden: E.J. Brill, 1993).

SOUTER, Alexander, *A Glossary of Later Latin to 600 AD* (Oxford: OUP, 1949).

BACKGROUND STUDIES

ARNOLD, Klaus, *Johannes Trithemius 1462–1516* (Würzburg: Kommissionsverlag Ferdinand Schöningh, 1971).

BARTLETT, R. 'The Conversion of a Pagan Society in the Middle Ages', *History*, 70 (1985), 185–201.

BECKER, Petrus, 'Die Hirsauische Erneuerung des St. Euchariuskloster in Trier', in *Consuetudines Monasticae: Eine Festgabe für Kassius*

Hallinger aus Anlaß Seines 70. Geburtstages (Rome: Pontificio Ateneo S. Anselmo, 1982), pp. 185–206.

BERNHARDI, Wilhelm, *Lothar von Supplinburg* (Leipzig: 1879; repr. Berlin: Ducker & Humbolt, 1975).

BLAMIRES, Alcuin, 'Women and Preaching in Medieval Orthodoxy, Heresy and Saints' Lives', *Viator*, 26 (1995), 135–152.

BRANN, Noel L., *The Abbot Trithemius (1462–1516): The Renaissance of Monastic Humanism* (Leiden: Brill, 1981).

BUTLER, Alban, *Lives of the Saints*, ed. by Herbert Thurston and Donald Attwater, 4 vols. (New York: P.J. Kennedy & Sons, 1956).

The Cambridge Medieval History, vol. 5, *Contest of Empire and Papacy*, ed. by J.R. Tanner (Cambridge: University Press, 1957).

CLARK, Anne L., *Elisabeth of Schönau: A Twelfth-Century Visionary* (Philadelphia: University of Pennsylvania Press, 1992).

CONSTABLE, Giles, *The Reformation of the Twelfth Century* (Cambridge: University Press, 1996).

DE VOGÜÉ, A., 'Twenty-five Years of Benedictine Hermeneutics—An Examination of Conscience', *American Benedictine Review*, 36 (1985), 402–52.

DOERR, Otmar, *Das Institut der Inclusen in Süddeutschland*, Beiträge zur Geschichte des alten Mönchtums und des Benediktinerorderns, 18 (Münster: Aschendorffsche Verlh., 1934).

ELM, Susanna, *Virgins of God* (Oxford: Clarendon Press, 1994).

FLANAGAN, Sabina, *Hildegard of Bingen, 1098–1179: A Visionary Life*, 2nd ed. (London: Routledge, 1998).

FLINT, V.I.J., *Honorius Augustodunensis of Regensberg*, Authors of the Middle Ages, 2, no. 6 (London: Variorum, 1995).

FRASER, Antonia, *Boadicea's Chariot* (London: Weidenfeld & Nicolson, 1988).

FÜRHRMAN, Horst, *Germany in the High Middle Ages 1050–1200*, trans. by Timothy Reuter (Cambridge: University Press, 1986).

GREENSPAN, Kate, 'Autohagiography and Medieval Women's Spiritual Autobiography', in *Gender and Text in the Later Middle Ages*, ed. by Jane Chance (Miami: University Press of Florida, 1996), pp. 216–36.

GROESCHEL, Benedict J., *A Still, Small Voice: A Practical Guide on Reported Revelations* (San Francisco: Ignatius Press, 1993).

HAUERKAMP, Alfred, *Medieval Germany 1056–1273*, 2nd edn, trans. by Helga Braun and Richard Mortimer (Oxford: OUP, 1992).

HILPISCH, Stephan, *Die Doppelklöster: Entstehung und Organisation*, Beiträge zur Geschichte des alten Mönchtums und des Benediktinerordens, 15 (Münster: Aschendorffsche Verlh., 1928).

LACKNER, Bede, *The Eleventh Century Background of Citeaux*, Cistercian Studies, 8 (Washington, DC: Cistercian Studies/Consortium Press, 1972).

LECLERCQ, Jean, 'Solitude and Sanctity: Medieval Women Recluses', in *Peaceweavers*, ed. by Lilian Thomas Shank and John A. Nichols (Kalamazoo, Michigan: Cistercian Publications, 1987), pp. 67–83.

LEYSER, Henrietta, *Hermits and the New Monasticism: A Study of Religious Communities in Western Europe, 1000–1050* (London: MacMillan, 1984).

LIFSCHITZE, Felice, 'Beyond Positivism and Genre: "Hagiographical" Texts as Historical Narrative', *Viator*, 25 (1994), 95–113.

MULDER-BAKKER, Anneke B., 'The Reclusorium as an Informal Centre of Learning', in *Centres of Learning: Learning and Location in Pre-Modern Europe and the Near East*, ed. by Jan Willem Drijvers and A.A. MacDonald (Leiden: E.J. Brill, 1995), pp. 245–54.

PIUS XI (Pope), 'Gia da qualche tempo', *Acta Apostolicae Sedis*, 22 (1930), 87–88.

ROISIN, Simone, *L'Hagiographie Cistercienne dans le diocèse de Liège au XIIIe Siècle* (Louvain: Bibliothèque de l'Université, 1947).

ROY, Gopa, '"Sharpen your Mind with the Whetstone of Books": The Female Recluse as Reader in Goscelin's *Liber Confortatorius*, Aelred of Rievaulx's *De Institutione Inclusarium* and the *Ancrene Wisse*', in *Women, the Book and the Godly*, ed. by Lesley Smith and Jane H.M. Taylor (Cambrdge: D.S. Brewer, 1995), pp. 113–22.

RASSOW, Peter, 'Über Erzbischof Ruthard von Mainz 1089–1109', in *Universitas: Dienst an Wahrheit und Leben: Festschrift für Dr. Albert Stohr*, ed. by Ludwig Lenhart (Mainz: Matthias Grünewald, 1960), pp. 55–59.

SCHNEIDER, Reinhold, *Kaiser Lothars Krone: Leben und Herrschaft Lothars von Supplinburg* (Zürich: Manesse, 1986).

SEIBRICH, Wolfgang, *Die vier Gründungen des Klosters Sponheim* (Idar-Oberstein: Selbstverlag, Prinz-Druck, 1995).

——, 'Zur Geschichte des Disibodenbergs', in *Der Disibodenberg* (Weinsheim: Katholische-Bildungswerk Rhein-Nahe-Hunsruck, 1995), pp. 7–18.

SPEER, Ludwig, *Kaiser Lothar III und Erzbischof Adalbert I von Mainz. Eine Untersuchung zur Geschichte des Deutsches Reiches im frühen zwölften Jahrhundert*, Dissertationen zur Mittelalterlichen Geschichte, 3 (Cologne, Vienna: Böhlau, 1983).

The Spirituality of the Middle Ages, ed. by Dom Jean Leclercq, Dom Françoise Vandenbroucke and Louis Bouyer (London: Burns and Oates, 1968). 'The Benedictine Tradition' (including St Hildegard and St Elizabeth of Schönau), pp. 162–86.

TELLENBACH, Gerd, *The Church in Western Europe from the Tenth to the early Twelfth Century*, trans. by Timothy Reuter (Cambridge: University Press, 1993).

VAN ENGEN, John, 'The Crisis of Cenobitism Reconsidered: Benedictine Monasticism in the Years 1050–1150', *Speculum*, 61 (1986), 157–72.

WEGENER, Wilhelm, *Genealogische Tafeln zur mitteleuropäischen Geschichte* (Gottingen: H. Reise, 1962, 1969).

WEINRYB, Bernard Dov, 'Mainz', *Encyclopaedia Judaica* (Jerusalem: Keter Publishing House, 1972), vol. 11, cols 788–92.

SELECT DETAILED STUDIES

ALLEN, Prudence, 'Sex and Gender Differentiation in Hildegard of Bingen and Edith Stein', *Communio: International Catholic Review*, 20 (Summer 1993), 389–414.

BERG, Ludwig, 'Die Mainzer Kirche und die Heilige Hildegard', *Archiv für Mittelrheinische Kirchengeschichte*, 27 (1975), 49–70.

BENT, Ian D., 'Hildegard of Bingen', in The New Grove Dictionary of Music and Musicians, ed. Stanley Sadie (London: Macmillan, 1980), vol. 8, pp. 553–556.

DRONKE, Peter, 'Arbor Caritatis', in *Medieval Studies for J.A.W. Bennet* (Oxford: Clarendon Press, 1981), pp. 207–53.

———, 'Platonic-Christian Allegories in the Homilies of Hildegard of Bingen', in *From Athens to Chartres: Neoplatonism and Medieval Thought, Studies in Honour of Edouard Jeauneau*, ed. by Haijo Westra (Leiden: E.J. Brill, 1992), pp. 381–96.

———, 'Problemata Hildegardiana', *Mittellateinisches Jahrbuch*, 16 (1981), 97–131.

———, *Women Writers of the Middle Ages* (Cambridge: University Press, 1984), chapter entitled 'Hildegard of Bingen', pp. 144–201;

notes, pp. 306–15; edition of Hildegard's autobiographical sections, pp. 231–41.

FLANAGAN, Sabina, *Hildegard of Bingen, 1098–1179: A Visionary Life*, 2nd ed. (London: Routledge, 1998).

———, 'Hildegard and the Gendering of Sanctity', in *Hildegard of Bingen and Gendered Theology in Judaeo-Christian Tradition*, ed. by Julie S. Barton and Constant J. Mews (Clayton, Victoria: Centre for Studies in Religion and Theology, Monash University, 1995), pp. 81–92.

———, 'Oblation or Enclosure: Reflections on Hildegard of Bingen's Entry into Religion', in *Wisdom which Encircles Circles*, ed. by A.E. Davidson (Kalamazoo, Michigan: Medieval Institute Publications, 1996), pp. 1–14.

———, '*Spiritualis Amicitia* in a Twelfth-Century Convent? Hildegard of Bingen and Richardis of Stade', *Parergon*, 29 (April 1981), 15–21.

FÜHRKÖTTER, Adelgundis, 'Hildegard von Bingen und ihre Beziehungen zu Trier', *Kurtrierisches Jahrbuch*, 25 (1985), 70.

HERWEGEN, Ildephonse, 'Les collaborateurs de Sainte Hildegarde', *Revue Bénédictine*, 21 (1904), 182–203, 302–15, 381–403.

Hildegard of Bingen: The Context of Her Art and Thought, ed. by Charles Burnett and Peter Dronke (London: Warburg Institute, 1998).

HILPISCH, Stephan, 'Der Kult der heiligen Hildegard', *Pastor Bonus (Trierer Theologische Zeitschrift)* 45 (1934), pp. 118–33.

HOTCHIN, Julie, 'Enclosure and Containment: Jutta and Hildegard at the Abbey of Disibodenberg', *Magistra: A Journal of Women's Spirituality in History*, 2:2 (1996), 103–23.

———, 'Images and Their Places: Hildegard of Bingen and Her Communities', *Tjurunga*, 49 (1996), 23–38.

———, 'Saintly Expectations and Earthly Networks: The Construction of Hildegard's Sanctity' (unpublished MA thesis, Department of History, Monash University, 1997).

JOHN, Helen, 'Hildegard of Bingen: A New Twelfth-Century Woman Philosopher?', *Hypatia*, 7 (1992), 113–23.

JOHN-PAUL II (Pope), 'Pope's Letter to Cardinal Volk, Bishop of Mainz. The 800th anniversary of the death of Saint Hildegarde of Bingen', *L'Osservatore Romano*, 1 Oct. 1979, 10.

KERBY-FULTON, Kathryn, 'A Return to the "First Dawn of Justice": Hildegard's Visions of Clerical Reform and the Eremitical Life', *American Benedictine Review*, 40:4 (December 1989), 204–23.

LACKNER, Bede, 'Hildegard of Bingen and the White Monks', *Vox Benedictina*, 5:4 (1988), 313–24.

MEIER, Christel, 'Eriugena im Nonnenkloster? Überlegungen zum Verhältnis von Prophetentum und Werkgestalt in *Figmenta Prophetica* Hildegards von Bingen', *Frühmittelalterliche Studien*, 19 (1985), 466–97.

MEWS, Constant J., 'Hildegard of Bingen: Gender, Nature and Visionary Experience', in *Hildegard of Bingen and Gendered Theology in Judaeo-Christian Tradition*, ed. by Julie S. Barton and Constant J. Mews (Clayton, Victoria: Monash University, Centre for Studies in Religion and Theology, 1995), pp. 63–80.

——, 'Hildegard and the Schools', forthcoming in *Hildegard of Bingen: the Context of Her Thought and Art*, ed. by Charles Burnett and Peter Dronke (London: Warburg Institute, 1998).

——, 'Hildegard of Bingen: The Virgin, the Apocalypse and Exegetical Tradition', in *Wisdom which Encircles Circles*, ed. by A.E. Davidson (Kalamazoo, Michigan: Medieval Institute Publications, 1996), pp. 27–42.

——, 'Seeing is Believing: Hildegard of Bingen and the *Life of Jutta, Scivias*, and the *Commentary on the Rule of Benedict*', *Tjurunga*, 51 (1996), 9–40.

MÖTSCH, Johannes, 'Genealogie der Grafen von Sponheim', *Jahrbuch für westdeutsche Landesgeschichte*, 13 (1987), 63–179.

NAUMANN-HUMBECK, Anneliese, *Studien zur Geschichte der Grafen von Sponeim vom 11. bis 13. Jahrhundert*, Heimatkundliche Schriftenreihe des Landkreises Bad Kreuznach, 14 (Bad Kreuznach: Kreisverwaltung, 1983).

NEWMAN, Barbara, 'Hildegard and Her Hagiographers: The Remaking of Female Sainthood', in *Gendered Voices: Medieval Saints and Their Interpreters*, ed. by Catherine M. Mooney (Philadelphia: University of Pennsylvania Press, forthcoming 1999).

——, 'Hildegard of Bingen and the "Birth of Purgatory"', *Mystics Quarterly*, 19 (1993), 90–7.

——, 'Hildegard of Bingen: Visions and Validation', *Church History*, 54 (1985), 163–75.

——, 'Romancing the Past: A Critical Look at Matthew Fox and the Medieval "Creation Mystics"', *Touchstone: A Journal of Ecumenical Orthodoxy*, 5 (Summer 1992), 5–10.

————, *Sister of Wisdom: St Hildegard's Theology of the Feminine* (Berkeley: University of California Press, 1987). A second revised edition appeared in 1997.

————, 'Seherin-Prophetin-Mystikerin: Hildegard-Bilder in der hagiographischen Tradition', in *Hildegard von Bingen: Prophetin durch die Zeiten. Zum 900. Geburtstag*, ed. by E. Forster (Freiburg: Herder, 1977), pp. 126–52.

————, 'Three-part Invention: The *Vita S. Hildegardis* and Mystical Hagiography', forthcoming in *Hildegard of Bingen: the Context of her Thought and Art*, ed. by Charles Burnett and Peter Dronke (London: Warburg Institute, 1998).

————, *Voice of the Living Light: Hildegard of Bingen and Her World*, ed. by Barbara Newman (Berkeley: University of California Press, 1998).

SCHOLTZ, Bernard W., 'Hildegard on the Nature of Women', *American Benedictine Review*, 31:4 (1980), 361–83.

SCHRADER, Marianna, *Die Herkunft der heiligen Hildegard*, newly rev. by A. Führkötter, Quellen und Abhandlungen zur Mittelrheinischen Kirchengeschichte, 43 (Mainz: Gesellschaft für mittelrheinische Kirchengeschichte, 1981).

————, and Adelgundis Führkötter, *Die Echtheit des Schrifttums der heiligen Hildegard von Bingen*, Beihefte zum Archiv für Kulturgeschichte, 6 (Cologne: Böhlau, 1956).

SOMMERFELD, G., 'Die Prophetien der hl. Hildegard in einem Schreiben des Meisters Heinrich von Langenstein', *Historisches Jahrbuch*, 30 (1909), pp. 43–61, 297–307.

THOMPSON, Augustine, 'Hildegard of Bingen on Gender and the Priesthood', *Church History*, 63:3 (September 1994), 349–64.

VAN DOREN, Rombaut, 'Ildegard di Bingen', in *Bibliotheca Sanctorum* (Rome: Istituto Giovanni XXIII, Pontificia Università Lateranense, 1961–70), vol. 7, cols 762–5.

VAN ENGEN, John, 'Abbess, Mother and Teacher', in *Voice of the Living Light: Hildegard of Bingen and Her World*, ed. by Barbara Newman (Berkeley: University of California Press, 1998), pp. 30–51 and pp. 206–9 (endnotes).

VOGT, Werner, 'Führung über den Disibodenberg', in *Der Disibodenberg* (Weinsheim: Katholische Bildungswerk Rhein-Nahe-Hunsruck, 1995), pp. 25–35.

Wisdom which Encircles Circles, Papers on Hildegard of Bingen, ed. by Audrey Ekdahl Davidson (Kalamazoo, Michigan: Medieval Institute Publications, 1996).

INDEX OF NAMES

SCRIPTURAL INDEX